Disputed Decis
of World War II

Disputed Decisions
of World War II

Decision Science and
Game Theory Perspectives

MARK THOMPSON

To Bill,
With best wishes,
Mark

McFarland & Company, Inc., Publishers
Jefferson, North Carolina

ISBN (print) 978-1-4766-8004-0
ISBN (ebook) 978-1-4766-3838-6

LIBRARY OF CONGRESS AND BRITISH LIBRARY
CATALOGUING DATA ARE AVAILABLE

Front cover: Aftermath of the Dieppe Raid in France
on August 19, 1942 (Library and Archives Canada)

Printed in the United States of America

*McFarland & Company, Inc., Publishers
Box 611, Jefferson, North Carolina 28640
www.mcfarlandpub.com*

To the memory of Howard Raiffa, pioneering titan of decision
science and game theory, mentor of unstinted kindness

"I sometimes wonder if the P.M. feels the full weight of the decisions he has to make....
It is as if Winston has a family of twelve children and there is not enough food for
all of them—some of them must starve to death. He has to decide which."

> —Diary entry of January 1, 1942, of Sir Charles Wilson,
> physician of the Prime Minister[1]

"The President never 'thinks'! He decides."

> —The response of Eleanor Roosevelt to "Just how does
> the President *think?*"[2]

"Unexplained decisions rob military history of almost all its instruction to the future
soldier."

> —Douglas Southall Freeman, 1935 Pulitzer Prize–
> winning author of *Lee*, in a letter of November 5,
> 1943, to Dwight Eisenhower, in which he wrote that
> he had easily enough learned what had happened
> in the American Civil War, "but Hell's own time ...
> finding out why it happened" and urged Eisenhower
> to save the documents of his decisions[3]

"The essence of ultimate decision remains impenetrable to the observer–often, indeed
to the decider himself.... There will always be the dark and tangled stretches in the
decision making process even to those who may be most intimately involved."

> —John F. Kennedy[4]

Acknowledgments

This book owes untellably much to the insightful readings and constructive critiques of friends—standouts among them being James Ashton, Max Bazerman; Alan, Brandon, and Helaine Cohen; Ellen and Scott Fowler; Emmett Keeler; Ralph Keeney; Liam MacLean; Thomas Olshefski; and Lisa Voth; and to the deft editing of Susan Kilby of McFarland.

A debt of thanks is also due the efficient and helpful staffs of the Liddell Hart Centre for Military Archives at King's College in London, of the U.S. Army's Military History Institute within the Army Heritage and Education Center in Carlisle, Pennsylvania, and of Widener Library at Harvard University.

Rick Atkinson, Pulitzer Prize–winning author of *The Liberation Trilogy*, was on the money in praising "master cartographer Gene Thorp," "a delightful, innovative" man whose artistry and technical excellence is on display in all the maps of the *Trilogy* and of this book.

For counsel through the pitfalls and puzzles of contemporary publishing I am indebted to Lucy V. Cleland, Victor J. Paci, George N. Tobia, Jr., John Taylor Williams, and Bryn and Richard Zeckhauser, as well as to the advice and encouragement of Dylan Lightfoot at McFarland.

The emotional support of my wife, Cindy Lewis, and of my daughters Julia, Martha, and Sara has also been most valued.

Contents

ix

Introduction

American Brigadier General Lucian Truscott had been invited to observe Operation Jubilee, an attack of one Canadian division on the French port of Dieppe on the English Channel. He described the night of August 18/19, 1942, from the deck of the destroyer, HMS *Fernie*:

> The night was cool as the darkened armada ploughed its way toward the coast of France under a partial moon.... We saw the low, flat tank landing craft crawling along like great dark water beetles with white waves now and again splashing against their tall snout-like ramps. We passed the infantry assault ships gliding along like dark gray ghosts with moonlight reflecting like jewels in the trailing wakes. In the distance, dim shapes of other destroyers and gunboats were barely visible now and again through the slight surface haze. No lights. No noise. All was dark and still. There was only the hum of driving motors, with occasional low murmurs of voices.[1]

At 0347 hours, a star shell exploded and lit up the sky above the 22 ships on the eastern flank of the Allied flotilla. Seven miles from the coast of France, they had—to the surprise of both sides[2]—bumped into a German convoy of five merchant boats, escorted by two submarine-chasers and one minesweeper. The enemy reacted the more quickly and fired on Steam Gunboat 5, the main Allied escort ship. Within minutes, two fifths of the crew of SGB 5 had been hit, its radios knocked out, and its steering disabled. It slowed to an aimless drift. Its surviving gunners could, however, still shoot and were joined in the firefight by Landing Craft Flak 1. Their guns sank a submarine-chaser and a merchant ship. The other German boats saw themselves outgunned and fled southwestward down the Channel coast toward Dieppe. The battle for that town had begun.

Five thousand Canadian and eleven hundred British soldiers were to be landed that day at and on either side of Dieppe: the largest incursion of Western Allied forces in France since the evacuation from Dunkirk, over two years before. The men were to reembark later that day and to return to England.

What decisions had sent those men to that French shore? How good or how bad would be the results? How good or how bad were the decisions?

These questions are put in this book to four strategic moments of the Western Allies in the Second World War: the deliberations on Dieppe; those that led in November 1942 to the Allied invasion of North Africa; the non-decision that allowed 53,000 enemy soldiers in August 1943 to escape from Sicily; and the determination to undertake an amphibious landing in January 1944 at Anzio in Italy. In these situations the processes of pondering are described; the outcomes are assessed; and the qualities of the decisions are rated. All four have been debated—by participants in the decisions at the time and in their memoirs and later by historians. Inasmuch as these writings contain facts, assertions, arguments, insights, and conclusions of value, how can it be worthwhile once again to tromp over these battlegrounds of controversy set on battlegrounds of gore and of death?

The short answer is that the extents of these continuing disagreements cry out for reasoned

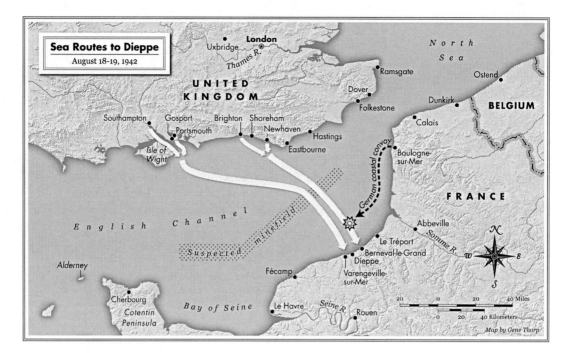

inquiry into whether these decisions, and one non-decision, and their outcomes were good or bad. Such inquiry should be based in part on critical reviews of the historical literature—not until now systematically undertaken. Fresh perspectives are also provided here by modern analytic approaches that shed new light on these points of contention of old.

*   *   *

The attack on Dieppe did not end well: at a cost of one thousand Allied deaths and three thousand other Anglo-Canadian casualties, next to nothing was gained. Did this abysmal result mean that the decision that had led to it was comparably bad? Who, if anyone, should be held responsible? Men (and they were all men) with the power to make such decisions did not achieve their positions by meekly accepting blame for their blunders. Common ploys of potentates whose choices work out poorly are to accentuate the good (at Dieppe the air battles) and to be inventive in finding positives (that Dieppe was beneficial in learning what not to do in future landings). Their memoirs minimize mention not just of bad aspects but also of entire disappointing episodes and of their personal roles in them.

When outcomes disappoint, scapegoats, often unfairly, are pointed to. Specs for fall guys typically are that they have sufficient stature for plausibility as fiasco factors but not so much sway that they can thwart their designation. Also in disfavor in the war were decision participants who issued unheeded warnings pre-disaster and who, post-disaster, insisted on pointing this out. One such person was swiftly sent off to a remote Atlantic island.

One striking example of the disagreements on decision outcomes was seen in the spring of 1943—after the Allied invasion of North Africa had culminated in the capture of one quarter million German and Italian soldiers. George Marshall, the leading general of America, then told his British counterpart, Sir Alan Brooke, that he still thought that the alternative strategy of attacking northern France would have been better: "We should finish the war quicker," to which Brooke responded, "Yes, probably, but not the way we hope to finish it!"[3]

Many histories, although excellent in narrative detail, tend simplistically to judge decisions by their outcomes: those leading to good results are reflexively thought good; those to bad, bad. Attacks and defenses, if successful, are presumed to have resulted from good decisions; if unsuccessful, from bad. Decision science and game theory, both but embryonic during the war, take a different tack. The two disciplines take into account what the decision makers knew and what they did not and then ask whether appropriately broad sets of alternatives were considered and whether the ones that were prospectively best were chosen. In these inquiries, the importance of certain analytic precepts appears.

One such precept, underlying and explaining many events of the war, although not explicitly recognized and named until 1979,[4] is the *planning fallacy*:

> the widespread tendency to have unrealistically rosy expectations of how well our undertakings will turn out. We think that we will complete our tasks and achieve our goals more quickly, at less cost, and with greater net benefits than experience suggests is likely.[5]

Decision scientists have documented such overconfidence among attorneys, engineers, negotiators, physicians, psychologists, security analysts, and testifying witnesses[6]: our estimates of how long it will take us to do something are typically based on best-case scenarios—even though our track records show that we have been, time after time, overly optimistic. This explains why public works projects end up costing multiples of their initial budgets, why we never seem to complete our home repairs as quickly as we thought we would, why students take years longer than planned to complete their dissertations, and why so many armed campaigns have ended in disappointment, if not disaster.

The planning fallacy has been ignored by most military writers and but tangentially and inexplicitly touched on by others—even though it is a leader among the factors that explain why nations go to war. Both the German invasion of Russia on June 22, 1941, and the Japanese attack later that year on Pearl Harbor were in significant part impelled by this behavioral tendency.

The role of the planning fallacy in clipping the wings of Dwight Eisenhower—preventing him from exercising in the battles to come a unified command—has also been overlooked by historians. The planning fallacy had underlain both the strategic expectations of the Allies for North Africa and, fortunately for them as matters played out, the response of Adolf Hitler. It also—although mostly unrecognized by those who have written about them—was a factor in each of the other three decision situations reviewed here.

Another concept of decision science and game theory of consequence in the war was the bluff—a ploy urged in 1942 by leading Americans to win British consent to their preferred strategy and a motivation two years later for an Allied amphibious attack. Both bluffs bombed. While such tricky moves have been made by generals for millennia, the first formal analytic study of bluffs appeared in 1944. It was authored by two fathers of game theory, who determined the optimal incorporation of such devious moves into overall strategies and the conditions required for their success. Had the generals of the early 1940s known such later findings, they ought not to have tried these bluffs—which only could have succeeded if their targets had been unaware of their nature.

Unawareness of the need to decide also can cost. Decision scientists have found that "failure to recognize that a deliberate decision has to be made is a serious source of poor decision making."[7] It might seem unlikely that the Allied decision makers of 1943—as able as in many ways they were—could have failed to realize that conscious choices had to be made and that active steps had to be taken to prevent the flight of 53,000 German soldiers from Sicily. This appears, however, to have been what happened—which subsequently resulted in the Allies suffering tens of thousands more casualties in the ensuing campaign in mainland Italy.

These and other concepts of decision science and game theory—such as the expected value of information, meta-decision-making, move-order considerations, other-side perception, principal-agent dynamics, and sunk-cost reasoning—were exemplified in the Second World War. None of these topics were then altogether new or unrecognized in combat. Generals and historians over the centuries have, for instance, noted the importance of the strategic initiative—which would later be rescrutinized by game theorists analyzing move-order pluses and minuses. Decision science and game theory have, however, reexamined these phenomena, have given them new names, have determined the conditions under which they have sway, and have shown how they may be heeded to gain best results. The insights of these two disciplines help us to judge how well the Allied commanders made their challenging choices.

The conclusions drawn on how good or how bad the decisions were derive in part from reconsidering the points made in the voluminous writings about them. Many of the conclusions reached here—particularly those concerning the explanations and justifications put forward for the decisions made—differ from those of the historical literature.

*　*　*

Less only than Adolf Hitler, Allied leaders Winston Churchill, Franklin Roosevelt, Alan Brooke, George Marshall, Dwight Eisenhower, Bernard Montgomery, Harold Alexander, and Omar Bradley, in roughly that order, had as decision makers—DMs—the most influence on the Western Front in the war. Of the millions of decisions affecting these fields of battle, this book reviews but a few—all of which have been, both at the time and in histories since, sharply questioned.

All in all, the Western-Ally decision makers of the war performed impressively well—not surprisingly, inasmuch as their nations had given these DMs their responsibilities because they had been thought likely to excel in them. The result was that—in concert with and in significant ways as the junior partner of the Soviet Union—they won the war. Throughout their deliberations and in later critiques of them there was awareness of what has been called "the central statistic of the Second World War": "that out of every five Germans killed in combat—that is, on the battlefield rather than in aerial bombing or through other means—four died on the Eastern Front."[8] Unlike modern decision scientists and game theorists, the DMs of the war pondered and conferred without putting numbers on probabilities (for the most part) or values (ever).

The epilogue looks, from the modern viewpoints of decision science and game theory, into whether poor choices may have resulted from weariness, from advanced years, from the particular fatigue that sets in when long series of decisions have to be made, from female companionship, from the interpersonal dynamics of deliberating groups, from insufficiently-critical reliance on recognized experts, or from flouting the millennia-old principle of command unity. It asks how all that has been—or still remains to be—learned from the tragedy that was the war may best guide future commanders.

1

Dieppe

The Strategic Decision: Should Dieppe in August 1942 Have Been Raided?

Details: Should Dieppe have been attacked frontally or indirectly via landings to the southwest and/or northeast? Should airborne troops have been employed? Should there have been bombardment by capital ships? Should Dieppe have been heavily bombed?

When made: in stages running from the first months of 1942 to mid–August.

The decision makers: Chief of Combined Operations Louis Mountbatten; Canadian Major General and Army Force Commander John Roberts; Air Force Commander Trafford Leigh-Mallory; Naval Force Commanders Harold Baillie-Grohman and John Hughes-Hallett; British Home Forces Commanders Bernard Montgomery and Bernard Paget, to both of whom Roberts reported; Canadian Lieutenant Generals Henry Crerar and Andrew McNaughton, to whom Roberts also reported; the War Committee of the Canadian Government with which McNaughton touched base and whose consent was required; the superiors of Leigh-Mallory within the Royal Air Force; the superiors of Baillie-Grohman and Hughes-Hallett within the Royal Navy; the British Chiefs of Staff, chaired by the Chief of the Imperial General Staff Sir Alan Brooke; and Prime Minister Winston Churchill.

Conclusions: the outcome: catastrophic, on a one-division scale, in disappointing the hopes entertained for the raid, in incurring losses that were as a panzer to a popgun relative to any gains achieved—but less bad, because of the limited scale, than the results at Kasserine and Messina; **the decision:** bad; **why made:** faulty meta-decisions in deciding how to decide; cascade expression of opinions whereby the early pronouncements of respected authorities induced others subsequently to agree—an aspect of groupthink, which will be considered in the epilogue; ununified command; the planning fallacy; insufficient awareness of uncertainties and their consequences—with respect to what enemy preparations and capabilities might be and to how battle events might play out in ways unanticipated by overly precise plans; excessive deference to air, land, and sea expertise; possible overestimation of the expected value of the information to be gained; **most to be lauded:** British commandos, Canadian troops, British and Canadian airmen; **most to be faulted:** Bernard Montgomery, for some of the unwise operational details and for not availing himself of whatever chance he had to call off the first incarnation of the raid; Alan Brooke, for not attempting to make more rational the jumble of responsibilities—which he had the best, if not great, possibility of doing; John Hughes-Hallett, for hijacking attempts to reconsider the operation.

The attacks of Germany and Russia on Poland in September 1939 had led at blitz pace to the conquest and shared occupation of that calamitously-located land. France and Britain had, on the third of the month, declared war on the Third Reich, but then had waited passively in defensive positions throughout the overrunning of Poland, the fall, and the winter. This period of inactivity on the Western Front known as the "Phoney War" ended in early April of 1940 with the briskly successful German invasions of Denmark and Norway. Britain, as urged by First Lord of the Admiralty Winston Churchill, had itself been planning to invade Norway but was beaten to the punch by Adolf Hitler. The United Kingdom landed forces at spots on the Norwegian coast but, by early June, had withdrawn them.

Churchill, on May 10, 1940, became Prime Minister. On the same day, the Germans attacked and soon took Luxembourg, the Netherlands, and Belgium, as their panzers raced to the English Channel. The troops England had sent to the continent were forced, late in the month through early June, to evacuate from Dunkirk, a French port on the Channel. Italy, on June 10, declared war on France and Britain. Wehrmacht columns, four days later, entered Paris. The French government had fled south and, on the sixteenth, made 84-year-old Maréchal Philippe Pétain, a hero of the Great War, its Premier Minister. An armistice ending Franco-German hostilities was signed on the twenty-second. It provided for German occupation of northern France and the Atlantic Coast, but that the French fleet would not be surrendered. Pétain, based in the centrally-located town of Vichy, would head the Nazi-friendly government of southern France. General Charles De Gaulle had foreseen that the demoralized leaders of his nation would make peace with Hitler, had fled on June 17 to London, and, the next day, had spoken via the BBC to his nation, urging continuation of the war against the invaders. Britain recognized De Gaulle as the leader of the Free French.

Adolf Hitler, after his victory over France, hoped to negotiate an end to the war with Britain but London, bucked up by the defiant rhetoric of Churchill, scorned the German overtures. The United Kingdom, fearing that the French Navy might fall into enemy hands, fired on July 3 on warships of its recent ally in the Algerian port of Mers-el-Kébir, sinking a battleship and killing 1,300.[1] The attack insulted and angered the French and signaled to Hitler and to the rest of the world that the UK was in earnest about fighting on. Germany responded one week later by opening the Battle of Britain: intensive bombing to force capitulation or to set the stage for an invasion. Although much damage was done to the airfields, factories, and cities of England, the Royal Air Force remained potent and Hitler opted not to challenge the supremacy of the Royal Navy by crossing the Channel.

On September 27, 1940, the Tripartite Pact among Germany, Italy, and Japan established the Axis Alliance—which Romania, Bulgaria, and Hungary would later join. Italy, earlier that month, had invaded British-held Egypt and, in October, attacked Greece. Both Benito-Mussolini-ordered offensives went poorly. Adolf Hitler in February 1941 sent Erwin Rommel to Libya—where he would command the Afrika Korps—and, two months later, invaded Yugoslavia and Greece, quickly conquering both.

On June 22, 1941, the so-far-overwhelmingly-triumphant Führer attacked Russia, to open a war unprecedented in size. Of its savagery, Churchill said to his nation two months later, "Since the Mongol invasions of Europe in the sixteenth century, there has never been methodical, merciless butchery on such a scale."[2] The Soviets were not fighting gently: before retreating, they moved their munitions factories eastward and destroyed homes, power plants, and foodstuffs to deny them to the invader; they left behind groups of partisans to sabotage and to murder in territory taken by the Germans; thousands of their own soldiers were shot for cowardice; their generals were executed for defeats.

The Prime Minister was not, however, speaking of the Soviets, to whom he had begun sending aid. The Wehrmacht had, in the first week of the war, captured a frontier village, then had killed its one hundred inhabitants. The slaughters of innocents grew exponentially: to thousands and then tens of thousands, on the way to more. The victims included gypsies, the mentally infirm, the aged, Communist officials, and, in greatest numbers, Jews. At the end of September in just one incident, 34,000 Jewish men, women, and children were machine-gunned and buried in a ravine near Kiev. By year end, between 500,000 and 1 million Jews of the USSR had been killed.

The war in Russia at first went well for the Germans and their allies: Finns, Hungarians, Italians, Romanians, and Slovaks. They had, by late October, taken 600,000 square miles of Soviet lands (more than the total 2019 areas of France, Germany, Italy, the Low Countries, Switzerland, Austria, the Czech Republic, and Denmark), home to 65 million, and had captured three million men of the Red Army, whom they treated so harshly that few survived. They were within 65 miles of Moscow and 25 miles of Leningrad—which was besieged and where deaths from starvation had begun and soon would rise to 1,500 per day. Vanguard units of the Wehrmacht would advance to within fifteen miles of the Kremlin.

The Germans would, however, take neither city. The Russians, having learned from a spy that they would not be attacked by Japan in the East, brought 30 divisions from Siberia to the Moscow front. Underequipped and underclothed for the winter of Russia, the German soldiers there had to heat their panzers with fires lit under their oil pans to keep them operational—while their opposite numbers, the 26-ton T-34 Soviet tanks, had been designed to function in temperatures that, in early December, dropped to 22 degrees Fahrenheit below zero. On December 5, 1941, the Red Army opened a counterattack that drove back the German lines near the Russian capital over 50 miles.

In Africa, the fortunes of war had swung back and forth. Rommel had driven forward in the spring four hundred miles from El Agheila in Libya to cross the border into Egypt, where he remained until November. A British counteroffensive then drove the Axis forces, by the end of the year, back to El Agheila.

Japan had, since 1937, been warring in China. A few days after the Japanese attack on Pearl Harbor on December 7, 1941, Germany and Italy declared war on the United States.

* * *

The evacuation of the British Expeditionary Force from Dunkirk had ended at 1423 hours on June 4, 1940. The next day—his 26th as Prime Minister—Winston Churchill approved a one-page proposal for hit-and-run raids on the coast of France. He instructed his Chiefs of Staff that "enterprises must be prepared, employing specially trained men of the hunter class, who can develop a reign of terror down the enemy coast."[3]

On the night of June 24-25, 1940, 115 British commandos crossed the Channel, landed south of Boulogne-sur-Mer, killed two sentries, and withdrew.

Three weeks after that, Churchill confirmed his serious interest in raiding by appointing Admiral Sir Roger Keyes Director of Combined Operations. Under Keyes, Combined Operations Headquarters—COHQ—secured landing craft and raised commando units. In March 1941, 500 commandos landed against no opposition on the Lofoten Islands off of Norway and destroyed factories producing fish oil, an ingredient in high explosives.

Admiral Keyes butted heads with the Royal Navy and Royal Air Force over who was to command the naval and air units in his raids. These squabbles led, in October 1941, to his dismissal and to his replacement by Captain Lord Louis Mountbatten. Lord Louis—"Dickie" to Churchill and the other high-level nicknamers of the war—was young, energetic, articulate, a favorite of Churchill, and a royal: King George VI and he being fellow great grandsons of Victoria and Albert. The second cousin of the King had had no experience in amphibious operations, but was thought by Churchill likely able to break through the military-bureaucratic roadblocks that had exasperated Keyes.

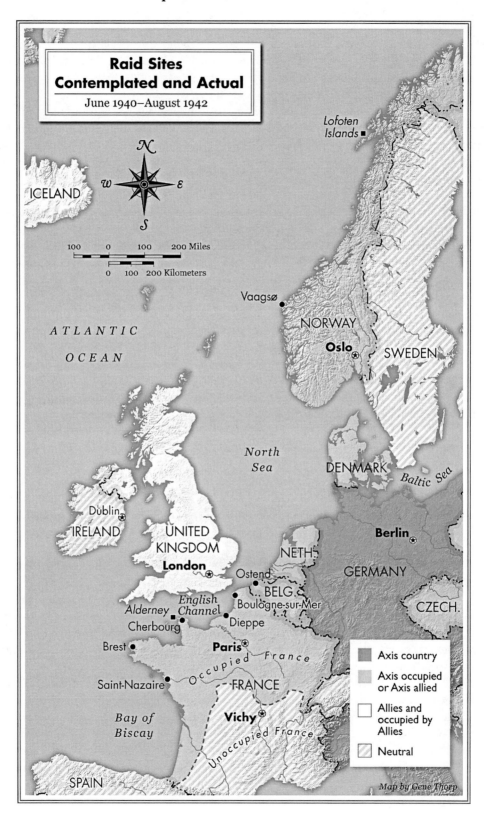

**Raid Sites
Contemplated and Actual**
June 1940–August 1942

ICELAND

Lofoten
Islands ■

ATLANTIC

OCEAN

Vaagsø ●

NORWAY

Oslo ⊛   SWEDEN

100   0   100   200 Miles

0   100   200 Kilometers

North
Sea

DENMARK

Baltic Sea

Dublin ⊛

IRELAND   UNITED
KINGDOM

Berlin ● ⊛

NETH.

GERMANY

London ⊛

Ostend ●

English   BELG.
Channel   Boulogne-sur-Mer ●   CZECH.

Alderney ■

Cherbourg ●   Dieppe ●

Brest ●   **Paris** ⊛

France

Saint-Nazaire ●   Occupied   **FRANCE**

Bay of
Biscay   **Vichy** ⊛

Unoccupied France

SPAIN

	Axis country
	Axis occupied or Axis allied
	Allies and occupied by Allies
	Neutral

Map by Gene Thorp

Sixty commandos, in November 1941, sought in Libya to kidnap or to kill Erwin Rommel. The Desert Fox had not, however, been at the targeted command post for weeks and was indignant that the British had thought that he would be so far from the front.

The next month, 626 Combined Operations commandos, with RN and RAF support, raided Vaagsø in Norway. In their six hours ashore, they overcame German resistance, inflicted 220 enemy casualties, secured a complete copy of the German naval code, destroyed fish-oil factories, and had thirteen of their own killed and 50 wounded. The exploit induced Adolf Hitler to send 30,000 more men to Norway. The Lofoten and Vaagsø raids have been called "Viking victories by the pick of the army over the small and third-rate garrisons of remote Norwegian fishing havens."[4]

Three months after Vaagsø, Combined Operations achieved what has been considered a spectacular success. Early on March 28, 1942, an obsolete destroyer, the HMS *Campbeltown*, disguised as a German vessel and accompanied by eighteen smaller craft, sailed into the estuary of the Loire. There, in the port city of St. Nazaire, was the only dry dock in France large enough to service Germany's super-battleships, the *Bismarck* and the *Tirpitz*—both of 43,000 tons. The *Bismarck* had, the previous May, been heading for St. Nazaire when found and sunk. The *Tirpitz*, blockaded by the Royal Navy on the Norwegian coast, had recently become operational. It was feared that, with the possibility of a retreat for repairs to St. Nazaire, she might break out into the Atlantic for a foray similar to that of the *Bismarck*. The *Campbeltown* at 0127 hours lowered her Swastika, raised British colors, and, seven minutes later, rammed into the dry dock. Her delayed demolition charges exploded hours later and destroyed the dock so severely that it could not again be used until after the war. Of the 630 raiders, one quarter were killed and one third captured.

(Whether St. Nazaire had a good outcome may be debated. It had achieved what was hoped for, with casualties of a magnitude that might have been expected. But did the gains justify the costs? Would it have been better to have forgone the raid? Churchill's referring to it as "the brilliant and heroic exploit" suggests a good outcome—although brilliance and heroism have sparkled in many a debacle. He did not state what the casualties had been.[5] Various historians have: conceded the heroism, while also noting the "frightening" losses[6]; have termed it "a hollow victory," thought "glorious" by the public[7]; and have called it a "success" with "a heavy cost."[8])

* * *

Mountbatten's Combined Operations Headquarters had begun early in 1942 the planning that would lead to Dieppe.[9] In addition to the main cross-Channel ferry ports in France, COHQ also considered such other possible landing sites as Ostend in Belgium and the island of Alderney off of the Cotentin Peninsula of France. Dieppe by February had been studied and the next month prioritized for intelligence gathering.[10] In early April, the town was chosen as the target for Operation Rutter: it was about the right size for a one-division assault; it was thought not to be strongly held; air cover could be provided by planes based in England; naval forces could leave England after dusk and be in supporting positions before dawn; and its beach seemed suitable for landing infantry and tanks. The objectives would be to bring invasion barges back to England "for our own use," to obtain documents from an enemy divisional headquarters, to take prisoners, and to destroy German coastal defenses, an airfield, radar installations, power stations, railroads, docks, and fuel dumps.[11] A force of infantry, paratroops, and armor was to hold the town and the area around it for a few hours, before re-embarking.

Officers of the Royal Air Force and Royal Navy joined in the planning for Rutter: Air Vice-Marshal Trafford Leigh-Mallory as Air Force Commander; Rear Admiral Harold Baillie-Grohman as Naval Force Commander. Ground-force units would be subordinate to the

South-Eastern Commander of the Home Forces, Bernard Montgomery, and to his superior, the Commander-in-Chief of the Home Forces, Sir Bernard Paget. Montgomery revamped substantially the original plan of COHQ. At the end of April, Montgomery asked Lieutenant General Henry Crerar, Commander of I Canadian Corps, if he would like the main ground force to be Dominion troops.

Crerar would. He picked the 2nd Canadian Division, led by Major General John Roberts. Montgomery deemed Roberts the best Canadian divisional commander—a distinction considered "faint praise," given Montgomery's low opinions of other Canadian generals.[12] Roberts became the Army Force Commander for Operation Rutter. He reported to Montgomery and to Crerar, who was subordinate to Lieutenant General Andrew McNaughton, Commander of the First Canadian Army. Canadian participation in the raid was subject to the consent of the War Committee in Ottawa, which, on May 15, was given. (McNaughton had been reproved by his government in 1940 for having agreed to send 1,300 Canadian soldiers to Norway, without having consulted Ottawa. He could, thereafter, on his own prerogative, assign Canadians only to "minor" undertakings. In anticipation of Rutter, he asked that his authority be expanded to larger operations, one of which, of division size, might occur soon. The War Committee consented to his request, without knowing the exact when, what, or where.[13])

The British Chiefs of Staff, on May 13, 1942, reviewed and "approved the outline plan" that had been agreed on by COHQ, the force commanders, Paget, and Montgomery "as a basis for detailed planning by the Force Commanders."[14] In a three-hour meeting ten days later, Churchill, Brooke, and Mountbatten discussed Rutter and other attack possibilities.[15]

While the U.S. had next to nothing to do with the planning of the Dieppe raid, the strategic paper George Marshall had presented on April 9, 1942, to the British Chiefs had called for "constant raiding by small task-forces at selected points along the entire accessible coastline held by the enemy."[16]

The forces for Rutter staged two landing exercises on the Isle of Wight. The first, on June 11 and 12, was so bungled that the date for the operation was put back; the second, eleven days later, went well enough that Rutter was scheduled to occur on July 4 or subsequent days, contingent on a favorable weather forecast. On July 1, Montgomery wrote that Rutter "has good prospects of success given:—(a) Favourable weather. (b) Average luck. (c) That the Navy put us ashore roughly in the right places, and at the right times" and officer confidence.[17] On July 3, Crerar and McNaughton gave separate Canadian approvals of the operation.[18]

*　*　*

Among the considerations that influenced the British and Canadian sign-offs on Rutter were events in Russia. Two Soviet armies had in May been surrounded and largely destroyed southeast of Kharkov and one quarter of a million men captured. The German armies were at mid-year readying to attack toward the Volga and the Caucasus.

*　*　*

In the first week of July, the skies above and the seas beside the French Channel Coast churned uncooperatively and, on July 7, Operation Rutter was called off—permanently, most thought. The Luftwaffe had, that day, discovered and bombed the ships assembled for the raid.

The resurrection of Rutter had begun one day before its death. On July 6, at Mountbatten's urging, the British Chiefs had agreed that the raid might be mounted later. A force-commander-level meeting was held on the eleventh. The operation was renamed Jubilee, but the essentials remained the same. The biggest change was to substitute commando landings for paratroop drops—for which the requisite weather was too rare.

Bernard Montgomery, upon learning that Rutter might live again as Jubilee, reported being "very upset."[19] The thousands of men who had been sequestered on the Isle of Wight had been dispersed to many sites. This, Montgomery said, meant that the operational secrecy of an attack on Dieppe had been irrevocably lost and that it should not be reconsidered. He was overruled, left England on August 10, and would command the British Eighth Army in Egypt.

In 1950, as Churchill researched Dieppe for his memoirs, he wrote that

> nothing in the papers I have now seen or my own record explains who took the decision to revive the attack.... Surely the decision could not have been taken without the Chiefs of Staff being informed? If so, why did they not bring it to my attention?... If the decision was made after I left the country [on August 3] was the Defence Committee or the War Cabinet informed? How did all this go?[20]

Documentation of the decision process had been scanty: few had been informed and little put on paper. Among the "extraordinary steps ... taken to ensure secrecy," Churchill would later write, were that "no records were kept."[21] The once and future Prime Minister was reminded that, having cabled on August 17 to ask about the timing of Jubilee, he must have known about it.[22] He had also, days earlier in Moscow, mentioned it to Stalin.

After reviewing events with Mountbatten and others, Churchill reported in his memoirs having thought "it most important that a large-scale operation should take place this summer."[23] With not enough time to plan a new attack, the only possibility was to have the forces of Rutter go ahead with the raid on Dieppe for which they had been trained. It was hoped that, with the imposition of extraordinary security measures, the operation would succeed. Churchill wrote that he had personally reviewed the plans with Brooke, Mountbatten, and Captain John Hughes-Hallett, who had replaced Harold Baillie-Grohman as the Naval Force Commander, and that the approval of the British Chiefs of Staff had been secured.[24]

Canadian assent was given in the week before the raid would take place: Henry Crerar on August 13 reported his satisfaction with the battle plan and Andrew McNaughton, three days later, followed suit.[25]

General Sir Archibald Nye, the Vice-Chief of the Imperial General Staff, had not been in the loop. With CIGS Brooke accompanying Churchill in August 1942 to Egypt and Russia, Nye headed the IGS. He knew nothing about Jubilee until action reports were received on August 19 and was not pleased to have been kept in the dark.[26]

The attack plan of Operation Jubilee, as the Allied flotilla, on the morning of August 19, 1942, approached the French coast, would have the scale of one division. Six Canadian infantry regiments, three British commando units, thirty tanks, eight destroyers, 250 other vessels, and 74 air force squadrons, along with miscellaneous other units, were committed to the attack. Six thousand one hundred men were slated to be landed, of whom 4,960 were Canadian, 1,075 British, 50 American, fifteen French, and five anti–Nazi Germans.[27]

The plan of Combined Operations Headquarters submitted to Bernard Montgomery called for landings miles west and east of Dieppe.[28] Montgomery, however, judged that there was not enough time for forces landed at a distance from Dieppe to reach and to take the town before they would have to re-embark. The tanks to be landed to the west would have had to cross two rivers, which could have been problematic. The better and perhaps only way to take the town, Montgomery held, would be via direct assault on its beach: a coup de main. Mountbatten thought such an attack too risky and counter-proposed the landing of infantry and tanks west of Dieppe. On

April 18 and 25, COHQ planners and Home Forces representatives reviewed the arguments for and against the frontal and lateral attacks. With Montgomery having by virtue of his command over all ground forces the final say, the beach at Dieppe would be directly attacked.[29]

Two German coastal batteries with six- and seven-inch guns and range of eleven miles were six miles east and west of Dieppe. To prevent them from firing on the naval craft of Jubilee, commando units were to take and to silence them. For flank protection of the main landing, attacks would also be made on the coastal villages of Puys and Pourville—a mile or two on either side of Dieppe.

The attacks would be made on a receding high tide—which at Dieppe on August 19 would have crested at 0403 hours.[30] It was judged that to make all attacks simultaneous would require excessively risky and difficult crowding and coordination of the boats. The four flank landings were scheduled for 0450 hours: nautical twilight. The sun would then be twelve degrees below the horizon; it would rise at 5:50. The pilots of the first landing craft would have just enough pre-dawn light to make out the main coastal features. The attack on Dieppe Beach was to be at 5:20. The landing, exploitation, and withdrawal were all to happen within one tide.[31]

Cover for the infantry assaults was to be provided by armor, navy, and air force. Nine tanks were to land with the first infantry on Dieppe Beach and to provide fire protection. Later waves were to include 21 more.

It had been proposed that at least one capital ship with eight-inch guns fire on the German defenses—which Naval Force Commander Harold Baillie-Grohman sought to arrange with the Royal Navy. The RN, however, nixed the idea. The previous December, Japanese planes in the South China Sea had sunk the battleship HMS *Prince of Wales* and the battlecruiser HMS *Repulse.* The RN would not allow the Luftwaffe to effect a like catastrophe in the Channel by sending any capital ship in daylight hours into the waters off of Dieppe. Naval fire protection would be limited in caliber to the four four-inch guns mounted by each of eight Hunt-Class, thousand-ton destroyers.

Initial attack plans called for heavy bombing of the defenses in and near Dieppe, for which Air Force Commander Trafford Leigh-Mallory sought Royal Air Force authorization.[32] The RAF, though, advised against this component of Rutter. It was felt that night bombing was unlikely to

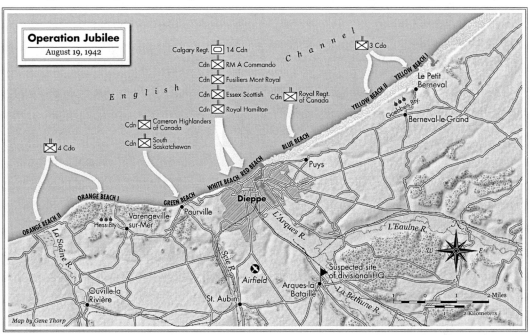

be accurate, would forfeit operational surprise, and would kill and anger French civilians. The elimination of the heavy bombing was approved in a planning meeting on June 5 chaired by Bernard Montgomery and attended by the three force commanders. Army Force Commander John Roberts, who feared that bombing Dieppe might clog its streets with rubble that would block the passage of his tanks, did not object.[33] Air support for the main attack would consist of ten minutes of cannon strafing by RAF Hurricane fighters. Combined Operations Headquarters had requested that a contingent force of bombers be in the air near Dieppe, on call to attack targets of opportunity. RAF Bomber Command had vetoed this idea because of difficulties in providing fighter protection and because the planes could not be spared from their main mission of blasting the Third Reich into submission.[34]

When heavy bombing was dropped from Jubilee, Admiral Baillie-Grohman again petitioned the Royal Navy for a capital ship or two—whose support had become the more urgently needed. The RN responded that none could be made available and that Rutter, instead "must depend on surprise"[35]: success would require getting ashore before the enemy became alert to its threat. This response made little sense. Surprise might have been achieved for the flank attacks but, at Dieppe itself, for which the large-bore guns had been requested, it was not possible. That the landings on its beaches were to follow those at Puys and Pourville by thirty minutes meant, as the Canadian Official History pointed out, that "there was no hope of surprise here."[36]

The Outcome: Minor Success; Profitless Movement; Major Disaster

The Allied fleet component that encountered a German convoy at 0347 hours was carrying British commandos bound for Le Petit Berneval and Berneval-le-Grand, six miles northeast of Dieppe, designated Yellow Beaches I and II. It was to have had 23 landing-craft-personnel vessels, plus three escorts. Four LCPs had, however, become disabled before the flotilla had run into the German boats and had headed back to England. Four more were damaged by enemy fire and also turned back. With only eight remaining close to the escort craft, the landing force for the Yellow Beaches seemed reduced by two thirds. Inasmuch as radio communications with the headquarters fleet in the Channel had also been lost, the attack on the Bernevals was called off.

Seven of the dispersed LCPs, however, did not get the message and continued on to France. One landed nineteen men on Yellow II Beach five minutes ahead of schedule—at 0445 hours—three quarters of a mile west of the village of Berneval-le-Grand. Five landed half an hour later—25 minutes late—and a sixth 30 minutes after that at Yellow I Beach, one and a quarter miles to the northeast of Yellow II at the hamlet of Le Petit Berneval. The Allies at Yellow I numbered about 115 British commandos and six U.S. Rangers. The objective for both commando groups was to silence the coastal guns—dubbed by the Allies the "Goebbels Battery"—of three seven-inch and four four-inch barrels. The commandos at Yellow II were too few to do any more than briefly shoot at the battery, before running low on ammunition and reboarding their LCP.

At 5:00, the Germans had sounded a general alarm and soon attacked the commandos at Yellow I. Some had gotten into the village of Le Petit Berneval, on their way to attack the Goebbels guns. The Germans drove them back to the beach, where they surrendered. During the raid at Yellow I, nineteen-year-old U.S. Ranger Lieutenant Edwin Loustalot had charged a machine gun and was shot, becoming the first American soldier killed in Europe in the war. Thirty-six other commandos were also killed and 81—most wounded—were captured.

A few minutes after the landing at Yellow II, 252 Allied commandos came ashore at Orange

Beaches I and II, six miles southwest of Dieppe. Groups from the two beaches converged on the coastal battery, which the Allies had code-named "Hess" and which had six six-inch guns. Supported by an air strike at 0630 hours, the commandos took the battery, blew up its guns and ammunition dumps, and re-embarked at 7:30. Thirty enemy had been killed—some bayonetted—and a comparable number wounded. Four prisoners were brought back to England. Twelve commandos had died, twenty were wounded, and seven captured.

Seven hundred and fifty men—three quarters of whom were of the Royal Regiment of Canada—had been assigned to attack Blue Beach at the village of Puys, a mile northeastward up the coast from Dieppe. Delays in forming up and heading for the shore put the Royals a quarter hour behind their scheduled landing at 0450 hours. They were to have controlled the eastern approaches to Dieppe and to have captured a field battery of four guns. The delay meant that the German defenders at Puys had been alerted by the earlier landings on other beaches and had enough pre-dawn light to fire accurately at the landing craft when within 100 yards of the shore.

The men in those boats could see that carnage awaited and—until naval officers threatened them with drawn revolvers—lost the inclination to jump out and to head toward the beach.[37] Once in the water, they sprinted through German bullets to the shore and to the apparent safety of a ten-foot sea wall. It was covered with barbed wire. To the left were pillboxes sited to machine-gun men desperate to get past the wall. Only twenty did. Second and third waves of landing craft only added to the number of trapped men. The defenders consisted of but one army and one Luftwaffe platoon, plus a few others: about 100 men.[38] They needed and received no reinforcements. At 0805 hours, the surviving Canadians on the beach surrendered.

Of the 554 of the Royal Regiment embarked, 95 percent became casualties, 264 were captured, 227 killed.[39] The Canadian Official History rated "the episode at Puys ... the grimmest of the whole grim operation.... Along the fatal sea-wall the lads from Toronto lay in heaps."[40]

The landing on Green Beach—at the coastal village of Pourville, a mile southwest of Dieppe—was almost on time at 0452 hours, but at the wrong spot. The South Saskatchewan Regiment of 500 men was to have come ashore on either side of the mouth of the Scie River and to have taken Pourville and a radar station to its east. Reinforced by 500 Cameron Highlanders—who would land, with bagpipes playing, at 550 hours—they were to meet up with tanks landed at Dieppe. The combined force was next to drive south and then east to capture the airfield north of St. Aubin and the German divisional headquarters at Arques-la-Bataille.

The South Saskatchewans landed, however, 400 yards from where they had intended to: not astride the Scie, but west of it. Surprise had been achieved and most of regiment landed without having been fired on. The men of the prairie quickly captured Pourville—also west of the Scie—but many of them were hit in crossing the river and they made little progress toward the higher ground to the northeast. The enemy had reacted quickly—rushing horse-drawn artillery and one platoon on bicycles into defensive positions. Although the Canadians penetrated more than a mile up the west bank of the Scie, they saw that they could not take their objectives and that no friendly tanks were coming from Dieppe. Withdrawal was ordered. By 1:30 PM, Pourville—the port of re-embarkation—was again in German hands. The attack at Green Beach had cost 160 Canadian lives; 245 were captured.

The main attack on the town of Dieppe was to touch down at 0520 hours. The pebbled shore—one mile long—before the town was designated Red and White Beaches: the former, on the invaders' left, to be assaulted by the Essex Scottish Regiment; the latter, to its right, by the Royal Hamilton Light Infantry; both supported by the 14th Canadian Tank Battalion. The attackers at Dieppe Beach totaled over 1,500 men, plus reserves. Between them and the buildings of the town at high tide were ninety yards of shingle, a barbed-wired, five-foot seawall, a grassy promenade 100 yards wide, and the Boulevard de Verdun. At the southwestern end of the promenade was a casino, which the Germans had partly demolished. On both sides of the beach were headland cliffs, within which artillery and machine guns covering the landing areas had been placed.

The Germans at Dieppe, forewarned by the earlier flank landings, had gone on alert at 0500 hours and, as dawn lightened the sky, shot at the incoming vessels. The defenders were themselves fired on by four Royal Navy destroyers and, from 5:15 to 5:25, by five squadrons of Hurricane fighters. The first Canadian infantry were thought to have reached the shore between 5:20, the targeted time, and 5:23; the first tanks, between 5:30 and 5:35—ten to fifteen minutes behind schedule.

The Canadians jumped from their landing craft, braved the fire of rifles, machine guns, and mortars, and hurried onto the beach. Some ran to the sea wall, while others dug into the stones for imperfect cover or lay still and played dead.

Three infantry parties totaling forty-plus men reached the buildings of the town. By noon, they had retreated to the casino or had been captured. Twenty-seven Churchill tanks were landed; two others were driven into too-deep water and drowned; one remained on its landing craft. Fifteen crossed the seawall onto the promenade, only to find that they could not get by concrete roadblocks—seven feet high, barbed-wired, and backed by anti-tank guns—barring their way into the town. Slated to take objectives four miles inland, no tanks made it past the first buildings of the town, 200 yards from the seawall.

Later Decisions: Should Reserves Have Been Sent to Red and White Beaches—As Was Done?

When made: at 0640 and 0817 hours.
The decision maker: Canadian Major General John Roberts.
Conclusions: the outcome: bad in all respects; **the decision:** bad, but somewhat understandable in the beclouded context; **most to be faulted:** John Roberts, but with recognition that many, if not most, would have done the same.

Smoke cloaked much. Royal Air Force planes laid wreaths of white on the beach, buildings, and bluffs of Dieppe. Royal Navy ships hid from coastal batteries by generating fat clouds about themselves and fired smoke shells to conceal the landing craft. Canadian soldiers ashore fired smoke mortars, operated hand-cranked, smoke-making machines, and threw smoke grenades. Houses and a factory in Dieppe and wrecked landing vessels burned and added to the smoke, which intermittently parted or lifted enough to expose as targets the desperate men in the boats and water and on the beach. German snipers high in the cliffs and buildings, using smokeless ammunition to avoid detection, picked them off.

But for the smoke, the command ship of John Roberts was close enough to Dieppe to have seen the calamity ashore. He remained in his operations cabin. He sought to sense the battle through radio communications—which, however, had largely broken down and afforded him but sparse, distorted glimpses of what his men were encountering, achieving, and suffering.

Jubilee planners had provided for interlocking and redundant radio networks that were thought "exquisitely designed."[41] They had anticipated that the enemy would intercept their conversations and would promote confusion with bogus transmissions and had devised countermeasures. They did not, however, expect that German gunners would especially target officers and radio operators,[42] thereby reducing Allied communication on the beach to a shambles. Inasmuch as Wehrmacht snipers throughout the war, including in Flanders in 1940, had prioritized those carrying radio sets—made conspicuous by the antennae—this should have been foreseen. Faulty interpretation compounded the confusion: virtually every transmission was subsequently judged to have been mangled or misunderstood on receipt.[43] The result was that Allied officers from General Roberts on down had little idea of what was happening.[44]

At 6:10 AM, a headquarters ship off of Dieppe logged in the message: "Essex Scot across the beaches and in houses." This likely derived from a transmission from the shore: "12 of our men in the buildings. Have not heard from them for some time." Roberts would later state that "information received indicated that 'Red' Beach was sufficiently cleared"—information that the Canadian Official History termed "very exaggerated"[45]—to justify sending reinforcements. At 6:40, he ordered Les Fusiliers Mont-Royal in to Red Beach.

The Royal Marine Commando was to have brought the landing barges captured in the harbors of Dieppe back to England. By 8:00, this was seen not to be possible. At 8:17, Roberts ordered the marines to reinforce his men on White Beach. He hoped that they might move through Dieppe to take and to silence German guns in the cliffs east of the town.

With poor operational vision, Roberts had had to determine what his division should do: to make what has been called "the most controversial decision in modern Canadian military history."[46] While some have criticized him for not securing a better sense of the battle before sending in his reserves,[47] the Canadian Official History came down softly on him: "Perhaps the general was unwise," but "deceptively encouraging intelligence was still being received."[48]

The Outcome: Wounding, Capture and Death

Les Fusiliers Mont-Royal, instead of landing on Red Beach, came ashore dispersed across both Red and White Beaches. This did not matter. Despite what one officer described as "the dash with which the men rushed ashore and charged up the shingle,"[49] Dieppe remained securely held by the enemy, whose fire swept the beach. Five hundred and thirteen of the Fusiliers—out of their original 584—became casualties. One hundred and five were killed in action; 344 were captured.

Upon emerging from their protective smoke-bank, the boats carrying the Royal Marine Commando came under fire and its commander, Lieutenant Colonel Joseph Picton-Phillipps, saw that the shore was a Canadian cataclysm. He stood in his boat to signal his seven landing craft to reverse course, to get back into the smoke, and to escape. In exposing himself to signal, Picton-Phillipps was shot dead. Three of his boats missed his message and continued on to the shore, where most of their men were killed or captured.

Still Later Decision: Should the Operation Have Been Called Off—As It Was?

When made: at 0900 hours.

The decision maker: Canadian Major General John Roberts, counseled by British Naval Force Commander, Captain John Hughes-Hallett.

Conclusions: the outcome: about the best that could have been salvaged from the disaster; **the decision:** somewhat good, poorer than if made earlier, better than if later; **most to be mildly lauded:** John Roberts and John Hughes-Hallett.

By nine o'clock it had become clear that enemy fire still controlled the beach and that only token parties on foot had entered the town. Roberts ordered withdrawal—a decision not subsequently questioned.

The Outcome: The Return of Twelve Hundred; Crowing in Berlin

At 1100 hours, Allied landing craft came in to Red and White Beaches—with covering Royal Navy gunfire and squadrons of Royal Air Force fighters overhead. The tanks on the promenade retreated to the beach to cover the withdrawal of the infantry. Between 350 and 400 men were taken off. Of the 1,135 men in the two regiments that had first landed at Dieppe—the Royal Hamiltons and the Essex Scottish—1,010 became casualties, 318 of them fatal. By shortly after 1300 hours, virtually all Canadians still ashore had surrendered. The only exceptions were the handful of men who had gotten over the sea wall at Puys. They laid down their arms later that afternoon.

About 1,000 of the Canadians designated for landing never made it onto French soil. Of the 4,000 who did, 1,200 returned to England. Half of them were wounded. Eight hundred Canadians had been killed in action and 1,950 taken prisoner—the latter number greater than the total of Canadians captured in the eleven months of fighting in northern Europe between June 1944 and May 1945.[50] Two hundred and seventy-five British soldiers and marines had become casualties, as had 550 sailors—the destroyer HMS *Berkeley* having been sunk by the Luftwaffe. The Royal Air Force suffered greater losses on August 19, 1942, than on any other day of the war. One hundred and six of its planes were shot down and 67 of its men killed. Ten pilots and thirteen planes of the Royal Canadian Air Force were lost.

The Germans had 600 casualties and were estimated to have lost 91 planes plus perhaps twice as many more significantly damaged.[51]

The Allies had feared that a repulse at Dieppe would be exploited by the propagandists of Joseph Goebbels, who might characterize it as a thwarted effort to establish a Second Front. To lessen this possibility, the BBC, once Jubilee was underway, broadcast to the French that the landings were but a short-term raid and urged them not to assist the invaders and thereby to invite reprisals.

Radio Berlin, soon after the raid, announced that an attempted invasion by an inept foe had been repulsed with scorn.

Field Marshal Gerd von Rundstedt reported that the local French had behaved admirably: providing refreshments for Wehrmacht troops and caring for their wounded. In gratitude, Hitler released 1,700 war prisoners from the area—returning them to their homes with immunity from conscription for slave labor. The Reich said, moreover, that it would give Dieppe ten million marks to repair the damage done by the Allies.[52]

Hitler and Goebbels had a propaganda coup. Maréchal Philippe Pétain volunteered to the Wehrmacht the forces of Vichy to beat off any such future landings.[53]

How Bad Was the Outcome? How Significant the Battle?

The only operational objective achieved by Jubilee—the only basis for any jubilation—was the destruction of the Hess Battery, accomplished by 252 men at a cost of 39 casualties. Of the others who landed, over four fifths became casualties—without doing anything of value.

Students of past wars had a variety of views and perspectives on Dieppe. To one historian, the raid "was one of the great tragedies of the Second World War; in percentage terms, the losses equalled or exceeded those in any First World War battle."[54] The four thousand Allied casualties were many times the hundreds of English dead and wounded at Agincourt, fought in 1415 sixty miles northeast of Dieppe; one sixth of those suffered by the allies of 1815 at Waterloo, one-hundred-plus miles further east; two thirds of those that the Americans would have in February 1943 at Kasserine; one half of America's on June 6, 1944; one two-hundred-and-eightieth of Russia's at Stalingrad.

The battle in the air that day was the largest fought on the Western Front in the war.

While dozens of books have been exclusively devoted to the raid at Dieppe or to aspects of it, Operation Jubilee has also escaped mention in numerous histories of the war.[55]

Churchill granted that "the casualties of this memorable action may seem out of proportion to the results," but asserted that "they must not class it as a failure. It was a costly but not unfruitful reconnaissance in force. Tactically it was a mine of experience."[56] After initially thinking Dieppe "a fiasco,"[57] Eisenhower, in his memoirs, found the same silver lining as Churchill: despite the "high percentage of losses... we learned a number of lessons that we later applied to our advantage."[58] Lord Lovat, who had commanded at the Orange Beaches, the only successful part of Jubilee, was not buying these sweeteners: he wrote in 1978 that "for thirty years the truth has been wrapped in pink ribbons, with saccharin added": "the raid itself was a disaster."[59]

The overwhelming majority of historians have disregarded Churchill's injunction that Jubilee not be seen as a failure: flatly calling it such, or a debacle, or a disaster.[60]

An Alternative Approach to Judging Decisions and Outcomes, That of Decision Science

To understand and to improve upon such deliberations as those that sent Allied soldiers to Dieppe have been main missions of *decision science*:

systematic inquiry—using the insights and tools of economics, game theory, psychology, statistics, and related disciplines—to structure and to guide choices made under uncertainty.[61]

As Soviet, Western, German, Italian, and Japanese soldiers killed and died, modern decision science did not exist. It was, in the decades after the war, pioneered by Ward Edwards, Ronald Howard, Howard Raiffa, and others. An influential, early exposition of DS was Raiffa's 1968 *Decision Analysis: Introductory Lectures on Choices Under Uncertainty*. The groundwork papers of these three founders have since been built on in hundreds of successor books: works that cover both commonsense and mathematically rigorous methods for making tough calls.

Decision science assesses both the soundness and the results of choices: whether good or bad decisions were made; whether good or bad outcomes ensued; and the extents to which the GDs or BDs may have caused the GOs or BOs.

Outcomes have been judged by different criteria:

Hopes. Choices are sensed to have had good outcomes if their results are what the decision makers both hoped for and judged to have had sufficient chances of occurring: that was why those choices were made. The Allies on August 19, 1942 had not come within German-coastal-artillery range of their expectations and hopes: a bad-outcome-per-hopes;

Net result. Some outcomes are not what were hoped for, but nevertheless have positive aspects outweighing the negative and are therefore good-outcomes-on-net. This was not the case for Jubilee, which had losses that swamped any gains and had set back the Allied cause: a BO-on-net; and

Comparison versus alternatives. While good and bad outcomes per hopes and net results are of interest and significance, for decision science the most critical question is whether or not an option not taken would likely have led to better results. That forgoing the raid on Dieppe would have been better than undertaking it meant that the actual result was a BO-v-alts.[62]

Different criteria give different ratings. Suppose that a city wants to improve the reading skills of its grade-school students and might implement either of two reading-enhancement programs of equal cost: Alpha and Bravo. Program Alpha is chosen hoping and expecting that it will yield test-measured reading gains of 0.6 grade level. Should it then achieve gains of but 0.45 grade level, it is a bad-outcome-per-hopes. A backer of the decision might, however, argue that the 0.45-grade-level gain was more than worth the program cost—signifying a good-outcome-on-net. If, though, Program Bravo would, per best estimates, have yielded still greater gains, choosing Alpha would have had a bad-outcome-versus-alternatives.

Among the criteria for judging outcomes, that of hopes is the easiest to apply; comparison versus alternatives, the most challenging and subject to dispute. Whether hopes have been fulfilled is generally known—even though different decision participants may have had variant versions of them. More problematic and debatable is the determination of net results and progress toward goal achievement—as involved decision makers and subsequent historians may value differently aspects of outcomes and therefore disagree on whether gains have exceeded costs and, if so, by how much. Still more difficult is the comparison with alternatives, which poses the possibly-insuperable challenge of speculating on what would have happened, had other courses been taken.[63]

Did the Lessons of Dieppe Make Its Outcome, on Net, Good?

Some—while conceding the short-term shortcomings of Jubilee—have held that, in a longer and broader perspective, it was both GO-on-net and GO-v-alts. Chief among the defenders of the raid was Louis Mountbatten. That both Churchill and Eisenhower wrote of its experiential pluses owed in part to personal briefings by Lord Louis. The account that Churchill gave in his memoirs of Dieppe had been drafted for him by Mountbatten.[64] The Chief of Combined Operations held that thousands of Allied casualties were on June 6, 1944, saved because of the earlier raid and that, for each death on the shingle of Dieppe, ten lives were saved 22 months later[65]:

> Dieppe was one of the most vital operations of the Second World War. It gave to the Allies the priceless secret of victory.[66]
>
> From the lessons we learnt at Dieppe all subsequent landings in the Mediterranean and elsewhere benefitted directly.... The successful landing in Normandy was won on the beaches of Dieppe.[67]

Others, however, have wondered if these assertions came from a desire to ennoble the last actions of the dead and/or from the wish to dodge blame for a bad decision in which Mountbatten had been front-row. Perhaps too, Mountbatten thought that Allied soldiers, sailors, and fliers might lose confidence in higher authorities and might fight less well, if they believed that their decision-making superiors had been dopey on Dieppe.

Mentions of Dieppe in histories of later amphibious operations were scant. The British Official Naval History mentioned Dieppe once in its account of the planning for the invasion of Sicily, as did Frederick Morgan, the initial chief planner for Overlord, in his memoirs.[68]

The after-action report of Combined Operations Headquarters listed many lessons taught by the raid, but especially stressed "*the need for overwhelming fire support* [emphasis in original]": including close support, heavy naval bombardment, and air action. General Henry Crerar related that, pre–Dieppe, the highest levels of command had thought that "an assault against a heavily defended coast could be carried out on the basis of securing tactical surprise, and without dependence on overwhelming fire support." Operation Sledgehammer, a possible 1942 invasion of northern France, had indeed been planned on that presumption—for which August 19, 1942, proved a "sobering influence."[69] For one historian, who thought that the lessons of Dieppe "were to save hundreds of Allied lives," they included seeing: the impossibility of directly assaulting a Channel port; the strength of Hitler's coastal defenses; and the need for close-support fire.[70]

Admiral Harold Baillie-Grohman disagreed, holding that most of the supposed lessons of Jubilee had been foreknown—indeed also published and disseminated—by the Royal Navy.[71] A later historian similarly dismissed the claim that Dieppe had secured any "priceless secret" as "tripe, unless the lesson of not attacking a well-defended town without proper intelligence and a preliminary aerial and naval bombardment is a 'priceless secret,' rather than the kind of assumption a lance-corporal might have made."[72]

Even if the lessons learned at Dieppe had been pre-raid non-obvious to generals as well as to lance-corporals, was the raid necessary to learn them? Another historian thought not—deeming the lessons of the raid either pre-known or learnable "far more easily and at less cost by other means."[73] The Allies and the Germans believed that much could be learned from war games. Could a simulation of Jubilee have learned virtually all that it taught? Bernard Montgomery granted that the lessons of Dieppe contributed importantly to Overlord's success, but also believed it possible to have secured them "without losing so many magnificent Canadian soldiers."[74] U.S. General Lucian Truscott disagreed, deeming Dieppe not "a failure," but "an essential though costly lesson."[75]

Alan Brooke had sided, pre-raid, with Mountbatten and Truscott. On June 30, 1942, days before Operation Rutter was to be launched, Churchill had asked Captain John Hughes-Hallett if he could guarantee success. The Chief of the Imperial General Staff jumped in: "If he, or anyone else, could guarantee success, there would indeed be no object in doing the operation. It is just because no one has the slightest idea what the outcome will be that the operation is necessary." With Tobruk having fallen to Rommel nine days earlier, Churchill said that "this was not a moment that he wanted to be taught by adversity." "In that case," Brooke responded, "you must abandon the idea of invading France because no responsible general will be associated with any planning for invasion until we have an operation at least the size of the Dieppe raid behind us to study and base our plan upon."[76]

Perhaps the Germans too would base future plans on the events of August 19, 1942: the learning from Jubilee was two-way. This objection to such raids had been raised before Dieppe, in a Royal Navy memorandum of July 25, 1942:

> The Germans welcome these raids for nothing shows up weakness in the defense more than an attack with a very limited objective. Every time we find a weak spot on the enemy's coast we point out his weakness, and there is ample evidence that he has taken and is taking full advantage of this information.... As it is our present intention ... to make an attack in force upon the enemy's coast, we are now [by raiding at Dieppe] doing our best to make that attack less likely to achieve success.[77]

The Germans would, in fact, learn not only from the battle but also from a copy of the operational plan for Jubilee, which they found on the corpse of a Canadian major. Field Marshal Rundstedt, Commander-in-Chief of Wehrmacht forces in the West, had the plan translated and, five days after the raid, urged his officers to study it to understand the Allied "method of landing and fighting" and to see how much the Allies knew about the coastal defenses. He cautioned, though, that the Allies would learn from their failure and would change their tactics.[78]

While Churchill, Eisenhower, Brooke, Mountbatten, Hughes-Hallett, Truscott, and some historians asserted that Jubilee was justified by its lessons, most later historians have disagreed—

writing that "Dieppe had been a disaster dressed up as lessons learned," with assertions that it had been "a necessary rehearsal" for Overlord being "much rubbish"[79]; that the claims of experiential value had been "entirely discredited"[80]; that the lessons learned were "obvious."[81]

What Pluses, Other Than Its Lessons, Did Operation Jubilee Have?

The Western Allies, having in 1942 superiority in aviation, welcomed air battles, such as that at Dieppe, in which they lost about as many planes as the Germans—which would increase their ratio of advantage. Churchill, shortly after the operation, reported to his War Cabinet that "the large scale air battle alone justified the raid."[82]

Authors have also noted other consequences of Dieppe—some perhaps intended, others likely unforeseen; any one of which might have constituted benefits more than justifying the 4,000 casualties suffered. Perhaps, for instance, those captures, wounds, and deaths demonstrated valuably to the Americans that an early invasion of northwest France was not feasible. The brunt of holding firm against American impatience for a true Second Front—not sideshow campaigns of limited size in Africa or other diversionary undertakings of like scale, but multi-division boots in France—had been borne by Churchill and Brooke. The debacle of Dieppe strengthened their case. Historians wrote that U.S. "illusions about the feasibility of invading France" in 1942 "must have been dispelled" by Dieppe[83] and that the raid "provided a useful argument for.... Brooke, who thought it would prove to the Americans once and for all that a second front across the Channel was unthinkable for at least another year."[84] It is possible that the casualty total of Dieppe, by giving pause to rash American impulses, saved the Allies multiples of that tragic number. As will be seen below, the tempering of American ardor to invade France was thought by some authors to have been not just an after-the-fact, consolational plus, but a prior intention.

Alternatively, the disaster at Dieppe may have been worth its costs to make the same point to the Russians. The UK had had also to hold firm in 1942 against the urgings of its other major ally for an early Second Front—for which Soviet Foreign Minister Vyacheslav Molotov came in late spring to London and Washington. To Molotov Churchill praised the Red Army and said that, given any plan, "provided it was sound and sensible," for further

> drawing the weight off Russia this year, we should not hesitate to put it into effect. Clearly, it would not further either the Russian cause or that of the Allies as a whole if, for the sake of action at any price, we embarked on some operation which ended in disaster and gave the enemy an opportunity for glorification at our discomfiture.[85]

Some have judged that Dieppe had been such a disaster.

Churchill told Molotov of his hopes that air attacks by the UK and U.S. would force the withdrawal of Luftwaffe units from Russia. While joining the U.S. in announcing on June 11 that complete understanding had been arrived at with Molotov "with regard to the urgent tasks of creating a second front in Europe in 1942," the UK simultaneously gave Molotov an aide-mémoire stating that "we are making preparations for a landing on the Continent in August or September 1942," which, however, could not be unconditionally promised.[86] The aide-mémoire also declared that the British "shall continue our policy of raids against selected points on the Continent. These raids will increase in size and scope as the summer goes on."[87] One historian wrote that "the British cannot have had much faith in [the success of Jubilee], other than to show the Russians that they were doing something and reinforcing the impossibility of invasion in 1942 to the Americans."[88] It is possible that Dieppe promoted Russian goodwill, the worth of which to the Western Allies may have been significant—or not.

The raid might also have gained in leading the Germans to divert to France forces that otherwise might have gone to the Eastern Front or have been available to oppose the impending Allied landings in Algeria and French Morocco. At the end of August, Hitler determined to augment his western defenses with seven additional divisions and, in early October, positioned elite units to fend off anticipated landings in Lower Normandy.[89] Churchill judged that these Dieppe-induced actions "did something to take the weight off Russia."[90] General Walter Warlimont of Hitler's HQ agreed with the Prime Minister: as a result of Jubilee, the Führer had "lost his nerve" and had transferred from East to West two crack divisions, "just when they might have turned the scales at Stalingrad."[91] The Canadian Official History concluded that Dieppe drew German attention toward France and away from Africa: "a dividend" of the raid, which was, however, "no part of the calculations of those who planned it."[92]

Also uncalculated were the possibilities that Jubilee might have induced the Germans to adopt an inferior defensive strategy or to become overconfident. The British Official History—with the official biographer of Mountbatten in agreement—judged it "probable that the Germans' success in repelling the Dieppe raid influenced their strategy, which proved fatal in 1944, of attempting to hold an attempt at invasion on the beaches instead of relying on a mobile reserve."[93] One historian wrote that "the disaster did create one major advantage. Hitler believed that what he would soon call his Atlantic Wall was virtually impregnable, and that his forces in France could easily defeat an invasion."[94] Field Marshal Albert Kesselring was said, because of Dieppe, to have overestimated German chances of beating off an Allied invasion of Sicily.[95] No record has been found that any Allied decision makers intended for Dieppe to be as botched and catastrophic as it was in order to trick the Germans into taking a poor strategic approach for beach defense or to lull them into relaxing their guard.

Judging Decisions Apart from Outcomes

It is tempting and relatively easy to judge decisions by their outcomes: those leading to good results are reflexively thought good; those to bad, bad. Does the consensus judgment that the Dieppe raid had turned out horrendously for the Allies necessarily mean that the decision to launch it was comparably bad?

The same question arises in sporting events—for instance, a golfer faced with a long shot over water to a green or a football coach mulling whether, on fourth down and short yardage, to punt or to go for a first down. If the golfer takes his risky option and hits a three-metal into a pond, it is often automatically concluded that he made a bad decision. If the football team conservatively punts, never gets the ball again, and ends up losing by two points, critics will call the decision too cautious. To decision scientists such snap judgments are examples of what they have termed *outcome bias:* rating decisions by their results.[96]

Decision science instead distinguishes the quality of the decision from the rating of the outcome. A decision for DS is optimal if and only if it is the alternative most likely—taking into account all that might happen and based on best available knowledge—to yield outcomes that are on expectation best for the decision maker. A bad decision is choosing a prospectively-inferior option.

For facile rating of decisions by their outcomes, the possibilities of good-decision-bad-outcome and of bad-decision-good-outcome cannot arise; for decision scientists, they do. Consider hypothetically a physician and patient together deciding on alternative cancer treatments A or B and suppose that they wish to maximize the likelihood that the patient will live at least five years.

Best data indicate that Treatment A offers this patient a 60-percent chance of five-year survival and Treatment B, a 40-percent chance. If A is chosen and followed soon by death, it is GDBO. (BO-hopes, because expectations and hopes were disappointed; also BO-on-net, with the non-attainment of the goal and the early death outweighing any positive aspects of the treatment. Judgment of the outcome via comparison versus alternatives must be based on comparison with the expected outcome with Treatment B.) To choose Treatment B and to survive over six years is BDGO-hopes, -on-net, and -v-alts.

Or, to take the football example, suppose that, using data from many games, estimates are made of what would happen if the fourth-and-short situation were to occur 100 times; that punting would lead on average to winning 21 of 100 times and that attempting to pick up a first down would win 36 of 100 games. The better choice is not to punt. Punting and still winning is bad-decision-good-outcome; having one's fourth-down play not pick up a first down and subsequently losing is good-decision-bad-outcome.[97]

Decision scientists have noted that Herodotus, over two millennia ago in discussing the actions of Persian kings, had remarked on the possibilities of GDBO and BDGO.[98]

Was Undertaking Jubilee a Good or a Bad Decision?

One way for decision makers to assert satisfaction with their choices and with the results obtained is to state that, if faced once more with the same choices and with knowledge of actual outcomes, they would do the same again. Louis Mountbatten, with respect to Dieppe, was unapologetic: "If I had the same decision to make again, I would do as I did before."[99]

The British Official History took a neutral position: "arguments whether or not the raid was justified in the circumstances are nicely balanced."[100]

Authors who judged that Jubilee had a bad outcome, had little good to say about the decision that had led to it: one judging the "fiasco"—like Operation Market Garden 25 months later—the product "of hasty planning, of obtuse enthusiasm on the part of those units desperate to see 'action,' and of amateur, even tragic, over-ambitiousness"[101]; another thinking the raid "in retrospect ... so recklessly hare-brained an enterprise that it is difficult to reconstruct the official state of mind which gave it birth and drove it forward"[102]; a third calling Jubilee "one of the most ill-conceived operations of the war," lacking even "the slightest chance of success"[103]; a fourth deeming that 3,400 Canadians had been "senselessly sacrificed," inasmuch as "sheer common sense ought to have told the Combined Chiefs of Staff that Mountbatten's plan was misconceived from the outset."[104]

Such critiques raise the question of how sound the Allied scheme for Dieppe was. The Germans, after studying the captured plan of their enemy for Jubilee, thought it "folly."[105] The Canadian Official History called it "unduly optimistic"; two other authors, "suicidal"; still others, stamped with "ignorance, incompetence," and "hubris" and, considered as a whole, "little short of criminal"; "bungled ... in every possible way"; and "fatally flawed."[106] (Brooke, when dining on August 29, 1942, with Churchill and Mountbatten, called the planning for Dieppe "all wrong." Mountbatten responded that it had been done as prescribed by the British Chiefs of Staff; should the CIGS persist in deeming it deficient, he must ask the Minister of Defence for a formal inquiry. Brooke, however, "presumably mollified Mountbatten" and the matter was not pursued.[107])

This was the same basic plan that Bernard Montgomery had largely crafted and signed off on, that Henry Crerar had judged "sound,"[108] and that he and Andrew McNaughton had twice approved. How could these three men have green-lighted an attack protocol that, when put to the test, proved—for so little possible gain—a warrant of death for one thousand men? (Montgomery stated in his *Memoirs* that the plan for Rutter had had—before being implemented as Jubilee—two modifications to which he would not have agreed: the dropping of the airborne component and of the preliminary bombing.[109] His authorized biographer thought this nonsense: considering the first change irrelevant to the sad outcome and noting that Montgomery had, on June 5, chaired the meeting at which the bombing had been dropped.[110]) One reason for the approvals of the plan was that able men had worked long and hard to produce a detailed document of three hundred pages. Aspects of the operation had had meticulous preparations. The men responsible for destroying targets had had specific instruction and rehearsals in the techniques to be employed. The withdrawal from Dieppe was to have had thirteen staged defensive lines.[111] It was reported that "nobody involved could afterwards recall a more thoroughly documented operational plan."[112]

Historian reviewers of the assiduously-prepared attack script have, however, found flaw upon flaw. One judged that the unfavorable terrain should have ruled out landing at or near Dieppe—making its selection "the first mistake."[113] To another author, changing the original plan of landings east and west of the town to a direct assault on its beaches was a "tragic and costly" mistake; to a third writer, "the fatal decision."[114] The Canadian Official History thought this part mistake and part lesson: "Dieppe killed the always more than dubious idea of frontal attack on a major fortified port."[115]

Faults also were found in the details of that frontal attack. It was, for instance, thought that the half-hour lapse between the flank and the main assaults was a "fatal change in plans."[116] Judged comparably fatal—indeed, "the most basic flaw of all"[117]—was Mountbatten's failure to provide for naval bombardment by capital ships. Without such support it was thought mistaken to have persisted with plans for the raid.[118] The cancellation of the heavy bombing was similarly deemed "a staggering decision."[119] The German after-action critique judged that "the strength of air and naval forces was not nearly sufficient to keep the defenders down during the landings."[120] One historian agreed and thought that, once the limitations on naval and air support had been imposed, the raid "probably should" have been canceled[121]; another judged the combination of the frontal attack and insufficient support for the assaulting infantry "the least explicable elements in our planning."[122]

Perhaps the explanation was the inexperience of the planners. The brittleness of the battle plan indicated to the Germans that it had been based on formalistic theory, rather than on practical familiarity with war.[123] Bernard Montgomery on first reading the draft plan of Combined Operations Headquarters, called it "the work of an amateur"[124]—which he then made worse by insisting on the frontal attack at Dieppe and by approving the flank assault at Puys[125] and the elimination of the heavy bombing. It was judged that those who had concocted Jubilee had had but "a slight grasp" of amphibious warfare.[126] The Germans noted that the plan had "fixed every detail of action for each unit." Given that the only certain expectation in war is that the unexpected will occur, the rigid pre-specification of unit orders ensured, the Germans judged, "the failure of the whole raid."[127] The COHQ after-action report and historians have agreed.[128]

Capping the critiques was their inability to identify any worthy objective for the raid. Orange Beach Commander Lord Lovat spoke for many who could find in Jubilee no goals of value close to commensurate to the resources deployed.[129] A later historian echoed that it was "hard to know what [it] was meant to achieve."[130] The Germans too were puzzled: was Dieppe to have been the opening move in a permanent invasion or was it just a raid? If the latter, why had the Allies thrown away thirty of their best tanks for so little possible gain? One Canadian officer, when captured and interrogated, was asked: Operation Jubilee had been "too big for a raid, and too small for an invasion"; what had the Allies been trying to do? The prisoner replied that, if they could tell him, he would be most grateful.[131]

The verdict on the plans for Rutter and Jubilee was initially rendered by the Wehrmacht and subsequently reiterated by historians: that, for little prospect of gain, they had condemned thousands of men to incapacitating wounds, captivity, and death—as should have been evident to any clear-eyed reviewer of them. The Canadian Official History recorded that "the enemy was astonished that, in spite of our generally accurate knowledge of his defences, we attempted an assault on an area strong both by nature and by art, with weapons which he considered inadequate."[132] The commander of the 302nd Wehrmacht Division found it "incomprehensible that it should be believed that a single Canadian division should be able to overrun a German infantry regiment reinforced with artillery."[133]

How Much Did Ill Luck, Flawed Execution, or Poor Intelligence Contribute to the Bad Outcome?

While Bernard Montgomery had predicated Rutter's "good prospects for success" on weather, luck, naval piloting, and officer confidence, the Canadian Official History and other accounts subsequently thought that Jubilee had had "bad luck," even "spectacularly bad luck"— citing such factors as the chance encounter with the German convoy and faulty intelligence that underestimated enemy strength.[134] (That the Germans at Dieppe on August 19 were in twice their anticipated strength was considered bad luck by some, but by others just the result of poor intelligence gathering.)

There had, though, also been elements of good fortune. Dieppe had, for instance, on August 19, 1942, had the clear sunny morning that the Royal Air Force had wanted—ideal for supporting the landed troops and for bringing the Luftwaffe out to battle. Fortunate too was that operational security had not been compromised, as Montgomery had feared it must be. The enemy on the day of Jubilee apparently knew nothing about either Rutter or it. The Canadian Official History, after reviewing German documents, had "complete certainty that [the enemy] had no foreknowledge whatever of the raid."[135]

They first had learned of it when the Allied ships and the German convoy had come together. The raid commanders feared that this chance engagement would forfeit surprise. In fact, though, the Germans thought it unexceptional: just a limited attack on a convoy, unconnected with any larger operation and not a cause for general alarm. Wehrmacht troops near the Bernevals—and possibly also those at Puys, but not those at Dieppe or further to the west—went on alert. The Canadian Official History, while terming the incident "bad luck," concluded that there had been no "general loss of the element of surprise."[136] The brief naval skirmish did cut by two thirds the commando force that landed at the Yellow Beaches and put paid to any chances it had had of success.

Possible success at each of the beaches had required surprise. The Germans had, in a general way, been alert to the possibility of a Channel-Coast raid. The communiqués issued by London and Washington on June 11, 1942, announcing agreement on a Second Front that year were thought by the Canadian Official History "notorious": they "would probably have been enough in themselves to lead the Germans to take special measures."[137] Hitler's directive of July 9, 1942, reasoned that Britain, to stave off Russian collapse, would undertake "a large-scale invasion"— with the French coast between Dieppe and Le Havre a target area of high likelihood.

Between July 20 and August 12, the 302nd Division defending Dieppe and adjacent coastline was reinforced with 2,503 untrained men. By August 18, German forces in France were, per the Canadian Official History, "in a full state of alert."[138] The men of the 302nd Division had been ordered that night to sleep in their battle clothes and to stay close to their weapons. The Luftwaffe unit supporting the 302nd, however, interpreted the weather forecast differently from the German Army and had given 24-hour leaves to one third of its pilots—most of whom attended forty miles from Dieppe a dance with female auxiliaries that lasted until dawn.[139] The raiders approaching the shore that morning were favored, in sum, by as much surprise as they could reasonably have hoped for.

Would those men, by performing well, benefit from the surprise they had achieved? One historian thought that, in execution, as well as in planning, "those responsible simply did not know what they were doing."[140] This judgment, however, seems too censorious.

The naval piloting had been a point of concern. Henry Crerar, like Bernard Montgomery, conditioned his prediction of success on good navigation. In the first training exercise for Rutter, two regiments had been landed two or more miles from their target beaches and the tanks had come ashore over an hour behind schedule. On August 19, however, the piloting proved both reasonably accurate and self-sacrificially courageous. The British Official History considered the performance of the Royal Navy "beyond praise."[141] The Canadian Official History, however, ascribed operational failure both to naval shortcomings and to the attack plan that did not allow for them. The landing at Green Beach—four hundred yards west of its target—had been a bull's eye in comparison with the misses of the training. The error had, however, in the judgment of the COH, forfeited the surprise achieved, prevented taking the heights to the east, and was "probably fatal" to this part of the operation.[142]

The Canadian Official History also attributed the repulse at Red and White Beaches to naval delays. That the landing infantry were perhaps as much as three minutes late meant that they "were to this extent less able to profit by the air attack." That the first tanks were ten to fifteen minutes behind schedule was, per the COH, "a more serious error.... In any opposed landing, the first minute or two after the craft touch down are of crucial importance; and it may be said that during that minute or two the Dieppe battle, on the main beaches, was lost. The impetus of the attack ebbed quickly away, and by the time the tanks arrived the psychological moment was past."[143] While most other authors have not linked the disaster to these delays, one exception also thought that, because of the fifteen minutes by which the attack at Puys was behind schedule, "the hinge jammed tight on Jubilee."[144] The COH concluded that Jubilee had demonstrated "that the military plan in such operations must not depend upon precise timing."[145]

Comparably proficient to the naval piloting was the air support. It was generally agreed that the pilots had performed superbly. Their actions in support of the men in the boats and on the beaches were described by the Canadian Official History as "beyond praise"; by General John Roberts, as "magnificent."[146]

Whether the ground forces took good advantage of their naval and air support to do well themselves has been disagreed on. Two German after-action assessments included ungenerous shots. The 81st Corps rated the commandos high and the Canadians low. One Wehrmacht general reported that the "English fought well. Canadians and Americans not so well."[147] These criticisms were, however, the exceptions. The German Fifteenth Army judged that "the enemy, almost entirely Canadian soldiers, fought—so far as he was able to fight at all—well and bravely." The 302nd German Infantry Division concluded similarly that the attacks at Dieppe, Pourville, and Puys had shown "great energy," while the "tank crews did not lack spirit." Churchill wrote that "the utmost gallantry and devotion were shown by all the troops and by the British Commandos and by the landing-craft and their escorts."[148] The problem for the Canadians had been, the

Germans judged, that underestimation of the defenses had put the attackers on the shore "in a hopeless position."[149]

Whether such underestimation was a failure of Allied intelligence was a question on which opinions clashed. The Canadian Official History rated "our own intelligence concerning the enemy's defenses and dispositions ... on the whole excellent ... there was not much we did not know about the defenses of the Dieppe area."[150] While some agreed,[151] others held the opposite.[152] Wehrmacht reviewers of the battle plan for Jubilee judged that "the British completely miscalculated the strength of the German defences," their knowledge of German troop dispositions being "extraordinarily inexact."[153] Combined Operations Headquarters had wrongly thought that the Wehrmacht's 302nd Division had been replaced by the 110th—entailing a 50-percent reduction in strength: to one historian, "a colossal British intelligence error."[154] The Canadian Official History, however, judged it without consequence.[155]

While Jubilee had been premised on surprising the Germans, the Allies too encountered the unexpected. They had, for instance at Puys, not anticipated that the sea wall and the main escape gully would be barbed-wired—which had not been seen in aerial photographs. Lieutenant-Colonel Douglas Catto, who would command at Puys, had said that, in the previous war, the Germans had always wired such features and had therefore asked for a heavy bombardment. His request was denied.[156]

Also not seen by the camera planes had been the German guns concealed in the chalk headlands on either side of Dieppe. The failure to detect this firepower led Lord Lovat to rate as "sketchy" the pre–Jubilee intelligence.[157]

Unexpected as well below those headlands was the nature of the beach at Dieppe. Fortunate for the Canadian tankers was that the armor of their Churchills proved invulnerable to the enemy's 37-millimeter anti-tank guns.[158] Unfortunately, however, many of the tanks became immobilized—either by enemy fire that knocked off their tracks or by the unanticipated nature of the shingle. It was of chert: flint-like stones so hard that, when caught in the tank tracks, they broke the links. The Germans had found before the raid that their own panzers became stuck in these rocks and concluded that they need not fear a tank attack. Allied planners had presumed that the beach composition would resemble the softer cobble of southeastern England—which was considered "another grave intelligence error."[159]

Nor were the strengths of the bridges over the Scie River accurately estimated. The option of landing tanks at Pourville was dismissed in part out of fear that those bridges would collapse under the weight of the Churchills. It was later found that the bridges could have borne the tanks.

An aspect of Allied intelligence faulted by Churchill and one historian was the fighting quality of the enemy: the opposition had been thought to consist of low-grade soldiers, which was judged to have been "far from" true.[160] To some extent, however, the assessments had been accurate. The enemy at Green Beach was hesitant in pursuing the retreating raiders. The Germans there were found to be "either very young men or very old."[161] Among the prisoners taken in the casino on Dieppe Beach were Poles who had been locked into their defensive positions with little food for four days. Many Poles serving with the Wehrmacht at Dieppe had been rejected for service in their nation's army.[162] What the raid planners may insufficiently have taken into account was that even troops of lesser quality could prove formidable—if they were confined with good weapons inside well-sited defensive positions and needed only to aim and shoot, knowing that their own lives hung on holding off the attack.

A less-defensible intelligence assessment concerned the headquarters location of the enemy division—which had been thought at Arques-la-Bataille and was to have been captured. The Allies had not learned that the HQ had on April 27 been moved six miles to the east. Inasmuch as there would be no chance of taking either spot, this misapprehension also did not matter.

How should the effects of luck, fighting performance, and intelligence be taken into account in judging the quality of the decisions that sent the Canadians to Dieppe? While the outcome was incontestably bad, might the decisions nevertheless have been justifiable—a case of good-decisions-bad-outcome owing to unforeseeable factors of bad luck, underperformance, and faulty intelligence?

That was not the case.

Perhaps the best judges of what had gone wrong for the Allies were the Germans—with three years of war experience and with their pre-raid assessments of what could and could not be done at Dieppe validated by the results. The defenders there doubted that any conceivable amount of luck, or excellence in execution, or upgraded intelligence could have made Jubilee a success. Even if the Allies had quickly taken Dieppe, the Germans perceived no objectives that might have been achieved that would have justified the resources committed to the raid.

Some accounts—notably the Canadian Official History—have taken issue with this German judgment. Most later authors have, however, agreed with the Wehrmacht's after-action critique: Lord Lovat, for instance, writing that "it was a bad plan, and it had no chance of success."[163]

The aspects of good and bad luck may have roughly canceled each other out and were, in any case, not so net bad as to have led good decisions to have a bad outcome. There were undeniable shortcomings of Allied intelligence, but it does not seem that the best information gathering that could realistically have been expected would substantially have improved either the decisions or the outcome.

The Canadians, from the privates to John Roberts, performed imperfectly—as in any army in any war has always been inevitable. Their shortfall from their likely-best-possible actions was, however, within the range of what the decision makers should reasonably have anticipated of men with their skills and experience.

Of all the aspects of ill luck of August 19, 1942, the worst was that visited on those men: they were horrendously unfortunate to have been assigned to an operation so poorly decided on and so badly planned.

Given the Retrospective Consensus That the Plans for Operations Rutter and Jubilee Were Disastrous, Why Had They Been Approved?

One factor that had led to the raid was the popular pressure for a Second Front. Since the cancellation of Rutter, calls for landing in France had grown louder, as Russian forces on the southern steppes recoiled further. The American, British, and Canadian publics and the Russian government did not understand why Western Allied troops were not already on the continent, fighting toward Berlin, easing pressure on the Red Army.[164] On July 23, Stalin telegraphed Churchill, bemoaning the suspension of supply convoys to Russia's Arctic ports and the continuing lack of a Second Front.[165] Churchill told the Soviet ambassador that significant continental raids were imminent. By then, Sledgehammer had been called off and Jubilee was the only planned European action of even its size. Out of a wish to do something, indeed anything, to take on the Germans and to help the Russians, the impulse to land at Dieppe—and to overlook any defects the operation might have—was strong.[166] The Canadian Official History judged that Jubilee "served as at least a partial substitute for" the Second Front for which the Americans and Russians had been calling, "and was welcomed in the highest circles accordingly."[167]

Those highest circles had their eyes on the lower circles of popular perceptions and wishes. Not only the original impulse for the raid but also the details of its ultimate mounting derived in significant part from attention to public opinion. Per one historian, "the raid's primary purpose was to grab headlines."[168] Churchill—after considering the risk that its failure would be seized on by Third Reich propagandists—favored attacking Dieppe in the belief that it would hearten Americans, British, and Canadians. Decisions on aspects of the raid also were guided by thoughts of public relations. Montgomery insisted on the frontal attack at Dieppe because, if flanking attacks lacked the time to take the town, the public would see the raid as a failure.[169] The Royal Navy vetoed sending a battleship to Dieppe out of fears that, if it were sunk, the Allies could not claim that the raid had been a victory—being concerned "to avoid a major public-relations reversal."[170]

An ongoing public-relations concern was Canadian frustration. The Dominion was itching to get into the war. It was ramping up its peacetime army of 4,500 men to a 1.1-million-man force that would distinguish itself in the European campaigns of 1943 through 1945. All-volunteer Canadian units had been in Britain since 1939. They wanted to do their life-risking part in defeating Nazi Germany but, so far, had had no chance to. Canadians in the spring of 1940 had not been included among British forces fighting in Norway and France. Only after the evacuation at Dunkirk were Dominion units sent briefly into Brittany, before being re-embarked, without having fought. Back in England, the Canadians trained and complained, patronized the pubs, brawled with the bobbies, and wondered if they ever would get into the war. Churchill wrote that the Canadian Army, by mid–1942, "had now for two years been eating its heart out in Britain."[171] General Bernard Montgomery and Canadian Prime Minister Mackenzie King, in addressing Canadian soldiers to hearten them, were both heckled. There was sensed "increasing pressure of public opinion in Canada for an active role for the [Dominion's] Army."[172] Henry Crerar had not hesitated in accepting Montgomery's offer of the lead role in Rutter. For him and his countrymen to decline to attack Dieppe, the battle plan would have had to be even more tragically and obviously flawed—if that was possible—than it was. The generals and men of Canada never came close to backing away from their proffered roles in the raid.

Not only the Canadians, but the Western Allies generally felt a need to show their mettle. Joseph Stalin—with Americans in less-confrontationally-expressed agreement—had ascribed the British reluctance to open a Second Front to "faint-heartedness." That Winston Churchill "bristled" at this charge was thought to have been one reason why he had approved Dieppe.[173]

The Prime Minister was joined in his approval of the raid by the British Chiefs of Staff—who, on May 13, 1942, and possibly also in July, gave it their blessing. In these endorsements, many factors may have influenced two of the service chiefs: First Sea Lord, Admiral Sir Dudley Pound and Air Chief Marshal Sir Charles Portal. Pound had been initially critical of Combined Operations Headquarters raiding plans but, historian Brian Villa concluded, for reasons of his own status and Royal Navy priorities, shifted position.[174] The First Sea Lord sensed that Churchill wished to oust him from his post, perhaps to replace him with Mountbatten.[175] To have opposed the raid would have reinforced charges that Pound was "too old, too sleepy, and too cautious"—in contrast to young, dynamic, daring Lord Louis.[176] The Royal Navy, especially as difficulties mounted with the Arctic convoys to the Soviets and forced their suspension, was criticized for insufficiently aiding Russia. Pound's going along with raiding Dieppe—even though he judged it militarily unsound—helped the RN both by appeasing Stalin and by deflecting Churchill from invading Norway.[177] Portal represented a service that, in May of 1942, mounted the first of its 1,000-plane raids on German cities. Such, the Royal Air Force thought, would win the war, with

Dieppe but a "side show."[178] Portal, however, did not oppose the raid, inasmuch as it might bring the Luftwaffe's fighters out to battle and, should it fail, would suggest the preferability of air over land operations.[179]

Joining Admiral Pound in wanting to kibosh Churchill's Norwegian schemes were two other decision makers on Dieppe—Canadian General Andrew McNaughton and CIGS Alan Brooke. McNaughton was thought to have hoped "that supporting Dieppe would more easily allow him to refuse [a Canadian-manned *Operation*] *Jupiter*." Brooke, fearing that he must not be so negative as to reject all of Churchill's ideas, approved Dieppe. In his view, "the disaster that resulted may be said to be part of the price paid for the slow strangulation of *Jupiter*."[180]

While McNaughton and Brooke deemed it essential to be negative on Jupiter, Bernard Montgomery was pushing an ethos of positivity on Rutter. In his approving report of July 1, he stated that "confidence" was an "essential ingredient for success." The British Home Forces Commander had feared that the Canadian officers—perhaps just in expressing their doubts about a defective battle plan—lacked sufficient self-assurance for the raid to go well, but said that he had became satisfied that this had been remedied.

The problem is fundamental to war: soldiers cannot conquer unless they think they can; yet—as the Light Brigade at Balaclava and the Army of the Potomac at Cold Harbor showed—no amount of resolution can prevail if orders are ill-conceived. Montgomery wrote that the invaders of Dieppe would need "an infectious optimism which will permeate right down to the rank and file."[181] Army Commander John Roberts may have been seeking such permeation when he was said—which he denied—to have told his subordinates that the raid would be a "piece of cake."[182] (After the war until his death in 1962, he would on each anniversary of the raid receive in the mail from an anonymous sender a piece of cake.)

The radio signalmen on Dieppe Beach may have felt that their reports should be rosy, which may have led them to mention the pluses—the handfuls of men who had gotten into the town—while failing to get across to the command vessels back in the Channel the bigger picture: the shambles on the shingle. A biographer suspected that Bernard Montgomery himself may, for the sake of perfused positivity, not have voiced his own misgivings about Rutter.[183] A similarly-sensed imperative to sound sunny may have underlain Mountbatten's post-raid wire to Churchill (in Cairo, after visiting Moscow): "Morale of returning troops reported to be excellent."[184]

For the regimental officers of the Second Canadian Division, display of the requisite optimism posed problems. Many had reservations about aspects of the planned raid and hoped that improvements could be made. To utter, however, such thoughts was taken to show unfitness for command—which must exude assurance. On August 14, the officers of Jubilee were briefed. Lieutenant Colonel Douglas Catto, who would command at Blue Beach, warned of "possible disaster." He was told by a planner superior to him, "If you want to keep your command, keep your mouth shut."[185] On July 9, John Roberts and Harold Baillie-Grohman, the Army and Navy Force Commanders, had requested a review of the operational plan. John Hughes-Hallett, then serving as naval advisor to Combined Operations Headquarters and junior in rank to the two, threatened them with an official inquiry if they did not back down—which they then did.[186] Their questioning had been quashed.

Consensus in multi-person choices can be achieved by such nixing of naysaying, by persuasion, by coercion, by purchase or barter of support, or by the calculated composition of the decision-making group. That Rutter was revived as Jubilee under strict security protocol enabled discretion as to who was informed and included among the decision makers. Louis Mountbatten and John Hughes-Hallett were alleged to have "cherry-pick[ed]" who was in the deciding circle.[187] Major Walter Skrine had been considered the Combined Operations Headquarters officer best-versed on the ground component of Rutter. He had, however, in June commented critically on the training exercises. He was not told about Jubilee until August 18.[188] Dissenters among the decision makers for Rutter were shown the door. By early July, that Harold Baillie-Grohman and Bernard Montgomery had reservations about Dieppe had become clear. The rear admiral—perhaps at his own request, perhaps at that of Mountbatten—was replaced as Naval Force Commander; the major general was relieved of involvement in Jubilee by his superior, Bernard Paget.[189]

Having next to no effect in bringing about Rutter/Jubilee were the stated military goals of barge bagging and defense and infrastructure destruction. General Julian Thompson described the projected capture of German landing barges in the harbor of Dieppe as "a classic example of a planning officer dreaming up a task for lack of finding anything better since there was no possibility of these craft being of any use to the British."[190] Neither decision makers at the time nor historians since have argued for the raid based on its assigned military objectives.

A higher level of military objective did, however, motivate the raid. The British Official History, after listing the asserted goals, suggested that they were somewhat bogus, inasmuch as "the real purpose was to test the German coast defences and discover what resistance would have to be met in the endeavor to seize a port. It was hoped also to inflict heavy wastage on the German Air Force."[191]

Most decisions in war should be and are made by selecting among alternatives those offering best prospects of net military gains. The decision to land at Dieppe was not reached by weighing whether the likely values of knocking out German batteries, learning German radar technology, and bringing barges back to England justified putting 10,000 lives at risk. It was instead made, among other reasons, because a Soviet dictator and Western publics clamored for battles, because Dudley Pound did not want perceived stodginess to cost him his First Sea Lordship, because failures on the ground could help the RAF get more bombers, and because generals wanted to be seen as gung-ho. More than virtually all other significant military decisions of the war—indeed any war—those on Dieppe were made not for military motives, but instead for reasons of diplomacy, personal purpose, service advantage, psychology, and public relations.

Could No One Have Prevented the Suicidal Folly? Did the Fault Lie in the Meta-Decisions—The Determinations of How the Decisions Would Be Made?

Winston Churchill led in questioning the decision-making of Rutter/Jubilee: first in December 1942; then again, eight years later. Self-interest was seen in the Prime Minister's queries: he was alleged to be "on the prowl" for a "sacrificial lamb" to bear the blame for Dieppe, thereby exculpating himself.[192] Churchill's leading candidates for scapegoathood were Mountbatten and Montgomery.[193] The Prime Minister, however, was persuaded by Mountbatten to describe the raid in his memoirs as a positive and not to get into a squabble over blame.

Later writers have written critically of the decision roles played by Churchill, Montgomery, Mountbatten, and others and have disagreed among themselves in assigning responsibility for Dieppe.[194] Such differences of informed opinion suggest that attention also should be paid to what decision scientists have termed *meta-decisions:* "choices about the decision process itself"[195]; "decisions about how to decide."[196] Did the best-suited persons have appropriate mandates to make the key judgments?

The roles and performances of leading decision participants for Rutter and Jubilee have been assessed, often beginning at the top, with Winston Churchill and Alan Brooke. Historians have not suggested a better arrangement for determining whether in 1942 division-scale raids should have been undertaken than by Churchill, as guided by Brooke at the head of the British Chiefs of Staff. The Prime Minister, supported by his CIGS, had on June 8 nixed Operation Imperator: a proposed hit-and-run scamper to Paris.[197] Either man could have done the same to Rutter/Jubilee. That Churchill did not was likely due to his regard for Brooke and Montgomery, to the appeal that bold raids had for him, and to his having told the Russians that they would be undertaken.

General responsibility for mounting such raids was that of Churchill's appointee, Louis Mountbatten, supported by his top lieutenant, John Hughes-Hallett—neither of whom had had experience in amphibious warfare.[198] In their previous commands of destroyers, they had had little to do with land operations. This observation can be taken as criticism of Churchill for appointing Mountbatten and/or as grounds for judging leniently Mountbatten's and Hughes-Hallett's roles in Dieppe. But how pertinent was their lack of amphibious background? No one in August 1942—except in war games—had had anything to do with an operation like Dieppe.[199] Mountbatten had had by then ten months to study the possibilities and problems of sea-launched assaults.

He and Hughes-Hallett had pushed Jubilee through—some thought by cheek, bluff, and panache. (Historian Nigel Hamilton savaged Mountbatten's performance as Chief of Combined Operations: blaming him for Dieppe and ascribing to him "intrigue, jealousy, and ineptitude ... even psychopathic ambition."[200]) But that Lord Louis could make things happen was a reason Churchill had promoted him. He and Hughes-Hallett were able men whose months of amphibious study might have led them to turn against Rutter/Jubilee, when it became a woefully-supported, frontal attack. They did indeed seek unsuccessfully to reverse the decisions depriving the raid of heavy bombing and broad-bore naval guns. Their remit, however, had been to launch raids—not, for whatever reason, to call them off. Like many in their posts would have done, Mountbatten and Hughes-Hallett swallowed their misgivings and hoped against hope for success.

Warnings that such success might not be forthcoming were voiced by Trafford Leigh-Mallory and Harold Baillie-Grohman, representatives respectively of the Royal Air Force and Royal Navy. Both the Air and the Naval Force Commanders had forebodings of disaster. Leigh-Mallory protested that the fire support at Dieppe would be inadequate and predicted Canadian massacre[201]; Baillie-Grohman was thought to have prompted Admiral Sir Bertram Ramsay to write Mountbatten on July 25 urging the cancellation of Jubilee and other raids.[202] In this letter, Ramsay threatened to bring the matter to the Chiefs of Staff, but was dissuaded by Mountbatten's reaction that "political reasons" ensured that the raiding would continue.

As an intimate of Churchill, Mountbatten had confidence that the Prime Minister was committed to significant continental attacks and would back him up. Moreover, Leigh-Mallory as an airman and Baillie-Grohman and Ramsay as sailors were not deemed competent to challenge Montgomery's judgment of raid feasibility in what was preeminently an army matter. The Royal Air Force should have had a say in the assignment of its squadrons to Dieppe and the Royal Navy in the commitment of its ships. The briskly dismissive responses of both services to the requests of Dieppe planners has suggested, however, to historians that insufficient priority in these decisions was accorded to the needs of the raid.[203]

Directly responsible for ensuring that those needs would be met were Bernard Paget, Andrew McNaughton, and Henry Crerar. The official chain of command was set on July 17 to run from Paget through the two top Canadian generals in England to John Roberts.[204] Even Paget, the top link, would have had difficulty in calling off an operation with Prime Ministerial backing.[205] The Canadians, McNaughton and Crerar, were concerned that they not be excluded from the decision-making and line of command for Dieppe. Once Rutter was launched, decisions on its air support were to be made at Fighter Group Headquarters in Uxbridge in West London by Leigh-Mallory, Montgomery, and Mountbatten. McNaughton asked that a Canadian be present. Paget, on July 4, rejected this request, because only Montgomery and not Crerar would have command[206] and there was to "no room for any more" at the HQ.

Crerar protested to Montgomery that the alleged insufficiency of space was a bogus pretext for Canadian exclusion and persuaded him to more than reverse Paget's rebuff and to invite both him and McNaughton to Uxbridge: an HQ, one Canadian historian wrote, "suddenly bursting with room."[207] Having had to exert themselves to be recognized and included as decision participants, it is not impossible that McNaughton and Crerar were subsequently, out of fears of being marginalized, reluctant to act other than cooperatively. Paget, McNaughton, and Crerar were, moreover, also heartened by Montgomery's endorsement: as McNaughton put it, his acceptance of "full responsibility for the operation" was on "the general basis of his confidence in the officers concerned."[208] None of the three opposed Rutter or Jubilee.

A major basis for their lack of opposition was Bernard Montgomery. The future field marshal was the linchpin decision maker for Rutter: its proponents felt confirmed by his support of it; its opponents, overridden by it. Of the dozen-odd decision voices, only Churchill, Brooke, McNaughton, Mountbatten, and Montgomery could have called off Rutter and only the first four could have canceled Jubilee. While Mountbatten was motivated by position to support the raid, any reservations that Churchill, Brooke, McNaughton, Crerar, and others in the seats of decision might have had were lessened by Montgomery's endorsement of it. When, in December 1942, Churchill asked General Sir Hastings Ismay why the decision to attack Dieppe frontally had been made, his short answer was that Montgomery mainly had made it happen.[209]

After his qualified statement of support for Rutter on July 1, even Montgomery would have had difficulty in keeping Jubilee from taking place.[210] His recommendation that the raid be canceled and his departure for Africa had negligible effect on Jubilee. Montgomery might, however, in the three preceding months have quashed Rutter. No one in the British military spoke with greater authority than he on the prospects and pitfalls of amphibious ops. He had, in the summer of 1940, been assigned responsibility for fending off a German invasion of England. The next fall, he had looked into the possibility of establishing a beachhead on the Cotentin Peninsula of Normandy.[211] The months he had spent planning British coastal defenses should have enabled him to envision how and how effectively the Germans would defend at Dieppe. He—arguably better than anyone else in the seats of decision—should have foreseen that disaster impended. Instead, however, of giving warning, he approved the battle plan. Had he forthrightly said, at any time over the preceding ten weeks, that the operation risked likely catastrophe, the Chiefs of Staff might well have withheld or withdrawn their own approval and the raid might not have gone forward.

One biographer thought that Montgomery may have been seduced by the audacity of Rutter to overlook its defects and may have muted any misgivings he had, lest the Canadians lose heart. Montgomery's subsequent self-disengagement from Jubilee may have arisen, it was speculated, from second thoughts about its feasibility. It was noted that Dieppe was for Montgomery but a tangential focus, less important than his other responsibilities[212]: the commander of the South-Eastern Army had devoted but limited time and attention to the raid and, it was claimed by a defender of the general, only "formally attended" one Combined Operations HQ conference on it: that of June 5, which he chaired.[213]

It is likely, moreover, that even on that day the focus of Montgomery on Rutter was not total. He had spent the better part of the previous two years developing tactical doctrine: how foot and armored units should be combined within divisions and corps; how divisions might be regrouped into new corps during battles; how tanks should be concentrated and supported by infantry, artillery, and air; how infantry carried by armored vehicles should conduct reconnaissance; how all units should conceal themselves from Luftwaffe observation. Montgomery's tenets had, by the spring of 1942, been broadly accepted and were said to have "revolutionized" British military thinking; he was deemed a general of "frightening professionalism."[214]

Montgomery had spent the first months of 1942 visiting the units under his command and conducting field exercises. The culminating war game, which he rated "the most strenuous" England had ever seen, ran from May 19 to May 30. In it, Montgomery pitted the two halves of his command—over 100,000 men—against each other. On June 4, the army commander lectured for two hours on the exercise and the principles of warfare it had brought out. The transcript of his address was circulated to high officers throughout the British Army. Alan Brooke read it and wrote Montgomery of his complete agreement with the doctrines expounded. It would be understandable if, after having put so much of himself into his presentation of June 4—the culmination of two years of study, thought, and experiment—Montgomery was the next day mentally and emotionally drained and unable to concentrate fully on Operation Rutter.

One man whose concentration on the operation was full was John Roberts. The major general, after having been strong-armed by John Hughes-Hallett to drop his objections, fretted, conferred with his subordinate officers, and went ahead with the raid.[215] He had studied amphibious operations for less than four months and had been told by the respected and omniscience-exuding Montgomery that Rutter could succeed. Should he voice further his doubts, he understood that another would take over his division in its first battle.[216] He determined to command in their war debut the men whom he was generally considered to have trained well.[217] By the eve of the raid, he had convinced himself that all would be fine and expected that, at 8:30 the next morning, he would join his troops on French soil.[218]

Disaster of Dieppe dimension demanded a scapegoat. It was John Roberts. While the careers of those who might have kept the landing craft away from Red, White, and Blue Beaches throve on, Roberts was the next spring reassigned from divisional command to run a recruiting station. Many have felt that he was unjustly given blame that should have been more widely borne—if he indeed deserved any.[219]

*   *   *

The upshot of the meta-decision-making was that the operational calls were spread so far and so thin that no one man—although Montgomery came closest—was responsible for the battle plan or, should disaster seem likely, for nixing the raid. The focus on Dieppe of each of the crowded cast of decision makers may have been further weakened by two reflections: first, that, in case of success, others would reap much of the credit; second, that, should calamity occur, each could point to the positions of others as bases for their own sign-offs and could expect that many would share any blame. In the latter thought, John Roberts was most wrong.

Meta-Decisional Issues: How Should Go-No-Go Determinations Be Made? How Were They Made on Dieppe?

Throughout the millennia of war, best decisions—and many of the worst—have been made by commanders acting on their own authority. This made sense: able decision makers, whose personal prospects hinged on battle outcomes, had incentives to act optimally for their armies and nations.

An alternative way of deciding would be seen for the landing at Anzio: as cases were made for and against the possible attack, whereupon several decision makers weighed the pluses and minuses and determined whether or not it would be undertaken.

Considered assessing of pros against cons works best when strongest cases are made for and against leading options. Mountbatten and Hughes-Hallett advocated well for the raid—as they were impelled by position to do. No one, however, had positional incentive comparable to theirs to speak against it. It was likely felt that negative aspects would be duly considered by Brooke, Montgomery, and their staffs. But both of these generals had other foci. Each may have felt that the involvement of the other lessened the attention that he personally should give to Dieppe. With respect to Rutter and Jubilee and with the lives of ten thousand in the balance, the weighing of possible gains against downsides was not well done.

Did the British Authorize Rutter/Jubilee Expecting Failure—Perhaps Also Hoping for It and Even Acting to Sabotage the Raid?

Historian Brian Villa believed that insufficient attention has been paid to "evidence that British planners knew perfectly well that the operation had virtually no hope of success."[220] Other authors have speculated similarly: perhaps the British knew Dieppe to be doomed but went ahead with it as an object lesson for the Americans and Russians.[221] One historian suggested that the British may have deliberately drawn German attention to "the very stretch of the French coast where Rutter was to go in"—thereby increasing the likelihood of disaster.[222]

If the British had been expecting and/or hoping for and/or acting to cause operational failure, Alan Brooke would have played a central role. Most historians would agree with the judgment that Brooke's "immense military experience would have told him that Dieppe had no prospect of success (had he stopped to question it)."[223] Brooke, as Chief of the Imperial General Staff, exerted himself, year after year, to veto what he thought the loonier strategic fantasies of Churchill and the Americans. On Rutter/Jubilee, however, he was largely disengaged and, at one key moment when Churchill raised sharp questions, a committed proponent.[224]

In Cairo, after having been cabled about the results of the raid, Brooke's reaction was observed: "'It is a lesson,' the C.I.G.S. grunted, 'to the people who are clamouring for the invasion of France.'"[225] He wrote on August 19 in his diary that he was "very comfortable. Very lovely night with the sound of the waves only a few yards away." He "went to bed that night with a wonderful feeling of contentment."[226] It is not impossible that Brooke's satisfaction that Dieppe had proved himself right and the clamorers wrong—the making of which point might ultimately save tens of thousands of lives—kept him then from allowing the one thousand deaths that had that day clinched his case to disturb his "wonderful feeling of contentment."[227]

Had Brooke approved the raid on Dieppe in the belief that it would fail, he could have seen the decision and result as good-decision-good-outcome: GO-hopes in that the actual result was what he had foreseen and wanted; GO-on-net in that it would enhance the war prospects of the Allies; and GO-v-alts in that he knew of no better way to achieve these ends.

Was this the reasoning of the Chief of the Imperial General Staff and, if so, was it sound? Such a decision calculus would have had four premises: that the Americans were bent on a disastrously premature landing in northern France, which was the opinion of Brooke and other British military leaders and may have been the case; that an amphibious debacle would change the mind-set of the Americans; that there was no better way to change American thinking; and that Dieppe would, in fact, be a debacle.

Brooke's diary suggests confidence that the tragedy of Dieppe would lead the U.S. and other clamorers for an early Second Front to see the folly of their thoughts. The British Official History asserted in the context of reporting the results of Dieppe that "the British Chiefs of Staff were correct in their belief that the German army in the West was amply sufficient to drive into the sea any force that the Allies might succeed in landing in the summer of 1942."[228] Whether the Americans drew the same conclusion from Dieppe, thereby weakening their advocacy of an early cross-Channel invasion, is not clear. As seen above, the main cited lessons of Jubilee concerned how a multi-division landing might best be undertaken—entailing some changes that might delay it—not whether it should be put back a year or two.

By August 19, 1942, the Allies had ruled out crossing the Channel that year. In the last months of 1942 and in early 1943, they progressively determined that Roundup/Overlord, the invasion of northern France, should not occur until 1944. In most accounts of that decision, little mention was made of Dieppe. One American official history was an exception: relating that, in late 1942, U.S. planners were thought "very much impressed" by the casualties suffered at Dieppe—which made them the more receptive to postponing Roundup/Overlord.[229] George Marshall, however, in December 1942, apparently undaunted by Dieppe, was said to be "think-ing not only in terms of raids but of seizing and holding the Brest peninsula."[230] At Casablanca in January 1943—when it was largely concluded that Overlord would have to wait for another year—there was negligible citing of Dieppe.[231] It is, however, possible that Dieppe significantly changed the attitudes of those who had pressed for an early Roundup and led to greater strategic wariness, yet was rarely spoken of in the war conferences out of basic good manners: avoiding mention of a point of pain.

Could American minds have been changed without incurring so many casualties? Could reasoned arguments, war games, or other means have been more persuasive to the Yanks and/or less costly? Brooke felt that his masterful presentations to Marshall and others had often been to no avail: "it is quite impossible to argue with him as he does not even begin to understand a strategic problem."[232]

Sapping Marshall's push for an early Roundup would also have been made more challenging if Operation Jubilee had been somewhat successful. Had it achieved its goals at modest costs, the logic behind staging it to fail would have been turned on its head: confirming to the Americans that their strategic optimism had basis, increasing the likelihood that they could force on their allies an insufficiently-prepared Roundup, and perhaps leading to the futile deaths of many times more than the one thousand of Dieppe. No record has been found of the pre-operation likelihood estimated by Brooke or others of mission fiasco. His reactions on the evening of August 19 suggest that the result had not been wholly unexpected.

If the four premises for launching Jubilee to fail had, indeed, been valid, launching a fore-doomed raid would have had non-negligible justification. For Brooke and other Britons to have not-unreasonably taken such a strategic approach does not require the validity of the premises, only that they had had grounds for believing them to be true.

Had this, in fact, been their thinking?

Possibly in part. Decisions are made for many reasons. Brooke's sign-off on Dieppe likely owed to: the crafting of the battle plan by the esteemed Montgomery; the need of the Allies to gain amphibious experience; his perceived need to approve at least one of "Churchill's fanciful hopes," of which Dieppe might prove "the least-costly"[233]; and also the reflection that, in the event of failure, better ultimate Allied strategy might result.

The Expected Value of Information

Alan Brooke before Rutter argued for it based on the insights it was likely to provide; Louis Mountbatten after Jubilee defended it on the grounds of the lessons it had yielded. Prospectively, actions may be justified by the expected value of the information—the EVI—they may secure; retrospectively, outcomes may be deemed good, because of the worth of the information actually obtained. The decision-scientific concept of EVI[234] may usefully have guided both pre-raid reconnaissance and the go-no-go decision on the operation itself.

The expected value of information may be estimated as follows:

> EVI = the probability that information might change a decision
>   multiplied by
>   the likely gain realized, if the decision is changed.

The expected value of information is vital to many decision makers: to political candidates, for instance, pondering whether to commission focus groups on campaign issues; to corporate CEOs wondering how much money to budget for market surveys; to physicians mulling which diagnostic tests to order for their patients. Focus groups, market surveys, and medical tests cost money. Some diagnostic tests and procedures also entail risks for patients. Whether or not these information-securing actions should be undertaken depends on the EVIs: whether their likely gains justify their costs. Such possible gains, in each case, derive from the chances of improving decisions—by enabling candidates to modify their position statements to secure more votes; by showing corporations how modifications of their product lines can increase profits; by helping doctors to take better therapeutic actions.

For Rutter/Jubilee, aspects of the expected value of information included: reconnaissance, port targeting, and the timing of Roundup. Whether the Allies should have dispatched additional camera-bearing planes to photograph the cliffs on either side of Dieppe should have been determined by weighing the likely gains—the EVI—against the likely costs.[235] The Allies in mid–1942 were undecided as to whether the sites of their landings in their ultimate full-scale invasion of northern France should include a major port. They might well have attacked such a harbor as Calais, Dieppe, Le Havre, Cherbourg, or Brest on the first day. The chance that Rutter/Jubilee might have beneficially changed that decision would have argued in its favor. Alan Brooke may have sensed that, without the possibly-sobering experience of a one-division Channel-Coast raid, the U.S. would insist on invading northern France in 1943. If so, the chance that raiding Dieppe would provide the information that would dissuade them from undertaking a catastrophically premature Roundup would have been of high prospective value.[236]

*   *   *

The concept of the expected value of information would not be formulated and the methods of calculating it not developed until years after the war. The nub of EVI—the prospects for improving later decisions—nevertheless underlay both Alan Brooke's pre–Rutter statement that a cross-Channel invasion required the learning that the raid could provide and Louis Mountbatten's post–Jubilee assertions of good-decision-good-outcome.

What Should the Allies Have Done?

The Allies, after Dieppe, mounted no more continental raids on anything like its scale—having evidently concluded that their prospective downsides multiply exceeded their likely gains. Such thinking, if earlier, might and perhaps should have ruled out Jubilee. There had been, however, a critical mass of Allied decision makers—led by Winston Churchill and George Marshall—favoring at least one temporary landing of significant size.

If such a raid was to be mounted, what might best have been done is suggested by the conclusions of most historians. While one deplored the selection of Dieppe and its environs as targets, most have not taken issue with the reasoning that led to this stretch of the Channel Coast. Although most writers have judged that, absent heavy bombing and capital-ship cannonading, the frontal-attack landings could not succeed, they did not go further to assert that the addition to Jubilee of bombers and of at least one battleship or cruiser would have made the raid a success. They did not dispute the German verdict that the Allies had sent too few to do too much for too little. Later planning for Overlord would presume—as many have felt that the architects of Rutter/Jubilee should have anticipated—that the costs, in resource and human terms, of frontally taking a defended port would be prohibitively high.

These judgments suggest that a raid should have been undertaken along the lines that Combined Operations Headquarters had proposed: a larger landing at Green Beach, perhaps with tanks, possibly accompanied by another attack northeast of Dieppe. The Germans thought that such an approach should have been taken.[237]

Against this alternative plan, objections were raised: landings peripheral to Dieppe might be too distant to take the town from landward; the bridges over the Scie might be too flimsy to support tanks; if Dieppe were not taken, the other raid objectives—even if all were achieved—would not suffice to dispel the perception of failure or futility.

The points had validity but could have been countered. Could not information on the Scie bridges have been obtained? How many more casualties would an unsuccessful frontal attack have had than a stymied peripheral approach and how much more sense of unsuccess? Would the brief taking of Dieppe have done anything more than mildly plump up a still-thin list of gains? These questions seem not to have been posed.

Models of Governmental Decision-Making

Much of this chapter has described factors that led the Allies to act otherwise than as they arguably should have. The gaps between the optimal and the actual behaviors of governments were addressed by Graham Allison in 1971 in *Essence of Decision: Explaining the Cuban Missile Crisis*—a revised second edition of which, written with Philip Zelikow, appeared in 1999. Allison pointed out that, when economists, historians, and political scientists have identified best choices and steps, they have, either explicitly or implicitly, presumed a unified, logical decision maker: the Rational Actor Model or Model I. However cogent Model I—per Allison, "the rational man of modern formal decision theory and game theory"[238]—might be in determining what a wise individual should do, it neither describes nor predicts well actual governmental behavior.

There was no single, cohesive, Model I decision maker for Dieppe. Instead, organizations and individuals interacted to put five thousand men on the cherty coast of France. Allison viewed such interactions through the alternative lenses of the Organizational Behavior Model (Model II) and the Governmental Politics Model (Model III). Model II holds that "a government is not an individual" but rather "a vast conglomerate of loosely allied organizations, each with a substantial life of its own."[239] Model III goes beyond Model II to "a further, more refined level of investigation," seeing each decision participant as, "in his or her own right, a player in a central competitive game. The name of the game is politics.... Governmental behavior can thus be understood ... as results of bargaining games."[240] Useful as Models II and III are for understanding governments, they are the more so for such international cooperative arrangements as those that sent 5,000 soldiers to Dieppe.

Allison's Organizational Behavior Model asks: "from what organizational context, pressures, and procedures did this decision emerge?"[241] This question of Model II had pertinence for Operation Rutter/Jubilee: the Royal Air Force and Royal Navy had in the words of Allison "their fixed procedures and programs,"[242] from which they preferred not to stray. They wanted to bomb Germany into surrender and to maintain and to enhance Allied dominance of the seas. Heavy bombing and bombardment in support of a one-day raid were outside their standard repertoires and priorities and therefore would not secure their consents.

The Governmental Politics Model seeks to know: "what *particular* [emphasis in original] characteristics of multi-person decision processes have consequences for the content of the decisions and actions that emerge?"[243] When personal positions differ, what is "the established procedure ... for aggregating competing preferences?"[244] For Rutter and Jubilee, the protocols for dealing with competing preferences were but partially established and would differ across the two versions of the operation. When Montgomery and Mountbatten disagreed on frontal versus peripheral attacks, the resolutional rule understood by both men was that Montgomery would get his way. As to whether the raid should or should not be mounted—the go-no-go decision—no single person had total say. Neither Brooke, Churchill, McNaughton, Montgomery, nor Mountbatten could have pushed Rutter through against the determined opposition of any one of the other four: a scenario of quintuple-veto that would become for Jubilee, with the departure of Montgomery, one of quadruple-quashability. Had any one of these five had go-no-go authority, he would likely have focused more and better on the decision and have had greater incentive to get it right. Other duties diluted the attention of all five. Had there been more awareness of such Model III phenomena, what happened at Dieppe and what went wrong there would have been better foreseen.

Conclusions

The Canadian Official History and other authors noted ways in which the disaster at Dieppe valuably guided Overlord: while the Royal Navy dared not risk a single big-gun boat for Rutter/Jubilee, six battleships and 23 cruisers would be off of Normandy on June 6, 1944; instead of ten minutes of cannon fire from Hurricane fighters, 1.1 million tons of bombs would be dropped; creatively-designed tanks—including swimmers, minefield-clearers, and flamethrowers—were developed for Overlord; and, with direct assaults on ports no longer deemed sensible, the Allies invented new means for supplying their armies over beaches.[245]

The greatest lesson of Dieppe related, however, not to weapons, tactics, or logistics but, instead, to the meta-decision of how to decide. Bernard Montgomery concluded from Jubilee "that there were far too many authorities with a hand in it," and no unique, designated commander preeminently in charge.[246] The Canadian Official History phrased it that the disaster had occurred in part because "the Dieppe plan was the work of a large and somewhat indefinitely composed committee, whose composition, moreover, changed steadily." That "there were a great many cooks ...

probably had much to do with spoiling the broth."[247] As with other purported lessons of Rutter/Jubilee, it could be argued that this one—the importance of command unity—also should have been obvious beforehand.

The Allies would for Overlord give first the Combined Chiefs, then Dwight Eisenhower, the mandate that would enable the later invasion to avoid many problems of the raid of 22 months before. For starters, the go-no-go decision of June 1944 would be made by one entity. The Combined Chiefs of Staff—led by Brooke and Marshall and significantly influenced by Churchill and Roosevelt—was the decision maker.

The top-level decision makers also arranged that those who would command the operation would also command its planning. This principle, deemed basic by the Canadian Official History,[248] had been honored in the breach for Dieppe. John Roberts had had among the many decision makers who scripted Rutter and Jubilee minor influence. While much planning for Overlord occurred before Eisenhower and Montgomery were assigned its two lead command roles, they subsequently assumed ownership of it and made substantial changes. Unlike Montgomery in 1942 with much else of import to deal with, he and Eisenhower two springs later had no other responsibilities that remotely rivaled their imperative of having Overlord succeed.

Their mandates then meant that needs for air and naval support, instead of being at the discretion of the two services, had become commands to them. The Allied air forces in 1944, as in 1942, thought that the other services should have minor, supporting roles, while strategic bombing conquered Germany. Although in 1942 the RAF had refused even to deploy a contingent reserve of twelve bombers off of Dieppe, Eisenhower, two years later, demanded and secured command over thousands of bombers, which he targeted on the bridges and railroads of France.

The prerogatives of the Supreme Commander in 1944 were such that not even the Prime Minister could veto aspects of strategy. Churchill, indeed, sought to limit the bombing of French railroads, lest it nettle the French, and wanted the landings of August 1944 in southern France to be scrapped. To sway Eisenhower, he threatened resignation and appealed to Roosevelt for support. The commander of Overlord, however, was backed by his President, had decision authority transformatively greater than anyone had had for Dieppe, and held to his best judgments.

2

North Africa

At three in the morning of November 8, 1942, the warship HMS *Walney*[1] entered the Algerian port of Oran. On the jetty of the harbor, painted in white letters, were the words: *"Honneur, Travail, Patrie."* It was the grand, if imbecilic, slogan of the regime, headquartered in Vichy, 200 miles south of Paris, that for the past 28 months had governed the south of the nation and its colonies.

On the upper bridge of the *Walney*, Lieutenant Paul Duncan of the Royal Navy spoke through loudspeakers: *"Ne tirez pas. Nous sommes vos amis. Ne tirez pas."* He had practiced his lines, intending them to sound like American-accented French—as Vichy's defenders of the city were thought less hostile to Americans than to British. Operation Torch—the Allied invasion of French North Africa, "the greatest amphibious operation since Xerxes crossed the Hellespont in 480 BC"[2]—was about to come ashore.

One hour later, 200 miles to the east, the destroyers HMS *Broke* and HMS *Malcolm* neared the port of Algiers and, just after four a.m., were fired on.

One hour after that, 26 landing craft bearing the U.S. 30th Infantry Regiment headed in toward the Moroccan port city of Fedala, 20 miles northeast of Casablanca.

The Allies approaching North Africa did not know how they would be received. U.S. Army Chief of Staff George Marshall had ordered his men to refrain from firing first.[3] Franklin Roosevelt had taped in both French and English an appeal to Vichy's Africa: "We come among you solely to destroy your enemies and not to harm you." He asked them not to resist and closed with, *"Vive la France éternelle!"* The BBC broadcast the President's message every thirty minutes. George Patton, commanding the force invading French Morocco was—as was not uncommon—irate: his troops would be coming ashore hours after those in Algeria and his Commander-in-Chief was forfeiting any chance for surprise.

The Grand-Strategic Decision: Should the Allies in November 1942 Have Landed in North Africa?

Alternatives: 1942 landings in northern or southern France, Norway, Belgium, Holland, Portugal, Spain, Sicily, mainland Italy, or on the Atlantic islands of the Azores, the Cape Verdes, the Canaries, or the Madeiras; or large European raids, of Dieppe scale or larger; or reinforcing the Middle East; or sending more divisions to the Pacific Theater; or building up forces in Britain throughout 1942, preparatory to invading France in 1943.

When made: on Friday, July 24, 1942, after on-and-off pondering for over a year.

The decision makers: Prime Minister Winston Churchill, President Franklin Roosevelt, and their military leaders, headed by Chief of the Imperial General Staff Alan Brooke and U.S. Army Chief of Staff George Marshall.

Conclusions: the ultimate outcome: excellent: in surpassing original hopes, in yielding benefits that eclipsed costs and brought final Allied victory closer, and in comparison with the likely results of alternative actions; **the decision:** most likely best—per the current historical consensus; **why the initial outcome disappointed the Allies:** the planning fallacy, poor other-side perception; **most to be lauded:** Winston Churchill and Franklin Roosevelt, roughly equally and with appreciation for their not allowing themselves to be too much pushed around by the flaunted expertise of their military men in many groupthink situations; Alan Brooke, for leading the resistance to proposed Operations Jupiter and Sledgehammer; **most to be faulted:** Adolf Hitler, for falling into the planning fallacy.

British military planners had in June 1941 already been looking forward to American entry into the war. They foresaw then that the impact of the U.S. would be "most marked" in the South Atlantic and that the UK and U.S., acting together, might occupy the Atlantic islands of Portugal and Spain, as well as the ports of French West Africa. From the latter,

> American forces ... may be able to push northwards. Friendly elements in the French Empire ... may be strong enough then to overthrow the authority of Vichy and re-establish their independence. If the enemies of the Axis were once again established on the southern shores of the Mediterranean, new opportunities would be opened out for the growing might of the American forces to close in on German-occupied Europe.[4]

British officers, when Churchill and Roosevelt met in Placentia Bay off of Newfoundland in August, suggested that UK and U.S. troops might jointly enter French North Africa.[5]

One month earlier, as Nazi armies sped through Russia and Japanese attacks in the western Pacific were feared, Franklin Roosevelt had sensed that his nation might soon be more than just an interested watcher of war. On July 9, he had asked his Departments of the Navy and War what might be "required to defeat our potential enemies." The response came two months later, on September 11, in a strategic report signed jointly by George Marshall as "General, U.S. Army, Chief of Staff" and Harold Stark as "Admiral, U.S. Navy, Chief of Naval Operations." Marshall and Stark conceded the infeasibility "in the near future" of "a sustained and successful land offensive

Map by Gene Thorp

against the center of the German power." They therefore recommended that the U.S. and its prospective Allies instead blockade, bomb, support resistance in Nazi-occupied lands, and undertake "land offensives in distant regions where German troops can exert only a fraction of their total strength." Northwest Africa—the Vichy-controlled colonies of French Morocco, Algeria, and Tunisia—was "a potential base for a future land offensive." Given that Britain was short of troops and on unfriendly terms with Vichy France, "it seems clear that a large proportion of the troops ... employed in this region necessarily must be United States troops."[6]

U.S. Navy Secretary Frank Knox on October 3 told the British ambassador to Washington that he and Roosevelt fancied sending 150,000 American soldiers to Casablanca—on the hopeful presumption that they would be welcomed into French Morocco by the Vichy officials.[7] The President asked General Marshall and Secretary of War Henry Stimson to look into sending an American force to West Africa.[8] On October 20, Churchill wrote to Roosevelt of the possibilities that British forces in Libya under General Sir Claude Auchinleck might soon sweep forward to Benghazi and beyond or that German demands on Vichy North Africa might lead it to join the war on the side of Britain. To capitalize on these contingencies, Britain would have four divisions ready by mid–November to land either in French Morocco "upon French invitation or otherwise help to exploit in the Mediterranean a victory in Libya."[9] The Prime Minister also then considered landing in Sicily—which idea, however, his military chiefs disfavored and, within days, he would give it up.

On December 13, as Churchill wrote to his First Sea Lord, Sir Dudley Pound, about Mediterranean possibilities, much had changed: the U.S. was in the war; the Prime Minister described the results so far of the Russian counterattack near Moscow begun eight days earlier as "the growing disaster of the German armies"; General Auchinleck had advanced in eastern Libya; and Maréchal Pétain ailed—and might be replaced by a leader more partial to the Allies. The Prime Minister proposed to make "a joint offer of blessing or cursing to Vichy"—welcome us or suffer consequences—for North Africa. He thought it "worth trying" for an American force to offer to land at Casablanca and asked that his own troops be prepared to land at Livorno—90 miles southeast of Genoa, 160 miles northwest of Rome, on the Italian coast.[10]

One week later, as the Prime Minister sailed over the Atlantic for the Arcadia Conference in Washington of UK and U.S. leaders, he prioritized getting from Roosevelt "assistance in a forward policy in French North Africa and in West Africa."[11] He penned memoranda for his chiefs, which would also be given to Roosevelt. In that applying to the Atlantic Front, he foresaw the "impending victory" of Auchinleck and hoped that Vichy would allow French North Africa to join the Allies. To act on that possibility, Britain was holding 55,000 men ready for "Operation Gymnast"—under which landings might be made in French Morocco, Algeria, and/or Tunisia. He hoped that the U.S. soon could send to Africa 25,000 men and 150,000-plus within six months.[12]

Arcadia opened on the evening of December 22 as Churchill conferred with Roosevelt in the White House. The President had not responded to the Prime Minister's note of October 20. When, however, the two met, the Prime Minister immediately sensed "that the President was thinking very much along the same lines as I about action in French North-West Africa."[13] On December 23, Churchill reported to his war cabinet agreement with the Americans "that it was vital to forestall the Germans in North-West Africa and the Atlantic islands [the Azores and Canaries]" and that it had been suggested that "it would be desirable to have all plans made for going into North Africa, *with or without invitation* [author's italics]."[14] Roosevelt that day told the assembled war leaders of the two nations "that he considered it very important to morale, to give this country a feeling that they are in the war, to give the Germans the reverse effect, to have American troops somewhere in active fighting across the Atlantic."[15]

On the day after Christmas, American and British officers agreed on a draft plan for landings in North Africa. It was premised on minimal opposition and a breathing spell of three months before the Germans could counterattack through Spain and Spanish Morocco. The plan envisioned in the first three months a commitment of 385 planes, anti-aircraft units, and six divisions, of which two would be armored. The UK and U.S. would each contribute three divisions.[16]

Ten days into 1942, First Sea Lord Pound thought that Allied troops might land at Algiers and Casablanca on March 3.[17] Two days later, in a meeting of fifteen Anglo-American leaders in the White House, Roosevelt asked that the North African operation—then planned to comprise 90,000 UK and 90,000 U.S. troops, plus air units[18]—be the first topic of discussion. (The President called it "Super-Gymnast"—"Super-" indicating the augmentation of Churchill's original concept with U.S. troops.[19]) Churchill responded that it had been intended that the invasion be synchronized with Auchinleck's advance to Tripoli. That Rommel's Afrika Korps was resisting more staunchly than had been expected meant, the Prime Minister said, that it would be longer before Auchinleck neared the Libyan capital and that there would therefore be more time to prepare for Super-Gymnast—which, given the other demands on Allied shipping, could not take place before March 23. U.S. Admiral Ernest King said that, while 15,000 American troops could be dispatched at any time to North Africa, they should not count on loading for the full operation until mid–April—which would push their landing back to early May. Roosevelt and Churchill agreed on calling for Super-Gymnast "at the earliest possible date."[20]

The two national leaders had their last meeting of Arcadia in the White House on January 14. It was there agreed that the date for the North African operation had to be put back further: the needed shipping would not be available until May; the first landings could not take place until June. The two leaders agreed, however, that, should the Germans move at any time into Vichy-controlled Northwest Africa, the Allies would have to counter with whatever forces they could muster—perhaps resorting, the Prime Minister suggested, to guerrilla operations.[21]

More than any specific strategic decision taken at Arcadia, Churchill wrote:

> It may well be thought by future historians that the most valuable and lasting result of our first Washington conference ... was the setting up of the now famous "Combined Chiefs of Staff Committee."
> There never was a more serviceable war machinery established among allies.[22]

Historian John Keegan would indeed render the judgment that Churchill had predicted.[23] The Combined Chiefs would be headquartered and would usually meet in Washington, where Field Marshal Sir John Dill would represent the London-based British Chiefs of Staff. The committee would convene in what Churchill termed "full-dress meetings" at the major war conferences in Casablanca, Washington, Quebec, Tehran, Cairo, Malta, and the Crimea, with Alan Brooke and George Marshall there heading the two national contingents.[24]

Brooke—who, as Chief of the Imperial General Staff, was Britain's soldier of highest rank—was initially skeptical of the Combined Chiefs, calling it one of "the false arrangements made in Washington." However, the CIGS reported, "My views altered completely as time went on and I grew to have the greatest faith in the Combined Chiefs of Staff organisation as the most efficient that had ever been evolved for co-ordinating and correlating the war strategy and effort of two allies."[25] Marshall agreed.[26]

Events in the East soon pushed Gymnast further back on the Allied stovetop. Japanese forces in February 1942: took Singapore, Sumatra, and Borneo; advanced in Burma and the Philippines; and destroyed an Allied fleet in the Java Sea. In consequence, Churchill wrote on March 4 to Roosevelt, "we are scraping together every ton of man-lift shipping we can lay our hands on" for convoys to India, Ceylon, Australia, and the Middle East. This and the success of Rommel's counterattack against Auchinleck in Libya made Gymnast "out of the question for several months"[27]—to which Roosevelt agreed.[28]

Dwight Eisenhower—who had one year before been an obscure lieutenant colonel and who had since risen meteorically to become the chief war planner of U.S. Army Chief of Staff George Marshall—expressed on February 19 the American strategic view:

> We've got to go on a harassing defensive west of Hawaii; hold India and Ceylon; build up air and land forces in England, and when we're strong enough, go after Germany's vitals. And we've got to do it while Russia is still in the war—in fact, only by doing it soon can we keep Russia in.[29]

In line with these thoughts, Marshall wanted Gymnast permanently shelved. Over the indirect grand-strategic approach of landings in Norway and/or North Africa, he favored the direct alternative of invading northern France, then proceeding to Berlin. He had his planners, led by Eisenhower, work out the details. Three strategic schemes—complementary parts of the same optimistic, aggressive outlook—resulted: Bolero, the build-up of American forces in Britain; Sledgehammer, a landing of five to nine divisions in northern France in the fall of 1942; and Roundup, a cross-Channel invasion of 48 divisions in the spring of 1943.[30] In meetings with Roosevelt on March 24 and April 1, Marshall persuaded the President to back his approach. The next step was to have the British sign on.

On April 8, 1942, an American delegation headed by George Marshall and Presidential intimate Harry Hopkins landed in London. Late that afternoon, they pitched the general's ideas to the Prime Minister and, the next morning, to the British Chiefs of Staff. Led by Chief of the Imperial General Staff Alan Brooke, His Majesty's top officers were skeptical: neither the land nor the air components of Sledgehammer seemed sufficient to prevent swift German erasure of an Allied beachhead. Days earlier to the British War Cabinet, the CIGS had mocked the operation: the best it might do was secure a front of twenty miles across the base of the Cotentin Peninsula; compared with the Russian fighting line of 1,500 miles, such an achievement would be "ridiculous"; for the Western Allies to claim it as substantial succor for the Soviets would make them "the laughing stock of the world."[31] On April 12, however, Churchill cabled Roosevelt that he was "in entire agreement in principle with all you propose, and so are the Chiefs of Staff."[32]

Five days later, Hopkins and Marshall left London thinking that, while reservations had been voiced about Sledgehammer in 1942, the British at least were on board for Roundup the next year. The chiefs of both allies had in their April meetings spoken mostly about invading northern France—any possible landings in North Africa going unmentioned.

Churchill had, however, kept his thoughts of Gymnast. He reported having deemed it undiplomatic to bring up in these meetings his own partiality for the operation.[33] After several weeks in which the military planners of both nations prepared for and analyzed Sledgehammer, Churchill on May 28 cabled Roosevelt: "We must never let GYMNAST pass from our minds." This cable was to the U.S. "the first danger signal" that the UK, instead of focusing on direct, cross-Channel attack, "was beginning to veer toward diversionary operations."[34] The UK was more than "beginning to veer": on May 8, six commanders had reported to the British Chiefs that Sledgehammer "is not a sound military operation"[35]—from which conclusion the British would not retreat.

Roosevelt had himself remained intent on fighting the Germans soon and again on May 6 had remade the point. In a memorandum addressed to the Secretaries of War and the Navy, his Joint Chiefs of Staff, and Harry Hopkins, he reported that "I have been disturbed by American and British naval objections to operations in the European Theatre prior to 1943. I regard it as essential that active operations be conducted in 1942."[36] He voiced the impatience of his nation.

A British delegation, traveling by flying-boat and headed by Churchill and Brooke, arrived in Washington on Thursday, June 18. Churchill flew north the next day to two days at the Hyde Park home of the President.

*   *   *

In the months leading up to that weekend: the loss of two Soviet Armies in the Ukraine had been accompanied by German progress in the siege of Sevastopol in the Crimea; the British-held Mediterranean island of Malta was in danger of capture or starvation, as but two of seventeen ships sent in mid–June to resupply it made it through; Rommel's Afrika Korps had surged forward and neared Tobruk—75 miles west of the Libya-Egypt border; the last Americans resisting the Japanese conquest of the Philippines had surrendered on Corregidor Island; Japan had taken the islands of Kiska and Attu in the Aleutians; the Japanese threat to control the Indian Ocean had, however, receded and the navy of Dai Nippon had been held to a draw at the Coral Sea and defeated at Midway; over one thousand Royal Air Force planes had taken part in a bombing raid on Cologne.

*   *   *

With Churchill off to Hyde Park, Brooke, Marshall, and supporting officers met on June 19 in Washington. They agreed that, in 1942, Sledgehammer landings directed at Brest, the Channel Islands, or Cherbourg or the invasion of Norway would all "be preferable to undertaking GYM-NAST."[37] Brooke summarized in his diary: "we made further progress towards defining our policy for 1942 and 1943 ... but am a little doubtful as to what P.M. and President may be brewing up together."[38] War Secretary Stimson confided that night to his own diary the same worry.[39]

PM and POTUS, as it turned out, were doing precisely what Brooke, Stimson, and Marshall feared: in mulling what next steps would be best for their countries, they largely disregarded—and were strategizing counter to—the advice of their generals and ministers. Both national leaders, before coming together, had leaned toward Gymnast. Roosevelt had pushed it in a meeting of U.S. officers and officials on June 17—leading Stimson to call it the "President's great secret baby."[40] Churchill gave Roosevelt a note making the points that "no responsible British military authority has so far been able to make a plan for [Sledgehammer in] September 1942 which had any chance of success unless the Germans became utterly demoralized, of which there is no likelihood" and that "the French North-West Africa operation should be studied." Knowing the President's urgent wish to fight the Nazis, the note asked rhetorically and disingenuously: "Can we afford to stand idle in the Atlantic theatre during the whole of 1942?"[41] If, it has been judged, the President had not already been fully for Gymnast, Churchill sold him on it in Hyde Park.[42]

On Sunday, June 21, having returned to Washington on the Presidential train, Churchill was with Roosevelt in the White House when a secretary brought a telegram to the President.[43] He read it silently, then handed it to the Prime Minister: Tobruk had fallen that day to Rommel. The fortified Libyan port had, the previous year, held out for over seven months when invested by the Afrika Korps; it had, this time, taken Rommel just four days for its capture. Churchill could not believe the news and had an aide call London for confirmation. London confirmed: 33,000 Commonwealth men had surrendered to about half as many Axis soldiers. Churchill thought it "one of the heaviest blows I can recall during the war.... Defeat is one thing; disgrace is another."[44]

After a moment of stunned silence, Roosevelt asked, "What can we do to help?" Churchill requested "as many Sherman tanks as you can spare." Roosevelt summoned Marshall, who said that "the Shermans are only just coming into production. The first few hundred have been issued to our own armoured divisions, who have hitherto had to be content with obsolete equipment.... Nevertheless, if the British need is so great they must have them."[45] It was a pinnacle moment for the U.S. as ally.[46] Almost half of the tanks with which Bernard Montgomery in October would attack at El Alamein would be American.[47]

A memorandum summarized the conclusions of the June discussions: preparations were to be pushed for a cross-Channel invasion in 1943, as well as for landings in France or the Low Countries in 1942; should these latter appear unlikely to succeed, "we must be ready for an alternative"; to this end, plans for Gymnast would be prepared and operations in Norway and the Iberian Peninsula considered.[48] The British party flew back to London.

Churchill wrote that "the purpose of my visit to Washington ... had been to obtain this decision [on Gymnast]."[49] But that decision had not been obtained. The Prime Minister had argued with his customary eloquence on June 21 for Gymnast over Sledgehammer, but Marshall and Hopkins had opposed him. Churchill felt that "the loss of prestige of the British after the fall of Tobruk" had prevented his closing an agreement on Gymnast.[50] He thought himself more frustrated than any compatriot going back to the loser of the Battle of Saratoga in 1777: he was "the unhappiest Englishman in North America since General Burgoyne."[51] (General Cornwallis eluded mention. The Americans in May 1943, hosting top British officers in restored Colonial Williamsburg, arranged for a somewhat-tactless side visit to the Yorktown Victory Monument. Marshall felt "humbled," that some of the UK party had no idea of what it was about.[52]) Though thwarted by Marshall and Hopkins in getting Gymnast, Churchill and Roosevelt had in return counter-thwarted the efforts of Marshall, Brooke, and Hopkins to push the North African operation off the table of consideration.

As June turned into July, the two national leaders became the more determined to break the decisional deadlock. Roosevelt would press the more urgently for what, since the previous December, he had wanted on behalf of his electorate: their army fighting Germans soon. Churchill described his own mindset: "I had to get from the United States the decision which, for good or ill, dominated the next two years of the war.... The moment had come to bury 'Sledgehammer.'"[53] PM and POTUS had both had enough of what seemed to have been happening, month after month: "meetings are held, discussions take place, and time slips by."[54]

To have German-fighting boots on the ground in 1942 with the British vetoing Sledgehammer, Roosevelt had to get Marshall to toe the Presidential line. The U.S. Army Chief of Staff had continued to plug Sledgehammer and thought Gymnast—in jeopardizing Roundup in 1943—worse than nothing. After what was described by Henry Stimson as a "thumping argument" over strategy between the President and the army chief on July 15,[55] Roosevelt directed Marshall and Hopkins to return to London and gave them written instructions: they must "carefully investigate the possibility of executing SLEDGEHAMMER ... If SLEDGEHAMMER is finally and definitely out of the picture, I want you to ... determine upon another place for U.S. Troops to fight in 1942."[56] Unusually for him, the paper was signed "Franklin D. Roosevelt Commander-in-Chief." It was an order: the President was fed up with having his expressed wishes countered by memoranda and succeeded by dithering. Privately, Roosevelt had pitched Gymnast to Hopkins.[57]

*   *   *

In the four weeks following the fall of Tobruk: Rommel had advanced to El Alamein in Egypt; no supply ships had even attempted to reach increasingly-short-rationed Malta; the convoy code-named PQ17 had set out from Iceland for Archangel in northern Russia with 34 merchant ships, of which 23 were sunk, their crews either dying in the Arctic Sea or, in Churchill's words, enduring "incredible hardships and mutilation by frostbite"[58]; Sevastopol had fallen to the Germans, Russian resistance in the Crimea had ended, and Nazi armies were advancing toward the Volga and the Caucasus; the Japanese had apparently abandoned their plan of attacking Midway Island, but had landed troops on New Guinea.

*   *   *

Against this global backdrop, American and British chiefs met at 10 Downing Street on the afternoon of Monday, July 20, 1942, for what for Churchill would be "perhaps the hardest-fought strategic debate in the war."[59] Marshall argued that, given the current German offensive, something had to be done to help the Russians. He spoke for the latest version of Sledgehammer: a beachhead of six divisions that would be gained in the fall, would be supplied through Cherbourg, would survive the winter, and would be the base for expanded operations in 1943. Most of the attacking troops would have to be British. Two days later, the British War Cabinet, heeding the judgment of the Chief of the Imperial General Staff, Alan Brooke, that there was "no hope of our still being in Cherbourg by next spring,"[60] unanimously rejected the American plan. Roosevelt had effectively leaked to the British via Hopkins that he would not be displeased if the nixing of Sledgehammer led to Gymnast.[61]

Roosevelt, on learning of the British position, accepted that Sledgehammer was out and reiterated to Hopkins and Marshall that American ground forces must battle Germans before the end of the year. The leading possibilities were in North Africa and Norway.

Marshall had anticipated the British response and, good soldier above all else that he was, set to obeying his Commander-in-Chief. Resignedly deeming it the "least harmful" choice, he opted for North Africa. He was not happy: not only was Sledgehammer the more conclusively off the table, but prospects for Roundup in 1943 had become bleaker. In consequence, to him "it looked like the Russians were going to be destroyed."[62]

In his room in Claridge's Hotel in the Mayfair District of London in the morning of July 24, Marshall drafted a proposal to undertake Gymnast. In writing it, he "had to bear in mind that we didn't have much and that much of what we had was in an amateurish stage." He outlined the "operations, limits, nature" of the attack. He asked that the Allies continue their preparations for Sledgehammer—largely as a deceptive measure, but also on the slight chance that circumstances would so change that it might be mounted. He wrote that, given essential commitments to the Pacific Theater, a consequence of Gymnast was that "ROUNDUP could not be executed in 1943." He showed his paper to Admiral King who, to Marshall's surprise, "accepted it without a quibble. Usually he argued over all our plans."[63]

The American delegation met at noon with the British Chiefs of Staff. In a session of ninety minutes, agreement was reached on Marshall's paper, with but minor changes. At 4:30, the paper was presented to Churchill, who at once approved it. The British War Cabinet was then convened and Churchill had Brooke present the Marshall memorandum. The Cabinet balked at the announced ruling out of Roundup. The ministers, Marshall recalled, "didn't want it used against them politically if they prevented ROUNDUP in 1943, thus delaying the freeing of Europe."[64] Perspiring heavily, Brooke "engaged in heated arguments" with the wary politicians, eventually triumphing: the paper was approved unaltered. Per Brooke: "Any change would have been fatal. The Americans had gone a long way to meet us, and I should have hated to ask them for more."[65]

The decision—on Friday, July 24, after over one year of mulling—had been made.[66]

For Churchill the strategic choice was "a great joy." He "now hastened to rechristen my favourite"—changing its name from "Gymnast" to "Torch."[67]

One leading decision participant was, however, in denial that the decisive step had in fact been taken. George Marshall had couched his memorandum—as confirmed by the Combined Chiefs—in contingent terms: preparations for the North African operation would go forward but the Allies would not until September 15 determine, based mainly on how the war was going in Russia, whether the attack would indeed be mounted.[68] Marshall returned from London thinking that the true decision was a month and a half in the future. Roosevelt, however, flatly disregarded the provisional language of Marshall and the Combined Chiefs: Torch for him was on—without question or any more talking.[69] He cabled Churchill on July 28 his sense that "the past week"—in committing the Allies to land in North Africa—"represented a turning-point in the whole war."[70] He told U.S. military leaders on July 30 "that he, as Commander-in-Chief, had made the decision that TORCH should be undertaken at the earliest possible date."[71] Neither the President nor the British ever wavered in considering the decision of July 24 to be final.[72] There would in mid–September be no mulling of whether Torch would happen.

The Four Steps of Decision Science

The decision-scientific approach to difficult choices typically has four steps:

- identifying alternatives for consideration: what are the choices?
- estimating the likelihoods of the various possible outcomes for each possible choice: how likely are good, bad, and intermediate results?
- valuing those outcomes: how good or how bad would they be?
- identifying the alternatives that are prospectively best: what would it be best to do?

Evaluating a decision entails addressing four questions. Were all reasonable alternatives duly considered? Were outcome likelihoods well estimated? Were possible outcomes appropriately valued? Was the best alternative[73] chosen? These questions are posed to the deliberations, discussions, and determinations that put Allied soldiers on the shores of Algeria and French Morocco:

Identifying alternatives. Throughout their military mulling, Allied leaders had to have in mind the globality of the conflict: that any grand-strategic allocations of resources to any continent or to any sea meant less for others. With this awareness as backdrop, selection among the main options was sequentially split: the Allied decision makers first, from June 1941 through July 24, 1942, pondered various strategic actions, finally settling on that of invading North Africa, and, over the next six weeks, chose among their tactical possibilities just how they would mount their attacks[74];

Estimating the likelihoods of possible outcomes. The chances of the outcomes that might result from the actions of the Allies were pondered—although usually not in numerical terms. Such mulling of what might happen drew attention to the critical uncertainties;

Valuing the outcomes. Britain and America saw the war and the world differently. This affected both the probabilities they estimated for and the values they ascribed to the possible outcomes; and

Choosing the prospectively-best option. The decision participants for Gymnast/Torch took varied actions to secure the actions they personally wanted.

Competing Grand-Strategic Priorities

At the meeting in August 1941 of Churchill, Roosevelt, and their beribboned officers in Placentia Bay, there was a general expectation that the war of twenty-three months was about to expand: that the roster of Western Allies soon would include the U.S. and that they before long would be fighting not just Germany and Italy but also their Axis partner, the Empire of Japan.

America and Britain confirmed in Placentia Bay the center beam of their grand strategy for the imminently larger war: they would first defeat Germany, before attending to Japan. When, four months later, American fury was drawn westward by Pearl Harbor, Britain feared that the U.S. might prioritize avenging herself on her surprise attacker. These fears would, however, prove to be without ground. Although the U.S. Navy, led by Admiral Ernest King, repeatedly urged more effort in the Pacific Theater, even if at the expense of all others, America would reaffirm at the end of 1941—and would subsequently remain committed to—the goal order of "Germany First," then Japan.

This principle, important as it would be throughout the war, did not, however, resolve all inter-theater choices. Neither America nor Britain understood it to mean that whenever any resource would have any value in fighting Germany, it must be taken from the war against Japan. The Western Allies in the first months of 1942 felt that they could do little for the moment against Germany, while Japan threatened imminently to advance toward India and to sever the sea lanes between the U.S. and Australia. Japan had at least to be slowed down, before heavy force would be wielded against Germany.

Roosevelt in January personally, if reluctantly, approved transferring seven cargo ships from supplying the Soviet Union to runs to the South Pacific.[75] In the first two and one half months of 1942, 90,000 of the 130,000 men America sent overseas went to the Pacific.[76] Most of the nation's aircraft carriers also were deployed against Japan—to devastating effect in June at Midway. By November, however, the U.S. Navy in the Pacific was down to but one floating flattop, the *Enterprise,* which was still so damaged from the Battle of the Eastern Solomons in August that it would not until the end of the month return to action. With Operation Torch coming ashore that month, the only remaining, large, intact carrier of the nation was the *Ranger*—then urgently needed in two oceans. The tenet of "Germany First" meant that the ship had to remain in the Atlantic to cover the landings of Patton in French Morocco.

Similar quandaries would recur: with so many areas pleading for resources, how much should each be allotted? If limited matériel might gain more in a theater of lower priority, should it go there? If so, how much? How should degrees of immediate urgency and of long-term priority be weighed against each other? Such questions were faced and resolved throughout the war by the Combined Chiefs of Staff.

Guidance for the CCS on the tough trade-offs between theaters was provided by the highest Allied authorities, who variously expressed the precedence order of their objectives. In December of 1941, the British Chiefs of Staff asserted "that only the minimum of force necessary for the safeguarding of vital interests in other theaters should be diverted from operations against Germany."[77] The U.S. would agree.[78] But what would constitute adequate safeguarding? Which interests were vital?

As George Marshall's lead war planner in February 1942, Dwight Eisenhower expressed the relative rankings of competing goals by distinguishing between two categories:

> those deemed "necessary," which included securing the United Kingdom and the North Atlantic sea lanes to her, keeping Russia in the war, and holding from the Middle East to India to prevent a juncture of Germany and Japan as well as to sustain China; and those considered "desirable," such as the security of Alaska, Hawaii, Burma, South America, Australia, and West Africa.[79]

On August 14, 1942, the Combined Chiefs of Staff ranked priorities in five levels: (1) Operation Torch, the Middle East, the Pacific, and supplying Russia; (2) the dispatching of American air units to Britain and China; (3) sending U.S. troops to Iceland to relieve UK troops there; (4) Bolero; and (5) India and China.[80]

Helpful and revealing as such rankings were, challenging choices still had to be made in allocating specific resources. American planners early in 1942 judged the most pressing logistic shortage to be of cargo ships; in the middle months of the year, "troop transports would become the limiting factor … after which the availability of cargo shipping would again control."[81] Later, as the Allies prepared to land in northern France, the shortage in landing craft became comparably constraining to those in cargo and troop shipping.[82] The need for landing craft was for a time so acute as to preempt in the shipyards of the Allied navies the construction of aircraft carriers and escort ships.[83]

The pleading for resources in different theaters was incessant. Prime Minister John Curtin of Australia in late 1941 and early 1942 felt that his nation was insufficiently defended and demanded the return of his nation's divisions serving in the Middle East. The retention there and in the Indian Ocean of Australian and New Zealand divisions was secured by having U.S. troops sent to their home nations. This troop-lift required, though, in March 1942 that 25 cargo ships be reassigned from runs to support forces in the Middle East and China.[84] Chiang Kai-shek protested in May that such disregard for the needs of his front meant that his nation's resistance to the Japanese might collapse.[85]

The main tensions and most-crucial trade-off decisions were between Allied needs in the Atlantic and the Pacific. In early 1942, the urgency of sending 22,000 Americans to the southwest Pacific required that the planned shipping of 24,000 U.S. troops to Iceland and Northern Ireland be reduced by three quarters.[86] That Churchill in April so quickly accepted Marshall's plans for Bolero/Sledgehammer/Roundup has been attributed to his desire to have the U.S. send its resources not westward to the Pacific but eastward over the Atlantic.[87] The ensuing build-up of troops and supplies in the British Isles was undertaken at the expense of the Middle East, China, shipments to Russia, and the Pacific.[88] The U.S. 3rd Infantry Division had been trained for service against the Japanese but was reassigned to Torch—leaving the Allied commanders in the South Pacific to make do with a less-trained unit.[89] The situation there—as the battling in Guadalcanal raged on—was then deemed "critical" and was vying directly with TORCH in the allocation of resources.[90] U.S. plans to oust the Japanese from the Aleutians were of lower priority than the landings in North Africa and the crisis in the Solomons and were put on hold.[91]

It was in this context of competing grand-strategic demands—from the islands of Alaska to the steppes of Russia, from the tropical sands of the South Pacific to the bleak plains of Iceland, from the deserts of the Middle East to the jungles of Burma—that the Allied commanders had to decide in 1942 where to send their ships, planes, guns, and men.

Strategic Alternatives

The decision makers of Gymnast/Torch considered many major options.

Winston Churchill, from before he became Prime Minister until after the Allies were committed to Overlord, favored operations in Norway. He had been the prime pusher for the unsuccessful British landings in Norway in April 1940 and continued through early 1944 to urge Allied attacks there—in 1941 code-named Ajax; in 1942, Jupiter. While many saw a Norwegian invasion as an alternative to Gymnast/Torch, the Prime Minister wanted both. Despite his persistent advocacy of Ajax and Jupiter, his chiefs saw the impossibility of providing adequate air cover as an irremediable flaw and never came close to approving either. "For steering Churchill off" Jupiter, Alan Brooke has been given "immense credit."[92] Given the resistance of the British Chiefs to his Norwegian schemes, the Prime Minister at various times proposed to the Americans and Canadians that they undertake these operations. They declined.[93]

Consistently thwarted on his Norwegian proposals, Churchill in the last three months of 1941 pondered an imaginative range of possibilities: from reinforcing the Russians in Murmansk to landings in Sicily or at Livorno.[94] The Sicilian idea, then Operation Whipcord, was scuttled in October 1941 by his chiefs, but would be refloated as Operation Husky and sent ashore 21 months later.

The Americans, after entering the war, extended the range of strategic thinking. Eisenhower reported that, in early 1942, "one senior officer seriously proposed that we make our initial landing in Liberia, and begin from there to fight our way laboriously up the coast of Africa toward Europe."[95] More seriously proposed—but thought comparably delusional by the British—was the combination idea of Bolero/Sledgehammer/Roundup. For Marshall, Eisenhower, Stimson, and other Americans from March 1942 through and beyond July 24, it was the favored approach. Throughout this time, many in the U.S. Navy, led by Admiral Ernest King, preferred to forgo strategic operations in the Atlantic Theater until 1943 to enable greater immediate allocations to the Pacific.

The British delegation headed by Churchill, when in the U.S. from the eighteenth to the twenty-fifth of June, revealed that the UK had been mulling five main options for actions that year: Sledgehammer-variant landings near Calais, Cherbourg, or Brest; Jupiter in Norway; and extended raids, of perhaps two or three days.[96] One spectacular foray that had been considered and rejected was Operation Imperator—under which a division augmented with tanks was to land, raid Paris, speed to a shore, and re-embark.[97] Churchill, Roosevelt, and others on the twenty-first discussed possible operations in Spain and Portugal in the last few months of 1942.[98]

After several meetings that day, Roosevelt asked Marshall to remain with him. The President then proposed sending U.S. troops to secure for the Allies territory stretching from Egypt to Iran—an extreme variant of the kind of force dispersion that Marshall deplored. The army chief was so fatigued and exasperated that he thought it best not then to respond and departed. He sent the President the next morning a paper quashing the idea.

Upon the emphatic British rejection of Sledgehammer on July 22, Roosevelt insisted on an alternative and suggested in priority order two versions of Gymnast, Jupiter, reinforcement of the British in Egypt, and "American operations through Iran into the Caucasus."[99] To Roosevelt's list of post–Sledgehammer-demise options, Eisenhower, in a memorandum of July 23 to Marshall, added that of taking the Azores, the Cape Verdes, the Canaries, and the Madeiras.[100]

French General Henri Giraud, upon arriving at Eisenhower's HQ on November 7, 1942, wanted to scrap Torch, then hours from going ashore, in favor of landing in southern France.[101]

Tactical Choices

Specifics of Gymnast/Torch—the when, the where, and the who—were pondered somewhat before and more intensively after July 24, 1942.

Roosevelt cared about the timing of Torch. Knowing the urgent desires of his public for Americans to be fighting Germans and fearing the effects of this impatience on the Congressional elections of November 3, he pled with Marshall: "Please make it before Election Day."[102] This request could be seen as a selfish elevation of personal and partisan concerns over what might be best for GIs with their lives on the line. Historian Andrew Roberts, though, defended the President's action: an electoral triumph of "the isolationists and Republicans" might jeopardize the Anglo-American approach to the war.[103]

Roosevelt had stipulated on July 25 that the landings must take place by October 30. Perhaps to enhance the chances for pre-election landings, he pressed repeatedly in August for advancing the date—cabling Churchill on the thirtieth that "I would still hope for October 14."[104] Unless the Allies landed by October 15, Torch was thought unlikely to help the Soviets—just why not being particularly clear.[105] Delays caused by plan changes and resource unavailability pushed the date back to November 8. In the elections held five days before Torch, the Democrats lost 44 seats in the House and nine in the Senate.

Decision participants prioritize what they push for. While Roosevelt had been primarily urging an early invasion, the British had emphasized making it more to the east. Throughout August, the two Allies had debated landing sites: the UK daring; the U.S. dreading. Foremost in the British mind was to drive rapidly—"within 26 days of passing Gibraltar and preferably within 14 days"[106]—to Tunis, thereby cutting off the Afrika Korps; foremost in the American was the possibility of Germans, perhaps aided by Generalísimo Francisco Franco, speeding through Spain to take Gibraltar, thereby severing communications to the Allies in the Mediterranean and putting their "heads in a noose."[107] (Gibraltar had been captured in 1704 from Spain by an Anglo-Dutch force and held ever since by Britain.)

British operational planners—backed by Dwight Eisenhower, whom in London they had won over to their view[108]—thought the key landing to be in Algiers, 400 miles from Tunis. They favored landing at Oran—600 miles west of Tunis—and Algiers on Day 1 and, two days later, at Philippeville (modern-day Skikda) and Bône (now Annaba).[109] That Bône was within 200 miles of Tunis (182 by road, 134 by air) was to the British a compelling consideration. George Marshall—backed by U.S. War Department planners—instead prioritized taking Casablanca, a base on the Atlantic, 1,500 land miles from Tunis. The Washingtonians proposed to disembark in French Morocco around Casablanca and in western Algeria around Oran. The lodgement area in Algeria was to extend sixty miles eastward from Oran—less than one quarter of the distance from Oran to Algiers.[110] Washington thought Algiers an excessively risky stretch; London, that the U.S. worries were unfounded and that Casablanca was therefore unnecessary. With the planners of the two nations at loggerheads, Churchill and Roosevelt stepped in, debated by cable, and compromised in early September on landings at Casablanca, Oran, and Algiers. It would later be judged that American over-caution had cost the Allies the quick capture of Tunisia, thereby committing a "strategic mistake."[111]

Another mistake of the U.S., to UK eyes, was its insistence on an overwhelmingly American character of Torch. Pétain's France, remembering the murderous bombardment of 1940 at Mers-el-Kébir, disliked Churchill's Britain. The U.S. had not only maintained diplomatic relations with Pétain but, at the insistence of Roosevelt, had also sent food to Vichy France and North Africa.[112] Americans, from the President on down, thought that the French particularly liked them. Future Prime Minister Harold Macmillan, Churchill's political envoy to North Africa after Torch had gone ashore, described the "delusion" of the Americans "that they were especially popular in France.... The French, owing to Lafayette ... were traditional friends of America. Moreover, the long-expressed preference of many American travelers for Paris over any other city was supposed to have considerable political influence."[113]

Churchill wrote that "I did not wholly share the American view that either they were so beloved by Vichy or we so hated as to make the difference between fighting and submission, but I was very willing that ... we should keep as much in the background as was physically possible."[114] He therefore proposed that an American command Torch—to which role the U.S. in early August of 1942 named Eisenhower. Later that month, the British, in order to have a first-day landing at Algiers, proposed manning it with their forces and just enough Americans to support the fiction that it was their invasion. Roosevelt cabled back: "I feel very strongly that the initial attacks must be made by an exclusively American ground force."[115] Churchill proposed having UK troops wear U.S. uniforms—which offer was declined. The U.S., however, softened its position to requiring that the attackers, as much as possible, seem to be American and agreed that the landings at Algiers would be made by troops of the two nations: on November 8, 47,000 Americans and 27,000 British would come into North Africa.

With Churchill and Roosevelt having stepped in to resolve the differences between their two militaries, basic agreement was reached on September 5.

Uncertainties

Incertitudes raise blood pressures, spawn ulcers, and cause hairs to fall out and financial markets to plummet. It is comforting, invigorating, and seductive to deny doubts, to pretend that all is sure. In councils of decision, speakers who belittle or ignore uncertainties sound thrillingly more persuasive than others who frankly confess their worries. Speakers to soldiers and to citizens in the war were the more inspirational, the more definite their words. Winston Churchill would not have changed "We will never surrender" to the possibly more accurate "The chance that we ever will surrender has been estimated at 8.7 percent"—the latter the kind of phrasing of decision scientists and game theorists. Lawyers in courtrooms, pundits in the media, and military historians in their battle critiques are the more impressive and convincing the less they mention or concede any possibility of error. One persuades the better and better pleases audiences, the more assuredly one speaks and the less notice is given to the limits of knowledge and grasp. Uncertainties are, in consequence, slighted, denied, and ignored.

Fortunately, however, in many ways—for how much less wonderful would our world be without surprises?—unfortunately in others, uncertainties exist.

"In no human activity other than war," the Prussian military theorist Carl von Clausewitz wrote, "are the connections with chance happenings—inclusive of the accidental and the lucky—as constant." Indeed, per Clausewitz, "the context of war comprises the four elements of danger, physical exertion, uncertainty, and chance." War was, for him, "the province of the uncertain: three fourths of what one deals with in war lies in the fog of greater or lesser uncertainty." War, therefore, often entails reliance on the laws of probability and "Bonaparte," Clausewitz thought, "had been quite right in saying that many decisions faced by military commanders would require mathematical calculations not unworthy of a Newton or an Euler."[116]

Allied decision makers in the war had much knowledge, interspersed with much ignorance. Their intelligence services produced excellent estimates of German troop dispositions before the landings on Sicily, at Salerno, and in Normandy but poor ones before the battles of Arnhem and the Ardennes. The Ultra decryption of German messages was providential for the Allies, but could not eliminate all puzzlement about enemy locations, strengths, and intentions.

Decision science was largely developed to cope with uncertainty. More than other disciplines, DS recognizes, addresses, bounds, and measures what is not known. Along with game theory, it seeks best actions when just what is happening or what might is unclear. At times, research or reconnaissance can resolve doubts; at others, they cannot; at still others, partial elucidation may be achieved. Before main decisions, decision science and game theory inquire into how much time and effort should go into seeking better understanding of present situations and of possible future events. Most often, incertitudes cannot be fully dispelled and prospectively best actions must be sought amid doubts.

Just how uncertainty in war is best dealt with remains an open question. Optimal decision-making requires accurate sense of what is and is not known. After, however, a decision has been made, many have felt that maximally-effective operations demand the presumption of certainty and troop-heartening suppression of doubt. Daniel Kahneman, a 2002 Nobelist for his work in decision science, has documented the excessive confidence that individuals often have in their judgments, their undue downplaying of uncertainties, and their over-sanguineness in risky undertakings. He has also, though, conceded that "when action is needed, optimism, even of the mildly delusional variety, may be a good thing."[117] Dwight Eisenhower (citing his need "to keep up, in front of everybody, a proper attitude of confidence and optimism") and George Patton ("Generals must never show doubt, discouragement, or fatigue") agreed.[118]

Barack Obama, in 2012, thought along the same lines and spoke in the quantified language of decision science about his challenges: "So you wind up dealing with probabilities. Any given decision you make you'll wind up with a 30 to 40 percent chance that it isn't going to work." In the end, "on top of all of this, after you have made your decision, you need to feign total certainty about it. People being led do not want to think probabilistically."[119]

*　*　*

Unsure factors pondered before, on, and after July 24, 1942, included the French, the Spanish, the Germans, the Russians, 1943, and the weather.

The attitude of Pétain's France toward an Allied invasion of North Africa was speculated on for over a year, until—and after—the Allies were ashore. There would be in French Morocco, Algeria, and Tunisia in November 1942 120,000 French soldiers.[120] Initial hopes that Vichy officials in these colonies might invite in Allied forces and even, perhaps, declare war on the Axis turned into questions: absent an invitation, would the forces of Vichy resist and, if so, how strongly? If Maréchal Pétain and his cabinet remained subservient to Germany, could his subordinates in Africa independently declare themselves for the Allies? Anglo-American views on these possibilities bounced about. In January 1942, Allied planners presumed French cooperation with Gymnast, with the possibility of minimal, uncoordinated resistance. Two months later, the UK and U.S. both thought that Vichy North Africa would resist any invasion, until it became clear that "the Axis is on the run."[121] Eisenhower said on July 5, 1943, that he had made a "big mistake" in overestimating the resistance the French would make in Algiers and other Mediterranean ports: had he better allocated his forces, the Afrika Korps would have been bagged months sooner.[122]

Eisenhower also, hindsight would reveal, had overfeared what Francisco Franco might do. Churchill wrote in December 1941: "We cannot tell what will happen in Spain. *It seems probable that the Spaniards will not give the Germans a free passage through Spain to attack Gibraltar and invade North Africa* [emphasis in original]."[123] American and British planners the next month predicated Gymnast on high confidence that German attacks through Spain to Africa would encounter Spanish resistance, would therefore be slowed by three months, and would lead the Spanish to welcome Allied forces into Spanish Morocco.[124]

Probably unknown to the Allies, Generalísimo Franco had—in June 1940, when German conquest of the Low Countries and northern France made Nazi victory in the war seem imminent—told Bundeskanzler Hitler that he was "ready under certain conditions to enter the war on the side of Germany and Italy."[125] His price had included chunks of French Morocco and Algeria, economic and military aid, and assistance in conquering Gibraltar for Spain. A month later, however, with Churchill's Britain having made clear its resolve to continue the war, the Caudillo voiced to the Germans his second thoughts: he had concern about what the British fleet might do to his peninsular nation and about possible American limiting of the oil provided to Spain.

On October 23, 1940, the German and Spanish dictators met at Hendaye, a French town on the border with Spain. Franco expressed desire to join the Axis, but regretted that his nation was poor, had had a bad harvest, was vulnerable to Anglo-American reprisals, and was therefore reluctant to come into the war. Hitler proposed taking Gibraltar, which Spain could then keep. Franco made positive noises, but refused to commit to the undertaking. Britain, her dominions, and the U.S. were then bribing with economic carrots and threatening with naval sticks to keep Spain out of the war. The Spanish at Hendaye asked the Germans to keep their talks secret, lest the imminent receipt of 250,000 tons of food from Canada be put at risk.[126] Franco understood that entry into the war was likely to lead to the immediate loss of Spain's Canary Islands and to the invasion of his mainland.

Hitler, on the day after Hendaye, traveled to Montoire on the Loire to meet with Philippe Pétain. He there persuaded the aged maréchal to cede French territory in Africa to Spain, if it should join the Axis—for which France would be compensated from British possessions. For months thereafter, German officers with Spanish assistance reconnoitered Gibraltar and planned its conquest and Hitler and Mussolini reminded Franco of how much he owed them for their support in the Spanish Civil War. While the Generalísimo expressed confidence that the Axis would be victorious and intent ultimately to enter the alliance and the war, he declined to set a date for such action.[127] The Axis nations, in consequence, like the Allies, were uncertain about Spain: whether Franco ever would join their coalition; whether, in the event of an Allied invasion of Spain, the Spanish would resist and possibly invite German divisions into their land to assist in its defense.[128] As 1942 progressed, British worries about Spain diminished, while those of the Americans remained significant.[129] UK General Sir Hastings Ismay summarized that, pre-invasion, the Americans, led by Marshall, fretted the German capture of Gibraltar "as a trap which might be sprung at any moment," while the British "scarcely gave it a thought."[130]

With American worries about the Mediterranean focused on the western strait, British uncertainties in the sea were to the east. The incertitude relating to the Afrika Korps of Erwin Rommel extended over more than the 1,100 miles separating the capital cities of Libya and Egypt: Churchill, in proposing Gymnast, presumed in the fall of 1941 that the Panzer general would soon be driven west to Tripoli and beyond by the British Eighth Army of Claude Auchinleck; the U.S. Army thought in mid–1942, after the fall of Tobruk, that Rommel might well take Cairo within two weeks.[131] British diplomats in the Egyptian capital were then burning their papers. Alan Brooke in late 1941 considered the PM's "elated and optimistic mood" for Gymnast unjustified, given the difficulties that the Eighth Army would face.[132] Soon, Churchill too appreciated how much of a challenge Auchinleck had in his opposing commander. The Prime Minister said to the House of Commons on January 27, 1942, "We have a very daring and skilful opponent against us, and, may I say across the havoc of war, a great general."[133]

Just how much effect a great general could have on the outcome of Gymnast/Torch would depend on how much support Adolf Hitler would give him. Would the Germans, in response to Allied landings, send forces into Tunisia and, if so, how quickly? The thinking in Eisenhower's HQ in late August was that "the Germans and/or the Italians could get into Tunisia in strength in twenty-eight days."[134]

If Axis troops were sent to Tunisia, how well would they fight? Allied decision makers—both the soldiers and, even more, the political leaders—pondered the psychology of their enemy and sought to affect it. Churchill and Roosevelt recalled that German fighting spirit had plummeted in the last months of the previous war and wanted to make it happen again; George Marshall in April 1942 urged the British Chiefs to be ready to exploit "a break in German morale" by launching Sledgehammer[135]; operations were argued for on the basis that they would dishearten the enemy; Stalin told Churchill that he appreciated the British bombing campaign, for its effects on German civilian morale.[136] Throughout the war, the Allies would be overly optimistic about how much their successes might discourage the Germans and impair their fighting.

Just how optimistic the Americans and British should be about their Soviet ally was, at the time of the decisions on Sledgehammer and Gymnast/Torch, not clear. Eisenhower, on July 19, 1942, sent Marshall a memorandum titled "Russia is the great question mark of the war."[137] Allied decision makers had conflicting thoughts about how events in Russia should affect Sledgehammer: should it be undertaken only if the Red Army was doing so poorly that a landing in France was essential to draw German divisions westward or only if it was doing so well that German spirits sank and the Wehrmacht had to strip the Channel Coast of troops? George Marshall touched on both points to the British Chiefs on April 14, 1942: the Allies might be forced to act in Europe "either because we might not be able to hold back while the Russians were being driven back or borne down or because a favourable opportunity had presented itself."[138] The report of the Combined Chiefs of June 21 stated, without revealing its reasoning and with what turned out to be excessive certainty: "The issue in Russia will be decided one way or the other by September, 1942."[139] One month later, during the visit of Marshall and Hopkins to London, the U.S. army chief still inclined toward "waiting a while to see what happened on the Eastern Front before deciding."[140]

The Western Allies wondered also if they should wait another year—until 1944—before invading northern France and also if launching Gymnast/Torch would make such a wait more likely. Would invading North Africa in 1942 preclude landing in France in 1943? Dwight Eisenhower, Ernest King, George Marshall, Dudley Pound, and Henry Stimson, at the moment of decision on Gymnast/Torch, asserted so; Winston Churchill and Franklin Roosevelt believed not—with which belief Alan Brooke, and British Air Chief Marshal Sir Charles Portal voiced agreement.[141] Historian Leo Meyer believed that the military decision makers of both nations "saw clearly" that Torch would delay Roundup until 1944, even though the British "never admitted it openly in conference."[142]

Not seen clearly by the Anglo-American DMs were the effects of weather on the optimal timing of Gymnast/Torch and on its outcome. Weather had set the stage for the demise of Napoleon's Grande Armée of 1812 and for the successful Russian counterattacks of late 1941 and early 1942. Should the landings in North Africa be launched early enough to relieve pressure on the Red Army before the climate came to its aid? Would waiting too long for the landings mean that the Germans would transfer many air squadrons from the inclement conditions in the east to the North African theater? The feasibility of landing in French Morocco would depend on the ocean conditions. Bad weather could hamper air support at all landing sites.[143]

Britain, in retrospect, was more right than her ally with respect to Spain: there had been in 1942 no danger of Germans moving through Franco's nation to Gibraltar. The Americans were right—and suspected that Alan Brooke (as he subsequently admitted[144]) had secretly agreed with them all along—that Torch precluded Roundup in 1943. Whether emphasizing the American nature of Torch significantly lowered French resistance is not clear—although Vichy forces would in December refuse to serve under British command, while accepting subordination to Americans.[145] Both nations were monumentally wrong about what Adolf Hitler would do.

Values: Anglo-American Differences in Outlook and Priority

To prosecute the war, the two leading Western Allies had mutually to accommodate their divergent views of the world: their differing expectations of what might happen and their conflicting thoughts on how good or how bad various possible events might be. In December 1941, for instance, the British were surprised to learn that the Americans fretted potential Axis threats to South America and the Caribbean—the U.S. noting that the Guianas produced 95 percent of the oil for its East Coast and half of that sent to Britain under Lend Lease.[146] While this particular concern would recede, one fundamental disparity in thinking about the war would persist until 1945. Churchill described it:

> In the military as in the commercial or production spheres the American mind runs naturally to broad, sweeping, logical conclusions on the largest scale. It is on these that they build their practical thought and action. They feel that once the foundation has been planned on true and comprehensive lines all other stages will follow naturally and almost inevitably. The British mind does not work quite in this way. We do not think that logic and clear-cut principles are necessarily the sole keys to what ought to be done in swiftly changing and indefinable situations. In war particularly we assign a larger importance to opportunism and improvisation, seeking rather to live and conquer in accordance with the unfolding event than to aspire to dominate it often by fundamental decisions. There is room for much argument about both views. The difference is one of emphasis, but it is deep-seated.[147]

Harold Macmillan also, at the time of Torch, described

> the fundamental difference between the American and British conception of war. Broadly, the Americans felt that you should find a convenient place to fight the main forces of your enemy of the moment, and regarded a battle as somewhat in the nature of an athletic contest, without much regard as to what would happen afterwards. The British tended to take a more sophisticated view; war is a continuation of policy, and policies and purposes may fluctuate and change.[148]

The attitudinal Atlantic divide had aspects and explanations. The U.S. thought the UK traumatized by what had happened between 1914 and 1918 and in 1940. To Marshall's advocacy of an early landing in France one Briton responded, "It's no use—you are arguing against the casualties on the Somme [in 1916]."[149] U.S. Secretary of War Henry Stimson wrote Roosevelt in August 1943 that "the shadows of Passchendaele and Dunkerque still hang too heavily over" the British leaders.[150] Churchill described his sadness as, in the House of Commons, he looked around him "at the faces that are not there"—because of the earlier conflict.[151] The UK had had in the Great War, out of a population less than half that of the U.S., fourteen times as many battle deaths.

While the Americans thought the British too borne down by their recent war history, the nation that had been at war since September 1939 saw the newcomers as so unleavened by fighting experience as to be strategically naïve. Alan Brooke considered that Harry Hopkins and George Marshall in early 1942 "had no idea of what modern war entailed and of how unprepared they were for it."[152] He was later echoed by British historians: that the U.S. was "hot to wage war in Europe, yet without the remotest strategical conception of how to do so or the problems involved."[153]

From one experience—the First World War—that the two nations had to some extent in common, divergent conclusions were drawn. The British thought that their peripheral approach had triumphed by effecting "the collapse of the German economy and will"; the Americans, that "their first direct offensives" had briskly brought victory[154]—like cavalry riding to the rescue.

The variant views on the earlier conflict have also been ascribed to differing theories of war: the Americans, devotees of Clausewitz, believing that war is best waged by confronting and defeating the enemy via concentration of forces on the main front; the British, followers of the pre–Christian-Era Chinese military theorist Sun Tzu, that peripheral attacks to weaken a strong opponent should precede full engagement.[155]

That such peripheral attacks in the Second World War often furthered the interests of the British Empire sparked American suspicions. Many in the U.S. sensed ulterior imperial motives in the tilt of the UK toward the Mediterranean. Henry Stimson in 1942 thought that Churchill was "more interested in saving British interests in Egypt and the Middle East [Iraq and Palestine] ... than in attacking Nazi Germany."[156]

As to such attacking, it was clear to all that the less the UK and U.S. did against Germany, the more the USSR would have to. Limited, peripheral attacks on the Axis—such as in North Africa or Norway, instead of across the Channel—meant that the Bear would bear even more of the brunt and would thereby likely spare hundreds of thousands of Anglo-American lives. This went largely unsaid in the councils of the Western Allies, but the point was so patent as not to need voicing. The Americans saw net positive value in a foredoomed, multi-division invasion of France that could draw Wehrmacht divisions from Russia and would demonstrate to Stalin a commitment to defeating Germany—not just a noble, but also a worthwhile sacrifice[157]; the British could see in such an undertaking nothing but the waste of matériel, deaths to no purpose, and gloating headlines for Nazi journals. Two British historians described the stances of Churchill and Brooke: their readiness "to fight not to the last American, but rather to the last Russian"[158]; their "willingness to allow the Russians to bleed the German Army," which "was a great service to [Britain]."[159] War-time Americans joined in these judgments and were irked that the British, intent on self-preservation, seemed to hang back from whole-hearted participation in the war.[160] Churchill in September 1941 had written to his chiefs of "the moral need of ... freeing ourselves from the imputation, however unjust, of always using other people's troops and blood."[161]

In 1942, the U.S. was, in pushing for Sledgehammer, itself advocating using other people's troops and blood: the operation would have had to be overwhelmingly British. The U.S., swaggeringly more confident in July 1942 than the UK that Hitler's France could be assaulted, became weeks later the less bold ally—showing "unexpected reluctance" to attack within the Mediterranean.[162] U.S. historian Rick Atkinson explained this attitudinal shift: in contrast to the predominantly British Sledgehammer; "with American soldiers predominant in TORCH, caution prevailed and audacity stole away."[163]

American audacity also stole away with respect to British urging later in the war to have the Anglo-Americans meet the Russians as far east as possible: the more Axis capitals and the more of the Balkans taken by the Western Allies, Churchill held, the better. The Americans were focused more on the present war and less on preparing for its aftermath. To the extent that they did ponder the post-war, they wanted to promote good faith with the Soviets—who would not welcome the West either leaving most of the fighting to them or pushing into Eastern Europe. Henry Stimson wrote to Roosevelt in August 1943 that the favored British "methods of pinprick warfare" were unlikely "to fool Stalin into the belief that" the Western pledge of a true second front had been kept—which, after the war, could prove "terribly dangerous."[164]

Such divergences in background and view challenged decision-making. The British, compared to the Americans, judged the prospects of Sledgehammer harshly: with less value ascribed to the most-optimistic scenario of a lasting lodgement in France and a judgment that even that was unlikely. For Gymnast/Torch, the relative assessments of values and probabilities of the two nations were reversed.

To agree on action in 1942, these gulfs of difference had to be bridged. That they were owed much to the PM and the POTUS.

Modes of Decision Influence

To secure their preferred courses of action, the decision participants of Gymnast/Torch acted in many ways. A persistently-pursued tactic of George Marshall was to pen memoranda. To enhance their impacts, he obtained and highlighted their endorsements by top officers. Marshall, by January 9, 1942, disfavored Gymnast and forwarded to Roosevelt that day a paper detailing its dangers and other drawbacks. More memoranda in the same vein followed. By mid–June, the army chief sensed that Roosevelt leaned again toward North Africa. On the seventeenth and twenty-third of the month, he gave memos to his Commander in Chief, reiterating how bad an idea—he, the Navy, the Air Corps, and their planners agreed—Gymnast was.[165]

Another paper prepared by George Marshall in the spring of 1942 outlined his plan for operations in Western Europe: the combination of Bolero, Sledgehammer, and Roundup. In a meeting on March 24, 1942, Roosevelt, Hopkins, and U.S. brass agreed that British support for Marshall's strategy should be sought. The President proposed presenting it to the British via submission to the Combined Chiefs. Harry Hopkins, however, fearing that the U.S. proposals would there be "pulled to pieces and emasculated," nixed the suggestion.[166] His own ploy for decision influence was to "deliberately try to bypass the Joint Planners of the Combined Chiefs," in order to preclude the British having "had their refutations prepared even before Marshall's plane touched down" in England early in April.[167] Hopkins wanted to keep the British in the dark, to have the advantage of springing Marshall's proposal on unprepared decision participants. Roosevelt and Marshall went along with the sly approach of Hopkins.

This American tactic to secure British acquiescence was not wise. The British Chiefs of Staff in London had been discussing Sledgehammer—which, by March 17, they had understood well enough to oppose.[168] Their performance throughout the war suggests moreover that, even if the U.S. had kept any word of Marshall's strategy from leaking to Britain before his trip, minimal advantage would have been gained: Churchill's chiefs—an un-shy group in conference with Americans—would have voiced their misgivings. As it was, the U.S. leaders had shown themselves to be not playing straight with their allies—a larger loss than any potential gain. It is possible that U.S. cloaking of what it had in mind lowered the level of UK candor in the meetings with Hopkins and Marshall in London.

The craftiness of Hopkins may indeed have led the British in responding to Marshall's plans to feel justified in not being fully straight with the Americans—in their own artful mode of swaying decisions. The tack of Churchill and Brooke when Marshall and Hopkins came to London in April was one of feigned concurrence: of signaling enthusiastic agreement in principle, while knowing that stipulated reservations and consideration of operational details would enable them not to follow through.

The high command of the United Kingdom was appalled by the Marshall-Eisenhower proposal of Sledgehammer, believing that an Allied landing in France in 1942 could only end in disaster. Neither Churchill nor Brooke, however, deemed it well to respond with total frankness to the American ideas—for candid rejection of them might lead the U.S. to send more of its forces to the Pacific. The British opted instead to seem more in step with their ally than they were. They agreed in principle, highlighted points of concurrence, and downplayed differences. The Americans took Churchill's "entire agreement in principle with all that you propose" to mean more than the British did—which may have been what the latter had intended.

Churchill's tactic of agreeing in principle has been called a "brilliant stroke": one that he had learned from his own officers. When they had wanted to kibosh one of his pet schemes, they had agreed in principle, then had "drown[ed] the idea in a sea of reasoned objection."[169] In October 1943, the Soviet Union would propose pressuring Turkey to enter the war and urging Sweden to make air bases available for bombing Germany. Churchill advised his Foreign Secretary, Anthony Eden, not to oppose these Russian suggestions. He did not want the situation to become one of the Soviets urging an approach and of the British "simply making difficulties. We should agree in principle and let the difficulties manifest themselves, as they will certainly do, in the discussion of ways and means ... we ought not to begin by crabbing everything."[170]

Eighteen months earlier, the British had taken the same approach in responding to Marshall. They had, in accepting his plans in principle, been confident that the difficulties of Sledgehammer would become clear. Consideration of its details, Churchill wrote, led to "a certain lack of conviction and ardour ... not only among the British but among our American colleagues. I did not have to argue against 'Sledgehammer' myself. It fell of its own weakness."[171]

Churchill was relying on his own intuitive grasp of the planning fallacy: our proposed undertakings tend to appear progressively harder, the more we get into the details of what has to be done.

Had the British dissembled in April 1942? Alan Brooke had conceded for Sledgehammer its "desirability ... if, and only if, conditions at the time made its success seem probable."[172] The concession was illusory: he could conceive of no possibility of such conditions occurring. No European attack could be undertaken, the CIGS stipulated, until the Allies were secure in their control of the Indian Ocean—which has been characterized as requiring "an open-ended commitment" of the Americans to that sea.[173]

George Marshall, the main target of any disingenuousness, may not have been taken in. He noted at the time that the agreement reached had only been in principle and that "many if not most hold reservations regarding this or that."[174] Churchill recounted that he had never favored Sledgehammer but was willing to give it "a fair run" with the planners—although he was "almost certain the more it was looked at the less it would be liked." He felt, though, that he "had to work by influence and diplomacy in order to secure agreed and harmonious action with our cherished Ally, without whose aid nothing but ruin faced the world. I did not therefore open any of these alternatives [Gymnast and Jupiter] at our meeting on [April] 14th."[175] Nor did he say what he thought of Sledgehammer.

Two top British generals were more apologetic about what their nation had and had not said to Marshall. Per Sir Hastings Ismay, in April 1942 a major general and Churchill's personal military assistant:

> Our American friends went happily homewards under the mistaken impression that we had committed ourselves to both ROUND-UP and SLEDGEHAMMER. This misunderstanding was to have unfortunate results. For, when we had to tell them, after the most thorough study of SLEDGEHAMMER, that we were absolutely opposed to it, they felt that we had broken faith with them.[176]
>
> I think we should have come clean, much cleaner than we did.[177]

Sir Ian Jacob, Military Assistant Secretary to the British War Cabinet, said, "We were convinced that [Sledgehammer could not be launched in 1942] but we were reluctant to say so too strongly lest Marshall should pack up his divisions and take them to the Pacific.... Marshall went home thinking that an attack could be launched that year."[178]

Among the British historians who held that Churchill and Brooke had deliberately misled the U.S. delegation in April through June of 1942 was Sir Max Hastings—who minced no words: in deceiving the Americans with "persistent dissimulation," his countrymen had "prevaricated."[179]

While feigning to agree with an abhorrent proposal partook of subtlety, there was nothing subtle in what ultimately killed Sledgehammer: it was bluntly vetoed. Churchill's assertion that the operation "fell of its own weakness" overstated the case: its difficulties and perils were indeed better understood in July than in April, but had been well enough grasped by the British in March as then to clinch their opposition; any misgivings the Americans may have acquired between the two meetings in London about Sledgehammer did not keep them from urging it until the July 22 moment of its categorical rejection by the British War Cabinet. No option requiring the cooperation of any decision participant can be chosen, if such cooperation is denied. Sledgehammer fell not so much from any inherent weakness discovered in mulling its details as because the British looked into the eyes of George Marshall and Harry Hopkins and said not a chance.

Related to feigning agreement as a stratagem in securing desired choices is not divulging thoughts and aims. Historian Samuel Morison judged that Alan Brooke had intended that Torch/Gymnast lead next to Italy, only then to France. The CIGS, however, "disclosed [this strategy] only bit by bit, which naturally gave the Americans the feeling that they had been 'had.'"[180] Since alerting the Americans to British ideas of Italy after North Africa would have cooled them on Gymnast, they were not to be brought up.[181] Brooke had, indeed, in February 1942, written to Auchinleck that "North Africa would provide an excellent base of attack on Italy"[182]—not an insight to be shared with the U.S. The CIGS was, however, not the only Briton keeping his cards close to his chest. He recorded in his diary on July 23, 1942, "Winston anxious that I should not put Marshall off Africa by referring to Middle East dangers in 1943."[183] Brooke, the next August before the First Quebec Conference, would return Churchill's favor by advising the Prime Minister to keep to himself his hopes to proceed from the Po Valley into Austria or the Balkans.[184] Although neither man urged that untruths be told, both felt it best not to reveal all their thinking.

While historians have confidently inferred various thoughts and motives of Churchill, Roosevelt, Brooke, and Marshall in seeking to win their trans-Atlantic ally to their own strategic approach, there is greater scholarly uncertainty about what had led to the White House statement of June 11, 1942. That announcement reported on the discussions that the President and other American leaders had had with Stalin's envoy, Vyacheslav Molotov: "In the course of the conversations full understanding was reached with regard to the urgent tasks of creating a Second Front in Europe in 1942." Molotov had proposed the wording. George Marshall had thought it too strong and had urged no mention of a date, but Roosevelt had overruled his top general.

It was subsequently judged that FDR had in the statement "all but committed himself to a cross-Channel invasion in August."[185] Speculation as to the Presidential purposes ensued. Did he believe a 1942 landing in France to be feasible? Was he just heartening the Soviets—the main reason he gave both to his military and to Churchill?[186] Was the statement—as Churchill asserted[187]—designed to worry the Germans into holding more divisions in the West and thereby providing relief for Russia? (Churchill later wrote to Stalin that this had been achieved.[188]) Was the President saying what he thought his public wanted to hear? Was he pressuring the British to support Sledgehammer? Was he lighting a fire under his own military?

Historians have reached no conclusions as to Roosevelt's reasons, which "we do not know."[189] The President had earlier "authorized Mr Molotov to inform Mr Stalin that we expect the formation of a Second Front this year"—which has been judged "reprehensible."[190] Roosevelt wrote Churchill that "the Russians are a bit down in the mouth," which made him "especially anxious that Molotov shall carry back some real results of his mission and give a favourable report to Stalin."[191] Stalin would in August complain to Churchill in Moscow: "It will be easily understood that the Soviet Command built their plan of summer and autumn operations calculating on the creation of a second front in Europe in 1942."[192]

Like Stalin had done with Vyacheslav Molotov, Churchill made use of Louis Mountbatten: sending him to Washington. The purposes of the two envoys included both reconnaissance and persuasion. Like the General Secretary, the Prime Minister sought insights on American thinking and to push the U.S. in desired directions. While American military planners in June still thought Sledgehammer both feasible and advantageous, their British counterparts had concluded the opposite. To begin to bridge the decision divide, Mountbatten came to Washington. That the lord was a prominent member of the British royal family was a plus: for Roosevelt liked regality.

Mountbatten in the U.S. capital sought both to learn the mindset of Roosevelt and to throw dirt on Sledgehammer. He dined on June 9 at the White House with the President and Hopkins.[193] George Marshall was not pleased not to have been invited. Mountbatten sensed that Roosevelt might back Gymnast—which was what Churchill had hoped to hear. The news spurred the Prime Minister to leave Britain on the evening of the seventeenth, bound for America.

Once in the U.S., Churchill was thought to have deliberately arranged to speak one-on-one with Roosevelt. In Hyde Park on the nineteenth and twentieth of June, the Prime Minister was judged to have gained "a considerable advantage" in exploiting the absence of Marshall and other advisors. With the army chief back in Washington, Roosevelt may have deferred more to the military expertise of his Sandhurst-educated guest.[194]

One tack of persuasion of Churchill in the early summer of 1942 was that of flattery via the—possibly fraudulent—gift of authorship credit: I want you to back Option Z; I tell you and others of your sagacity in formulating and/or backing that choice; in your swell of pride, you forgive any overstatement of your role and do support Z. Churchill, in urging Gymnast to Roosevelt on July 8, 1942, called it "your commanding idea."[195] (Just which of the two national leaders deserved more credit for originating the North African strategy is not clear. Each may, independently, have come to it. Historian Nigel Hamilton judged that Churchill in his memoirs—by stressing his message of October 20, 1941, and his suggestion to Roosevelt on December 22 of "Anglo-American intervention in French North Africa"—had overstated his own role; that Churchill had sought "to paint himself ... as a successful wartime prime minister"; and that, to that end, he had made himself the proposer and Roosevelt the consenter, when "the reverse, however, was the truth."[196]) George Patton on August 14, 1944, would take the same approach in getting Omar Bradley to agree to let three corps of Third Army drive toward the Seine: "It is really a great plan, wholly my own, and I made Bradley think he thought of it. 'Oh, what a tangled web we weave when first we practice to deceive.'"[197]

Churchill's conferring the credit for Gymnast on Roosevelt has been seen as part of a general strategy of "stroking of the president's ego."[198] The Prime Minister said that, in the Allied strategic debates of 1942, "No lover ever studied every whim of his mistress as I did those of President Roosevelt."[199]

Signally failing to grasp the whims and the will of Roosevelt that summer, as he maneuvered to get his preferred strategy, was George Marshall. The army chief of staff on the tenth of July, knowing himself supported by War Secretary Stimson and Admiral King, telegraphed to the President, who was in Hyde Park, yet another memorandum. He and the other U.S. chiefs had learned of the British distaste for Sledgehammer and of the increasing tilt of Churchill toward Gymnast. They stated that, with the British pushing operations in France in 1942 off the table, the U.S. "should turn to the Pacific ... assume a defensive attitude against Germany, except for air operations; and use all available means in the Pacific."[200]

Game theorists might have seen this memorandum either as a response to the anticipated British veto of Sledgehammer or as a threat to induce British support of both Sledgehammer and Roundup. If a threat, what would the U.S. do should its ally hang tough: would it indeed "turn to the Pacific" or would it fail to follow through, thereby revealing the pressure tactic to have been but a bluff? While the language of much of the memorandum was in the mode of recommending what the U.S. ought to do, given the UK stance, it also asked the President to "urge the Prime Minister 'that we go through with full Bolero plans [inclusive of Sledgehammer and Roundup] and that we attempt no other operation.'" That this was a threat, rather than just a reaction, was confirmed by a follow-on memorandum Marshall sent the same day: "My object is again to force the British into acceptance of a concentrated effort against Germany."[201]

Were the two memoranda proposing a threat that would indeed be carried out or were they urging a grand-strategic bluff? The memoirs of Henry Stimson called it starkly "the bluff."[202] George Marshall in 1956 said that "in my case it was a bluff, but King wanted the [Pacific] alternative."[203] If, for two of the three main persons behind the memoranda, they were a bluff and, for one, a wish; the missives were in one sense whole-cloth bluff: there were no plans for the radical grand-strategic shift suggested. The President either knew of or instinctively suspected this lack and reacted to the memoranda by asking on July 12 for a report that very afternoon "in detail outlining the steps that would be necessary" to shift the American emphasis from the Atlantic to the Pacific: "Roosevelt," per historian Nigel Hamilton, "was calling their bluff." Marshall had lamely to confess to his Commander in Chief that "there is no completed detailed plan for major offensive operations in the Pacific."[204]

Hamilton—with Roosevelt seeming somewhat to agree—considered the first memorandum of July 10 "perhaps the worst-argued strategic document ever produced by America's highest military officers."[205] Frustrated that he could not hold Roosevelt to his own strategic views, Marshall, per Hamilton, had committed an iconic series of errors: attempting to daunt his C-in-C by referencing a consensus of expert military support for his position; criticizing Roosevelt's preferred operation as "indecisive" and "ineffective"; proposing in a Pacific focus an alternative to Gymnast that had not been thought through; and buttressing his position with the argument that shifting U.S. resources to the Pacific would aid Russia, should it be attacked by Japan—which Hamilton, in the absence of any indication that Tokyo might do so, thought "utterly without merit."[206]

Supreme Court Justice Oliver Wendell Holmes judged Franklin Roosevelt a "second-class intellect, but a first-class temperament." Neither attribute of the President, in responding to Marshall, showed deficiency. He could not have welcomed being pressured by the weight of expert military opinion blasting his preferred option; he saw through the more flimsy of Marshall's points; he thought the message to Britain an ignoble threat of "taking up your dishes and going away."[207] He sensed, moreover, the emptiness of the bluff.

Upon receiving Marshall's admission that there had been no planning for a Pacific-ward pivot, Roosevelt responded that the proposal before him was

> exactly what Germany hoped the United States would do...
> Therefore it is disapproved of at present.
> Roosevelt C-in-C[208]

This memorandum accorded with the sixteenth maxim of Napoleon, which had advised "never to do what your enemy wishes." (It also anticipated later theory of zero-sum games, in which to do what an able opponent would want you to is to blunder.)

Hamilton, more than other authors, judged that this episode lowered Marshall's standing with Roosevelt: that it put the general's career at risk; that FDR's rejection was one of contempt; and that Marshall's actions cost him his chance to command Overlord.[209]

If reading Marshall's mass of memoranda did not change Roosevelt's mind, perhaps reading the thoughts of another general would. Marshall and Stimson in the summer of 1942 read *Soldiers and Statesmen,* the memoir of Field Marshal Sir William Robertson, who from 1915 to 1918 had been Chief of the Imperial General Staff. Robertson had lambasted the role of Churchill, in 1915 as First Lord of the Admiralty, in persuading a reluctant British military to invade Gallipoli—with calamitous results both for the attack force and for his own governmental standing. Robertson particularly criticized Churchill's espousal of the indirect strategic approach and his bureaucratic maneuvering. Marshall and Stimson saw the same cabinet politician thinking the same thoughts and using the same methods to get Gymnast. Stimson on July 15 touted the book to Roosevelt and left with him a copy, having flagged the key pages, and a cover note: "I beg you to read it without delay and <u>before you decide upon your present action</u> [emphasis in original]."[210] Churchill was not pleased to learn of this.[211]

Even after the decision on North Africa was made on July 24, Stimson continued to machinate to reverse it. He turned to the time-honored bureaucratic ploy of the motivated leak: the arranging for reports to appear in the press designed to move decision makers toward or away from specific actions.[212] The Secretary of War deplored Torch and may have thought that a good way to undo a bad decision would be to plant articles stating that a politician without military training was dangerously overruling his admirals and generals. Such pieces appeared and riled Roosevelt. At a cabinet meeting early in August, he denounced them and said that he and his armed forces were acting in harmony and that he only stepped in "when the Army and Navy differed and it was necessary for someone to decide between them"[213]—which Presidential statements have been called "lies."[214] Secretaries Knox and Stimson held contrary opinions, yet did not speak in the cabinet to contradict the President, and Roosevelt held firm in insisting on Torch.

* * *

One approach to strategic resolution not taken by the Allied decision makers was one that decision science—if in full-fledged existence—would have urged: estimating numerically the likelihoods that alternative actions would lead to various outcomes; judging quantitatively how favorable or unfavorable those outcomes might be; and systematically determining which alternative offered best overall prospects.[215]

Decision science was in the early 1940s but emergent and little known. Even in the decades after its theoretical soundness has been shown, major military decisions and national policy choices are not based on such numeric methods as those of DS. Nevertheless, to a limited extent and without quantification, the American and British decision makers of June 1941 through July 1942 sought the same goal that later decision scientists would have: actions based on the combined understandings of many that offered the best promise of achieving their generally-agreed-on objectives. They did—albeit without numbers—ponder and debate the likelihoods and the values of possible outcomes.

Roosevelt and Marshall

The President and the U.S. Army Chief of Staff from 1939 through 1945 have been considered the best-ever civilian-military partnership at the head of U.S. fighting forces. For Thomas Ricks, whose *The Generals* in 2012 critiqued American command from the Second World War through the conflicts in Iraq and Afghanistan, George Marshall was the gold standard. Praised aspects of the ascetic Virginian included: his stressing of broad-perspective strategic grasp over circumscribed tactical mastery; his preference for flexibly-applicable education over set-piece training ("less on what to think and more on how to think"[216]); his valuing of ambition directed to furthering the success of the team; his promotion of inspiring leadership and abhorrence of micro-management (which would be symbolized in Vietnam by helicoptered generals hovering over and directing company battles); his policy of rapidly relieving general officers who underperformed (with the occasionally-exercised options of second-chance reappointments). The touchstone question of Ricks over seven decades was "What would George Marshall do?"[217]

Notwithstanding the consensually-acknowledged excellence of GCM in much, he was, in the grand-strategic decisions of 1940 and 1942, outperformed by FDR—who, with more-flexible thinking and wider-horizon view than his highest officer, pondered the options of their nation. In June of 1940, when the British had fled from Dunkirk, abandoning most of their equipment—including 680 of their 700 tanks—Marshall had opposed sending to England B-17 bombers that were there desperately needed. Thinking in the narrowly-military mode that Ricks disparaged and indeed considered anti–Marshallian, the army chief then held that dispatching the B-17s "would be seriously prejudicial to our own defensive situation."[218] The President had a broader perspective—thinking globally, symbolically, politically, and psychologically—and overruled "the unanimous opinion of his military advisers, key legislative leaders, and his own secretary of war."[219]

One month later upon the collapse of France, Marshall urged ending all aid to Britain and transferring most of the U.S. fleet from the Pacific to the Atlantic. Roosevelt rejected both parts of this advice—thereby sustaining the main opponent of Germany and better positioning the U.S. to withstand the forthcoming attacks of Japan. These missteps of 1940 would be followed two years later by further fumblings of the U.S. Army Chief of Staff: his pushing of Sledgehammer, his failed bluff to win British acceptance of it, his overdone disparagement of Gymnast, and his misguided emphases in the planning of Torch. The President in these matters showed the better judgment.

The Outcome: Brief Opposition in Landing; Loss of the Race for Tunis; Capturing Thrice as Many Men as Had Been in the Afrika Korps

Since their decision of July 24, 1942, the Allies had had successes and setbacks.

In the South Pacific, U.S. Marines in August had invaded the Japanese-held island of Guadalcanal in the Solomons and had made a hit-and-run raid on Makin Atoll in the Gilberts. In the latter operation, nine marines were captured and beheaded. Later that month through early September, a mostly-Australian force had defeated a Japanese attempt to land at Milne Bay, on the eastern end of New Guinea.

Thousands of miles to the northwest, fourteen Allied merchant ships had headed eastward on August 10 from Gibraltar toward Malta. They and their Royal Navy escorts were attacked by the submarines, torpedo boats, and planes of the Axis. The Germans and Italians sank two cruisers, one destroyer, and one aircraft carrier of the RN and nine of the cargo ships. The five Allied merchantmen that stayed afloat brought 50,000 tons of supplies. Those cargoes, plus Spitfire fighters flown in from the convoy, reprieved the island. Malta-based planes would continue to attack the supply lines of Erwin Rommel. On the other side of the mine fields and barbed wire in front of his Korps, the British Eighth Army—commanded since mid–August by Bernard Montgomery—was reinforcing, refitting, and readying to attack.

Also in August, the forced deportation of Frenchmen to become slave labor for Nazi war factories began. The gendarmes of the Vichy government—with French citizens often observing—rounded up Jews in the unoccupied zone of France and, by September 5, had sent 10,000 to Paris, to be put on trains to Auschwitz.

Churchill, in 1953, judged September and October of 1942 to have been "the two most anxious months of the war."[220]

Not until October 23 did Montgomery feel strong and ready enough to attack the El Alamein lines of the Afrika Korps. For more than a week the British, Australians, New Zealanders,

South Africans, Germans, and Italians killed each other on the sands of Egypt—until, on November 3, the impending breakthrough of the Eighth Army forced its enemy to begin a retreat that would extend fifteen hundred miles. (The propagandists of Joseph Goebbels called it a "westward advance."[221])

For the Wehrmacht—indeed for the world—in these months, the predominant front was in Russia. Nazi forces in mid–August had reached the Caucasus Mountains and, two weeks later, the suburbs of Stalingrad. By the thirteenth of September, the German semicircle of lines around the namesake city of the Soviet leader ended at the Volga north and south of the city. Supplies and reinforcements for the Russian defenders were ferried, under fire, across the river. Adolf Hitler decreed that every male inhabitant of Stalingrad—Communists all, he thought they must be— would be killed and prematurely he proclaimed the capture of the city.

* * *

The Allied landings of November 8, 1942, surprised some Germans, but not others. General Walter Warlimont wrote that Wehrmacht headquarters "was taken completely by surprise." But he had himself, one week before, penned a report fingering French North Africa as the most likely Allied target. This conclusion, moreover, had been frequently advanced and once had been shared by Hitler.[222] Nothing, however, had been done.

When, two days before the landings, Allied ships had been seen sailing eastward past Gibraltar, Axis leaders had speculated on their destinations: Benito Mussolini thought North Africa[223]; German naval intelligence thought Malta, then Tripoli, then Algeria[224]; Hermann Göring guessed Corsica, Sardinia, or Libya[225]; Hitler's HQ thought southern France.[226]

The reaction of Vichy's forces in the harbor of Oran was not perceptibly softened by the attempt of Lieutenant Paul Duncan to make his *français* sound *américain*. They fired on and soon sank both the *Walney* and her sister ship, the *Hartland*. Of the 393-man half-battalion the two ships carried, 189 were killed and 157 wounded. Of accompanying naval personnel, 118—including Lieutenant Duncan—were killed and 93 wounded. Eleven soldiers reached shore on a raft and were captured. Subsequent spinning that the valor of these men so moved the French that it "contributed to the half-hearted manner" in which the harbor was wrecked has been rejected: "there was nothing half-hearted about it": 27 French ships and three floating dry docks were scuttled.[227]

The highest-ranking American naval officer in the Oran force was Rear Admiral Andrew Bennett, who had protested to Eisenhower that, inasmuch as the Vichy French were likely to resist, the plan to send the *Walney* into the harbor was "suicidal and absolutely unsound." Eisenhower, however, had felt that, in the interests of Allied harmony, he had to heed the counsel of British four-star Admiral Sir Bertram Ramsay. Ramsay had urged sending the ships into the harbor: "If it doesn't do anything else, it's good for the spirit of people.... If successful, it's a wonderful boost for morale."[228]

Bennett had been right; Ramsay, lethally wrong. Eisenhower took responsibility for the tragedy. Bennett could not keep to himself the thought that the attack, both in prospect and in retrospect, had been a blunder—which was not what the higher-ups of either nation wanted to hear. He found himself soon posted to Iceland.[229]

The Allied assault on the port of Algiers fared little better. The *Malcolm* was soon disabled and retreated at four knots back out into the sea. The *Broke* made it into the harbor and landed 250 soldiers but then was sunk by Vichy gunners. The men ashore formed a defensive perimeter that the French attacked with tanks. After 24 of their number were killed and 55 wounded and with no relief imminent, the survivors surrendered shortly after noon.

Patton's men landed in French Morocco against negligible opposition and his main force at Fedala began to advance toward Casablanca, then were slowed by logistic difficulties and Vichy bullets.

Before the Allies had come ashore, their agents in Algeria and French Morocco had sought to persuade the potentates of Vichy North Africa to welcome them as liberators. These initiatives had had mixed results. They had achieved greatest success at Algiers, where sympathetic Vichyites had seized strategic points, had prevented ammunition from being issued to some French troops, had sent officers to the beaches to guide the invaders, and had arrested officials who insisted on opposing the Allies. On the outskirts of Algiers, however, as also near Casablanca and Oran, the Vichy French fought the invaders.

Admiral Jean Darlan, the commander of all the armed forces of Vichy, happened on November 8 to be in Algiers. His son, hospitalized for polio in the city, had recently taken a turn for the worse and, three days earlier, the admiral had flown in to be with him. Informed of the invasion early on the eighth by Allied conspirators, Darlan first unburdened himself of the thought that he now knew the Americans to be as stupid as the British. For two days he wavered, wondering what authority he still had under Maréchal Pétain, who was in Vichy being pressured by the Germans. The admiral, on November 10 under effective arrest by the Allies and deeming Pétain a German prisoner, ordered all Vichy troops in North Africa to cease resisting Torch. Adolf Hitler immediately ordered the invasion by German and Italian troops of previously unoccupied France.

Darlan had been regarded by many in the UK and U.S. as a reprehensible, Nazi-soft opportunist. In May 1941, he had allowed the Axis to supply Rommel through Tunisia—an accommodation that had been denied by another Vichy official. Eisenhower, to "sav[e] time and lives"[230] opted to work with Darlan and to place him in charge of French North Africa. Although this deal with the despicable was widely criticized, Churchill and Roosevelt backed their general. This awkward situation for the Allies (which Churchill in his memoirs called an "embarrassment"[231]) was resolved on December 24, 1942, when Darlan was killed by a 20-year-old Frenchman. Within two days, the assassin was tried by a court martial and executed—without learning his motives or whether he had accomplices. The court martial had been ordered by General Henri Giraud, who, as the subordinate of Darlan, had commanded since November the French armed forces in Africa. He succeeded to Darlan's position.

The 74,000 men landed by the Allies on November 8 at nine sites on both sides of Casablanca, Oran, and Algiers were soon augmented. By the first of December, the Americans and British had put 253,000 into North Africa.[232] They could not—even without the ceasefire ordered by Darlan—have long been resisted by the outnumbered forces of Vichy, wielding outmoded weapons. Algiers was surrendered to the Allies on the evening of November 8 and Oran, at noon the next day. With the capitulation of Vichy troops in French Morocco on the morning of the eleventh, significant Vichy opposition to Torch was ended. The Allies had suffered 2,000 casualties, half of them deaths; the French, about one third more.[233] The soldiers of Vichy in Africa soon would be fighting alongside the Americans and British. The Allies had feared worse, had hoped for better, but were in any case securely ashore and could now turn to the east: toward the two key ports of northern Tunisia: Bizerte and Tunis.

El Alamein and Torch changed the tenor of the war. Churchill spoke of them on November 10, 1942: "This is not the end. It is not even the beginning of the end. But it is, perhaps, the end of the beginning." Five days later, the church bells of Britain—silenced for more than two years by the bleakness of war—rang in victory. On November 20 with the arrival of a four-ship convoy from the east, the siege of Malta was effectively ended.

Well begun by that date was what would become known as the race for Tunis: would the

Allies or the Axis, in the next few weeks, first gain control of that strategic port, along with Bizerte? Should the British and the Americans take them soon, Erwin Rommel—now retreating across Libya—would be trapped between the converging armies of Eisenhower and Montgomery. Given growing Allied strength on the sea and in the skies between Italy and Tunisia, the men of the Desert Fox would be doomed.

But two main things went wrong for the Anglo-Americans: the Axis reacted more quickly than the Allies had thought they would or could and the French in Tunisia did not interfere with the immediate Axis response: the first German fighter planes coming in on November 9, followed three days later by the advance units of the Italian Superga Division. Further flights would bring in 750 Germans per day. With an additional 1,900 Wehrmacht men coming in by sea, the Germans in northern Tunisia would total 17,000 by the end of the month—joined by 11,000 Italians.[234] Per the American Official History, "the rapidity of the Axis build-up ... greatly exceeded the estimates of the pre-invasion planners."[235]

The Allies had had thoughts of sending commandos and paratroops to take Bizerte and Tunis by November 13. With, however, the Allied airborne units having gotten somewhat scattered on the eighth and with Vichy's officials and forces in Tunisia cooperating more with the Axis than with the Anglo-Americans, this optimistic undertaking was scrapped. Instead, British troops sailed on the eleventh eastward from Algiers to take the port of Bougie (Béjaïa today) and a combined UK-U.S. force of commandos landed the next day at Bône—125 miles east of Bougie, 200 miles from Tunis. While neither of these moves was opposed on land, the air was another matter. German planes could attack the advancing Allies from airfields in Sardinia and Sicily and soon would have seven in Tunisia. With the Allies short of all-weather airfields in the North African mud, the Axis, for the moment, was superior in the skies. Luftwaffe bombs destroyed the train station and eighteen of the 22 piers in Bône.

In charge of the Allied drive toward Tunis was British Lieutenant General Sir Kenneth Anderson, described as "a commander of congenital pessimism."[236] Both he and Eisenhower were, however, talking aggressively: Anderson vowing that he would "kick Rommel in the pants as soon as possible"; Eisenhower telling his Scottish subordinate, "I applaud your dash and energy," which was good because "boldness is now more important than numbers. Good luck."[237]

On November 14, Anderson ordered 12,000 men eastward in a three-pronged drive, hoping that he would, in one week, be attacking Bizerte and Tunis. Key battles over the next half-year would be fought along a 23-mile stretch of the winding Medjerda River: from Medjez-el-Bab, 33 miles west-southwest of Tunis, to Djedeïda, fourteen miles west of the capital. Hannibal was said to have said that Medjez-el-Bab, where the Medjerda cut through the Eastern Dorsal Mountains into the coastal plain, was the key to Tunisia.[238]

Complicating the picture was a force of 9,000 Vichy troops, retreating westward from Tunis, badly armed, and stalling for time with the Germans by holding out the prize of their possible surrender. At Medjez-el-Bab the French stopped retreating and summoned Anglo-American help from the west. The Germans, under Captain Wilhelm Knoche, on November 19 opened fire on the French, British, and Americans in the town. Knoche had small units swim the river, which led the Allied defenders to believe that they were being attacked by a superior force. They evacuated Medjez and withdrew eight miles: "a striking example of bluff achieved by boldness by a small detachment less than a tenth of the size of" its enemy.[239]

In southern Tunisia, an American paratroop battalion dispatched by Eisenhower had, on the seventeenth, taken Gafsa, an oasis town 70 miles from the Gulf of Gabès. The paratroops contemplated hurrying southeast to take the city of Gabès—which would have cut the line of communications and retreat for Rommel's army. The Americans were, however, beaten to the

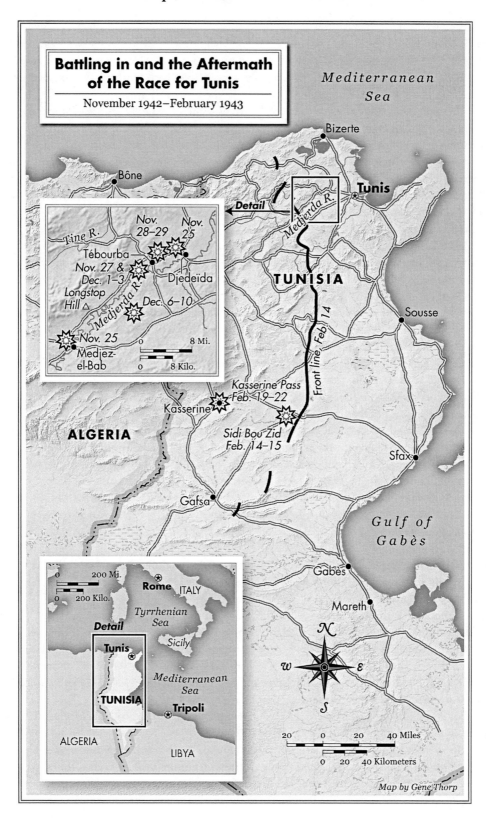

Battling in and the Aftermath
of the Race for Tunis
November 1942–February 1943

Mediterranean
Sea

Bizerte

Bône

Tunis

← Detail

Medjerda R.

TUNISIA

Detail inset:

Tine R.

Nov.
28–29

Nov.
25

Tébourba
Nov. 27 &
Dec. 1–3
Longstop
Hill △

Medjerda R.

Djedeïda

Dec. 6–10

Nov. 25

Medjez-
el-Bab

0   8 Mi.

0   8 Kilo.

Sousse

Front line, Feb. 14

Kasserine Pass
Feb. 19–22

Kasserine

Sidi Bou Zid
Feb. 14–15

ALGERIA

Sfax

Gafsa

Gulf of
Gabès

Gabès

Mareth

N
W   E
S

Lower inset:

0   200 Mi.

0   200 Kilo.

Rome   ITALY

Tyrrhenian
Sea

Detail

Sicily

Tunis

Mediterranean
Sea

TUNISIA

Tripoli

ALGERIA

LIBYA

20   0   20   40 Miles

0   20   40 Kilometers

Map by Gene Thorp

punch by small German units sent south from Tunis to take the ports of Sousse, Sfax, and Gabès. Fifty Wehrmacht paratroopers had "bluffed the French garrison into evacuating Gabès."[240]

Disconcerted by the setback at Medjez-el-Bab, Kenneth Anderson ordered a halt in his drives on Bizerte and Tunis. On November 25, he resumed his offensive with an attack on Medjez-el-Bab that was beaten off. A few miles to the north on the same day, however, a force of 54 light tanks commanded by Lieutenant Colonel John Waters, the son-in-law of George Patton, rolled eastward through the valley of the Tine River. Seventeen of the Stuart tanks bypassed the town of Tébourba to arrive at the village of Djedeïda, within sight of the minarets of Tunis. There, the U.S. armored company surprised and attacked a German airfield, destroying twenty-plus planes, while losing one tank, before pulling back.

That raid led the Germans to withdraw from Medjez-el-Bab and Tébourba and to take up a defensive position at Djedeïda. In fighting on the twenty-seventh through the twenty-ninth, the Allies failed to take that village. Then, in the first four days of December, German counterattacks recaptured Tébourba. Further Axis attacks on the sixth through the tenth forced the Allies to retreat to within six miles of Medjez-el-Bab, whereupon both sides paused to recover.

Late on December 22, it was the turn of the Allies to advance—as Eisenhower estimated their chance of taking Tunis at "not more than 50–50."[241] Difficult fighting in the cold rain northeast of Medjez-el-Bab did not gain even the initial tactical objectives of the Anglo-Americans and Eisenhower on Christmas Eve called off the attack. He told his press corps, "Gentlemen, we have lost the race for Tunis."[242] His troops would endure a dreary winter in the African hills as Adolf Hitler and Benito Mussolini sent tens of thousands more men to Tunisia.

* * *

The Axis might well have done better to have sent those soldiers instead to southern Russia. On November 19, Soviet forces, as planned by Marshal Georgy Zhukov, had attacked the Axis lines—held by inexperienced Romanian troops—north of Stalingrad. The Red Army, the next day, also attacked south of the city. The two Soviet prongs, on the twenty-second, came together, surrounding in Stalingrad the German Sixth Army. That force would have done best to retreat from the city, but Hitler would not hear of it. Futile attempts to relieve the Sixth Army were beaten off and—on February 2, 1943, ending the greatest of battles—it surrendered.

* * *

At dawn on Valentine's Day of 1943, 100-plus tanks of the Tenth Panzer Division clanked west toward American positions arrayed in a winding, protective arc north, east, and south of the Tunisian town of Sidi Bou Zid. The U.S. troops were caught unawares, still battle-green, poorly led, operating tanks inferior to the panzers rolling toward them, and badly positioned: dispersed, dug in mainly in the valleys and not on the high ground.[243] Unsurprisingly, except to themselves, they panicked, ran, and were killed and captured.

Erwin Rommel, having retreated from Egypt across Libya into southern Tunisia, took command of the Axis vanguard advancing westward from Sidi Bou Zid—at times accompanying in person its leading units. By February 20, his war-seasoned Germans and Italians had advanced fifty miles to take the Kasserine Pass—2,000 feet above sea level and one mile wide—through the Grand Dorsal Mountain Chain. From there, the field marshal attacked both westward toward Allied supply depots and northward to threaten the rear of the British First Army. With reinforcements having strengthened the Allied defenses and with his own forces being lessened by losses and finding themselves locally outnumbered, Rommel was stopped. He judged further attacks to be pointless and, on the night of February 22–23, began withdrawing back through the pass. He would turn his attention southward to fending off the advance of the British Eighth Army of Bernard Montgomery, his pursuer since early November.

Churchill's judgment that the Americans had been "mauled"[244] at Sidi Bou Zid and Kasserine was all too accurate. The battling there had cost the U.S. 6,000 casualties and 183 tanks—versus fewer than 1,000 German casualties.

But that Axis success could only be fleeting: the Americans would gain lessons, resolve, and new commanders from their defeat. Eisenhower brought George Patton over from Morocco to replace Lloyd Fredendall at the head of the American II Corps. Allied planes, based on airfields built in eastern Algeria and western Tunisia and behind Montgomery's advancing Eighth Army, gained dominance in the air. The Germans and Italians could not adequately support their forces or even nimbly withdraw them as the Allies tightened their mastery of the water and air between Italy and Africa. On May 13, 1943, the last of the Axis units in Africa surrendered.

American casualties in North Africa approximated 19,000; British, 38,000; and French, 20,000. At least 8,500 Germans and 3,700 Italians were killed in Tunisia, with total Axis wounded of about 45,000. One quarter million Axis soldiers—of whom 102,000 were German—laid down their arms.[245]

The Sequence of Outcome Ratings for Torch: First Good; Then Bad; Ultimately, Better Than Good

Torch had three objectives in the order of getting ashore; taking Tunisia; and destroying or capturing all Axis forces in Africa. The first of these, landing, was called by Churchill "a brilliant success"[246]—with which judgment historians have agreed[247]; achieving the second quickly would bring about the third. But the good outcome of the landings was succeeded by loss of the race for Tunis—which the American Official History bleakly called "a failure"[248]: a bad-outcome-per-hopes, which put in doubt the possibility of bagging the Afrika Korps.

Why had the Allies lost the race?

Churchill wrote that, after the "brilliant success" of the landings, the slowness of the French in Tunisia in rallying to the Anglo-Americans and their allowing the Axis takeover of the colony "robbed" the Allies "of complete success."[249]

Eisenhower, like Churchill, blamed the men of Vichy, but also had other explanations for the bad-outcome-per-hopes. He had written to Marshall on November 9 of his exasperations with the Vichy French: "I am so impatient to get eastward and seize the ground in the Tunisian area that I find myself getting absolutely furious with these stupid Frogs."[250] At the end of the month, he reiterated to his army chief that he had "made the decision to rush our forces into Tunisia as rapidly as possible" and continued to act "so that everything is coordinated to the single objective of taking Tunisia."[251]

A few days later, Eisenhower cabled Churchill: "If" the French in Tunisia "had resisted [the Axis] even feebly our gamble would have won." The Allies would also have triumphed, he said, had they had but "a half-dozen [more] motor transport companies."[252] Eisenhower told an aide early in 1943 that if "Anderson had been willing to gamble a bit more on his logistics ... then we would have had the necessary wallop to take Tunis."[253] Years later in his memoirs, the Supreme Commander of Torch gave further reasons for the Allied disappointment: the "overall weakness of [Anderson's] force" and "unseasonable rains."[254]

The British Official History described the weather: "rain, which fell in 'torrential buckets for three days' and was expected to continue in spasms for six to eight weeks, was making it practically impossible for wheels to move off the roads; any manoeuvre was out of the question."[255] Neither the British nor the American Official Histories nor other accounts have indicated that the wetness was "unseasonable"—rather than what might have been somewhat expected.

Although Eisenhower privately criticized Anderson for excessive risk aversion, he did not do so in his memoirs. There, he wrote that Anderson had been "remarkable … in accepting this bold[256] order from an American": Eisenhower's directive "to exert every effort to capture Bizerte and Tunis with the least possible delay." Anderson "was a true ally—and a courageous fighter."[257] Others, however, have come down hard on the Scotsman: both for the "bad British plan" of splitting his forces into three prongs instead of concentrating them "for a single hammer blow at the brittle Axis defense" and for pausing to ready his forces before attacking.[258] Bernard Montgomery wrote in his diary in April 1943: "ANDERSON (First Army) is not fit to command an Army in the field; everyone knows it, including his own Army."[259] Anderson would return to England to be knighted, but would not again command fighting men.

An additional battlefield factor, unmentioned by Churchill and Eisenhower but noted by historians, was German military prowess: "It was an unequal struggle against a much more proficient and better-armed enemy."[260]

That Eisenhower offered so many reasons for not taking Tunis may have been a response to his sense that many British, led by Alan Brooke, thought that he was reason number one. Eisenhower, the CIGS later wrote,

> seemed to be unable to grasp urgency of pushing on to Tunis before Germans built up their resistance there.… Eisenhower … was far too much immersed in the political aspects of the situation. He should have left his Deputy, [U.S. General Mark] Clark, to handle these, and devoted himself to the tactical situation.… It must be remembered that Eisenhower had never even commanded a battalion in action when he found himself commanding a group of Armies in North Africa. No wonder he was at a loss as to what to do.… I had little confidence in his having the ability to handle the military situation confronting him.[261]

General Sir Ian Jacob put it that "there was general feeling that Eisenhower was totally inexperienced—didn't know what to do—was too far back—ought to have had an advanced headquarters."[262] George Marshall seemed somewhat to agree with these British criticisms when, on December 22, he cabled Eisenhower: "Delegate your international problems to your subordinates and give your complete attention to the battle in Tunisia."[263]

Had Eisenhower, as per the wishes of Brooke and Jacob, been closer to the front, focusing on tactics and pushing Allied forces toward Tunis, would it have made much of a difference? Brooke's reasoning seems inconsistent: if the Supreme Commander was as lacking in military acumen as the CIGS and Montgomery judged throughout the war, how could his proximity to the fighting have gained Tunis for the Allies? Even if Eisenhower had performed up to the highest standards aspired to by Brooke, the obstacles and hindrances faced would likely have kept the Allies out of Tunis.

The Planning Fallacy

The meta-reason why the Axis beat the Allies to Tunis—implicit in some of the explanations advanced, but not close to being adequately recognized by anyone at the time—was the planning fallacy: that events rarely play out as favorably as foreseen. The Allies, before November 8, were woefully unaware of this. They thought then that Tunis could be taken in two weeks. They had not realized the likelihoods that and the extents to which plans and schedules might be overoptimistic. In consequence, they had not made allowances and contingent provisions for the possibilities: that the Vichy French might not act as cooperatively as desired; that the Axis might respond with rapid audacity; that shortages of equipment types might occur; that such officers as Kenneth Anderson, commanding in a situation of befogged incertitude, might take actions that in retrospect would seem misguided; and that the weather might prove troublesome. The shortfall from what the Allies had hoped and expected would happen was dismaying.

From before its beginning to after its end, Gymnast/Torch was a poster case for the importance in war of the planning fallacy. That we overestimate how easily and how quickly we will complete our tasks was seen in the deciding on, the planning for, and the executing of the operation: beginning with the optimistic general thoughts of 1941; succeeded on January 10, 1942, by the specific assertion that the Allies could be in French Morocco and Algeria by the third of March; followed by successive movebacks over the next four days of the landing date to March 23, then to May, and then to early June; before, in early March, indefinite postponement. Later slippages of targeted times included delaying the invasion until November 8 and not taking Tunis until five-plus months after envisioned. Had the pervasiveness of the planning fallacy been as understood then as it would be decades later: this series of events would have been better anticipated; more steps should have been taken to prevent time loss and to lessen its consequences; and the Allies ought not to have been as surprised and disconcerted as they were by the events of November and December 1942.

All Allied decision makers had had enough experience to know that glitches and setbacks happen; none had awareness of how likely it was that untoward events and unforeseen factors would derail the drive toward Tunis.

A significant result of such Allied unawareness was that Eisenhower's power was pruned.

The British, especially Brooke, wanted more British and less American command authority. They believed that they were militarily more capable and more deserving of high position. The Americans believed the opposite. Obliviousness on both sides to the planning fallacy gave advantage in argument to the United Kingdom: with so much having gone wrong in the last two months of 1942, with the failure to take Tunis having been so disappointing, with the most obvious target to blame being the Kansan in charge of it all.

Led by Alan Brooke, the British at the Casablanca Conference of January 1943 held that, with Eisenhower having so bungled the race for Tunis—as apparently proven by the chasm between hope and result—somewhat autonomous commanders must be inserted between him and the air, ground, and sea forces of the Mediterranean Theater. The Americans, also chagrined by the lost race, acceded to these British demands—an abject retreat from Marshall's previous pitches for command unity.

Had the Allies been more aware of the planning fallacy, matters might have been otherwise settled. Brooke, however genuine his belief that Eisenhower had fumbled the Allied ball, did not articulate just what it was that the man from Abilene had done wrong—except in wishing that he had delegated politics to Clark and had provided better "drive and co-ordination."[264] Eisenhower had, in many ways, pushed to take Tunisia: including sending an American paratroop force to the south of the country, beefing up Anderson's attack with American armor, and pressing him unsuccessfully to accept more. Eisenhower's defenders might have argued: that, disappointing as the lost race was, it was not predominantly his fault; that such shortfalls from hopeful plans were not uncommon and indeed somewhat to be expected; that the paramount principle of command unity ought not to be cast aside just because a result that should have been thought not unlikely had in fact occurred.

Such a case was not made for the commander of Torch. The resultant splintering of authority would lead to Allied frustrations and failures in the battles yet to be waged.

Consequences of the Allied Failure to Take Tunis Quickly

Most failures have costs. How bad were those of the Allies' lost race?

In terms of time, having been beaten to Tunis cost, per the American Official History, about two months. The history judged that "under the most favorable circumstances," north Tunisia would be taken in mid–December, leading "at the earliest by March" to complete Allied control of Africa—two months before that actually occurred.[265]

In terms of harm not done to the Wehrmacht, the lost race might have had a significant cost: the successful flight of the Axis forces from Africa. Taking Tunis by the end of 1942 would have bagged Rommel's Afrika Korps—which would number 78,000 when in late January and early February of 1943 it crossed over from Libya into southern Tunisia.[266] The German capture of Tunis and its retention into 1943 meant that Rommel, and virtually all other Axis troops in Africa, might escape across the Sicilian Narrows to Italy.

But that did not happen.

Hitler and Mussolini, instead of getting out of Africa every man they could, opted to reinforce and to maintain their bridgehead on the continent. Optimistic about their ability to do so, they did not foresee how quickly the Allies could complete their conquest of Tunisia and were able to pull out but a few of their men before the end came. In consequence, they lost not just the Afrika Korps, but also their reinforcements: not 78,000, but 250,000. The Allies, by losing the race for Tunis, had captured 172,000 more enemy than they would have, if they had won.

Admiral William Leahy, Chairman of the U.S. Joint Chiefs under Roosevelt and Truman, called the result of the six-month Anglo-American campaign in Africa "the ultimate success"[267]; Albert Kesselring, the German of highest responsibility in Africa at the time of Torch through May 1943, conceded that his enemy had achieved "a total victory."[268]

Was Undertaking Operation Gymnast/Torch a Good or a Bad Decision?

To judge military actions fairly challenges decision science, as it has soldiers and historians. Libraries teem with books pointing out the oversights, misconceptions, and unsound strategies of decisions in war that turned out badly. It has been noted that "writers on military subjects ... necessarily know more than the generals, admirals and statesmen did who had to make decisions on imperfect knowledge, and too readily conclude that everyone at the time made mistakes."[269] Many such criticisms are just; many are not. It is not hard, after military disasters, to compile lists of factors that were known or should have been known or might have been known and that, if properly appreciated, would have led to better actions and outcomes. The responsibility of later critics and of decision science is to appreciate reasonably the situations of decision makers in history, based on the information they had, plus that they should also have obtained. Such DMs generally had clouds of indications pointing in all directions. If they failed to make sensible inferences of what was happening and of what steps to take, they should be censured. It is, however, all too easy but unjust to succumb to a type of *hindsight bias:* to cherry-pick with the advantage of retrospection from the welter of reports available to historical decision makers precisely those data that might have led to better actions and outcomes.[270]

Judging the decision on Gymnast/Torch can be parsed into two questions: whether the Allies did well in not landing in France in 1942; whether they were wise in undertaking Gymnast/Torch. Related to both is the issue of whether the effect that Gymnast/Torch had on delaying Roundup/Overlord until 1944 was good or bad.

The prevailing historical consensus is that Gymnast/Torch was a better choice than Sledgehammer would have been,[271] indeed that Sledgehammer would have been a bad decision, with a likely bad outcome.[272]

Arguments that Sledgehammer could have succeeded and might have been better than Torch have been, since the war, without traction—even though this has been called a "debate" that "will last for ever."[273] Despite broad agreement with the judgment that "a cross-Channel invasion in 1942 would certainly have ended in catastrophe,"[274] this verdict may be challenged—if only by the weight of military acumen on which Sledgehammer once stood.

Nearly all the leading military minds of the United States consulted on Sledgehammer judged that it had sufficient prospects for success that it should have been undertaken—while a comparably high proportion of their British counterparts believed the opposite. At lower levels, however, many planners of Britain sided with the Americans in believing the operation feasible.[275] When, on July 18 in London, George Marshall and Harry Hopkins met with the Americans who had been planning Sledgehammer, U.S. Generals Dwight Eisenhower, Mark Clark, and Carl Spaatz—who commanded the U.S. Eighth Air Force—urged the operation. Harold Stark, the commander of U.S. naval forces in Europe, was "lukewarm" in his support.[276] General Lucian Truscott prepared an advocacy brief for Marshall to present to the British.[277]

Eisenhower, throughout most of 1942 a proponent of Sledgehammer, would, however, change his mind. Having in March fashioned the plan and the case for Bolero-Sledgehammer-Roundup, he reiterated in June in a meeting of the Combined Chiefs of Staff his belief in the feasibility of a 1942 landing in northern France. Alan Brooke reported there that the British Chiefs, after "exhaustively" studying Sledgehammer, "had not been able to discover any worth-while objective." Eisenhower argued in response for the "possibility at least of securing a bridgehead and holding it as Malta or Tobruk had been held."[278] That Tobruk fell the next day did not strengthen his case. When, on July 22, the British War Cabinet rejected Sledgehammer, Eisenhower thought that that vote might have made that moment the "blackest day in history."[279] On October 9 and November 6, the commander of Torch shared with British and American generals his opinion that it was "unsound strategically."[280] By the time, however, that he penned his memoirs, his assessment had changed: Sledgehammer would, indeed, have been "unwise": the requisite air cover could not have been provided; the benefits, even in a best-case scenario, would have been eclipsed by those actually yielded by Torch.[281]

Most authors have made Torch good-decision-good-outcome.[282]

One high official who disagreed cited the factor of luck—as the unpredictabilities of war can make good decisions have bad outcomes and the reverse. While George Marshall—consistent even after the Axis surrender in Tunisia in preferring Bolero/Sledgehammer/Roundup—made Torch bad-decision-bad-outcome, his co-slammer of the operation, Henry Stimson, conceded the good outcome. The combination of BDGO had resulted, he thought, because Torch had been "the luckiest operation of the war"—while knowing that Torch proponents would not concede the BD.[283] Fortunate factors he cited were the Russian victory at Stalingrad, the landings (perhaps he meant the abnormally gentle surf in Morocco), and the "success over submarines." Given that

Torch was judged a triumph long before the Russians prevailed at Stalingrad or the battle against the U-boats was won, Stimson's logic has been questioned.[284]

To Eisenhower the non-incursion of the Germans through Spain was good fortune and the failure of the Vichy forces to rally quickly to General Giraud, bad. Ten days before the invasion, he had fretted the weather and German submarines[285]—neither of which proved problematic. That Admiral Darlan was in Algiers on November 8 was described by Churchill as a "highly fortunate complication."[286] Eisenhower called it without doubt "entirely accidental" but Harold Macmillan, 25 years later, was unsure whether Darlan had been there "by chance or calculation."[287] (On October 17, 1942, an Eisenhower aide had written that "representatives of Darlan" were passing on Vichy's intelligence to the Allies and hinting that the admiral might defect to them, bringing with him the sequestered French fleet.[288] Eisenhower, that day, wrote to Marshall that Darlan had indicated that he might cooperate with Torch and considered arranging for the admiral to command all Vichy forces in North Africa.[289] Joseph Goebbels on December 11, 1942, cited a German research report, which "proves convincingly that Darlan started for North Africa to desert us and that his son's illness was only an excuse."[290] It seems more likely than not that Goebbels was right and Churchill and Eisenhower, wrong.)

Allied good luck has also been seen in that Hitler learned of the Torch landings while traveling to Munich for the annual celebration of his Beer Hall Putsch of nineteen years before, while the German high command he had left behind in East Prussia was in "disarray."[291]

For historian B. H. Liddell Hart most fortunate was that

> by the irony of luck, this failure [in the race for Tunis] turned out one of the biggest blessings in disguise that could have happened. For without such a failure Hitler and Mussolini would not have had the time or encouragement to pour very large reinforcements into Tunisia.... But for the Allied failure in December ... it is all too probable that the Allied re-entry into Europe would have been repelled.[292]

Via what Liddell Hart thought ironic luck, factors that originally seemed unfortunate for the Allies became positive. That the Vichy French acted so favorably for the Axis, that torrential rain fell in the Tunisian hills at first seemed to Eisenhower elements of bad luck that resulted in not taking Tunis. With, however, Hitler's decision to hold on in Africa, the noncooperation of the French, the shortage of trucks, the unwillingness of Anderson to gamble, and the rain flipped from being bad to good for the Allies.

Also unclear in being either bad or good for the Allies was the effect that Torch may have had in delaying Roundup/Overlord until 1944. Winston Churchill shifted his thoughts on when best to invade France. In late November of 1942, he pressed the British Chiefs to commit to launching Roundup the next year—a stance that, given the insufficiencies of troops and ships, exasperated Alan Brooke.[293] Subsequently, the Prime Minister came to believe that the result of Torch—together with Hitler's decision to send more men to Africa—in pushing Overlord back to 1944 was "fortunate":

> The year's delay in the expedition saved us from what would at that date have been at the best an enterprise of extreme hazard, with the probability of a world-shaking disaster.... I am sure now that ... the attempt to cross the Channel in 1943 would have led to a bloody defeat of the first magnitude, with measureless reactions upon the result of the war.[294]

Alan Brooke in 1961 agreed: "Any idea of a cross Channel operation was completely out of the picture during 1942 and '43, except in the event of the German forces beginning to crack up, which was very unlikely."[295] Later writers have agreed with the Prime Minister and his CIGS that delaying Roundup/Overlord until 1944 was good-decision-good-outcome.[296]

By October of 1943 Churchill wished to postpone Overlord even beyond the following spring. He thought then that the importance of completing the conquest of Italy meant that Stalin should be informed that Overlord might have to be moved back.[297] At Tehran, however, the next month, the Americans and Russians pressured the Prime Minister into agreeing to invade France in the coming spring. A few days later, Churchill prioritized enlisting Turkey in the war—largely because "this alone can delay a second front in France."[298] On April 19, 1944, he lamented in a minute to his Foreign Office that Overlord "has been forced upon us by the Russians and the United States." (This sentence was deleted from his reproduction of the minute in *Closing the Ring*—excised along with others in similar vein, with the result that any misgivings of Churchill at this time about Overlord were not to be found in his memoirs.[299])

Henry Stimson believed that neither Churchill nor Brooke wanted Overlord in 1944.[300]

Was the Decision of Adolf Hitler to Send More Troops to Africa Good or Bad?

Adolf Hitler, between November 1942 and April 1943, sent 142,000 Germans to North Africa: 21,000 in November, 31,000 in December, 29,000 in both January and February, 20,000 in March, and 11,000 in April. Benito Mussolini sent at least 31,000 Italians.[301] Most of these men would in Tunisia be wounded, captured, or killed.

Both Erwin Rommel and Adolf Hitler's headquarters staff, after the Torch landings, had concluded that an Axis presence in North Africa was no longer tenable[302]—which warnings Hitler ignored. Twice—in November 1942 and March 1943—Rommel flew from Africa to the Führer's HQ to press the point; both times to no avail. Hitler in March responded that an Axis retreat from Africa so soon after the surrender of the German Sixth Army in Stalingrad would significantly impair German prestige.[303] The Führer concluded that Rommel had become a pessimist—which meant that his forebodings could be disregarded. The general was ordered to take sick leave, after which, Hitler said, he would command operations that would drive the Anglo-Americans back to Casablanca, as a prelude to expelling them from Africa altogether.[304]

In early February of 1943, General Walter Warlimont of Hitler's staff had traveled to Tunisia and had spoken with the Axis commanders there. He concluded that an orderly retreat to Sicily was still possible and should immediately be undertaken.[305] Upon returning, he attended a strategic conference at the Führer's headquarters in East Prussia. There, Albert Kesselring spoke first, voicing optimism about Axis prospects in Africa.[306] Hitler then turned to Warlimont and asked with curt condescension for his thoughts: "Und Sie?" When Warlimont's first words signaled his thinking, Hitler cut him off: "Have we anything else?" Hermann Göring then rebuked Warlimont for his impertinence in disagreeing as an outranked officer with Kesselring, a field marshal of his Luftwaffe, and for irking the Führer.[307]

Hitler and Mussolini met on April 8, 1943, at Schloss Klessheim near Salzburg. The Duce urged that peace be made with Stalin, whereupon the Axis could concentrate on defeating the Western Allies; the Führer could not see how an accommodation could be reached with Russia and asserted that a bridgehead in Tunisia could be indefinitely held. For so long as the Axis remained in Tunisia, the Anglo-Americans would not attack in Sicily, mainland Italy, or southern France. The Duce deferred to the Führer's judgment: Tunis was at all costs to be held; no arrangements were to be made for evacuating troops; the possibility of defeat in Africa was not to be considered.[308]

Albert Kesselring, Commander-in-Chief, South, of the Wehrmacht, joined Hitler in supporting Axis reinforcement of Africa and did not in his memoirs criticize this decision of his

Führer. He instead saw four main reasons for the Axis failure in the continent: the original under-estimation of Mediterranean importance; supply breakdown; the challenges of coordination with Italy; and excessive German deference in dealing with Vichy France.[309]

Churchill in his memoirs called Hitler's reinforcement of the Axis in Africa "a grave strategic error."[310] On February 11, 1943, he had spoken to the Commons of the Führer's decision:

> While I always hesitate to say anything which might afterwards look like over-confidence, I cannot resist the remark that one seems to discern in this policy the touch of the master hand, the same master hand that planned the attack on Stalingrad, and that has brought upon the German armies the greatest disaster that they have ever suffered in all their military history.[311]

Others have also considered Hitler's action bad-decision-bad-outcome.[312]

Two German histories did not explicitly call Hitler's response to Torch an error, but advanced judgments indicating as much. One thought the Axis leadership to have been in denial that, in the wake of El Alamein, Torch, and hardening Russian resistance at Stalingrad, it had lost the strategic initiative. It underestimated the fighting strength of the Allies and overestimated Axis capabilities. Deeming the Americans and British in Tunisia unused to war ("kriegsunge-wohnt"), the German high command envisioned soon driving all the way to Morocco.[313] (Hitler had been told that U.S. soldiers were "rowdies who cannot stand up under an emergency." He had replied that "[American] farmers are so miserable. I have seen pictures of them. Too pitiful and stunted; something altogether uprooted that wanders around."[314]) Another German perspective was that Hitler: had "clung to his illusions"; had thought in early December that he could with but seven divisions attack both eastwards to take the Suez Canal and westwards to chase his enemy from Africa; and had "shrugged off" the logistic challenges to his conceptions.[315] Hermann Göring had assured his Führer that, the distance from Sicily to Tunis being but the mere "leap of a panther," there would be no problem in supplying Axis forces in Africa.[316]

Hitler, on May 10, 1942, met with Rommel and conceded bad-decision-bad-outcome: "I should have listened to you before."[317] Two months later, however, the Führer said that he had reflected on his dispatching more divisions to Africa after Torch and had concluded GDGO: had he not so acted, it would have accelerated by six months the Allied invasion of Europe, have led Italy to defect from the Axis Alliance, have enabled the Allies to land unopposed in Italy and to push quickly forward to the Brenner Pass, and "would inevitably have led rapidly to the loss of the war."[318]

By contesting Allied control of Africa after Torch, Hitler had, per the American Official History, gained not the six months he claimed, but only two[319]; his decision had cost one quarter of one million men. Historians have sided with the view expressed by Churchill: "If Hitler had been wise he would have cut his losses in North Africa and would have met us in France with double the strength he had in 1944"[320]; the Führer had had not the good-decision-good-outcome he claimed, but BDBO.

Hitler's African decisions in late 1942 and early 1943 had two parts: first, putting more men in and, second, not getting them out. His dispatching of troops and planes to Tunisia has been questioned: should he not have realized that those resources were then more urgently needed in Russia?[321] Assessment of that decision depends on judging the importance of delaying Allied control of the Mediterranean and on estimating the effects those divisions and squadrons would have had on the Stalingrad front.

Whether or not Hitler decided well in moving men into Tunisia, he blundered in not getting them out. He should have done there what he soon would Sicily: prioritize bringing his troops back; not holding onto the Axis bridgehead so long that it would jeopardize the chances of orderly escape.

Two behavioral bases underlay this error of Hitler: excessive reliance on expertise—which topic will be discussed in the epilogue—and the planning fallacy. The Führer trusted too much his Luftwaffe experts, Göring and Kesselring, in convincing himself that he need not heed the warnings of Erwin Rommel and Walter Warlimont. The over-sanguineness of all three—Hitler, Göring and Kesselring—that an augmented Afrika Korps could be adequately supplied was yet another instance of the planning fallacy.

Game Theory

Assessing the quality of decisions in adversarial situations—such as those of the Allies and Axis in North Africa—has been a main focus of *game theory*:

the analysis of strategies in contexts—usually competitive, occasionally cooperative—where the outcomes for two or more participants depend not only on their own actions, but also on those of others.

Like decision science, game theory in the early 1940s was but budding. It was born as a discipline during the war—as its first landmark treatise, *Theory of Games and Economic Behavior*, by John von Neumann and Oskar Morgenstern, appeared in 1944. Sixteen years earlier, Neumann had published a result that since has been seen as vital for GT as was Amatino Manucci's late-thirteenth-century development of double-entry bookkeeping for accountancy and as William Harvey's 1628 description of blood circulation for medicine: his 1928 proof of the Minimax Theorem.[322] Since 1944, tens of thousands of game-theoretic books and papers have been published and work in the discipline has won numerous Nobel Prizes in Economics.

A century before John von Neumann's proof of the Minimax Theorem, Carl von Clausewitz had seen war as "fundamentally a game: a game through the fabric of which run the thick and fine threads of possibilities and probabilities, of good and bad luck—making war, of all human activities, that most like a game of cards." "While the objective nature of war makes it a calculation of probabilities," Clausewitz held, "its component of chance makes it a game.... The subjective nature of war—the personal qualities with which it must be waged and the noblest of which is courage—makes it appear to us that much more as a game."[323]

Neumann's Minimax Theorem paper addressed a special class of strategic games in which gains and losses balance out: what one side loses is exactly what the other side wins. Such games are termed *constant-sum* or, more commonly, *zero-sum*.

The Second World War, like every war ever, was non-zero-sum: its losses, totaled over all participants, dwarfed its gains. In Europe, the three main players were the Axis, the USSR, and the Western Allies. Had the main Axis power, Germany, surrendered unconditionally on, say, September 1, 1944, most would agree that all three players would have been better off: the same basic post-war outcome could have resulted; all three would have suffered fewer casualties—78,000 Soviet soldiers died just in taking Berlin; and Germany would have been spared much harm.

The Second World War also, however, had zero-sum aspects: to the extent that each side felt it essential to defeat the other, it was zero-sum.[324] Both sides—from 1942 through 1944, when the decisions reviewed here were made—treated the war as zero-sum: the Germans, feeling betrayed by the Treaty of Versailles in 1919, had, 20-plus years later, no interest in a mutually-advantageous, negotiated pact; the Allies—not wanting any future German leader to be able to claim non-loss of the war and/or national hoodwinking via the malicious violation of armistice understandings and judging therefore that lasting peace required the irrefutable defeat of their opponent—committed themselves to achieving unconditional surrender. Given this context, many battles and maneuvers of the war may be analyzed as zero-sum, two-player confrontations of the type much studied by game theorists: any increase in the chances that one side would achieve clear-cut victory entailed an equal reduction in the chances of the other.

Along with two-player, zero-sum games, Neumann and Morgenstern in 1944 also analyzed multi-player and non-zero-sum games, both of which would give rise to extensive literatures. While outside the scope of this book, significant game-theoretic developments in these areas with applicability to the Second World War include:

Non-zero-sum games. John Nash would in the early 1950s prove the existence of equilibria in non-zero-sum games and would in 1994 receive a Nobel Prize in Economics. The 2001 movie directed by Ron Howard, *A Beautiful Mind,* was based on the life of Nash and won four Academy Awards, including that for Best Picture;

The prisoners' dilemma. Among the best-studied of non-zero-sum games is this situation, in which all players, by acting in their own best individual interests, achieve outcomes that are worse for all than if all acted in their best collective interests. Front-line behavior in the First World War has been explained as a prisoners' dilemma of the trenches[325];

Competition with incomplete information. While game theorists often presume certain, accurate grasp of competitive context, military decisions are typically made with but imperfect—and often strikingly flawed—understanding of circumstance. Pursuant to the judgment of Clausewitz that wars are quintessential examples of games in which the contestants have but partial knowledge of their situations, John Harsanyi studied such scenarios and, in 1994, was with John Nash a co-Nobelist[326];

Coalition creation. The object in many multi-player games is to form a profitable or a victorious partnership. Historical situations analyzable as such games include the strategic diplomacy that set the sides for the European wars of the seventeenth and eighteenth centuries, the seven coalitions that opposed revolutionary and Napoleonic France, and the negotiations of alliance pacts before both world wars. In June 1940, Mussolini's Italy was persuaded by Hitler to fight alongside Germany, while Churchill sought throughout the first war years to enlist Turkey as an ally, but, until February 1945, did not succeed. Lloyd Shapley in the 1950s analyzed the options and powers of potential coalition members and in 2012 became a Nobelist; and

Promises and threats. Advantage in the creation of coalitions and in many other forms of non-zero-sum games may be gained by promises and threats. Both were applied in the war as both Adolf Hitler and the Western Allies sought to enlist Spain as an ally. The actions of Japan and the US prior to December 1941 were designed to deter each other from taking undesired steps. Both failed. The optimization of promises, threats, commitments, and deterrence was in 1960 addressed in *The Strategy of Conflict* by Thomas Schelling, a Nobelist in 2005.

Other-Side Perception

In game situations—whether zero-sum or non-zero-sum, two- or multi-player—and in war, participants do better the sharper is their *other-side perception*: their ability to imagine themselves in the places of their opponents. Ulysses Grant, in his memoirs, described a personal moment of OSP. In 1861, he approached his first encounter as a commanding officer with his enemy, Confederates under Colonel Thomas Harris:

My heart kept getting higher and higher until it felt to me as though it was in my throat. I would have given anything then to have been back in Illinois, but I had not the moral courage to halt and consider what to do: I kept right on. When we reached a point from which the valley below was in full view I halted.... The [Confederate] troops were gone. My heart resumed its place. It occurred to me at once that Harris had been as much afraid of me as I had been of him. This was a view of the question I had never taken before; but one that I never forgot afterwards.[327]

Such understanding of how one's opponents emote, perceive, reason, act, and react has long been of value in war. Hannibal, for instance, at the Trebbia River in 218 BCE, anticipated how the Roman consul Sempronius Longus could be made overconfident by having his Carthaginians suffer small defeats; how he could be provoked to offer battle by having his African cavalry throw javelins into the Roman camp; and how the legions of Sempronius would be panicked by a surprise attack on their rear. Hannibal learned the next year that the new Roman consul Flaminius had been speaking boastfully, deduced that he would advance precipitately, irked Flaminius into greater rashness by laying waste to Tuscan fields, and, at Lake Trasimene, crushingly ambushed the Roman army.

Game theorists have written of that quality of Hannibal. One called it "a talent for anticipating [one's] opponent's choices" and considered its applicability in a situation equivalent to the rudimentary game of Matching Pennies that had been discussed by Neumann.[328] In this game of two players, A and B, each holds one coin and reveals simultaneously to the other whether the coin held is heads or tails. Should the two coins match—both heads or both tails—A keeps both; should they not match, B does. To come out ahead, you must be better in predicting your opponent's actions than your opponent is in predicting yours: you must have better other-side perception. An eight-year-old boy described by Edgar Allan Poe in *The Purloined Letter* has been cited as an example. Poe's boy had remarkable success in such a game and related how he achieved his superior OSP: "I fashion the expression of my face, as accurately as possible, in accordance with the expression of [my opponent's], and then wait to see what thoughts or sentiments arise in my mind or heart, as if to match or correspond with the expression."[329] Success in such games has been seen as depending on being "'more perceptive' than one's opponent"; "able to anticipate [one's opponent's moves] sooner or more accurately than" vice versa.[330] Reviews of studies in which subjects sought to understand the thinking and to anticipate the plays of their opponents led to the conclusion that "most subjects are simply unable to put themselves in the shoes of their opponents."[331]

Such inability, Winston Churchill noted, handicaps both generals and politicians. He touted OSP: "In war and policy one should always try to put oneself in the position of what [Prussian, then German, Chancellor Otto von] Bismarck called 'the Other Man.' The more fully and sympathetically a Minister can do this the better are his chances of being right."[332]

Bernard Montgomery and Albert Kesselring sought OSP; George Patton thought he had it. On the walls of Montgomery's command caravan in Normandy were photographs of Erwin Rommel and Gerd von Rundstedt—along with 30 of himself.[333] The Allied ground commander looked at them and

> sought to project himself into their minds, to see the battle as they saw it and to gauge their reactions. He was determined to conduct his own operations in such a way that he could force his opponents into courses of action which would appear to them to provide logical and intelligent counterstrokes, but which would in fact contribute to their own undoing.[334]

Kesselring was said to have "imagin[ed] himself in the enemy's shoes."[335] Patton wrote to his wife during the Sicilian campaign that "I can put myself inside the enemies [sic] head."[336]

Other-side perception includes sensing: what one's opponents know; how they are likely to interpret the intelligence available to them; how they view their priorities and options; how they would react in different situations; how they value possible outcomes; what processes of reasoning they follow; how daring they might be; and how they regard and predict the actions of their opponents.

The OSP of both sides in mid-fall of 1942 would prove faulty: that of the Axis in misanticipating where the Allies would strike; that of the Allies in misforeseeing the reactions of Hitler and Mussolini.

Move-Order Plusses and Minuses

In addition to the other-side perception of the Americans, British, and Axis in the lead-up to Torch, a further game-theoretic issue of that moment was the meta-strategic question facing Adolf Hitler and Benito Mussolini: suspecting that the Anglo-Americans might soon attack in the Mediterranean, would the Axis do best to be the *first* or the *second mover*? Some in the Wehrmacht HQ had predicted that the Allies would land in Algeria with the aim of taking Tunisia and thereby cutting off the Afrika Korps. Acting on this expectation, the Axis might have opted to move first by sending forces, perhaps in October, to Tunis. Or, it might—by awaiting any Allied landings, then reacting to them—have chosen to be the second mover.

Moving first would, if the Allies had been planning to land in Algeria, have clinched for the Germans and Italians victory in the race for Tunis. Moving second would have put the Axis, without having sent troops to Tunis, in better position to respond if the Allies happened to have had Libya, Sardinia, Corsica, southern France, or other targets in mind. Adolf Hitler also favored being the second mover for diplomatic reasons. Like the Anglo-Americans, the Axis wondered how the Vichy French would respond to Allied entry into North Africa. The Führer did not want to pressure the French, in advance of any Allied landings, to accept Axis troops into French Morocco, Algeria, and/or Tunisia—lest that increase the likelihood that the Vichyites there would go over to the Allies.

The advantages and disadvantages of first and second moving have been seen in historical warfare. First movers, such as Alexander and Caesar, have typically been aggressors and have exploited possession of the initiative. Second movers—like Wellington in many campaigns—have tended to be defenders, seeking to capitalize opportunistically on any openings afforded by attackers. Robert E. Lee was more successful as a second mover in such victories as Second Manassas and Chancellorsville than as a first mover in the campaigns of Antietam and Gettysburg. Ulysses Grant saw first-mover advantage at Fort Donelson in 1862, after a Confederate attempt to escape encirclement had been desperately beaten back, with resultant demoralization on both sides. He sensed that "the one who attacks first now will be victorious." He struck first and took the fort.[337]

The Soviet high command in the spring of 1943 anticipated that the Wehrmacht would attack its salient centered at Kursk and debated whether to be the first or second mover. Stalin feared that awaiting the enemy attack would allow the Germans to choose the time and place of battle, as they had one year earlier in their breakout toward the Caucasus. While one Russian general in the salient urged a preemptive attack, the counsel of Marshal Georgy Zhukov prevailed[338]: the Red Army waited in place for the German assault. The Soviets initially gave up ground, before stiffening and counterattacking.

Perceptions of first-mover advantage and second-mover disadvantage have started wars: significant factors in igniting the First World War were the senses of great powers that they could not risk being second movers in the race to mobilize; that Japan attacked at Pearl Harbor was based in part on the anticipation of first-mover advantage that, indeed, gained it victory upon victory in the first months of its war against the UK and the U.S.

In checkers, chess, and go, having the first move in the game is advantageous. In multi-person games of poker, being last to bet provides information on the hands of the other players, possibly enabling successful bluffs, and has positional advantage.

In non-zero-sum games, moving first may be best. One such scenario studied by game theorists[339] is the game of chicken—engaged in by American teenagers in the 1950s. In this potentially-deadly game, two drivers speed toward each other: should just one swerve to avoid a head-on collision, the non-swerver wins and the swerver loses; should both swerve, there is no winner or loser; should neither swerve, their crash is a likely-lethal double loss.[340]

It has been observed that the first driver to commit in a credible manner to continuing straight will be the winner, inasmuch as that commitment gives the other the choice between losing the game but surviving uninjured and the much-worse outcome of crashing. Inasmuch as any rational driver would prefer swerving and losing to a head-on collision, the first firm and understood commitment to continue straight wins the game. Game theorist Thomas Schelling noted that, in a variety of situations including bargaining negotiations, "commitment is a means of gaining *first move* in a game in which first move carries an advantage."[341]

Superpower brinksmanship was in the 1950s likened scornfully by Bertrand Russell to the game of chicken—with both the Soviet Union and the United States threatening and risking thermonuclear war in order to secure relatively small advantages, perhaps just the prideful satisfaction of getting the other side to give way.[342]

First-mover advantages in business include preemptively cornering resources and customer loyalty. Disadvantages are that later entrants into markets may copy successful products, while sparing themselves the expensive processes of research, development, trial, and error that led to them.

Conclusions

Flawed presumptions by all concerned drove the North African decisions. Adolf Hitler, the main decision maker of the Axis, disastrously misappraised the likely result of reinforcing without preserving the ability to withdraw. American thinking was premised on the fearfully overestimated chance of an Axis attack on Gibraltar. The British saw through these misapprehensions of their enemy and ally to have of the three parties the most accurate view. Yet they too, like the Americans, had deficient other-side perception: neither had more than the faintest of thoughts that the Axis, having secured a Tunisian bridgehead, would take anything other than its self-evidently-best-for-the-Axis course of withdrawing to Italy. The OSP of both Allies failed to anticipate even as a low-probability event the actual outcome of Torch: the capture of one quarter million men. This result has been called "Tunisgrad"—if pretentiously in its evocation of the apocalyptic battle on the Volga, which inflicted thrice as many Axis casualties,[343] still, until 1944, the greatest victory in the war of the Western Allies.

The possibility of a Tunisgrad does not seem to have been mentioned in the year-plus of Allied strategizing through July 24, 1942, nor in the subsequent fifteen weeks of tactical planning. At Casablanca in January 1943, the Allies based their discussions of future operations on the supposition that their conquest of Tunisia was but a matter of time[344]—yet generally did not mention any chance of winning on Tunisgrad scale. One exception was Churchill who, on January 15—already scenting the possible size of victory—spoke of having the Germans in Africa "in the bag eventually."[345] On February 9, he wrote to Stalin of Allied hopes "to destroy or expel" by April the Axis forces in Africa.[346] A few days later, however—as Rommel was exposing and exploiting the incompetence of the Americans at Kasserine—he called the Allied situation in Tunisia "anxious."[347] By February 24, he was back to telling Stalin that the Axis forces "will now be brought into the grip of the vice."[348] General Sir Harold Alexander—as 18th Army Group Commander, Montgomery's superior—was then not so optimistic and cautioned his Prime Minister that the end was in fact not imminent.[349] On March 11, Eisenhower indicated to Marshall that a Tunisgrad might be glimpsed, suggesting that continuing Axis reinforcement of its forces in Tunisia might be "a serious mistake," based on overestimation of its logistic capabilities.[350] On April 6, Churchill wrote to Stalin of Allied forces closing in for the kill, and of their acting "to prevent a Dunkirk escape."[351]

Top Axis leaders were even slower to sense that a Tunisgrad could happen. The requests of Kesselring in the early spring of 1943 to withdraw personnel from Tunisia were rejected by Hitler because such actions might impair fighting morale.[352] Erwin Rommel reported that the collapse and surrender of the Axis armies came as "a complete surprise" to the Führer's HQ.[353]

Decision science might have helped the Allies to have at least considered in their strategic deliberations—and to have acted in their tactical planning to maximize their chances of achieving—the quarter-of-a-million-men surrender that in fact occurred. Tunisgrad was made possible by the reaction to Torch of Adolf Hitler. Decision scientists, among whom Daniel Kahneman and Amos Tversky were prominent, have interviewed thousands and have found that in "choices that involve moderate or high probabilities, people tend to be risk averse in the domain of gains and risk seeking in the domain of losses."[354] Kahneman wrote of the two situations:

> People are averse to risk when they consider prospects with substantial chance to achieve a large gain. They are willing to accept less than the expected value of a gamble to lock in a sure gain.
>
> People who face very bad options take desperate gambles, accepting a high probability of making things worse in exchange for a small hope of avoiding a large loss. Risk taking of this kind often turns manageable failures into disasters. The thought of accepting the large sure loss is too painful, and the hope of complete relief too enticing, to make the sensible decision that it is time to cut one's losses.[355]

The actions of Bernard Montgomery and of Adolf Hitler in the last two months of 1942 were in line with these decision-scientific findings. By prevailing at El Alamein by November 3, Montgomery had a bell-ringing gain. Many on the Allied side hoped that he would enhance that victory by taking chances to capture many of Rommel's retreating men. Montgomery preferred, however, not to risk the lessening of his gain by taking such chances. In the domain of gains, he was risk-averse.[356]

Adolf Hitler on November 8, 1942, faced the possible loss of the Afrika Korps and, with it, Africa. Like later research subjects of decision science, he was willing to chance "making things worse in exchange for a small hope of avoiding a large loss." Risk-seeking in the region of possible losses, the Führer upped the ante, immediately sending three German divisions to Tunisia, with more to follow. The other-side perception of the Allied decision makers had not anticipated Hitler's determination to hold on in Tunisia. Had they known the later findings of decision science, they could have foreseen better how their opponent would react and how vast a victory they might have.

3

Messina

Late on August 16, 1943, lead patrols of the U.S. 7th Infantry Regiment probed southeast-ward into the Sicilian city of Messina. Beyond its port on its eastern side were three miles of Mediterranean water separating Sicily from Calabria, the province that is the toe of the Italian boot. A Long Tom—a field cannon of six-inch caliber—was brought forward into the hills above the city. It fired across the Strait of Messina the first one hundred rounds of the war of U.S. artillery onto mainland Europe.

Early the next morning, as the last German soldiers embarked from Sicily, they towed behind them in the sea to chill it, a bottle of wine with which they would toast their escape.

At ten that morning, Lieutenant General George Patton reached the heights above Messina. He had forbidden subordinate officers to accept the surrender of the city. His convoy hurried down to the central square—as German guns shot at them from Calabria. The shells continued to land nearby as Patton formally took over Messina. Minutes later, a British patrol came from the southwest into the city.

Bent on beating the Brits to Messina, "Blood and Guts" Patton had lashed his Seventh Army forward and had finished a short nose ahead of the Eighth Army of General Sir Bernard Montgomery. This victory—although highlighted in the Best Picture, *Patton,* of 1970 of Franklin Schaffner—had limited luster in that it had entailed hurrying units into areas the Germans were no longer defending and in that Montgomery had not been pushing his men to win a race that he had little sense of being in.

Later that day, General Sir Harold Alexander—commander of 15th Army Group, which contained the Seventh and Eighth Armies—cabled his Prime Minister: "By 10 AM this morning, August 17, 1943, the last German soldier was flung out of Sicily and the whole island is now in our hands."[1]

The Sicilian campaign, Operation Husky, begun with Allied landings on July 10 on the southeastern shores of the island, was over.

The Strait of Messina, where Husky ended, had nearly been the grave of the mythical Odysseus. That hero of Ithaca had been advised by the sorceress Circe that, in sailing through the channel, he should hug the Calabrian coast—even though the six-headed monster Scylla dwelled there. To feed her mouths, she grabbed and devoured six sailors of each boat that passed by. That was better, though, than nearing the opposite, Sicilian, shore, the home of Charybdis—another monster, who specialized in sucking in so much water as to create whirlpools that engulfed and destroyed whole ships. Odysseus heeded the enchantress and lost six of his men.

The Germans of 1943 in crossing over the strait did better than had Odysseus in passing through it: they encountered no such monsters, indeed met with no noticeable resistance at all. While the Ithacan had mourned his devoured half dozen, the twentieth-century escapees rejoiced. Allied planes had sunk or destroyed seven Wehrmacht boats.[2] The Germans, however,

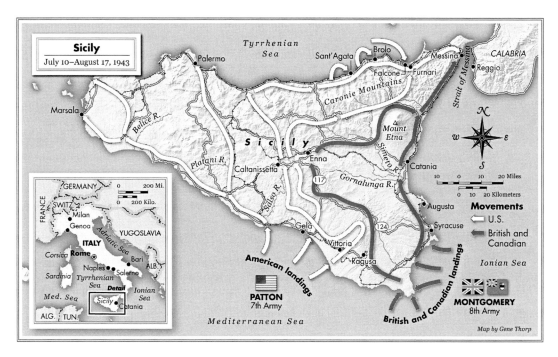

claimed to have lost in the crossing only one boatman and not a single transported soldier.[3] This had occurred despite Allied dominance in the water and the air.

Later, because his men had made a barbecue of the sacred Sicilian cattle of the sun-god Helios, the ship of Odysseus was swept into a maelstrom of Charybdis, from which only he survived. The German nation, in 1943, was being sucked ever deeper into a latter-day vortex in which the death toll would be, on a mythic scale, greater.

The Non-Decision: Should the Allies in July and August of 1943 Have Acted, More Than They Negligibly Did, to Prevent the Escape of 53,000 Germans Across the Strait of Messina?

While other chapters of this book have considered choices actively made, the Allied decision makers for Sicily never focused on preventing German flight from the island. By not forthrightly addressing possible German escape, eight might-have-been-decision-makers effectively, by default, made a non-decision—that of doing nothing effectual—that would prove as consequential as many a resolutely-arrived-at determination in the war. The MHBDMs did not even decide not to decide: they just did not decide. Each of the might-have-been-decision-makers had competing priorities to which their attention was given.

Alternatives: to take the city of Messina and its nearby shoreline before the Wehrmacht could use them as points of embarkation; to land in Calabria, which would have deprived the Germans in Sicily of their escape route; to encircle enemy forces on Sicily; to interdict via naval and air attack the crossing of the strait; not to take any of these actions—which was what happened.

When not made: January through August of 1943.

The might-have-been-decision-makers: the Combined Chiefs of Staff; Dwight Eisenhower, Supreme Commander in the Mediterranean Theater; Harold Alexander, Deputy Commander-in-Chief to Eisenhower; Admiral of the Fleet Sir Andrew Cunningham; Air Chief Marshal Sir Arthur Tedder; Bernard Montgomery; and George Patton.

The competing priorities: for the Combined Chiefs and Eisenhower especially and, to a lesser extent for Alexander, Cunningham, and Tedder, the arguably-more-important issues of possibly invading Sardinia and/or mainland Italy and of inducing Italy to quit the war; for Cunningham, the furtherance of Allied control of the Mediterranean; for Tedder, the strategic bombing of Nazi Europe; for Alexander, Montgomery, and Patton, the tactical challenges of defeating the Axis forces in Sicily; for Montgomery, the organizational details of moving on to the mainland.

Conclusions: the outcome: intermediate per hopes; good on net; bad in comparison with the likely results of alternatives; **the non-decision:** abysmal; **why not made:** ununified command resulting from Eisenhower, Alexander, Cunningham, Tedder, Montgomery, and Patton all being both principals and agents with ill-defined assignments and mandates; failure to perceive the need to decide, excessive risk aversion; **most to be lauded:** Albert Kesselring, Hans-Valentin Hube, and Ernst-Günter Baade; **most to be faulted:** the Combined Chiefs of Staff for botching at Casablanca the meta-decisions of setting the structure and the ethos of command—a judgment at variance with the historical literature, which has fingered in varying degrees the lesser culpabilities of George Marshall, Dwight Eisenhower, Harold Alexander, Andrew Cunningham, Arthur Tedder, Bernard Montgomery, and George Patton.

The war, in the first months of 1943, had been going better for the Allies.

After half a year of gruesome jungle combat, the Japanese on February 7 withdrew from Guadalcanal. That American victory would begin the island-hopping rollback of Japanese conquests in the Pacific. In March, Australian and U.S. flyers destroyed most of a Japanese troop convoy in the Battle of Bismarck Sea. By early June, the Japanese had evacuated the Aleutians.

South of Stalingrad, German forces retreated over three hundred miles from their furthest advances into the Caucasus Mountains. The Russians, pushing west, retook Kursk and Kharkov, but relost the latter to a German counterattack that also destroyed the Soviet 3rd Tank Army. Russian retention of a salient around Kursk set the stage for the greatest of all tank battles: that of Kursk, which began on July 5, 1943.

The Allies exploited their supremacy in the air, as the Americans joined the British in bombing the cities of the Reich. Allied planes were also instrumental in combating Nazi submarines. The U-boats had in 1942 sunk almost eight million tons of Allied shipping: the loss of merchant-fleet capacity exceeding even the product of what Churchill called "the immense shipbuilding programme of the United States." The number of operational U-boats peaked at 235 in April 1943. That would be the year, however, in which, Churchill wrote, "we could see the balance turn": as the amount of Allied tonnage sent to the bottom by the subs was less than half that of 1942.[4]

The Allied invasion of Sicily had been decided on in the Anglo-American conference held in January 1943 in Casablanca. Franklin Roosevelt had said there that the Allies would demand from Germany, Italy, and Japan their unconditional surrender.

The Outcome: Allied Conquest of Sicily; German Escape; Italian Forsaking of the Axis Alliance

The Germans had reacted to the landings of Operation Husky by doubling from two to four the number of their divisions in Sicily: bringing in from Calabria the 29th Panzer Grenadiers and, from southern France, the First Parachute Division. At peak strengths, the Allies outnumbered the Germans by more than five to one: 467,000 to 90,000.[5]

The fighting value of the 315,000 Italian soldiers on the island was uneven. Some—such as the artillerists—performed well. The hearts of most, however, were elsewhere than in assisting the Germans in the war. Tens of thousands deserted; 33,000 Sicilians accepted invitations to defect to be paroled to their homes[6]; over 100,000 were captured. The Italian commander in the eastern port of Augusta surrendered it without a fight—to the embarrassment of Benito Mussolini and the fury of Adolf Hitler. Albert Kesselring related that the Napoli Division in southeastern Sicily had "vanished without a trace."[7] He often asked himself whether the Germans might not have been better off without their purported allies—given their evident distaste for the war and their dubious loyalty to the Axis pact.[8]

Once the U.S. Seventh and UK Eighth Armies were securely ashore, their greater numbers of men, planes, and ships meant that it would only be a matter of time before Alexander could cable Churchill that the foe had fled. The main questions on the island had become how long it would take, how many casualties both sides would suffer, and how many Germans would get away.

The Allies made no special effort to interfere with the flight of their enemy.

American and British forces in Husky had 22,400 battle casualties, of which 5,200 were deaths. Five thousand Germans died in Sicilian battles and 6,000 were captured[9]; 130,000 Italians became casualties.[10]

Twelve thousand German support personnel left Sicily early in August. By the seventeenth, the Wehrmacht had evacuated over the Strait of Messina 53,000 men,[11] 10,000 vehicles, 47 tanks, many other heavy weapons, 1,100 tons of ammunition, and twelve thousand tons of supplies.[12] It had left behind 3,500 vehicles, 78 tanks, and 287 artillery pieces.[13]

Of greater import was that Husky had hustled Italy out of the war. On July 24, the Fascist Grand Council of the nation had met and, in the early hours of the next morning, had voted Benito Mussolini out of power. Marshal Pietro Badoglio would head the new Italian government; the deposed Duce was arrested and would be held in a ski resort northeast of Rome. Badoglio said that his nation would continue to honor the Axis Alliance and to wage war at the side of Germany. Few Italians, Germans, or Allies believed him. Eight German divisions took the Brenner Pass and other key points in north Italy. They and additional units were poised to race south, should Badoglio surrender to and join with the Allies.

How Good or Bad Was the Outcome of Operation Husky?

The fighting on Sicily had constituted, Churchill wrote, "a successful and skilful campaign of thirty-eight days."[14]

Later writers would deem the conquest of the island neither as successful nor as skillful as it might—indeed should—have been. The shortfall lay largely in what the Prime Minister did not mention: that 53,000 Germans had fled to fight again. The more able Germans who still had guns in their hands, the further the Allies were from victory in the war.

That 70,000 Italians[15]—few of whom were particularly interested in fighting the Allies—also got away was of lesser consequence.

The account of the Prime Minister suggests good-decision-good-outcome: GDGO, though, for the decision reached at Casablanca in January to invade Sicily, not for the non-decision not to act purposefully to prevent German escape—which he did not mention.

Operation Husky had: a good-outcome-per-hopes—in that the three main Allied goals, of engaging German forces and thereby keeping them from the Russian front, of consolidating Allied control of the Mediterranean, and of precipitating Italian withdrawal from the war, were met; a good-outcome-on-net—in that these three results, at acceptable costs, moved the Allies toward ultimate triumph; and a questionable good-outcome-versus-alternatives—in that some decision participants at Casablanca and commentators afterward thought that it would have been better to invade Sardinia and/or Corsica; others, to attack in the Eastern Mediterranean; still others, to minimize operations in the Middle Sea, while preparing for Overlord.[16] Eisenhower, on July 10, 1943, feared "that the Germans would breathe a sigh of relief to realize we were only going after Sicily."[17] Given that the situation in its game-theoretic essence was zero-sum, such a sigh would have meant an enemy judgment of an Allied bad-decision-bad-outcome-v-alts.

Judgments on the Non-Decision of Failing to Interdict German Flight and Its Outcome

Eisenhower said on August 14, 1943, that he had made "two 'mistakes'—the landing at Casablanca [which presumably, as per British thinking, should not have been made] and our super-cautious approach to Italy. On the latter Ike now thinks we should have made simultaneous landings on both sides of the Messina Strait, thus cutting off all Sicily and obtaining wholesale surrender."[18]

Ike's memoirs painted a rosier, muddier, less-candid picture. They described the results of Husky—including Mussolini's fall and Italy's exit from the war—as "more far-reaching than the mere capture of the enemy garrison."[19] That such a capture had not occurred was glossed over—although the theater commander admitted that "most of the badly battered German garrison" had gotten away.[20] Alexander, Eisenhower wrote, "had faintly hoped" that Montgomery's Eighth Army might drive swiftly on Messina, thereby blocking the enemy's escape. But that force had moved more slowly than Alexander had weakly wished.[21] Montgomery's own memoirs, while accepting no responsibility, put bleaker hues on the outcome: that so many enemy had fled was "an unsatisfactory ending" and an "iniquity."[22]

German leaders ascribed higher importance to the escape of their men from Sicily than did the Allied commanders. Adolf Hitler had long had the reflexive response to setbacks of forbidding retreats—enjoining instead hold-at-all-costs resistance until death. By July of 1943, however, the Axis catastrophes of Stalingrad and Tunisia had changed his thinking. On the evening of the 25th, shortly after learning of Mussolini's ouster, the Führer said to his headquarters generals that "under all circumstances we must rescue [our soldiers in Sicily]; they're no good [there]; they must cross, particularly the paratroops and the Göring Division. The equipment doesn't matter a damn.... But we must get the men back."[23] The next day, he ordered Albert Kesselring to prepare for German withdrawal from Sicily[24]—while reserving for himself the right to decide on the timing and specific unit movements.

Glimpses of the Führer's mindset at this time were given in private conversations with Erwin Rommel. Hitler had recently told the field marshal that Germany had little chance of victory in the war and faint hope also of making peace with the Western Allies—since their leaders with whom Germany might have negotiated a treaty were not in power. Hitler had therefore resolved, he said to Rommel one evening in late July, to fight for every house until nothing remained. For a great people, such a heroic death was historically necessary. Moreover, "If the German people are incapable of winning the war, then they can rot." Rommel confided to his family: "Sometimes you feel that he's no longer quite normal."[25]

Albert Kesselring, commander of all Germans in the Mediterranean, had anticipated the strategic thinking of his Führer on Sicily. He had on July 13 told Panzer General Hans-Valentin Hube, his subordinate who would be in charge on the island, that his highest priority was to make sure that the Germans got safely back to Calabria.[26] Both German generals had, however, to tread with delicacy, since the Führer's men on the island were nominally subordinated to Alfredo Guzzoni, at the head of the Italian Sixth Army. That so many of his men ultimately escaped from Sicily Kesselring rated an achievement at least on a par with Dunkirk.[27]

Others have held that the comparison with Dunkirk understated the German feat at Messina. The escapees in 1940 had been "exhausted, disorganized, dispirited" and without virtually all of their motorized equipment; the Germans arriving in Calabria were tough, determined, well-provided with heavy weapons, and proud of having held off a superior force with control of the air for 38 days.[28] Neither Kesselring nor historians were buying Eisenhower's description of the escaping Germans as "badly battered."

Colonel General Heinrich von Vietinghoff would command the German Tenth Army in mainland Italy, which would imperil the Allied landing in September at Salerno and would halt for months at the Gustav Line the Allied drive northward toward Rome. He wrote that the Germans could not understand why the Allies did not seize sooner the Strait of Messina—either simultaneously with the first landings of Husky or shortly afterward.[29] Vietinghoff would consider the escapees from Sicily the iron of his Tenth Army.[30]

The current historical consensus—which is not here disagreed with—holds that the non-decision and its outcome were bad in comparison with what might have been done: BnonDBO-v-alts. The American Official History judged Allied command performance in Sicily poor—finding that the German retreat over the strait had "proceeded unimpeded" and that it constituted "one of the most successful evacuations ever executed from a beleaguered shore."[31] "Nearly all military historians," it has been summarized, "condemn the campaign."[32]

Operation Husky has been seen as a template for repeated Allied failures to come: the inability "to translate captures of ground into destruction of enemy forces." It was the only Western Allied land operation of July and August 1943—during which time four million soldiers fought in Russia near Kursk and Orel. While 6,000 Western Allied soldiers died in Sicily, the Russian figure for that period was one half million—which was why the Soviets looked on Husky "with such contempt."[33]

* * *

The Sicilian non-decision had an intermediate outcome with respect to expectations and hopes: although Churchill did not mention any higher aspirations for Husky in terms of bagging Germans, Eisenhower and Montgomery did; those of Alexander were optimistic long shots, while Patton never focused on preventing German escape. Even though many Wehrmacht men had been allowed to get away, the taking of Sicily moved the Allies closer to final victory: a good-outcome-on-net.

What Affected How Bad or How Good the Outcome of Operation Husky Was?

After a poor start, the Germans fought superbly. The Wehrmacht had soon dispensed with the fiction of supreme Italian command in Sicily. On July 16, Hans-Valentin Hube assumed control of all sectors with German troops, with orders from Albert Kesselring to delay for as long as possible Axis retreat from the island. Fifteen days later, the Italian Comando Supremo subordinated to Hube all Axis forces in Sicily. This occasioned moments of friction—as when Italian units resisted German appropriation of their motor vehicles and opened a firefight with deaths on both sides.[34] Such incidents, however, were few, as Alfredo Guzzoni did not oppose the transition from covert to overt German command. Kesselring and Hube judged accurately what their men could and could not do and, with sensitive other-side perception, with how much urgency the Allies would push forward.

The Hermann Göring Division had not performed well in attacking the Seventh Army soon after its landing[35] and George Patton initially judged that the Germans were "not fighting as well as in Tunisia."[36] Wehrmacht paratroopers, rushed in from France to block Montgomery's shoreline route to Messina were, however, superlative. By late July, Patton had changed his assessment: "The Germans are SOB but great soldiers and are sticking to the death."[37] Their withdrawal in five stages toward Messina was precisely planned and deftly brought off. Colonel Ernst-Günter Baade commanded the naval, artillery, and anti-aircraft units on both sides of the strait. He arranged for the waterway to be covered by 500 guns, ranging up to four batteries of eleven-inch cannons. Two thirds of these weapons were anti-aircraft and threw up what has been thought the most intensive flak concentration of the war—greater than those of central London and the Ruhr Valley.[38]

Not warring as well as the Germans were the Allies, who learned in Sicily that airborne actions were trickier than they had thought. Their naval guns on the night of July 11/12 fired on incoming friendly paratroopers, downing 23 planes and causing 290 casualties. Two nights later, same-side guns shot at another airborne op, with the result that but 295 of 1,856 men were landed close to their targets. German officers took advantage of what they called the "Anglo-Saxon habits" they observed: scheduling their movements for the times when the Allies had lunch, tea, and dinner and few of their planes were aloft.[39] While Omar Bradley and George Patton thought Montgomery's generalship too cautious, Eisenhower, after study, concluded that an all-out northward attack by the Eighth Army in mid–July would have been repulsed. The Americans, he wrote, had "sincere enthusiasm for the fighting qualities of their British and Canadian partners."[40]

The Allies had benefited at first from successful deception—as the Germans were taken in by a monumental ruse. British intelligence officers had had a body wash up on the shore of Spain, carrying documents indicating that the Allies would next attack in the eastern Mediterranean. The Wehrmacht was duped and ordered Kesselring on May 21 to prioritize defending Sardinia and the Peloponnese. The First Panzer Division—considered "a unit whose presence in Sicily might have been decisive"[41]—was in early June moved from southern France to the Peloponnese. Only two German divisions would be in Sicily on the morning of July 10.[42]

That morning would have factors of luck that affected the battle outcome. The day before, Montgomery had fretted in his diary: "I consider that if we are to succeed *we must have* [emphasis in original] average luck, and probably 60 or 70 percent luck.... I consider that we shall require all our resources to capture SICILY, and that the further exploitation on to the mainland ... is definitely unlikely to be possible."[43] The Allies were unlucky that the weather on the night of July 9/10 was an unseasonal gale, which was partly responsible for forcing 69 gliders to land in the sea, drowning 252[44]; lucky that resistance to their landings was slight[45] and that most Italian soldiers wanted out of the war and did not fight well—Eisenhower and Montgomery having feared that they would perform as well in Sicily as they had in Africa.[46] Kesselring considered the Axis forces "mighty lucky" in "the Allied conception of operations," which featured ploddingly methodical advances and attempted neither large-scale encirclements of the defenders, nor moves on Calabria, nor concerted naval and air attacks on forces crossing the Strait of Messina.[47]

What Steps Might the Allies Have Taken to Have Captured or Killed Tens of Thousands More Germans in Sicily?

It has been suggested that the Allies could have enhanced their Sicilian victory by landing in Calabria before, simultaneously with, or after the landings in southeastern Sicily. Albert Kesselring reported having "been anxiously expecting ... throughout the Sicilian campaign" Allied landings in Calabria—which he had no troops to oppose and which would, he thought, have led to "an overwhelming Allied victory"[48]; Alfredo Guzzoni and other Axis generals also deemed such possible attacks their most worrisome threats and wondered why their enemy did not undertake them.

The Allies had in fact in May considered making amphibious attacks near Reggio (on the tip of the Italian toe, seven miles southeast of Messina across the strait), near Crotone (one-hundred-plus miles northeast of Messina in eastern Calabria), and at Taranto (deep in the instep of the Italian boot, over 200 miles northeast of Messina). Operation Buttress, the landing near Reggio, would have put the Allies on the Calabrian shore, in position to secure the landing points of Axis soldiers fleeing Sicily. Operation Goblet, near Crotone, would have positioned the Allies to control the twenty-mile-wide Calabrian isthmus between the Tyrrhenian and Ionian Seas, cutting the enemy's route of escape. A similar effect might have been achieved by the Operation Musket landing at Taranto.

Allied planners originally pondered Buttress, Goblet, and Musket not as blockers of escape from Sicily, but as next steps after the victory in Tunisia. As such, the proposed operations, in the words of the American Official History, "inspired little enthusiasm"[49] and were not seriously reconsidered until after the Allies, ashore in Sicily, had determined to attack the mainland.[50] One historian judged that amphibious landings in late July on the two sides of the Strait of Messina—given the availability of landing craft and Allied control of the air—"would not have been too difficult."[51]

The actual landings in Sicily might have been made closer to Messina. German commanders expressed wonder that the Allies had not come ashore nearer to the strait on either the northern or the eastern coasts. One historian considered the landings so far from Messina, "the major tactical error of the campaign."[52] An early plan for Husky had had the American Seventh Army landing near Palermo. It was, however, scrapped by Montgomery, who wanted Patton protectively positioned on his left, not 120 miles away to the northwest. Another historian thought that landing Patton close to Palermo would have placed him "well on the way to the Straits of Messina" and to trapping "all the enemy forces in Sicily."[53] Alexander—citing the difficulties of terrain—disagreed.[54] Both he and Montgomery, insistent on ample air cover, ruled out having the Eighth Army land much further north than it did.[55]

Even disembarking where they did, the Eighth Army might have clinched a more complete victory by pushing immediately toward Messina. The American Official History—with historians in agreement[56]—thought that Montgomery on July 12 should have driven with all his strength directly up the east coast of Sicily, thereby "finishing off the Axis defenders quickly and pushing on through to Messina." Instead, however, the Eighth Army commander proposed on that day to split his efforts between westward and northward attacks—to which Alexander agreed. The result, per the AOH, was for the Eighth Army an "ill-fated two-pronged offensive" that "completely nullified" the advantages gained in the landings.[57]

That disparaged two-pronged scheme might itself have achieved better results had the two Allied armies moved in coordination against the Germans. Montgomery judged on July 12 that he and Patton, if acting in concert, "could inflict a disaster on the enemy and capture all his

Central Mediterranean
Summer 1943

AUSTRIA

HUNGARY

Po

YUGOSLAVIA

Apennine

Livorno
Florence

ITALY

Adriatic Sea

CORSICA

Mountains

Rome
Cassino

Anzio

Naples   Salerno

Taranto

SARDINIA

Tyrrhenian
Sea

Crotone

Catanzaro

Palermo   Messina

Reggio

SICILY

Ionian
Sea

Tunis

Pantelleria

MALTA

TUNISIA

Mediterranean
Sea

20   0   40   80 Miles

0   40   80 Kilometers

Map by Gene Thorp

troops."[58] Nine days later, after disjointed movements of the two Allied forces had continued, Montgomery still was optimistic that they could converge on the Germans—whereupon he "did not see how the enemy could get his army away from SICILY; it was doomed if we acted properly."[59] Kesselring and Hube were not as concerned about this doom of their divisions as Montgomery's assessment—which was seconded by the AOH and others—suggested that they should have been. Relying on the abilities of their men, the mountainous ground, and the tactical tendencies of their foes, they judged finely just how long they could linger on the island.

One striking instance of Allied malcoordination occurred on July 12, when Montgomery decided to attack westward with part of his force, which would put it on collision course with the Americans. To make room for the British left, Alexander shifted southwestward the boundary that had been set between the armies: the capture and use of Highway 124 would no longer be assigned to Patton's Seventh Army, but instead to Montgomery's Eighth. Before being pulled back, leading U.S. units had fought to within one thousand yards of the highway. Lieutenant General Omar Bradley, who commanded under Patton, described it as "the only good road available for a northward thrust west of Mount Etna," which, when taken, "would open a path to [the city of] Enna [in the center of Sicily]."[60] Patton would have to truck his 45th Division a dozen-plus miles back to the southern beaches, to swing it around to his left.

The Yanks, before being yanked back, had—per the American Official History—"been ready and willing to take Highway 124 and Enna, thus encircling the German defenders facing Eighth Army."[61] The British Official History agreed that Alexander had, indeed, "made a mistake."[62] Omar Bradley called the bouncing of the Seventh Army to make room for the Eighth "the most arrogant, egotistical, selfish and dangerous move in the whole of combined operations in World War II."[63] To a historian, it was "the most damaging misjudgment of the Sicily campaign."[64] Patton wrote to his wife that "had I not been interfered with ... by a fool change of plan, I would have taken Messina in ten days."[65]

Having been bumped away from Highway 124, Patton proposed to Alexander to head for Palermo. Montgomery thought that the Deputy Commander-in-Chief had then erred in permitting the Seventh Army "to wheel west towards Palermo. It thereby missed the opportunity to direct its main thrust-line northwards in order to cut the island in two: as a preliminary to the encirclement of the [Mount] Etna position and the capture of Messina."[66] Kesselring disparaged Patton's taking of Palermo as a pointless dispersion of force.[67]

The Allies might alternatively have gotten sooner to Messina by undertaking amphibious assaults—expediting the drives along both the northern and eastern coasts and also trapping enemy defenders. Admiral of the Fleet Sir Andrew Cunningham wondered whether the Allies might not have taken better advantage of their command of the sea. Landing craft had been available for amphibious moves by the Eighth Army, but not until August 16—after the Germans had broken off battle contact and were retreating to their embarkation sites—did Montgomery undertake a sea-borne end run that accomplished nothing.[68] Cunningham asked "whether much time and costly fighting could not be saved by even minor flank moves which must necessarily be unsettling to the enemy."[69] German commanders admitted having feared such actions.[70]

Patton thrice—on August 8, 11, and 16—threw amphibious left hooks on the northern coast. The American Official History judged that the first landing "probably did encourage the Germans to give up [a defensive ridge] a few hours earlier than they had intended."[71] The second—at Brolo on the eleventh—landed 650 men five miles ahead of the American front line. There were anxious moments when it was feared that the force would be wiped out by the German rear guard.[72] It held out, however, until reached by Patton's advancing infantry, but had been too small to block the enemy retreat. The AOH conceded that the landing, at a cost of 177 casualties while inflicting roughly the same number, had "accomplished little" but asserted that it "had come close to trapping" much of the 29th Panzer Grenadier Division and "even closer to rolling up the whole northern sector of [the German] defensive line."[73] One historian agreed with the AOH on the lack of payoff, believing that Patton had erred in not mounting a larger, better-supported landing.[74]

Omar Bradley, in his memoirs, disparaged such amphibious actions. He had urged delaying the landing at Brolo until the front line was further forward, had had his request turned down by Patton, and termed the episode "a complete fiasco."[75] Bradley thought the third landing silly and had advised against it. Patton, however, liked the press coverage his sea-borne moves generated and put another task force ashore before dawn on the sixteenth. It was welcomed by his own infantry, which had advanced beyond that point. Montgomery, despite himself refraining from amphibious moves, thought on August 10 that Patton should launch one at Furnari, 25 miles west of Messina, which "would cut off the enemy completely." Montgomery's biographer retrospectively agreed, provided that Patton "put in a bigger assault" than he had at Brolo.[76]

But that provision was the problem: the transport needed to bulk up such an attack may not have been at hand. To achieve the result envisioned by Montgomery, the AOH, and other historians, Patton needed more than the nine craft that had borne his men ashore at Brolo. Hundreds of landing vessels had been used on July 10.[77] Just how many were subsequently available is unclear— with British landing craft being sidelined by the need for spare parts and American withdrawn to Tunisia to prepare for the landing at Salerno.[78] It should—the British Official Naval History believed[79]—have been possible to gather together enough of them to make the landings strategic blows, instead of desperate scrambles to survive. As actually mounted, the BONH judged that Patton's amphibious end runs had had minimal impact.[80]

Greater impact might have been achieved had air and naval supremacy been exploited to interdict escape. Montgomery had posited, pre-invasion, that a main goal of Husky was to "prevent the escape of [the Axis] garrison back to Italy."[81] This was, however, he thought, not the responsibility of his army but, instead, "a matter of first importance for our naval and air forces."[82] Alexander saw things similarly and on August 3 asked Air Chief Marshal Sir Arthur Tedder and Admiral Sir Andrew Cunningham to coordinate in cutting off the Axis retreat. Cunningham responded that Allied small craft already were operating in the strait at night and that, once the coastal batteries were silenced, the navy would send "surface forces to operate further into the straits."[83] Air Vice-Marshal Arthur Coningham on August 11 gave assurance that Allied boats and planes could "handle" any large-scale enemy retreat.[84]

Whether or not they could have, they did not. Upon reconsideration, both the navies and the air forces of the Allies decided that the massed guns of Colonel Baade precluded concerted attacks on the strait. Admiral Cunningham would write in his memoirs that "there was no effective way of stopping [German escape], either by sea or air."[85] Others disagreed. Albert Kesselring thought it axiomatic that flak positions could not survive committed bombing. He also judged that Baade's gunners could not have protected the sea-lanes of evacuation, had the Allies resolutely attacked them.[86] One historian suggested specifics: having air reconnaissance locate Baade's heaviest batteries and battleships fire at ranges of five to nine miles to knock them out, whereupon naval craft of intermediate size could enter the strait to put out of action the 88- and 90-millimeter guns and to enable smaller craft to take on the Axis ferries.[87] Allied bombers might also have destroyed the roads on either side of the strait.

In addition to destroying roads, the Allies might have done better to have had more off-road capability: to have had more hooves. Lucian Truscott, who commanded the U.S. 3rd Infantry Division in Sicily, and George Patton had as young men been cavalry officers. They noted in their memoirs that the mountainous terrain of Sicily had necessitated using mules, horses, burros, and bullocks for supply. Patton wished that he had had "a complete American cavalry division with pack artillery. Had we possessed such a unit, not a German would have escaped."[88] Truscott echoed.[89] It has also been thought that the Eighth army had blundered in not arranging for pack-animal transport.[90]

The common theme of these critiques is that the Allies would have done better to have truly challenged German escape from Sicily: bad-non-decision-bad-outcome-versus-alternatives.

Not part of this consensus were the memoirs of four leading Allied decision makers among those most responsible for not opting to cut off German flight: Eisenhower, Alexander, Cunningham, and Tedder. Their common authorial tack was to mention minimally the non-decision, to overstate the achievements of the Allies generally in Sicily and specifically at Messina, and to disagree tersely with those who thought that more could and should have been done.[91] Cunningham, reported "almost nightly raids on the Straits of Messina by our motor torpedo boats ... at great risk to themselves" while Tedder wrote of his "bombers ... directed against bottlenecks around Messina to block the routes to the north-eastern beaches," as his "night bombers concentrated on those beaches that might be used for evacuation and on possible points of assembly"—all of which by both services, however impressive it might have sounded in these memoirs, but negligibly inconvenienced the Germans. Historian Carlo D'Este found in the writings of Alexander, Cunningham, and Tedder with respect to Messina "a complete absence of candour": while Cunningham and Tedder avoided mention of Allied strategic shortcomings and "chose to ignore the unsatisfactory ending," Alexander "lived in a fool's paradise."[92] These memoirs, in sum, insofar as they related to German flight through Messina, were self-serving fictions.

Why Did the Allies in Sicily Not Take Any of Many Possible Decision Alternatives, Instead of Drifting into Their Actual, Inferior Non-Decision?

One explanation offered is the somewhat-understandable British scorn for the Americans. Alexander's approval of Montgomery's proposal on July 12 to attack both northward and westward—which bounced Patton backward and leftward—the American Official History speculated, "has never been satisfactorily explained," but may have owed to his "distrust of the American fighting man."[93] That the cocky newcomers to the war had, in February at Kasserine, been "humiliated"[94] by Erwin Rommel had not been forgotten by British generals. Eisenhower thought that Alexander should not be blamed for initially relegating Patton's Americans to a secondary role—since, as the result of their debacle debut in Tunisia, "the British command completely lost confidence in them as offensive troops."[95] UK officers occasionally referred to Yanks as "our Italians" or, sexistly, as "Alice."[96]

But the GIs and their generals had learned from their opening incompetence. British Lieutenant-General Sir Oliver Leese, commander of the British 30th Corps in Sicily, admitted that he "did not realize the immense development in experience and technique which [the Americans] had made in the last weeks of the North African campaign." Leese felt that earlier trust in U.S. troops in Sicily might have enabled the Allies to "end this frustrating campaign sooner."[97] While official praise of troops may be suspected to be feel-good pabulum, the words of Alexander in his cable of August 3 to Churchill did shine sunnily on Patton's men: "The American Seventh

Army have done a grand job and are fighting really well"[98]—a judgment topped by that of the American Official History that it "had done more than well."[99]

Another explanation for Allied underperformance in Sicily was the lack of a plan to block German escape. Two persons who—arguably above all others on earth—should have known whether there was an Allied strategy to thwart German escape were Harold Alexander and Bernard Montgomery. Neither did. Both thought in early August that there was such a plan; both were wrong.[100] It was later thought "astonishing ... that no Allied plan for halting the Axis evacuation ever existed."[101] Pre-invasion planning had not extended beyond securing the beachheads.[102] The planners had presumed that Alexander's HQ would take over from there; Alexander, that the planning would have gone further.[103] Both Alexander and Montgomery ought to have inquired earlier than they did into planning to prevent German flight and, on learning of its nonexistence, to have had it undertaken.

In the absence of plans to seal off the strait, the Allies had to decide and to act on the fly. Unfortunately for them, the Germans in Sicily improvised faster and better.

The requisite improvisation would have been the more readily achieved, had the Allied armies, navies, and air forces been acting in harmony. Instead, their coordination was poor. While Admiral Cunningham would not send large ships into the strait until bombing had neutralized the coastal batteries, the air forces were wary of challenging Baade's flak and more interested in bombing the oilfields of Romania and the airfields and railroads of mainland Italy. On August 12, as 409 U.S. planes attacked Rome, thousands of Wehrmacht soldiers were being ferried—in daylight and unmolested—from Sicily to Calabria.

Such blatant getaways were facilitated by poor Allied intelligence. Kenneth Strong, Eisenhower's chief intelligence officer, has been faulted for obliviousness to the impending German escape. While Eighth Army intelligence had on August 5 called attention to the empty German ferries arriving in Messina, Strong, five days later, reported "at present no adequate intentions [sic?] that the enemy envisages evacuation of MESSINA bridgehead."[104] It has been judged "reasonable to assume that had [Strong] warned of the Axis evacuation, as indeed he ought to have, that Eisenhower would have intervened in time to counteract at least a portion of the evacuation."[105]

The failure of the Royal Navy to interdict that evacuation was blamed in part on long memories. Many Royal Navy officers off of Sicily recalled the unsuccessful attempt in 1915 to take control of the Dardanelles—a waterway with geographic similarities to the Strait of Messina. Historians have attributed RN reluctance to enter the Sicilian channel to the setback of 28 years before.[106]

The ill-coordination of the three armed services in Sicily had a parallel in the lack of strategic concert between America and Britain. The two nations had, since Casablanca in January, not been in step about continuing on from Sicily to continental Italy: the UK fervidly for; the U.S. leerily reluctant. Not until July 20 did the Combined Chiefs of Staff approve the mainland invasion. Its earlier authorization might, historians have thought, have led to timely operations in Calabria to trap the Germans in Sicily.[107]

Relatively unmentioned by historians as a reason that 53,000 Germans were permitted to sail off unharried to Calabria was that Allied decision makers had been attending to other issues.[108] Dwight Eisenhower, in his report of July 19, 1942, to the Combined Chiefs of Staff and the British Chiefs of Staff, noted that

> the United States and British governments prescribed two objectives for operation HUSKY which would also apply to post–HUSKY. (a) The military objective of eliminating Italy from the war, *i.e.*, destroying and rendering ineffective the Italian land, sea and air forces wherever they may be; (b) the political objective of delivering the Italian people from the Fascist regime which led them into the war and of restoring Italy as a free nation.[109]

These two goals were the main subjects when Eisenhower met on the seventeenth and twenty-sixth of July and on the first and ninth of August with Alexander, Cunningham, and Tedder. In his reports to the CCS and BCS of these meetings, Eisenhower also briefly mentioned the challenges to the fighting on Sicily posed by the terrain and, on August 2, that "with the support of naval gun fire on the right, we should be able to cut off a large part of the German garrison now in Catania and hasten the destruction of the enemy."[110]

But the prospect of such cutting off was an afterthought—subordinated in the minds of the four commanders to the issue of how best to move on to the mainland. The mostly-unmentioned meta-reasons why so many Germans escaped—why there was no plan to forestall enemy escape, why extemporized interdiction coordinated among the three services did not happen—were that overall command was ununified and that the four top decision makers in the area were other-focused. All four were intent mainly on the military goal of getting Italy out of the war and Eisenhower on the political objective of ending Fascism—two prime priorities assigned by their nations. But that so much attention went to those paired objectives, as well as to other personal foci of the four commanders, resulted in the Allies not doing as well as, most judge, they should have at Messina.

Who, If Anyone, Was at Fault?

Prominent among those censured for Allied messing up at Messina was George Marshall. The Allied delay until July 20 in deciding to invade mainland Italy was attributed to the U.S. Army Chief of Staff—in particular for the stance he took in May in Algiers. There, knowing that Roosevelt would back him, Marshall had refused to endorse the on-to-continental-Italy proposals of Brooke and Churchill—with "the result," some judged, "that tens of thousands of Germans escaped Sicily."[111]

Next-highest-ranking among those blamed was Dwight Eisenhower. The Supreme Commander of Husky was seen as "juggling too many balls in the air—with the result that all tumbled."[112] One of the balls was attending to civil affairs in French North Africa—where rational governance had somehow to be fashioned out of mutually-back-stabbing De Gaullists, Giraudists, and Vichyites. (While Eisenhower indeed took no steps to stop German escape and was, undeniably, "juggling too many balls," two of his most important—conquering the island and getting Italy out of the war—hardly could be judged to have been dropped.) Omar Bradley thought that his West Point classmate had come up short in Sicily: Ike alone had the position "to conceive the operation as a whole, impose his imprint, see it through and accept responsibility for the consequences. But Ike did not rise to the challenge."[113] The British Official Naval History asked why the Supreme Commander did not convene Alexander, Cunningham, and Tedder to formulate how they might best thwart German escape—their four meetings during Husky having instead mainly addressed invading the mainland.[114]

None of the attendees at those meetings escaped censure. Bernard Montgomery in mid–July 1943 was not high on Harold Alexander, his immediate superior: "He does not take a very firm grip himself and I generally have to suggest things to him, but he always acts on my suggestions."[115] Alexander was criticized by the American Official History for allowing Montgomery on July 12 to split his attack; by Montgomery for allowing Patton six days later to head off to Palermo; by historians for allowing Montgomery on July 20 to push on his left, while holding on his right. "Meekly" and "lamely" were the repeated adverbs of one historian for how the overall ground commander went along with the urgings of his "two prima donna army commanders," whom he guided but limply[116]—with other authors piling on in such knocking of Alexander.[117]

The more influential of the two prima donnas was Bernard Montgomery, who commanded in the more critical sector, who had greater access to Alexander's ear, and who, more than anyone else, determined how Husky played out. The victor of El Alamein, in opting on July 12 for a two-pronged drive to the north and west, counted on his superior to rubber-stamp his idea. Nine days later, in downgrading his northward thrust to a holding of position and in putting his offensive emphasis into a clockwise circling of Mount Etna, Montgomery did not bother even to touch base with his compatriot boss. One biographer—supported by other writers[118]—described a progression in the general from the delusional optimism of the first three days ashore, to a mistaken dispersion into multiple thrusts, followed by passively turning over the closure of the campaign to Patton, as he prepared to invade the mainland.[119]

Montgomery's strategy of having the two Allied armies jointly crush the Germans was seen to have fallen apart when prima donna number two on July 19 headed northwest for Palermo and large-font headlines, instead of northeast for Messina and conclusive victory.[120] Omar Bradley thought that Patton had sent his left wing "off in the wrong direction in what was essentially a public relations gesture" that "generated the headlines he so craved."[121] Patton was on the July 26 covers of both Newsweek and Time. His vainglorious "obsession with Palermo and Monty's over-ambitiousness" were alleged to have combined to "wreck the Allied offensive in Sicily."[122] Among others down on Patton in Sicily were Montgomery's chief of staff Francis De Guingand and the American Official History.[123]

Joining the army generals in shouldering criticism were the leaders of the air forces and navies, Arthur Tedder and Andrew Cunningham. It has been judged that the Allies had "failed to use intelligently" their dominance in the air and on the seas.[124] The British Official Naval History faulted the navies for "weak effort"; the air forces for being so busy with mainland bombing that they were not available when needed at the strait.[125] One historian thought "the biggest failure of [Husky] to be the complete and utter failure of both the Air Forces and the Navies to prevent" enemy escape—with "most of the blame" put "at the Navy's doorstep."[126] Another, however, especially blamed the flyers: "the Allied failure to employ their strategic bombing capability was undoubtedly the most costly mistake of all."[127] Generals Lucian Truscott and Omar Bradley and the AOH criticized the air forces for refusing to cooperate and coordinate with the other services.[128] Per Bradley: "the airmen had studiously–and arrogantly—avoided the tactical planning.... Even when pressed, they would tell us nothing about how they would support our landings.... The air support provided us on Sicily was scandalously casual, careless and ineffective."[129] Other authors joined in faulting the commanders of the Allied planes and boats.[130]

With so many attributions of Sicilian blame floating around, one historian was absolutional: concluding that none of the above and no one else was at fault. Samuel Morison judged "that the entire HUSKY plan was wrong," but also, astoundingly, that—owing to such circumstances as the perceived need for air cover, memories of the Dardanelles, and preparations for the mainland assault—"no blame should be attached to the Allied commanders."[131]

What Should the Allies Not Have Done?

Despite general agreement that the Allies should somehow have acted to prevent German escape, relatively little attention has been paid to the key meta-decisions for Husky—who would be the decision makers, what their mandates would be, how they would interact, and who would be issuing orders to whom. These determinations were made at Casablanca and largely led to the military non-decisions.

Allied bumbling in Sicily showed that the main lesson of Dieppe—the importance of command unity—had not yet been learned. If the UK and the U.S. had consciously wanted to increase the likelihood of flawed decisions and non-decisions, they should, in certain meta-decisional respects, have done just what they did for Husky.

A significant step in increasing the likelihood of bad decisions and non-decisions was to attenuate the control of the Supreme Commander. Alan Brooke, having blamed Dwight Eisenhower for the feebleness and the slowness in late 1942 of the Allied push toward Tunis, determined to limit the chances for the Kansan commander to botch the next op as well. How, though, could he do this, given the sense of the British—and it is hardly conceivable that they were not right—that the U.S. wished recognition of its importance? Brooke's solution at Casablanca was that of "flattering and pleasing the Americans" by elevating Eisenhower to Supreme Command[132] but for Husky slyly inserting between him and his forces three British buffers: Alexander, as deputy commander-in-chief; Cunningham, as naval commander; and Tedder, as air commander. The three Britons were to exercise "the active direction of the land, sea and air operations."[133]

The American Official History described the mandate of the Supreme Commander as "to act as a sort of chairman of the board, to enter into the final decision-making process only when the board members presented him with unsolved problems.... Eisenhower was raised involuntarily far above the operational level; only indirectly could he influence the course of operations once that course had been agreed on by his committee of three."[134] Harry Butcher, Eisenhower's friend and aide, on July 8, 1943, sensed "great difference" between Torch and Husky: "in the former Ike had direct control of all operations"; in the latter, Alexander, Cunningham, and Tedder commanded, "with Ike sitting as referee to settle contrary desires of the services.... The only major decision Ike can make in this operation is to call it off."[135]

The upshot of the meta-decisional machinations at Casablanca was that the two leading commanders of Husky would be two relatively unassertive men, one of whom was back on his heels. Dwight Eisenhower in early 1943 was disconcerted by recent events and not as forceful as he would be the next year. In Casablanca, he had proposed to attack toward the Tunisian seaport of Sfax, thereby separating Jürgen von Arnim's Fifth Panzer Army in northern Tunisia from Erwin Rommel's Afrika Korps, retreating through Libya. Alexander and Brooke had criticized the plan, in that it would expose the Allied forces in Sfax to attacks from both sides. Per one historian: "Brooke had assailed Eisenhower over [the suggested attack]. Unprepared and intimidated, Eisenhower had mounted a halfhearted defense before retreating in disarray from the room."[136] (The leading German and Italian commanders in Africa had not shared Brooke's scorn for Eisenhower's proposal. They had feared just such an attack toward the Gulf of Gabès and had taken steps to forestall it.[137] Erwin Rommel stated that [such an attack toward the Mediterranean coast southwest of Sfax, close to Gabès] was "my main fear." The threat of such a stroke had spurred him to hurry his Korps westward. This fear of Rommel was the reverse of the German sigh of relief that Eisenhower would imagine on July 10: it implied—zero-sum-game-theoretically—his judgment that Eisenhower's proposal would have been a good action for the Allies: in his words, their "correct operational decision."[138] Eisenhower, uncandidly and untruthfully in his memoirs, did not mention having pushed this idea at Casablanca and, instead, related only that he had "disapproved" this plan about which "a portion of the staff became obsessed."[139])

It was a low moment for the Supreme Commander. His chief proponent, Marshall, was "irked at Eisenhower's limp showing before the combined chiefs."[140] Inasmuch as neither Churchill nor Roosevelt either thanked him for what he had done or more than perfunctorily praised him at Casablanca, he felt that "his neck is in a noose."[141]

On April 7, 1943, Eisenhower reported that, should the Germans have more than two divisions in Sicily, Husky would have "scant promise of success." Churchill erupted, responding that, for Husky, convoys to Russia had been suspended. Should the operation be canceled because of two-plus Wehrmacht divisions, "what Stalin would think of this, when he has 185 German divisions on his front, I cannot imagine." The Chiefs of Staff of the UK and the U.S. backed up the Prime Minister. Eisenhower, described by Omar Bradley as "much-chastened," cabled on April 12 that Husky would go forward.[142] George Patton, the next month, diagnosed "inferiority complex-[es]" in both Eisenhower and Alexander. He wrote to his diary and his wife of the fear that both Ike and Alex had of Monty. Eisenhower sensed that to get on the wrong side of the man whom El Alamein had made an imperial hero was to risk being fired.[143] Ike, on May 8, asked George to write to Marshall praising his diligence, audacity, and adroit handling of the British. Patton, out of gratitude to Eisenhower, wrote the requested letter, feeling that he "lied in a good cause."[144]

While Eisenhower was then so shaken as to ask friends to write such letters, the initial planning for Husky was dysfunctional, undertaken by men of low standing who would not command it, ill-directed and -supported by their superiors and with unclarity as to their mandate. Force 141, named for the room in the St. George Hotel in Algiers in which its first meeting was held, first planned Husky. It was led by British Major General Charles Gairdner, described as "ill-equipped" and "out of his depth."[145] Eisenhower, Alexander, and Montgomery were, in the early months of 1943, too involved in the Tunisian campaign and other matters to devote much time to Husky. Montgomery, first notified in February that he would command in Sicily, reacted to the initial plans much as he had to those for Dieppe: finding them "a dog's breakfast"[146] and revamping them. Gairdner resigned—sensing his lack of clout and seeing the work of his task force as an exercise in futility.

Once the forces of Husky were ashore, the physical separation of the top officers by hundreds of miles—was another obstacle to adept decisions. For much of the campaign, Eisenhower was in Algiers; Alexander, in Sicily; Cunningham, in Malta; and Tedder, in Tunis. Many—including the British Chiefs of Staff, Bernard Montgomery, and the British and American Official Histories—were astonished and appalled by such separation.[147]

*   *   *

The synopsis of Allied words on possibly interdicting German flight consisted of: prior assurances by the air forces and navies that, when the German withdrawal got going in earnest, they would ramp up and blast and stop the retreaters; air force explanation that intense flak and inviting targets elsewhere precluded sending many planes to the strait; naval explanation that Baade's unsilenced guns ruled out sailing significant vessels into the waterway; and untrue assertions after the fact by both services that they had done much. For effective interdiction to have occurred, either Eisenhower or Alexander would have had to work out with Cunningham and Tedder the requisite actions, have issued the necessary orders, and have monitored events to make sure that both services were doing what they had to. Such a positive scenario was made the less possible by the interleaved leadership structure concocted at Casablanca, by the passivity of Eisenhower and Alexander, and by the hundreds of miles separating them from each other and from the air force and naval commands. It was, above all, a failure of meta-decision.

Principals and Agents; Unity of Command

Underlying each of these poor meta-decisions was a topic studied by decision scientists, game theorists, economists, lawyers, and management specialists: the *principal-agent* relationship—a preeminent aspect of which for the military is the issue of *command unity*. Per decision scientists John Pratt and Richard Zeckhauser:

> Whenever one individual depends on the action of another, an *agency relationship* arises. The individual taking the action is called the *agent*. The affected party is the *principal*. In common parlance, the doctor is the agent, the patient the principal. The consultant is the agent, the client the principal. The corporate executive is the principal, his subordinates the agents. The corporate executive in turn is an agent for the shareholders.[148]

In the Second World War, the foremost principals were the citizens of the fighting countries; their agents, their national leaders—who were in turn principals with respect to their military chiefs; who were principals toward their top subordinates; and so on, down to the rifle-toting privates, the ultimate agents.

Among the findings of researchers on the principal-agent relationship pertinent to war is that of "information asymmetries—agents typically know more about their tasks than their principals do, though principals may know more about what they want accomplished."[149] Your dentist knows more than you about what could and should be done for your teeth. The company commanders at Brolo knew more about the individual hills in front of them and the enemy behind those hills than did George Patton; Ernst-Günter Baade knew more about where to position individual guns to command the Strait of Messina than did Albert Kesselring. Patton, however, knew more than his company commanders what might be strategically achieved by amphibious end runs; Kesselring knew better than Baade how command of the strait might set the stage for a sequenced retreat out of Sicily.

Another focus of principal-agent research is that of agency loss. Neither businesses nor armies "function as well as [they] would if all information were costlessly shared or if the incentives of principal and agent(s) could be costlessly aligned." When agents do not do what their principals would want them to "*agency loss* or *agency costs*" result. "The agency loss is the most severe when the interests or values of the principal and agent diverge substantially, and information monitoring is costly."[150] In Spain in July of 1812, Spanish general Carlos de España was told by Viscount Wellington—acting as principal to España as his agent—to hold the bridge at Alba de Tormes. De España did not. The result was that the French army, when soon defeated near Salamanca, slipped away. The shortfall from what would have been gained, had de España done as Wellington had wished, was agency loss.

Agency losses are likely greater when principals and agents have different levels of risk aversion—as Kenneth Arrow, a 1972 Nobelist in Economics, has noted.[151] Abraham Lincoln, in July 1863 after the battle of Gettysburg, wanted the victorious general, George Meade, to attack Robert E. Lee before the defeated Confederates could escape across the swollen Potomac River. The President, as agent of the Northerners who had elected him and as principal over Meade, was willing to risk the attack for what he, and historians since, have viewed as a huge potential gain: the destruction of Lee's Army of Northern Virginia. Just what Meade, Lincoln's agent, thought is not fully known. His recent victory in what remains the largest battle ever fought in the Western Hemisphere had made him a national hero. Perhaps he did not wish to risk the loss of much of that status that a reverse at the Potomac might bring, while the possible enhancement of his status that a further victory there might achieve was not so great in his mind as to justify the risk.

Meade did not attack and Lee got away—from Lincoln's perspective, a tragic agency loss. Such motivation and resulting agency loss was similarly seen in Bernard Montgomery's cautious pursuit of Erwin Rommel after El Alamein.[152] Eisenhower wrote to Marshall in May 1943 that Montgomery was "so proud of his success to date that he will never willingly make a single move until he is absolutely certain of success."[153]

Bryn Zeckhauser and Aaron Sandoski—researchers into decision-making at high levels of business and government—have noted that analogous situations occur in corporations: as executives may shy away from steps offering expected gains to their companies, if they sense that unfortunate results might hurt them personally. Their suggested key to effective management is to recognize the distinction made by decision science between the quality of the decision and that of the outcome. They judged that to "overcome loss aversion and take calculated risks is a core element in turning risks into competitive advantages.... The most important incentive is to reward people in whatever way you wish—money, promotions, awards—for simply *making* a smart decision, not on the outcome of their decisions."[154] Finding best ways to do so in war should be a priority for commanders.

Professor Arrow also noted that "multiple principals" make agency relationships "more complicated."[155] Dwight Eisenhower in the summer of 1943 could not disagree. Fair assessment of his performance in Sicily must consider the context in which he commanded: not just his overstuffed roster of responsibilities, but also the challenges of being simultaneously the beleaguered agent of many and the principal of more. Harold Macmillan described the Supreme Commander on July 29: "Poor Eisenhower is getting pretty harassed. Telegrams (private, personal, and most immediate) pour in upon him from" the Combined Chiefs of Staff, Marshall, Roosevelt, Secretary of State Cordell Hull, Churchill, and Foreign Secretary Anthony Eden. "All these instructions are naturally contradictory and conflicting." In consequence, per Macmillan, Ike became "rather rattled by their constant pressure of telegraphic advice on every conceivable point."[156]

Getting one general to do what the superior entity—in Eisenhower's case, the Western Alliance—wanted had similarities to the managerial challenges of private companies. Determining the best working arrangements for employees—the structuring of their contracts, the monitoring of their work, their incentivizing with productivity bonuses, and the like—has been a leading area of research into principal-agent relationships.

Principal-agent researchers have inquired into the agency losses that result: when physicians are so concerned about possible malpractice liability as to order tests and procedures that cost far more than their expected values of information would justify and that might on net be harmful to their patients; when lawyers take legal actions that promise to increase their fees while not serving the best interests of their clients; when financial advisors invest client funds in excessively risky securities that pay them (at-times-undisclosed) commissions. To what extent should the Combined Chiefs have worried that Eisenhower, as their agent, might have different levels of risk aversion, or different priorities, from their own? Might he act in ways that would not well serve them and/or their nations?

Kenneth Arrow noted that theorists have long focused on the optimal motivation of employees as agents using such levers as salaries, bonuses, and firings. In "real-world practice," however, he observed that such motivation may be achieved instead by "systems of ethics, internalized during the education process and enforced in some measure by formal punishments and more broadly by reputations"—thereby obviating the "very complex fee functions" derived from theoretical models.[157] In armies over the centuries, the predominant ethos has been one of obedience to superiors: whereby subordinates ideally seek to do what their immediate bosses wish them to. Inasmuch as Eisenhower seems in fact to have aspired to do what the Combined Chiefs—and especially Marshall—wanted him to, the possibility of his causing worrisome agency loss was reduced. For other generals in the war—the motives of Clark, Montgomery, and Patton, among others, have been questioned—this seems not so much to have been the case.

In the United States, the principle of obedience to superiors was linked to that of unity of command: each subordinate soldier and officer was to follow the orders of one immediate superior. Boot camps drove this point home to privates, who obeyed their corporals and they their sergeants and so on up to the top of the pyramid, where each military theater commander was to defer to the highest civilian authorities. In the first months of the UK and U.S. as fighting Allies, this was modified: theater commanders reported to the Combined Chiefs of Staff and they to the top civilians.

The U.S. Joint Chiefs of Staff in 2017 defined *unity of command,* to mean that

> all forces operate under a single commander with the requisite authority to direct all forces employed in pursuit of a common purpose;

the objective being

> to ensure unity of effort under one responsible commander for every objective.[158]

In private companies, unity of command now denotes strict, unambiguous hierarchy: each employee reporting to one superior.

The great generals of history—Alexander, Hannibal, Scipio, Caesar, Genghis Khan, and their successors—had had unified authorities. The sixty-fourth maxim of Napoleon was that "nothing is so important in war as an undivided command."

American respect for the principle of command unity derived in part from the Civil War: as Ulysses Grant was in 1864 made General-in-Chief and the next year achieved victory. The U.S. War Department in 1914 laid down that "unity of command is essential to success.... All troops assigned to the execution of a distinct tactical task must be placed under one command."[159] Disregard for this principle has been seen as a factor underlying American military disappointments in Vietnam and Afghanistan.[160]

U.S. belief in the essential unity of authority was strengthened by the First World War. The takeaway of Americans and of many others on the conflict was: that the Western Allies in the first years of the conflict floundered and foundered from ill-coordination; that the crisis created by German attacks in March 1918 forced the Allies[161] to assign to French general Ferdinand Foch unified command on the Western Front; and that victory soon resulted. George Marshall, at the Arcadia Conference on Christmas Day of 1941, referenced the earlier war in pitching the principle:

> As a result of what I saw in France [in 1917 and 1918] ... I feel very strongly that the most important consideration is the question of unity of command.... I am convinced that there must be one man in command of the entire theater—air, ground, and ships. We can not manage by cooperation.... If we make a plan for unified command now, it will solve nine-tenths of our troubles.

While speaking of one theater—that of the western Pacific and Southeast Asia had been under discussion—Marshall was touting a tenet for all. In the earlier conflict, "it was," he said, "not until 1918" that "we had to come to this"—with the result that "much valuable time, blood, and treasure had been needlessly sacrificed. If we could decide on a unified command now, it would be a great advance over what was accomplished during the World War."[162]

Two days later, Marshall proposed to Churchill and other UK leaders in Washington that British General Sir Archibald Wavell be assigned unified command over a region extending from Australia and the Philippines to India. The Royal Navy was said to have "kicked like bay steers" against the idea of having to obey any soldier.[163] Brooke, back in London, thought the concept "wild and half-baked" and that Wavell was being set up as the fall guy for the inevitable initial defeats that would be inflicted by Japan.[164] Churchill, also foreseeing "the Japanese onslaught," at first resisted Marshall's proposal but then, having been lobbied by the U.S. Army chief, Hopkins, and Roosevelt, concluded that "we must meet the American view."[165] Wavell established the HQ for his unified theater command in Java on January 15, 1942, but could not prevent the imminent Allied loss of Singapore and of much of the Dutch East Indies. His command was dissolved on March 1.

The U.S., undaunted by this Eastern experience, continued to press for undivided commands. In a meeting of the Combined Chiefs on May 28, 1942, Eisenhower made a major point of it, arguing that "committee command could not conduct a major battle."[166] Later that year, the U.S. directive for the North African landings laid down that "The Commander in Chief, Allied Force, [Eisenhower] will command all forces assigned to Operation TORCH, under the principle of unity of command." The actual lines of authority established for that operation, however, interwove American and British officers in what has been termed "a mixed command" that "endeavored to reconcile the principle of 'unity of command' with that of 'balanced national representation.'"[167] The challenges of such reconciliation would persist for the remainder of the war.

Alan Brooke, in writing of the Casablanca Conference, conceded "that centralised command was essential," but also expressed in the same paragraph his satisfaction at having undermined Eisenhower by putting Alexander under him to exercise effective authority. He explained his thinking:

> From many points of view it was desirable to hand [command in Africa] over to the Americans, but unfortunately up to now Eisenhower ... had neither the tactical nor strategical experience required for such a task. By bringing Alexander over from the Middle East and appointing him as Deputy to Eisenhower, we were carrying out a move which could not help flattering and pleasing the Americans in so far as we were placing our senior and experienced commander to function under their commander who had no war experience.... We were pushing Eisenhower up into the stratosphere and rarefied atmosphere of a Supreme Commander, where he would be free to devote his time to the political and inter-allied problems, whilst we inserted under him one of our own commanders to deal with the military situations and to restore the necessary drive and co-ordination which had been so seriously lacking.[168]

The same line of thought led to the insertion of Cunningham in the command structure between Eisenhower and the navies and of Tedder between him and the air forces. The CIGS, as he frankly wrote in his diary and told his fellow Britons, thought little of the strategic acumen of the U.S. decision makers—from Roosevelt and Marshall on down—with whom he dealt.[169] Eisenhower was to him but a genial and lucky but militarily-dense American, whose authority it would be well to undermine—even though such undermining should have been expected to lead to calamities of intermediate size, like that that actually ensued at Messina. To accept the chances of such shots in the Allies' feet was better, Brooke may have thought, than to risk the chest wounds to the cause that turning all over to the smiling Yank could easily lead to.

Eisenhower, when it came to command unity, was not the clueless Kansan that Brooke deemed him—not so flattered by the exalted title bestowed on him at Casablanca as not to notice that it was a sugar coating on a bitter pill, laid on to conceal that he was being stripped of much authority. He was described on February 10, 1943, as "burning inside" that the Combined Chiefs were giving directives to his subordinates. They should, he held, receive their orders only from him, while he should answer to the Chiefs.[170] Eisenhower had, two days earlier, voiced these frustrations to Marshall: that the British wanted "'committee' rather than 'single' command." He was irked that the Combined Chiefs had ordered Alexander "to *cooperate* [his emphasis] with Cunningham and Tedder in executing [Husky]. Manifestly, responsibility again falls directly on me." In their present mode, the Combined Chiefs might well take an action that he would deem "a definite invasion of my own proper field.... Naturally, there are many broad naval and air problems that will be solved by the respective Commanders in Chief under my direction, but it seems impossible for the British to grasp the utter simplicity of the system that we employ."[171]

Eisenhower would not get the unified command he wanted. The British continued to resist having their proven commanders be totally answerable to an underaccomplished American and Marshall did not secure undiluted authority for him. Eisenhower came to see that he had to do the best that he could as a committee head. By April of 1943, he was reduced "to plaintively begging General Alexander, his subordinate, for the 'essentials of your broad tactical plan' for the attack on Tunis." Churchill then intervened, asking Alex to keep Ike better informed, since "so much depends on going through the ceremonial processes"—rites presumably meant to promote the fiction of Eisenhower's operational control. As Harold Macmillan expressed the arrangement, the British would manage matters in the Mediterranean as "the Greek slaves ran the operations of the Emperor Claudius."[172]

Two British commanders, Arthur Tedder and Alan Brooke, voiced lip-service allegiance to command unity but seem never to have believed in it. Tedder wrote that the key to Allied success in the Mediterranean pre–Husky had been "unity of command," by which the air forces had been "co-ordinated with land and sea power."[173] One page later, he stated that the successes of Allied air in the North African campaign "proved co-operation with, but not subordination to, the Army, to be the right way of employing the Air Force in support of land power."[174] Tedder disliked the subordination of his planes not just to "the Army" but also to any other higher authority. Autonomous, somewhat-voluntary cooperation with other services rather than subordination to one commander was, however, not an elaboration of how command unity should be achieved but, instead, a repudiation of it. Tedder's air forces believed that they had the wisdom and the right to determine where they should strafe and bomb. They did not let the ground and naval commanders—from the initial Husky landings through the ultimate German getaway at Messina—even know how much they could be counted on. This attitude of entitled independence truncated the Sicilian triumph.

Brooke wrote and thought similarly to Tedder. His postulation at Casablanca that "centralised command was essential"[175] was an empty endorsement of America-pushed theory—which, however, he disemboweled practically by limiting Eisenhower to titular preeminence, while giving hands-on direction to Alexander, Cunningham, and Tedder.

The British, in and between the world wars, had not agreed with the Americans on the importance of command unity. Instead, as indicated by the take of Tedder, they felt that cooperation among forces should be the guiding tenet.[176] Churchill, on October 20, 1941, wrote to Roosevelt that "'Unity of Command' could not be extended to cover the Navy.... In combined operations, of which we have a long and variegated experience, we have never followed the practice of subordinating the Navy to the Army, or vice versa."[177] Britain, by giving Eisenhower an impressive title that would prove as hollow operationally as they had hoped it would, got the command structure they wanted: three significantly autonomous commanders under Eisenhower being asked to cooperate; with the four commanders meeting occasionally to further their coordination.

Whether the shortfall of the Sicilian victory owed more to the failure of the commanders to focus on preventing German flight or to the diffusion of authority is moot. Both factors were implicated. No commander, had he realized the importance of forestalling German getaway, had the clout to make it happen. One American historian, in assigning blame for the Allied bumbling, would side with Eisenhower, considering that the British imposition at Casablanca of "their own committee system of separate C-in-Cs for air, ground and sea operations" proved in Sicily "wholly ineffective."[178] The 53,000 German escapees could in this view be deemed the price paid for the Allied adoption of Brooke's command arrangement. The CIGS may have felt that worse might have happened, had Eisenhower had the authority he thought appropriate.

On May 2, 1943, Bernard Montgomery had proposed to Brooke a unified command for Sicily: "I should run HUSKY ... it is a nice tidy command for one Army HQ and Eighth Army should run the whole thing." Patton, in Montgomery's scenario, would command an American corps under him; Alexander would finish off the campaign in Tunisia and have nothing to do with the next op.[179] That the Americans would never have accepted such an arrangement should have made it easier for them to understand why the British did not want comparable authority to be given to Eisenhower.

The Allies would at Messina pay the price for Brooke's ever-so-clever circumvention of command unity—which had vanished into clouds of Casablanca hashish haze—and for Marshall's having allowed it to happen.

Why Did the Germans in Sicily Do Better Than the Allies?

The Axis Alliance in early July of 1943 linked Germany with a co-belligerent that wanted out of the war, that by the end of the month would have ousted its leader, and that in two months would have signed an armistice. The tasks of the German commanders in Sicily were, moreover, made the more challenging by having in Adolf Hitler and Hermann Göring two superiors, who, although more than 1,000 miles to the north, issued orders to them on matters large and small. Nevertheless, in the quality of the decisions made and in the results achieved, Albert Kesselring, Hans-Valentin Hube, and their subordinates outperformed the Western Allies.

Why had it happened?

One advantage that German decision makers in Sicily had over those of the Allies was that the differences between the national approaches of the Axis Allies had less effect. The Germans and Italians, like the Americans and British, often regarded one another with disdain and ill feeling. These attitudes of the UK and U.S. made each unwilling to defer too much to the other and led to independent actions and lapses of coordination. The Italians, after the first few days of Husky, acceded to the overall command of Kesselring and Hube.

That Kesselring and his subordinates were on the same page was in beneficial contrast to the divergent aims of those below Eisenhower. Kesselring, Hube, and their division commanders were in sync: devoted to delaying the Allied conquest of Sicily, before slipping back to Calabria.

Kesselring, moreover, acted assertively—in contrast to the somewhat-abashed Eisenhower—in exercising, indeed exceeding, his authority. While Kesselring was subject to many of the same constraints placed on other Wehrmacht leaders—such as lacking authority to order withdrawals without the prior approval of Hitler—he ignored them. On August 8, when, in his judgment, the time had come to move his men over the strait, he ordered it without awaiting the Führer's okay. This action, he said, made him for a considerable time *"persona ingrata"* in Hitler's headquarters—which, given the successful retreat, did not unduly bother him.[180] (Per one historian, absent Kesselring's order, "the entire German corps in Sicily would have been lost."[181] Given that the Allies did not come close to effective interdiction and that Hitler had already approved the evacuation, if not the precise timing, this seems an overstatement.) Had Dwight Eisenhower or Harold Alexander had anything like the self-confidence and focus of Albert Kesselring, either might have acted to prevent so many of their enemy from escaping.

The Perspective of Game Theory

Game theorists might have viewed the confrontation in Sicily in the simplified form of one basic decision for each side. For the Germans the choice was between

running: briskly withdrawing from the island; or

reinforcing: sending in more troops to slow the Allied conquest, while hoping that all units would eventually be safely withdrawn.

The Allies could have acted either

aggressively: undertaking actions that risked increasing their own casualties in order to prevent large-scale German getaway; or

deliberately: moving cautiously toward Messina, minimizing the risks to their own men while also lowering the chances of significantly capturing or destroying enemy units.

Most commentators, beginning with Dwight Eisenhower, believe that the Allies—whether their opponent ran or reinforced—would have done better to have acted aggressively, thereby getting a substantially better expected outcome. The Germans knew that to reinforce before running, rather than to run at once, was to risk the major loss of 50,000 men for the marginal, possible gain of delaying the Allies by at most a few weeks.[182] Albert Kesselring was, however, so sure of his other-side perception—which told him that the Allies would make their inferior choice—as to take the major risk for the marginal upside and was backed by Adolf Hitler.

Risk Aversion

The OSP of Kesselring was significantly based on his sense of Allied risk aversion. One biographer of Harold Alexander, judged that the assignment of the overall ground commander in Sicily had been to achieve "continued success," without incurring "the risk of defeat"—which "the Allies, and Churchill in particular, could not afford." Alexander was seen to have had limited appetite for or tolerance of risk: the "hazards of the landing" had been so great as "to preclude Alexander from taking any further risks"—such as attempting to surround German divisions.[183]

Albert Kesselring had the same view of the fighting in Sicily. He saw in the Allied command pervasive shunning of hazards—which he expressed as "a dominating thought ... to make sure of success, a thought that led it to use orthodox methods." In consequence, "it was almost always possible for me, despite [poor intelligence] to foresee the next strategic or tactical move of my opponents."[184] Later, in mainland Italy, Kesselring faced Mark Clark and, per one historian, soon sensed his risk aversion—which he "would use ... to his advantage for months."[185]

Many have thought American generals, in war after war, overly reluctant to take risks. To Patton in October 1944, that was a shortcoming of Bradley: "I wish he had a little daring."[186] American historians have deemed U.S. generals in the European campaign of 1944 and 1945 characterized by "unimaginative caution ... competent but addicted to playing it safe."[187] General James Gavin believed that the war could have been won by the end of 1944 "at considerably less cost in blood and resources, if [Allied leaders] were willing to take more chances."[188] Thomas Ricks, having reviewed American generalship from George Marshall to David Petraeus, concluded that the national trait of excessive risk aversion extended from Omar Bradley ("prudent to a fault"[189]) through Korea and Vietnam to Afghanistan and Iraq.[190]

Organizational Behavior

As at Dieppe, the Organizational Behavior Model of Graham Allison helps to explain what happened and what did not. Organizations, per Allison, are "oriented toward doing whatever they do."[191] They determine what they want to do, then seek to tweak the overall goals of governments and alliances toward "objectives most congruent with their special capacities and ... beliefs."[192] The Allied air forces in the Mediterranean wanted to bomb mainland Italy; the navies, to cement their control of the sea. Both resisted diversion from their dominant desires to prevent German flight from Sicily. Had General Eisenhower asked Admiral Cunningham or Air Marshal Tedder what the Allies should prioritize, each would have emphasized what his service force wished to do. When Alexander actually asked what the air forces and navies could do to keep the Germans from slipping away, neither gave the considered and objective answers that might have sealed off the Strait of Messina—but that would also have pulled their pilots and helmsmen away from what they wanted to do.

How Bad Were the Consequences of the Non-Decision at Messina?

In summary, while there is consensus that the Allies bungled in letting 53,000 Germans cross over from Sicily to Calabria, there is none on what the Allies should have done nor on which potential Allied decision maker should have made it happen. Nor has there been analysis of how bad the escape of 53,000 Germans was for the Allies.

Several suggested steps for the Allies—initially landing closer to Messina or landing in Calabria or thrusting soon and hard toward Messina or coordinating better the drives of the two armies or better combining those drives with amphibious outflankings or having their planes and boats prevent escape—have been touted as likely to have reduced the number of fleeing Germans. The actions would have had costs for the Allies in terms of resources committed and casualties incurred, as well as in such opportunity costs as having to cut back on bombing mainland Europe.

To estimate the consequences of not acting to prevent German escape, one possible Allied step that was suggested by Dwight Eisenhower, Alfredo Guzzoni, and Albert Kesselring may be considered: landing in Calabria. We might suppose that the Allies, once securely ashore in Sicily and having established airfields there, had landed at the Catanzaro neck of Calabria and had there blocked the eighteen-mile-wide isthmus. This would have been a modification and elaboration of Operation Goblet—a landing near Crotone—which had earlier been contingently planned. The Axis, per Kesselring, had no forces to prevent such an action.

Once the Allies were ashore at Catanzaro and quickly dug in, the Axis could have drawn on forces in Sicily to attack from the south and on forces in mainland Italy to attack from the north. Since, however, the Allies in the neck would have been supported by naval guns and air cover, Axis assaults on positions in the neck would likely have failed—as would later German attacks on the Allied beachheads at Salerno and Anzio. The best German reaction to Allied capture of the Catanzaro Isthmus would seem to have been to attack only from the south. Such an attack would likely have led, as was the case at Anzio, to more German than Allied casualties—perhaps 10,000 versus 5,000. The ultimate result would have been that the 53,000 Germans on Sicily would have been captured or killed, at a cost of 5,000 Allied casualties.

This hypothetical result may be compared with the actual outcome of 53,000 Germans having gotten away to become the rock ribs of resistance to subsequent Allied advances northward in mainland Italy. Those advances had the objects of drawing Germans from other fronts to the peninsula, of removing German soldiers from the war, and of taking territory—especially locations for airfields and such symbolic prizes as Rome.

In fighting from May 11 to June 4 of 1944—from the opening of the successful attack on the Gustav Line through the taking of Rome—Allied casualties totaled 44,000 versus 38,000

German.[193] These numbers suggest that, in their fighting slog up the Italian Peninsula, the Allies suffered eight casualties for every seven German casualties inflicted. Well over 53,000 Wehrmacht men were put out of action in the twenty months of fighting in mainland Italy. To the extent that the Allies were battling to remove German soldiers from the war, allowing 53,000 Wehrmacht men to flee Sicily meant that 61,000 (8/7 of 53,000, rounded off) additional Allied casualties would occur—casualties that would be suffered later to diminish German forces by 53,000. To have landed at the Catanzaro Neck versus what the Allies actually did and did not do would have saved them about 56,000 (= 61,000 minus 5,000) casualties.

Of the Allied casualties between May 11 and June 4, 1944, eighteen percent were deaths, three fourths woundings, and seven percent missing. Prorating the 56,000 Allied casualties that would presumptively have been saved by landing at Catanzaro by these proportions means that about 10,100 of them would have been deaths; 42,000, woundings; and 3,900 missing. The bottom line is that by not landing at Catanzaro, the actual actions and nonactions of the Allies resulted in an estimated 10,100 additional dead, 42,000 additional wounded, and 3,900 additional missing Allied soldiers.

This quantification of the consequences of not landing at the Catanzaro Neck is suppositious. Perhaps alternative Allied actions would have been better. Perhaps the numerical assumptions made here are off the mark. Perhaps way off—by a factor of two or more. If so, it would be well to redo the bare-bones analysis above—to arrive at better estimates of the results of alternative Allied actions.

That 4,000 Allied casualties and 1,000 Allied deaths were incurred at Dieppe made clear how catastrophic that raid was and led to its decision making being judged "hare-brained" and worse. Because no attempt, until now, has been made to estimate the consequences of the mass escape at Messina—an order of magnitude or so worse than Dieppe—there has been no comparable grasp of how bad that outcome was and no comparable sense of how flawed were the earlier meta-decisions and subsequent non-decision that had led to it.

The virtual unanimity that the Allies blundered in Sicily means that thousands of Allied soldiers—maybe about 56,000—were later killed, or were badly wounded, or went missing because better Anglo-American actions were not taken.

Conclusions

The unscathed sailing away of so many Germans to Calabria owed to two main decision-impairing factors: the Combined Chiefs of Staff, the meta-decision makers, having disregarded the principle of command unity—as noted by many authors and reprising the main cause of the disaster at Dieppe; and the strategic decision makers having "lost sight of" a crucial "objective: to seal the Strait of Messina."[194]

Would the main decision makers, Dwight Eisenhower or Harold Alexander, have done better in Sicily had they had on their staffs management specialists, decision scientists, and/or game theorists of the twenty-first century?

Perhaps.

Both generals knew that they did not have unified commands and likely expected the kinds of problems that that led to. They evidently, however, both inferred from the contexts in which they had been placed that that could not be remedied. They might well have benefited from latter-day management mavins with insights on situations in which loosely-controlled subordinates or co-decision-makers have variant agendas and with tips on how to optimize outcomes in such settings. (Like game theory, management science has also been seen to have been born in the Second World War.[195])

The decision-scientific and game-theoretic habit of quantification might have helped at Messina. With much else on their minds, the Western Allies neglected to focus on interdicting German flight—with the result that Eisenhower saw too late that such passive non-decisions can have effects as significant as those of active choices. What was needed was a way to apportion attention among multiple concerns. Decision science and game theory would later have such a way: in quantifying the importance of different—and occasionally competing—objectives.

That the Combined Chiefs of Staff, Eisenhower, Alexander, Cunningham, and Tedder, once their armies were securely ashore in Sicily, were mainly intent on knocking Italy out of the war was not unreasonable: it should indeed have been their lead focus. What was regrettable, though, was that this number-one priority so preoccupied these decision makers that they lost sight of number two: thwarting German flight. Decision science and game theory could have expressed numerically the relative importance of progress toward the two objectives—perhaps in terms of expected contributions to ultimate victory—and have helped to ensure that each received due attention. These disciplines might also have quantified the connections between the two goals: estimating the effects that allowing German escape would have on subsequent operations in Italy—which turned out to be significant.

Appropriately dealing with plural priorities tests decision makers and has been addressed by management experts and by such decision scientists as Ward Edwards, Ralph Keeney, and Howard Raiffa.[196] It nevertheless remains an imperfectly-resolved challenge.[197] It has been felt that, for many organizations, as few as two goals are too many; that even acknowledging a second priority distracts and detracts from realizing the first.

The Wehrmacht, however, balanced well the attention it paid to the same two considerations.

In a two-player, zero-sum game with full information, which Sicily effectively was, both sides should have the same levels of concern for all factors affecting results—since all gains and losses are felt equally, if oppositely, by the two opponents. The Allies and the Wehrmacht should, game-theoretically, have cared roughly the same about the Allied conquest of Sicily being slowed by a few weeks, about German escape, and about Italy staying in or exiting the war. The Germans knew that the war status of Italy and the extraction of their troops from Sicily were more important than delaying the Allied conquest of the island—but also that the last had positive, if relatively minor, value. Throughout the last 35 days of the 38-day campaign, the Wehrmacht high command kept in mind the priority in Sicily of getting its men to Calabria. The Allies would have done better to have accorded about the same level of attention and urgency as their enemy to the possibility of German getaway across the strait of Scylla and Charybdis.

4

Anzio

At 0200 hours on January 22, 1944, American and British forces began splashing onto the shore at and near Anzio and Nettuno, Italy, two beach resorts on the Tyrrhenian Sea, thirty miles south of Rome. Opposition was minimal, as but one German company had been posted there. The Allied invaders were designated VI Corps; their attack, Operation Shingle. American Major General John Lucas commanded. His immediate superior was his countryman, Lieutenant General Mark Clark, heading the American Fifth Army, the II Corps of which was fighting on the southern front north of Naples. Clark reported to British General Sir Harold Alexander, in overall charge of Allied ground forces in Italy: Fifteenth Army Group—which also included on the Adriatic Coast the British Eighth Army under Lieutenant-General Sir Oliver Leese.

* * *

Operation Shingle was a smaller part of a smaller part of a smaller part: less than half of all Allied troops in Italy; with those combined armies towered over in importance by Operation Overlord, which would be launched 136 days later; itself involving but a fraction of the forces engaged on the Eastern Front.

Two decisions for Shingle stand out over others. More than anyone else and more on December 25, 1943, than on any other day, Winston Churchill had made the first: whether to undertake the landing. John Lucas, on January 22, 1944—once ashore and meeting no resistance to speak of—faced the second: how aggressively to move inland.

The Strategic Decision: Should the Allies in January 1944 Have Landed at Anzio?

Alternatives: to persevere with the attacks northward in Italy that, since October 1943, had been progressing slowly or passively to hold the Allied positions that had been gained by the late fall.

When made: on Saturday, December 25, 1943—after months of on-and-off mulling; before another week-plus of wavering.

The decision makers: Churchill, Roosevelt, and their leading generals.

Conclusions: the outcome: disappointing per hopes, possibly a plus but probably a minus on net and in comparison with alternatives; **the decision:** neither clearly good nor clearly bad; **suboptimal aspects:** poor other-side perception—which possibly induced an ill-conceived bluff, dissuasion of dissent via groupthink and the marginalization and exclusion of possible disagreers from decision discussions; possible delusion by the sunk-cost fallacy; **most to be lauded:** Albert Kesselring; **most to be faulted:** no one.

The Battle of Kursk in midsummer 1943 had seen initial German gains that were halted after ten days and were succeeded by Russian counterattacks that again recaptured Kharkov and, by the end of the year, had also recovered Orel, Smolensk, and Kiev.

U.S. forces in the Pacific in the second half of 1943 advanced in the Solomon Islands and on New Guinea and took Makin and Tarawa in the Gilberts.

From November 28 through December 1, 1943, Winston Churchill, Franklin Roosevelt, and Joseph Stalin met in Tehran. They there agreed that the Western Allies would launch Operation Overlord the next spring and that, after Germany had been defeated, the Soviet Union would declare war on Japan.

*   *   *

The British Eighth Army of Bernard Montgomery had, on September 3, 1943, crossed over unopposed from Messina to Calabria. Five days later, the Italian government of Marshal Pietro Badoglio announced that it had surrendered to the Allies, who the next day landed at Salerno, 25 miles southeast of Naples. The Germans seized most of Italy and their Tenth Army counterattacked at Salerno so sharply that the Allies considered re-embarking, before stabilizing the situation. The Tenth Army retreated to the north of Naples. German intelligence had learned where Benito Mussolini was being held and, on September 12, the deposed Duce was rescued by German commandos and installed as the puppet head of government in German-controlled northern Italy.

In early October, Allied forces approached the Volturno River, twenty miles north of Naples. Generals Dwight Eisenhower and Harold Alexander thought that they would take Rome, 100 miles beyond the Volturno, before the end of the month.[1] Franklin Roosevelt passed this assessment on to Joseph Stalin, as Winston Churchill readied for a triumphal visit to the Eternal City.[2] But the Allied advance soon slowed. Field Marshal Albert Kesselring conscripted Italians to prepare defensive lines in the Apennine Mountains—whose heights could interdict passage up the 85-mile-wide peninsula—while his Germans defended with skill and courage. Eisenhower cabled on October 9 that the transfer of German forces from north Italy to the South meant that "there will be very hard and bitter fighting before we can hope to reach Rome."[3]

Adolf Hitler had in fact considered withdrawing his forces north of Rome—as urged on him by Erwin Rommel. In the autumn of 1943, 163 Axis divisions served on the Eastern Front; 34, in France, Belgium, and Holland; and seventeen, in Italy. The Allies, after seven divisions were withdrawn for Overlord, retained eleven in Italy, but would soon add three more. Kesselring persuaded Hitler that the mountainous peninsula was well-suited for defense; that (as Churchill had been saying to his own generals and allies) losing Rome would be a signal triumph for the Allies; and that the airfields given up in a withdrawal would facilitate Allied strategic bombing.[4]

Hitler's autumnal decision to contest the way to Rome meant that it would not fall for another eight months. By that time, the U.S. Fifth Army alone would have suffered in Italy 125,000 casualties.[5]

Shortly after the capture of Naples on October 1, 1943, Alexander had contemplated landing five divisions behind the German lines and planners in Clark's Fifth Army had thought Anzio the best site. It soon, however, appeared that neither so large a force nor sufficient transports would be available. Clark, in consequence, proposed that Lucian Truscott's Third Division, beefed up to 24,000 men, have the honor of taking and holding a limited lodgement, until the rest of his army would push through from the south and link up. Truscott foresaw in the proposition not honor but horror: "there will be no survivors."[6] Clark backed off the idea.

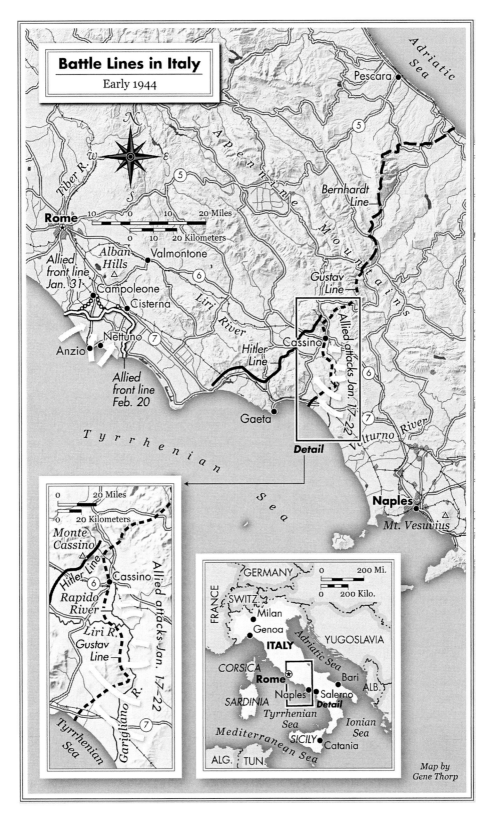

Battle Lines in Italy
Early 1944

Adriatic Sea

Pescara

5

Apennine Mountains

Bernhardt Line

Tiber R.

5

Rome

Gustav Line

Allied front line Jan. 31

Alban Hills

Valmontone

6

Campoleone

Cisterna

Liri River

Allied attacks Jan. 17–22

Nettuno

7

Cassino

6

Anzio

Hitler Line

7

Allied front line Feb. 20

Volturno River

Gaeta

Detail

T y r r h e n i a n   S e a

Naples

Mt. Vesuvius

0   20 Miles
0   20 Kilometers

Monte Cassino

Hitler Line

6   Cassino

Rapido River

Allied attacks Jan. 17–22

Liri R.
Gustav Line

7

Gariglian o R.

Tyrrhenian Sea

GERMANY

0   200 Mi.
0   200 Kilo.

FRANCE

SWITZ.

Milan

Genoa

ITALY

YUGOSLAVIA

Adriatic Sea

CORSICA

Rome

Bari

ALB.

Naples

Salerno

Detail

SARDINIA

Tyrrhenian Sea

Ionian Sea

Mediterranean Sea

SICILY

Catania

ALG.

TUN.

Map by
Gene Thorp

Eisenhower, however, kept open the possibility of an amphibious landing on the Tyrrhenian Coast: Operation Shingle. For it, he had secured approval from the Combined Chiefs of Staff that 68 landing ship, tanks (LSTs) be retained in the Mediterranean until December 15. On November 8, Eisenhower had the deadline for the craft extended to mid–January and directed Alexander to plan Shingle.[7] Clark, on December 18, judged that the landing could not be mounted by the middle of the next month and therefore recommended its cancellation—to which Alexander agreed.[8]

The demise of Shingle lasted one day. On December 19, Winston Churchill, in Carthage on the outskirts of Tunis recuperating from pneumonia, met with Alan Brooke. The PM and the CIGS found that they had each separately concluded that the slow Allied advance in Italy argued for an amphibious run around the southwestern end of the German line.[9] Churchill, that same day in a cable, pitched the idea to his Chiefs of Staff in London. The British Chiefs, three days later, having been briefed by Brooke, cabled back their agreement, which set the stage for Churchill to hold in Carthage a Christmas-morning conference of high officers. It was held in his bedroom, presided over in pajamas by the convalescing Prime Minister. (Churchill wore for the gathering that day what Harold Macmillan described as "a padded silk Chinese dressing-gown decorated with blue and gold dragons."[10]) It endorsed a landing at Anzio, sixty miles northwest of where Kesselring's Tenth Army—entrenched in its Gustav Line—faced Clark's Fifth. When, on December 28, Roosevelt cabled his assent, the decision was confirmed. The British Official History—with the American Official Histories and other authors in agreement[11]—summarized that "Mr. Churchill had decided ... and Mr. Roosevelt and the Combined Chiefs of Staff had concurred."[12]

The reasoning that led the Allies to the Tyrrhenian beaches of Anzio was laid out by Churchill in his Christmas-Day message to Roosevelt—with commentary in brackets.

25 Dec 43

I held a conference to-day with Eisenhower, and all [an overstatement, given the conspicuous absences of Clark and Lucas] his high officers. Report as follows:

General Alexander is prepared to execute the landing at Anzio about January 20 if he can get a lift of two divisions. This should decide the battle of Rome, and possibly achieve the destruction of a substantial part of enemy's army. To strike with less than two divisions would be to court disaster...

For this purpose eighty-eight L.S.T.s are required. These can only be obtained by delaying the return home of fifty-six L.S.T.s due to leave the Mediterranean from January 15 onward.... Nothing less than this will suffice...

It is believed that the lost three weeks [the delay of the LSTs] can be recovered and the existing prescribed build-up for "Overlord" maintained.

Having kept these fifty-six L.S.T.s in the Mediterranean so long [such past history being a superficially cogent, but irrelevant, detail: all that mattered was the best use going forward of the LSTs], it would seem irrational to remove them for the very week when they can render decisive service. What, also, could be more dangerous than to let the Italian battle stagnate and fester on for another three months? [? The Allied creep forward in Italy was disappointing and resource-costly but posed no risks remotely comparable to those of Shingle] We cannot afford to go forward leaving a vast half-finished job behind us. [Was this the "sunk-cost fallacy" noted by Daniel Kahneman and other decision scientists: the common phenomenon of misguidedly extending commitment to what has initially proven a disappointing decision, in hopes of gains that more than retrieve prior shortfalls, that turn an apparent bad-decision-bad-outcome into good-decision-good-outcome? Per Kahneman, "A rational decision maker is interested only in the future consequences."[13] Churchill's defenders might argue that his reference to the "half-finished job" was but a part of the sound argument that the initial goals in Italy might now be achieved via limited further commitment.] It therefore seemed to those present that every effort should be made to bring off Anzio.... If this opportunity is not grasped we must expect the ruin of the Mediterranean campaign of 1944. [Churchill here anticipated the research results of Amos Tversky and Daniel Kahneman with respect to the emotional impacts of decision framing. They found that the arbitrary wording of medical issues irrationally swayed even physicians and public health professionals.[14] Churchill's wording would be more likely to secure support for Shingle than if he had alternatively written that, in passing it on, "we must expect not to achieve the goals of the Mediterranean campaign of 1944"—the emotional difference between "expect the ruin of" and "expect not to achieve the goals of" being large]...[15]

The Prime Minister, the next day, described for his generals the results he foresaw: if the landing were made with "two full divisions plus paratroops it should be decisive, as it cuts the communications of the whole of the enemy forces facing the Fifth Army. The enemy must therefore annihilate the landing force by withdrawals from the Fifth Army front or immediately retreat."[16]

Years later, after Shingle's failure to achieve the results foreseen by Churchill, "two chapters of [his memoirs]," were, per one historian, "devoted to shifting responsibility for the Anzio debacle onto other shoulders."[17] The Prime Minister there admitted, "I had of course always been a partisan of the 'end run,' as the Americans call it."[18] He also, though, related that Alexander "thought the operation right and necessary" and that the stiff resistance of the Germans had "led General Eisenhower to contemplate an amphibious flanking attack"—to which, by late December, he "was already committed in principle."[19]

Eisenhower, in his own memoirs, counterspun: having no part of having at the end of 1943 been "committed in principle" to Operation Shingle. Like Churchill, he was seen as intent to put space between himself and Anzio Beach. His account of the war, written three years before the memoirs of Churchill on Shingle, featured the Prime Minister as prime mover: "the PM was almost exclusively responsible for the decision."[20] Eisenhower conceded having "agreed to the general desirability of continuing" the northward push in Italy,[21] but credited himself also with having voiced the problems that Shingle would face: that it would be risky and logistically difficult; that it "would not by itself compel" German withdrawal from their main front; and that "a force of several strong divisions would have to be established in Anzio before significant results could be achieved."[22]

But, Eisenhower said, "the Prime Minister was nevertheless determined to carry out the proposed operation. He and his staff ... felt certain that the assault would be a great and prompt success." The man who would in a week leave forever his Mediterranean command contented himself on Christmas Day, per his memoirs, with "repeat[ing] my warning as to the probable outcome" and acceded to Anzio.[23] (Julian Thompson, who had commanded a commando brigade in the Falklands War of 1982 and had retired a major general, labeled Eisenhower's claim to have been against Shingle in this meeting "a fabrication." He also noted that, soon after it, Eisenhower's Mediterranean HQ had cabled the Combined Chiefs that Shingle, notwithstanding its hazards had a prospective "prize ... so high that the risk may be worth taking."[24]) Eisenhower's memoirs did not mention his earlier role in ordering the planning for Shingle, nor his arranging for its landing craft, nor that, time after time, he had touted the operation to the Combined Chiefs,[25] nor that, in a press conference on December 23, he had predicted: "Jerry is going to write off this southern front.... I don't think he is going to defend it long."[26]

The minutes of the Christmas meeting paraphrased Eisenhower as having "felt strongly ... that the right course was to press on in Italy where the Germans were still full of fight. Nothing short of a bold venture such as SHINGLE would quicken up the successful prosecution of the campaign.... In his view there was no likelihood of the Germans suddenly breaking except under conditions which would be created by a successful SHINGLE."[27] Whatever caveats he spoke that day were muted enough that the meeting was characterized—by Churchill and others—as having unanimously supported the operation.[28]

On January 23, 1944, Eisenhower's aide, Harry Butcher, described Shingle as a "brilliant maneuver," about which Ike's HQ in London was excited. Butcher regretted, though, that Alexander was unjustly reaping in the British press the "credit for a long-layed plan which developed under Ike"—who truly deserved the plaudits. Butcher was seen soon to have joined in judging Shingle "a disaster"—which led him to not include this passage in his published diary.[29]

*   *   *

The Germans in early January were estimated to have 13 divisions on or near the Gustav Line, plus eleven and one half in northern Italy.[30] The Allies had beefed up their forces in the peninsula to eighteen divisions.[31]

The stage for Shingle would be set by two prior attacks on the Gustav Line: that of the British 10 Corps on the evening of January 17 over the Garigliano River and, three nights later on its right, that of the American II Corps over the Rapido. These assaults sought to draw German reserves to the southern front.[32]

The British crossing of the Garigliano led Kesselring to send two-plus divisions from Rome to reinforce his right in the South. The Americans took 1,700 casualties in being beaten off the north bank of the Rapido.[33]

The Operational Decision: Should Major General John Lucas, in His First Two Days Ashore, Have Pushed Boldly Forward—Which He Did Not Do?

Alternatives: what he did: to proceed with caution to establish a stoutly-defensible, relatively-shallow beachhead, rather than a much-deeper position, more threatening to enemy communications, but also harder to defend; or to adopt an intermediate course of pushing his line further forward to include the two villages of Campoleone and Cisterna.

When made: by Saturday, January 22, 1944.

The decision maker: John Lucas, his actions initially backed by his bosses, Mark Clark and Harold Alexander. Per the British Official History: "neither Alexander nor Clark instructed Lucas to rush at the Alban hills [high ground formed by long-inactive volcanos and the main topologic feature between Anzio and Rome, about halfway between the two] immediately after landing. They gave the Alban hills as the ultimate objective … but gave no particular objectives on the ground and imposed no timings. Very properly they left these matters to the commander on the spot."[34]

Conclusions: the outcome: likely about the best that could have been achieved; **the decision:** better most judge than opting for the aggressive alternative; **why made:** risk aversion—possibly approximating an optimal level; **to be sympathized with for having accepted unwanted assignment to a no-win command, in which (other than in making the one preeminent decision) he did not perform particularly well, but deserving credit at least for avoiding disaster:** John Lucas.

John Lucas, Commander of VI Corps, on January 22 faced the most consequential decision of his career: how far inland to push at once. He could dig in to solidify a beachhead on the Plain of Anzio or he could move aggressively inland: perhaps 20 miles northward, into the Alban Hills; perhaps a comparable distance northeastward to cut the communications of the German Tenth Army on the Gustav Line; perhaps beyond the Alban Hills all the way to Rome. Two main roads led from Rome to the southwestern half of the Gustav Line: Highways 6 and 7. Fourteen miles northeast of Anzio on Highway 7—which in the time of the Caesars had been the Appian Way—was the village of Cisterna. Thirteen miles north of Cisterna was the town of Valmontone, on higher ground, astride Highway 6. Should John Lucas have initially contented himself with hardening a modest shoreline position or should he have extended his perimeter to include the villages of Campoleone and Cisterna or should he have pushed on at once toward the Alban Hills and/or Valmontone?

Lucas—described by one historian as combining a "milquetoast demeanor" with a "keen tactical brain"[35]—had been appointed to command Operation Shingle, Alexander recounted, as the "logical choice": as "the only available corps commander who was not actively engaged" and as a member of Clark's Fifth Army. Churchill praised Lucas for having at Salerno "distinguished himself in command of a corps"[36] and Clark lauded his subordinate major general as "the man who had contributed so greatly to our successes since Salerno."[37] Clark had, though, preferred that Matthew Ridgway command VI Corps, and had but acquiesced to the appointment of Lucas.[38] Lucas had a long friendship with Eisenhower and at West Point had known Patton: "a close friend of mine since we played polo together on the Mexican Border."[39] Eisenhower had thought so highly of Lucas that he had, one month earlier, urged George Marshall that Clark be promoted to theater command and that Lucas take his place at the head of Fifth Army.[40]

Later, Alexander and Clark would in similar words voice misgivings about their corps commander: Alexander, that Lucas was "old physically and mentally"[41]; Clark, that he was "ill—tired physically and mentally—from the long responsibilities of command in battle."[42] A British officer wrote that, when Lucas visited troops in Italy, "our spirits sank as we watched this elderly figure puffing his way around."[43] Alexander on February 16 cabled to London that Lucas had "proved to be an old woman."[44] The commander of VI Corps had confided to his diary on January 14, 1944, his 54th birthday, that he felt every one of his years.[45] He would die in 1949.[46]

Alexander, on January 12, 1944, had set down the operational objectives for Operation Shingle. Lucas was to cut German communications, to threaten the Tenth Army rear, to "join hands" with Allied forces thrusting through the Gustav Line, then to hasten to Rome.[47] Clark's orders to Lucas of the same day have been judged by the American Official History "deliberately ambiguous"[48]: it was left to the VI Corps Commander to judge when, after "seiz[ing] and secur[ing] a beachhead," he might venture beyond it "to advance on [the Alban Hills]." Clark made it clear to Lucas that his preeminent priority was to make his coastal position invulnerable and then, if the Germans reacted weakly and passively, to advance further. "Don't stick your neck out, Johnny," he advised. "I did at Salerno and got into trouble.... You can forget about this goddam Rome business."[49]

* * *

The Allies at Anzio on January 22 would have two surprises. Their first was their half of a simultaneous double surprise: for John Lucas, that hardly any Germans were there[50]; for Albert Kesselring, that the Allies were. (Generals often resist admitting surprise. Kesselring wrote in his memoirs that it was clear that the Allies would land at or near Anzio: Alexander must become impatient with his slow progress and "must surely end it with a landing, which ... could only be expected in the region of Rome." Despite the ex post obviousness of the Allied action to Kesselring, he had ex ante stationed few defenders in the region where he said he had foreknown the Allies would land. He had stationed two divisions in Rome to counter a landing but, when the British attacked over the Garigliano, he transferred them to that front—even though it was, in his ex post retelling, to him "clear that such a landing would somehow be coupled with an offensive on the southern front."[51] He had thus done precisely what the Allies had hoped the British attack would induce him to do—even though he claimed to have known that the Allies would make such an attack for that purpose. He explained his actions as "perhaps relying too much" on a report by Admiral Wilhelm Canaris—Hitler's chief of intelligence.[52] Canaris had said that there were no indications that the Allies had any immediate amphibious intentions.[53])

The second Allied surprise followed closely the first: for Kesselring acted at once to dash the hopes and predictions of Churchill and Alexander that Anzio would impel the immediate retreat of his Tenth Army. By 0830 hours—six and one half after the Allied landings had begun—he had ordered the headquarters of his 1st Parachute Corps to coordinate and command Wehrmacht units immediately dispatched to contain the Allied beachhead. These troops were called in from northern and central Italy and included components of three infantry divisions, one panzer division, three panzer grenadier divisions, two parachute divisions, and the Hermann Göring Parachute-Panzer Division. From southern France and Yugoslavia, two additional infantry divisions were summoned. By nightfall, the parachute corps HQ was in place, the Allied way to the Alban Hills was blocked, and a thin defensive perimeter hemmed in the lodgement of Lucas.[54] The Wehrmacht's blocking positions between the beachhead and higher ground were designated its Fourteenth Army, commanded by Eberhard von Mackensen. Albert Kesselring would also have his Tenth Army, under Heinrich von Vietinghoff, continue to defend on the Gustav Line.

John Lucas is thought to have determined pre-landing not to move aggressively toward higher ground.[55] He had likely suspected how Kesselring would react and already decided on the actions that he would take: on January 22 he just held to the intention he had arrived at days before going ashore. It would have been reasonable for him to have identified recent situations similar to that that he expected to be in at Anzio and to have determined what actions would there have worked best. Anzio's obvious predecessors were the landings made on July 10, 1943, in Sicily and on September 9 at Salerno. The enemy had counterattacked both times—endangering Allied forces near Gela in Sicily and at Salerno. Lucas, rather than hurry inland, would harden his position. The unanticipated feebleness of the opposition he initially met at Anzio would not lead him to change his mind and to drive quickly up into the hills.

Kesselring, a dozen days later, would attack the corps of Lucas; critics, in the years to come, would assault the American major general's decision.

On learning of the landing, Churchill had cabled Alexander, "Am very glad you are pegging out claims rather than digging in bridgeheads."[56] But digging in, not pegging out, was precisely what Lucas was doing. The Prime Minister seems disingenuously to have been urging audacity.

The Outcome: Stalemate at the Beachhead

By midnight of D-Day, January 22, Allied troops in and around Anzio numbered 36,000: the "two full divisions plus paratroops" that Churchill had said "should be decisive." They had 3,000 vehicles, in a position fifteen miles long, ranging from two to four miles inland.[57] Thirteen Allied invaders had died. The BBC reported the next day that Rome would be reached within 48 hours.[58] Nineteen weeks would, instead, pass before the Allies took the city of Scipio and Caesar.

The two sides, in the days after the landing, shelled and bombed each other as their forces grew. By January 25, 56,000 Allied troops and 7,000 vehicles were ashore. Tempting immediate objectives for Lucas were the two villages of Campoleone, thirteen miles north of Anzio, and Cisterna, fourteen miles northeast of the port. These two positions might serve as staging areas for further advances, which was their main attraction as seen by Harold Alexander; or, as alternatively stressed by Mark Clark, they could be defensive strong points in the event of German counterattacks.[59] Should they not be taken, they would serve as coordinating nodes of enemy resistance.

On January 30, with 75,000 Germans confronting 69,000 Allies,[60] the British First Division attacked toward Campoleone and the American Third Division, toward Cisterna. The advance of the British created a four-mile-long Allied salient that reached almost to Campoleone.[61] The Americans were stopped a mile short of Cisterna. The Germans would, until late May, continue to hold both villages.

Adolf Hitler, hoping that elimination of the beachhead would be a devastating setback for the Allies, further reinforced his Fourteenth Army. By the night of February 3, the two sides at the beachhead had each between 90,000 and 100,000 men, as the Germans counterattacked.[62] The main assault began one hour before midnight and set the tactical template for Mackensen's assaults over the rest of the month: movements and fighting mainly at night in deference to Allied control of the air; initial infiltration around the flanks of the Anglo-American positions, before seeking to overrun them—which they occasionally did. Some aspects of the attacks, such as the massing of artillery for them and the particular lines of assault, were specified by Hitler—in what the British Official History called "his strange interventions in detailed tactics."[63]

The first target of Mackensen on the third and fourth of February was the salient pointing at Campoleone. In six days of fighting, the Allied line there was pushed back four miles. This German advance was but a prologue, Hitler thought, as he ordered a further "concentrated, overwhelming, ruthless" attack that was to end at the sea.[64] German forces containing the beachhead were reinforced to 125,000, against 100,000 Allies.[65] The Führer's renewed assault opened on February 16 and gained nearly a mile that day, nearly three by the morning of the eighteenth—putting the Germans five miles north of Anzio. But Allied infantry resistance—aided by 400 artillery pieces, naval guns, and 800 planes (which dropped 2,200 tons of bombs in battle support in the first 16 days of the month)—stiffened. On the nineteenth, two rested American regiments counterattacked. Over the next few days, the fighting petered out, both sides having taken 5,000 casualties. In the first month of the battle at Anzio, the Allies had total casualties of 19,000: 2,000 dead, 8,500 wounded, and 8,500, captured or missing. The Germans had lost a comparable number.[66]

* * *

John Lucas had not wanted to command at Anzio. He had told Mark Clark that VI Corps would be too weak to move toward the Alban Hills and Rome. Clark had responded that, if Lucas did not accept the assignment of Shingle, he would be relieved of all command.[67] Lucas had acquiesced. He recorded on January 10 that he "felt like a lamb being led to the slaughter."[68]

Once landed at Anzio, the prudence of Lucas in forgoing the aggressive drives desired by Churchill and Alexander had, he thought, gone far toward holding off the German attacks on the VI Corps beachhead that might otherwise have erased it. He could not, however, keep his doubts about Shingle from dispiriting the men he commanded. He had little confidence in his British troops nor they in him. He rarely ventured near the front to visit his units, but stayed mostly in his HQ by the shore.

John Lucas had, in his diary entry of January 14, foreseen that someone—who more likely than he?—would be blamed for the gap between hope and force sufficiency.[69] After the American repulse at Cisterna, it was judged that "no one bore greater responsibility for Anzio than Churchill, and he kept a pale eye peeled for possible scapegoats"—for which role Clark and Lucas were front-row prospects.[70] Lucas, on February 1, had sensed the displeasure of Alexander: "My head will probably fall in the basket but I have done my best."[71] Clark learned that George Marshall also thought that Lucas had not done well[72] and was told by Alexander that the failings of his subordinate might well lead to Clark's own firing.[73] The commander of the U.S. Fifth Army, on February 22, sacked Lucas.[74] Lucian Truscott, who had been commanding the U.S. Third Division under Lucas, took over beachhead command.

After further attacks at the end of the month, Albert Kesselring on March 1 ordered an end to the attempts to push VI Corps back into the sea. Adolf Hitler had a group of front-line officers from the Fourteenth Army come to his headquarters for his personal questioning. They arrived on March 7 and told their Führer that the main reason that their force had not fulfilled his hopes was the Allied artillery.[75]

The battle lines defining the Anzio beachhead would not appreciably change for another eleven weeks—two and one half bleak months for the front-line soldiers of crouching in soggy foxholes, their feet in ankle-deep water (the water table in many places but a foot or two below the surface), their enemies often a grenade throw away, with snipers sited to fire at anyone who in daytime failed to stay behind cover.

Did the Operational Decision of John Lucas Have a Good or a Bad Outcome?

Churchill thought, before and after the landings, that, had Lucas taken his aggressive alternative—not digging in, but pegging out—Kesselring would have had to retreat or to lose much of his Tenth Army: to him and Alexander, the actual result was bad-outcome-per-hopes and bad-outcome-versus-alternatives. The subordinate British division commander of Lucas, Major General Ronald Penney, "was," Churchill wrote, "anxious to push inland. His reserve brigade was however held back [presumably by Lucas].... By the evening of January 23 ... the opportunity for which great exertions had been made was gone."[76] (Churchill and Lucas were mutual non-admirers. Each blamed the other for the disappointing outcome at Anzio. Lucas, on January 9, 1944, criticized to Alexander the operation he was to command. To him it seemed likely to prove another Gallipoli—also, he wrote in his diary the next day, the misguided inspiration of "the same amateur."[77] To have had such a disbeliever as Lucas at the controls might have seemed bizarre, but was not without precedent: Eisenhower had also been such in North Africa.)

Three high officers seconded Churchill's rating of bad-outcome-versus-alternatives. The Prime Minister quoted German General Siegfried Westphal's judgment that Lucas could, in his first day or two ashore, have sent a force into Rome.[78] Albert Kesselring concluded in his first visit to the Anzio front on January 22 that "the Allies had missed a uniquely favourable chance of capturing Rome and of opening the door on the Garigliano front."[79] British Air Marshal Sir John Slessor thought that, if the invading force had been German or Russian, Highways 7 and 6 would have been captured by the twenty-fifth, leading to the immediate collapse of the German right on the Gustav Line.[80]

But two of those who had criticized Lucas changed their minds—joining in judgment other generals who supported the commander of VI Corps. Alexander himself reflected, after the war, that his unhappiness with Lucas at the time had been unjust: he had indeed been "right to wait and consolidate."[81] Albert Kesselring had a turn-around similar to Alexander's. His relief on January 22 that the Allies had failed to exploit a golden chance to take Rome changed after the war to the judgment that "it would have been the Anglo-American doom to over-extend themselves."[82] Alexander's chief of staff, John Harding, agreed with the later judgment of his superior that the caution of Lucas "probably saved the forces at Anzio from disaster."[83] What Alexander, Kesselring, and Harding concluded was that aggressive initial movements by Lucas would have so thinned out the Allied lines that German attacks at vulnerable points would have broken though and that the Allied beachhead would have been demolished: most of VI Corps would have been lost: a replay of Dieppe, times ten or more.

Mark Clark had thoughts in the same direction: if "advance deeply inland at the beginning" had been undertaken, "we most certainly would have suffered far more heavily, if not fatally."[84] Lucian Truscott dismissed as a "delusion" of "arm chair strategists" the notion of "a 'fleeting opportunity' at Anzio during which some Napoleonic figure would have charged over the [Alban Hills], played havoc with the German line of communications, and galloped on into Rome."[85] Any such "reckless advance," would, he thought, have led to "destruction of the landing forces."[86] Other generals in agreement that the prudence of Lucas had been essential included Ronald Penney and Gerald Templer, both of whom had commanded the First British Division at Anzio; U.S. First Armored Division Commander Ernest Harmon; Ira Eaker, Commander-in-Chief of Allied Air Forces in the Mediterranean; and British Field Marshal Sir Henry Wilson, who in January 1944 had succeeded Eisenhower as Mediterranean theater commander.[87] George Marshall thought that Lucas could likely have taken the Alban Hills, but that it would have entailed defending so extended a perimeter that his caution had been wise.[88] The verdict of these generals was good-outcome-versus-alternatives.

Major general and historian J. F. C. Fuller agreed with Churchill that Lucas, had let slip through his fingers a unique strategic opportunity.[89] Five other historians, however, held the opposite: basically that, had Clark and Lucas "made a dash for the Alban Hills ... on landing," it would have allowed their force to be cut off and the hills "turned into the largest POW camp in Italy."[90]

The greater weight of opinion holds that John Lucas did better by digging in than if he had pegged out: a good-outcome-versus-alternatives.

(This judgment implies a result less noted in the literature of principals and agents than that of agency loss: *agency gain.* Principal-agent theory, as applied to Anzio, would have noted that Churchill and Lucas—with the former acting as principal, five levels above the latter as agent—had divergent views on what the VI Corps, once landed, should have done. When Lucas did other than as Churchill wished, this caused, in the mind of the latter, agency loss—a frequent focus of principal-agent research. That most have since concluded that Churchill was wrong and Lucas, right changes the sign of the effect: Lucas, by straying from the intentions of Churchill, achieved an agency gain.)

Was the Operational Decision of John Lucas Good or Bad?

Decision science has found that connected, sequential choices are best analyzed in reverse chronologic order: the later before the earlier.[91] In health care, for instance, a decision on whether to order a medical test—or which test to order—would be followed, if a test is ordered, by learning its results, then, based on them, by making a therapeutic decision. The initial decision on testing is best made by first considering how the later, therapeutic choice should or would be resolved, if no test is ordered or, if ordered, based on its possible results. Similarly, one best critiques December's decisions on Anzio by first considering what might have happened in January: what the weather might have been; how the Germans might have disposed their troops; how they might have reacted; what tactical actions John Lucas might, should, and most likely would take; and what battle outcomes might have resulted—with probabilities estimated for all possibilities pondered. The choice made by John Lucas on the coastal plain of Anzio is therefore first assessed—before the earlier decision of his superiors that had put him there.

* * *

John Lucas could, in his first 24 hours ashore, have hunkered down close to the shore, have hurried into the hills, or have hedged between those two courses by taking such intermediate points as Campoleone and Cisterna, but not pressing on beyond them. He had hunkered. Subsequent reviews of his actions have focused mainly on whether he would have done better to have instead headed at once toward high ground.

Mark Clark on January 30, 1944, and some historians later thought that John Lucas, immediately after landing, ought to have taken his intermediate option: neither sticking as close to the shore as he did nor striking out to the Alban Hills or Valmontone, but instead soon capturing Campoleone and Cisterna, before digging in. To have attempted much more than that, they believed, would have been unwise.[92] Even if, however, VI Corps had quickly taken those two villages, its possession of them may well not have budged Kesselring from the Gustav Line.[93] Most critiques of John Lucas as decision maker on January 22 have ignored the limited, Campoleone-Cisterna, option and have focused on whether he ought to have taken a daringly-more-aggressive course.

Alexander and Clark, on January 25, visited Lucas: the former congratulating him for "a splendid piece of work"[94]; the latter, urging the capture of Campoleone and Cisterna[95] but also finding the progress toward Cisterna "satisfactory."[96] Two days later, though, Clark and Lucas both felt that Alexander—likely reflecting the impatience he was hearing from Churchill[97]—was disappointed in the modest progress made. Churchill, on January 28, criticized Lucas to Brooke—who "quiet[ed] the Prime Minister down," while not revealing that he shared his misgivings.[98]

On the last day of January, Alan Brooke also was ascribing the "little progress" largely "to lack of initiative in the early stages."[99] Historian Andrew Roberts saw matters in the same light, calling Lucas "the wrong man to command [Shingle]."[100] Roberts also, however, noted that Alexander and Clark had "rubber-stamped all Lucas' decisions but escaped censure."[101] Alexander thought that the experience of Lucas at Salerno had led him to expect that the landing at Anzio would be contested. When it was not, he lacked the flexibility "to adjust his mind to a new situation. A younger or more experienced soldier would have been quicker to react."[102]

Alexander on February 15 cabled to Brooke his dissatisfaction with Lucas and Churchill the next day wanted Alexander to go personally to the beachhead and take over VI Corps command. Brooke "rather lost my temper" in remonstrating to the PM against his propensity to interfere in military matters.[103]

Winston Churchill and Bernard Montgomery, reminiscing in 1953, agreed that, when Lucas had "clung to the beaches" at Anzio, he had committed one of the "five capital mistakes" made by Americans in the war. (The other U.S. blunders fingered were stopping Alexander from taking Tunis when he first could have, insisting on the invasion of southern France, adopting a broad-front strategy in northern Europe in late 1944, and letting the Russians capture Berlin, Prague, and Vienna.[104])

Lucas gave two main defenses of his decision: that he had been following orders and that he had saved his Corps. He noted with respect to his orders "a very significant change in mission" between those of January 8 and the final version of January 12: "Instead of advancing to seize [the Alban Hills], I was to 'advance on' that terrain feature and no mention of Rome was made whatever." In receiving this order, Lucas had been told "that much thought had been put on the wording ... so as not to force me to push on at the risk of sacrificing my Corps." He held that "the term 'advance on,' which is an established military term meaning 'to move in the direction of,' indicated in itself that the Army questioned my being able to reach this feature and, at the same time, hold a beachhead which would protect the port and beaches."[105] Had he not obeyed his orders, "Had I been able to rush to the [Alban Hills] immediately upon landing, nothing would have been accomplished except to weaken my force by that amount because the troops sent, being completely beyond supporting distance, would have been immediately destroyed. The only thing to do was what I did."[106]

As to the intermediate possibility of quickly taking the Rome-Cisterna railroad, Lucas blamed his ally: "The British were so slow getting ashore, though, that holding such advanced gains against the rapid German build-up in strength would have been, to say the least, difficult."[107] While praising British troops—"no braver men in the world"—Lucas questioned both the overall effort and the tactics of his allies and "lost confidence, to some extent at least, in the British Division and its commander. They seemed unable to make even a simple reconnaissance without getting into trouble."[108]

The greater weight of military and historical opinion sides with John Lucas: by not attempting too much, he avoided foreseeable calamity. While most authors have defended Lucas by arguing for the superiority of the outcome he achieved, two specifically praised the "sensibility" of his decision: concluding that he saw the unattainability of Churchill's gleaming goals and that reaching out for them would have invited disaster.[109] Instead, he secured a perimeter that Adolf Hitler could not rub out. In so doing and without resorting to numbers, he took the course that met the decision-scientific criterion for good choices: that offering highest prospective value: a good-decision-versus-alternatives.

Widespread belief that John Lucas had at Anzio performed about as well as he could have led later to his heading the U.S. Fourth Army, a training unit. While the rise from corps to army command was a technical promotion, Lucas—like Kenneth Anderson, Lloyd Fredendall, and John Roberts, each of whom had also been held responsible for disappointing Allied hopes— never again gave orders to men in battle. He wrote an account of his war experience in diary form: *From Algiers to Anzio.* The War Department was, however, not pleased with his criticism of Churchill, Alexander, and other Britons and forbade publication.[110]

Did Operation Shingle Have a Good or a Bad Outcome?

General Lucian Truscott asked in his memoirs whether the landing at Anzio had been "worth the cost"[111]: whether the decision of Christmas 1943 had had a good- or a bad-outcome-on-net.

That the Germans, nearly four months after the landing, still held the Gustav Line and Rome dismayed Churchill. He called the results of the assault "disaster" and "ruin in its prime purpose"[112]; "a story of high opportunity and shattered hopes, of skilful inception on our part and swift recovery by the enemy."[113] The Prime Minister had "hoped that we were hurling a wild cat to the shore, but all we had got was a stranded whale."[114] On May 15, 1944, to the assembled commanders for Overlord, Churchill exhorted, "We must not have another Anzio."[115] Historians have shared the Prime Minister's bleak judgment of mission failure: an undeniably-bad-outcome-per-hopes.[116]

But how bad had the outcome been? Should the Allies, after the fact, have wished that they had not undertaken Shingle? While Churchill thought that it had fallen calamitously short of his expectations, he also wrote that "the aggressive action of our armies in Italy, and specifically the Anzio stroke, made its full contribution towards the success of 'Overlord'" and also assisted in liberating Rome[117]: "reap[ing]" in the late spring "the harvest from our winter sowing at Anzio."[118] The gains Churchill saw in Shingle included drawing ten German divisions to the beachhead, causing enemy losses of 30,000 men to 25,000 for the Allies, and making "possible the kind of movement for which it was originally planned, only on a far larger scale"[119]: although a bad-outcome-per-hopes in the short run, a good-outcome-on-net in the longer view. (Truscott's casualty figures were 50,000 German and 43,000 Allied.[120] That both sets of numbers indicated greater enemy than Allied losses after the first month of Shingle, in which casualties were about equal, owed to greater German losses in their later attacks on the beachhead.) The Prime Minister, on February 8, 1944, also claimed for Shingle a back-handed, Dieppe-like, experiential gain: "we should also learn [from it] a good many lessons about how not to do it which will be valuable in Overlord."[121]

Like Churchill, Eisenhower gave mixed ratings. The "initial stages" of the operation had played out disappointingly—as, he said, his staff had expected—but the end result of inducing Hitler to send eight more divisions to Italy helped the Allies on other fronts: "in the final outcome the Anzio operation paid off handsomely."[122] (That Churchill's number of ten German divisions transferred to Italy differed from Eisenhower's eight is not of import. Divisions varied in size between and within national armies and over time and intelligence-service estimations of enemy strength were fallible. Clark believed that the Germans intentionally split up and scattered their divisions for deception—in which they had success, as Allied intelligence officers often erroneously inferred, after identifying a few enemy soldiers of a division, that the entire division was present.[123]) The commander of Overlord also, though, wrote that the Anzio landing had "partially ... for some months" been "a draining sore in the side of the attacker."[124] (Hitler had used the same metaphor: Anzio for him too was an "abscess."[125])

More positive on the outcome than Churchill or Eisenhower was Alexander:

> Anzio played a vital role in the capture of Rome by giving me the means to employ a double-handed punch—from the beachhead and from Cassino—which caught the Germans in a pincer movement. Without this double-handed punch I do not believe we should ever have been able to break through the German defences at Cassino.[126]

This judgment in his memoirs of good-outcome-on-net and good-outcome-versus-alternatives turned around what Alexander had on February 11, 1944, written to Churchill in terming Shingle "a great disappointment."[127] The previous month, the commander of all Allied ground forces in Italy had told Lucas "with great glee" that Shingle would make Overlord "unnecessary"[128]—making the actual result starkly a bad-outcome-per-hopes.

Lucian Truscott answered his own question by concluding—based on casualties, Wehrmacht divisions drawn to the beachhead, and German losses in equipment and supplies—"that Anzio was worth the cost"[129]: a good-outcome-on-net.

Pluses for the Allies of having mounted Shingle included that it drew nine or so enemy divisions to the beachhead, that it further showed that the Western Allies were not leaving all ground fighting to the Russians, and that it helped to take Rome. Minuses were that the operation took Allied resources from the Gustav Line and that it led to losing 1,700 men (not included in Churchill's casualty figures for Anzio) in the January assault over the Rapido—which Kesselring called an Allied error.[130] (Clark foreknew that the Rapido attack would be "costly." He would, however, accept the likely losses in hopes that the assault—whose rear was secure—would draw enemy forces from the Anzio Plain, where the rear of VI Corps would be the sea.[131] It would have been better for the American forces at the Rapido to have delayed their attack until the British on their left had secured high ground overlooking their crossing points. But Clark, because of the imminence of the landings at Anzio, would not agree to the postponement.[132])

Whether the estimated casualty figures of 30,000 German and 25,000 Allied losses—a ratio of 1.2 to 1—were net good or bad for the Allies depends on the value judgments of them. Total German casualties for the 601 days of fighting in mainland Italy from September 9, 1943, through May 2, 1945, were 435,000, versus 312,000 Allied[133]: a ratio of 1.39 to 1. In the three months of battles in northern France commencing on June 6, 1944, the respective figures were 500,000 German (of which 200,000 were surrounded in coastal strong points) losses, 220,000 Allied,[134] and a ratio of 2.27 to 1.

Clark later thought that the Anzio forces would have been better employed on the Gustav Line—making Shingle a bad-outcome-versus-alternatives.[135] Strengthened attacks there as an alternative to Shingle, would have induced responsive German reinforcements. Yet another alternative for the Western Allies would have been to suspend for months their attacks in Italy—which would have been, Churchill suggested to Parliament on February 22, 1944, to "stand still and watch the Russians."[136] (Churchill might have had for Shingle a motivation that had also underlain Jubilee: to show Stalin that the Western Allies, to aid the Red Army, were actively attacking Germans.) The choice for the Western Allies between limiting their own casualties and vigorously assisting the Russians was, throughout the war, bedeviling.

The psychological and political effects of Shingle are not easily judged. Whether Shingle produced Western-Ally benefits in dealing with Stalin is unknowable. Stalin had in November 1943 at Tehran said that he did not understand why his allies were slogging up through Italy toward Rome—which was not of importance.[137]

There was thus no unity of judgment among decision participants as to whether the Allies did best to have landed at Anzio: with Alexander affirming that it did; with Clark disagreeing; with Churchill and Eisenhower straddling the issue. There is, however, a general consensus among historians that the Fifth Army would have done better to have forgone Operation Shingle. Their most common characterization of the landing was that of failure—a judgment predicated largely on the operation's non-achievement of its stated aims but also indicating that such consolation benefits as those cited by Churchill, Eisenhower, and Alexander were outweighed by the costs.

Had the participants in Churchill's Tunis conference known what the results of the Anzio landing would be, they would not have backed it—which argues that the outcome was bad.

Deciding on Shingle

Had the decision on Anzio been made so that those with best insights on objectives, options, possibilities, uncertainties, and likely results had had appropriate influence?

Mark Clark thought not and summarized that "the Tunis decision to stage SHINGLE had been made a bit carelessly and without the participants in the conference understanding the requisites for a successful operation, though they had been clearly stated in advance by my staff."[138] This should not have been the case. Although Clark had not attended the conference, his superiors, Alexander and Eisenhower, had. The requirements flagged by Clark's staff should, via them, have been duly taken into account. Perhaps, owing to deficiencies in transmission from staff to Clark, to his superiors, and to the conference, the message of Clark's staff had not been considered in Tunis.

Critical premises of Shingle—although agreed on by persons of excellent credentials to judge—proved wrong. The uncertainties associated with these presumptions were underappreciated—as decision science has found often to happen. Two generals whose expectations out-stripped results ascribed their over-optimism to their underestimations of the Germans: Clark found that "the enemy had succeeded in rushing far greater strength than anticipated to the Anzio sector ... artillery was massed on high ground with more effectiveness than we had encountered anywhere in the drive northward"[139]; Alexander thought that "we may well have underestimated the remarkable resilience and toughness of the Germans."[140] Even Truscott, a pre-invasion pessi-mist, admitted that the decision makers and invasion planners, including himself, "did not know and failed to appreciate ... the technique which the German command had developed for rapid concentration against, and the sealing off of, any such landing."[141]

Alexander also wrote that he and the other DMs on Shingle had failed to appreciate the terrain:

> From the map, [Shingle] ... looks an attractive proposition. But when viewing the objective from the beach-head one appreciates in better perspective the formidability of the task. The Alban Hills are really a massive mountain terrain, much more difficult to gain and maintain than can be apparent from maps.[142]

Yet another misapprehension at the moment of decision was excessive confidence that Al-lied air superiority could interdict German movements.[143]

The decision makers of Anzio had sheaves of data and G-2—intelligence service—esti-mates and reached divergent conclusions. While Churchill and Alexander expected a speedy dislodging of the enemy from the Gustav Line, to be soon followed by the capture of Rome, Ei-senhower, Lucas, and Truscott did not, and Clark wavered between the two camps. In part, these differences of opinion stemmed from variant intelligence reports. The G-2 of Clark's Fifth Army had, on January 16, 1944, deemed it "likely that [Shingle] will cause [the enemy] to withdraw from his defensive position once he has appreciated the magnitude of that operation."[144] Trus-cott, however, wrote that "no one below Army level believed that the landing of two divisions at Anzio would cause a German withdrawal on the Southern front, or that there was more than a remote chance that the remainder of the Fifth Army would be able to ... join with us within a month."[145] George Patton, often delusionally optimistic, told Lucas on January 12, "You can't get out of this alive."[146]

Shingle decision makers and their intelligence analysts might reasonably have predicted either that Anzio would soon bring the Allies through the Gustav line or that it would not: ev-idence, precedent, and logic pointed in both directions. They should, however, whatever their advice and whatever their best estimations, have understood that the decision on Anzio was taken in the context of substantial uncertainty and that its outcome would be subject to the vagaries of luck.

Uncertainties

The words and actions of Mark Clark, at the time of Anzio and later, bespoke uncertainty. The title of his memoirs, *Calculated Risk*, has long been a focus of applied decision science. "A cal-culated risk" was also Clark's characterization of Churchill's mindset in pushing Shingle through. He thought it himself "a dangerous undertaking," but did "not desire to give any impression that I am disagreeing with the decision. On the contrary, I approved it on the condition that it was undertaken with sufficient strength."[147]

Clark fretted, though, especially after hearing from Lucas and Truscott, that the projected strength might, indeed, not suffice and in early 1944 voiced reservations—leading to "some doubt during the first week of January that the operation would take place."[148] But, after speaking with Alexander, Clark swung to the positive and Alexander reported to Churchill on January 4 that "Clark and I are confident that we have a great chance of pulling off something big if given the means with which to do it." It has been judged that this misstated the "ambivalent" mental state of Clark, who confided to his diary his sense that "a pistol was being held at [my] head" by Churchill.[149] "Perhaps to buck himself up," the general added to his journal, "I am convinced that we are going to do it, and that it is going to be a success."[150] Lucas, gloomier than Clark, penned similarly conflicting thoughts in his diary on January 21: despite his "many misgivings," he said that he was "also optimistic."[151]

Had decision science existed at the time of Shingle and had its practitioners been consulted in its deliberations, they would have inquired into the uncertainties. They would have urged contributors to Shingle's decisions to focus more than they did on the points of divergent view: inquiring of them just how sure or unsure they were or should have been about the weather, other battle-affecting conditions, enemy actions, outcome likelihoods, and outcome values. They would have identified and have sought to understand differences of opinion. By parsing the components of such opinions, they might have found the roots of disagreements, which might or might not have led to reconciliations of judgments among decision participants. They would not have wanted the holders of variant views to be pressured into modifying or abandoning them, solely to achieve imposed, apparent, but superficial consensus.

Special challenges in assessing uncertainty are cataclysmic risks. For Shingle, several authors have suggested that there was—even after Lucas had taken his cautious option—a substantial chance of having almost all beachhead soldiers killed, wounded, or captured. By the second week of February 1944, the beachhead was seen as "precarious"[152] and "imperiled"[153]: the Campoleone salient had fallen to the German attack; Lucas had been driven back to within three miles of his last line of defense. The history of the Fifth Army termed it "questionable whether the final beachhead line could hold."[154] Per the American Official History, "the [German] prospects of [erasing the beachhead] seemed good."[155] But what did "precarious," "imperiled," "questionable," and "prospects" that "seemed good" mean: what, numerically, were the chances pre-invasion through the first two weeks of February that Kesselring could erase the beachhead? Fifty percent? Thirty percent? Ten percent? No one said.

Harold Alexander, at one point of peril, had told Clark, "We may be pushed into the sea."[156] Clark himself later thought that "a powerful German counter-attack [at Anzio] might well have wrecked the entire Allied campaign in Italy."[157] John Lucas, on March 23, 1944, told a military audience that "there had never been any doubt in his mind that the beachhead would hold."[158] He had recorded in his diary on January 25 that he deemed the beachhead "safe."[159] Of his thought in early February, he said "that the possibility of being driven from the beachhead never occurred to me." On the fourth, however, he had recorded: "I think the old Hun is getting ready to have a go at me. He thinks he can drive me back into the ocean. Maybe so."[160] He did not put a probabilistic number on "maybe so." Three days later, he "hope[d]" his forces could repel the expected German attack.[161]

Decision scientists and game theorists, if involved, would have prioritized estimating numerically the chance of this catastrophic contingency.

The extent to which the decision makers of Shingle pondered a potentially-devastating repulse—Dieppe in spades—is not clear. Churchill's pitch to Roosevelt on Christmas did mention that landing "with less than two divisions would be to court disaster." Perhaps he believed that, once he had secured for the landings two-plus divisions, operational disaster would not be courted. More worrisomely on his mind than possible calamity on the Tyrrhenian shore seems to have been "the ruin of the Mediterranean campaign of 1944," if Shingle were not to go forward. Evidence that potential beachhead extinction was considered was provided by Harry Butcher of Eisenhower's HQ, who wrote on January 16 of "the great hazard of annihilation to the landing force if Fifth Army should be unable to reach it by land"[162]—as, in fact, for four months, would be the case.

From the perspective of the operational planners and decision makers, the inability of the Allied forces at the Gustav Line to drive quickly to the beachhead was bad luck—one of the factors of fortune influencing the outcome at Anzio. Good luck for the Allies was that German planes did not discover the concentration of ships in advance of Shingle and that German agents in Naples did not report preparations for the operation—with the result that surprise was achieved.[163] Countervailingly, the British Official History attributed the speed of the immediate German re-action to the landings not just to "a brilliant feat of staff work," but also to the bad luck of "weather unfavourable for flying."[164] Further poor weather for planes began on January 30 and extended into February.[165] One tack taken by Churchill in explaining the good-decision-bad-outcome of Shingle was the misfortune of his poor health: "if I had been well enough to be at [Alexander's] side as I had hoped at the critical moment I believe I could have given the necessary stimulus. Alas for time, distance, illness and advancing years."[166]

Luck affected not just the outcome at Anzio but also the decision on Shingle. The amphibious operation might not have been undertaken had it not happened: that Brooke and Churchill had met in Tunis on December 19, 1943; that the Prime Minister's convalescence had put him in the Mediterranean, conveniently sited to summon to his bedroom the theater commanders; that Eisenhower had had lame-duck status, which muted his reservations; or that Clark had not been at the Christmas-Day conference and could not voice there the criticisms of Shingle he heard from Lucas and Truscott.[167]

* * *

John Lucas at Anzio could not keep his skepticism about the premises and promises of Shingle from dampening the spirits of all about him. His was a gloomy HQ and an unenthusiastic army that might well, with a better attitude, have done more. Alexander wished that VI Corps had instead been commanded by "a thruster like George Patton."[168] But the battle conditions that enabled Patton to romp through Sicily and to break out of Normandy were not those of Anzio. "Old Blood and Guts," if in command there, would likely have had a more inspired and aggressive force that might, however, have ended up worse than that of Lucas.

Lucian Truscott, after succeeding John Lucas as commander of the Allied forces at Anzio, criticized his predecessor's headquarters for having radiated pessimism and uncertainty, for never having "been positive and confident either in planning or in directing operations."[169] It is a fine line for any leader to take into account, before deciding, all pertinent uncertainties; then, after deciding, to give orders with doubt-banishing vigor.

Values

The Allies hoped that landing at Anzio would lead to the early capture of Rome. What actually happened disappointed them. Hitler's orders foresaw a third outcome: erasing the Allied beachhead. Countless gradations of intermediate results were possible: including different dates for taking Rome and varying levels of Allied and German casualties. Decision scientists—if in existence and consulted—would have asked the Anzio decision makers their best estimates of just how valuable or costly to the Allies such outcomes would have been.

The two leading participants at the Christmas conference on Anzio—Churchill and Eisenhower—valued differently the aspects of the outcomes. Churchill coveted Rome. Mark Clark reported that the Prime Minister

> felt that the entire Allied position was prejudiced by the fact that the Germans were putting up such a successful defense of Rome. This, he believed, was having an unfavorable effect on both Turkey and Spain; it was, therefore, essential that the Italian capital be captured, and soon.[170]

Breaking through the Gustav Line and taking Rome were for Eisenhower but secondary considerations, subordinate to the invasion of France:

> Our problem [in Italy] became that of forcing the fighting, but with economy and caution so as to avoid unnecessary diversion of units and supplies that could be used in Overlord. We had to follow a plan that would avoid reverses, costly attacks, and great expenditures of supplies but which would continue to keep the enemy uneasy and, above all, would prevent him from reducing his Italian forces to reinforce his position in northwest Europe.[171]

Had outcome values been quantified, Eisenhower's and Churchill's numbers would have shown the different priorities they assigned to the two campaigns.

Decision scientists would have sought best estimates of—and, to the extent possible, a consensus on—the likelihoods and quantified values of the various outcomes that might have resulted from possible steps. With such figures, they could then determine which actions were on expectation in the best interests of the Allies: whether or not the landing at Anzio should have been undertaken and, if so, how.

Judgments of the Decision to Undertake Shingle

Were the prospective net benefits of the landing at Anzio not only positive (a good-decision-on-net), but did they also exceed for the Allies those of alternative actions (a good-decision-versus-alternatives)?

The accounts of Churchill and Eisenhower leave it unclear whether they thought the outcome of Shingle, on net, good or bad. The PM gave judgments both of GDBO-on-net and of good-decision-somewhat-positive-outcome-that-ought-to-have-been-better-on-net. Any uncertainty about the arithmetic sign of the outcome did not, for Churchill, apply to the decision. To Stalin he wrote on June 5, 1944: "Although the amphibious landing at Anzio … did not immediately fructify as I had hoped when it was planned, it was a correct strategic move, and brought its reward in the end." (Three months later, however, in what has been called "a rare moment of candor," Churchill told an intimate, "Anzio was my worst moment of the war. I had most to do with it."[172]) Kesselring made statements both ways. He agreed in his memoirs with Churchill that the thinking behind Shingle had been good: "I can only say that had I been the Allied Commander-in-Chief I would have at least attempted to shorten the Italian campaign by tactical landings."[173] The field marshal also, though, voiced a judgment similar to that of Eisenhower: that Shingle, with not enough infantry and no armor in its initial stage, was but "a half-way measure" and, therefore, an "error."[174] Others have agreed in judging that Shingle as mounted was too small for its aims and therefore a bad decision.[175]

The British Official History judged that Churchill's case for Anzio constituted "not very strong arguments in favour of a risky venture" and that the operation "was fathered by wishful strategical thinking and was not made the subject of a searching tactical analysis."[176]

John Lucas and other officers and authors agreed with these ratings of Shingle as a bad decision.[177]

Shingle as a Bluff

Harold Alexander said after the war that Shingle had been "a bluff" intended "to scare the Germans into pulling back ... all would depend on whether or not the Germans were fooled by our bluff. If the Germans on the southern front felt that their rear was threatened and exposed, they might pull back."[178] Some historians supported this view of the field marshal: holding that John Lucas ought to have hurried to take the Alban Hills: such "a bluff prosecuted with imagination and daring ... might have worked ... for not having tried, Lucas could not altogether, nor would he ever, be forgiven."[179]

Bluffs—long of interest to game theorists—are

false portrayals of strength, situation, or intent to lead others to take actions not in their best interests.

John von Neumann in 1944 described two types of bluff: "to give a (false) impression of strength in (real) weakness" and "to give a (false) impression of weakness in (real) strength."[180] These ploys were seen in his analysis of poker: players with bad hands might bet with aggressive bluster in hopes of inducing opponents to fold; players with strong hands would want to seem weak to lure opponents into putting more money into the pot. Subsequently, only the former situation has been commonly taken in poker to constitute bluffing. Neumann demonstrated mathematically that poker players do best with betting strategies that occasionally include bluffs of his first type: showing that players who refrain from ever raising on bad hands will, on expectation against able opponents, achieve poorer outcomes than they might have. He also determined the conditions under which bluffs can achieve competitive advantage and the optimal ways of making and calling them. Neumann's analysis could be extended to establish the basis for both of his types of bluffing in bridge: overbidding and underbidding to deceive opponents into taking actions inferior for them. Central to his analysis is the incompleteness of the information available to the competitors: your bluffing works in poker and bridge because your opponents do not know what cards you hold. The logic of Neumann indicates that bluffs should not occur in games—such as backgammon, checkers, chess, and go—in which both sides have complete information.[181]

A variety of bluff considered by game theorist Thomas Schelling is the threat that one does not, if it is unsuccessful, plan to follow through on.[182] A union, might, for example, threaten a strike to get management to raise wages. If the union does not intend to have its members walk out in the event that management does not budge, it is bluffing. Such bluffs are not uncommon in bargaining.[183] Suppose that you wish to sell me a car and will not accept less than $30,000 for it and that it is worth $40,000 to me. I may understand your position well enough to announce that I will not pay a penny more than $32,000. If I in fact would pay, say, $35,000 should you insist on that price, my announcement is a bluff. As was seen in Chapter 1, George Marshall and Henry Stimson later stated that they had in July 1942 indeed attempted to bluff the British into supporting their preferred grand strategy by making a threat that they did not intend to carry out if called on it.

Bluffs in war include many actions designed to mislead enemies as to one's strength, situation, or intent. An extended consideration of such ploys has been provided by Jon Latimer in *De-*

ception in War: The Art of the Bluff, the Value of Deceit, and the Most Thrilling Episodes of Cunning in Military History, from the Trojan Horse to the Gulf War. The first chapter of Latimer, "A History of Bluff in Warfare," includes, from the campaigns of Caesar through the First World War, examples of: luring or cowing opponents by making one's own forces look weaker or stronger than they actually were; feinting in one direction combined with moving in concealed fashion in another; and feigning disorder and desperation to induce overconfidence and rashness in the enemy.[184] Small German units in Tunisia in November 1942 successfully bluffed larger Allied forces into yielding Medjez-el-Bab and Gabès. The Wehrmacht was itself bluffed by deceptions to believe, after June 6, 1944, that another Allied army was preparing to attack at Calais and to keep there much of its Fifteenth Army.

Was Operation Shingle indeed a bluff? Might it as such have succeeded? Among the decision makers on Anzio, Alexander was alone in calling it a bluff. Churchill in pitching Shingle to Roosevelt did not suggest that its success depended on tricking Kesselring into making a bad move. Nor did he in his memoirs. The Prime Minister seems instead to have presumed that accurate German understanding of the situation would induce retreat: he was not pushing Shingle as a bluff. Per Eisenhower's memoirs, he had not thought that the operation would lead the Germans to retreat: the scale of Shingle being too small to make it their proper strategic response nor were they likely to be so deceived as to pull back when they did not need to.

Alexander's instructions to Lucas "to cut the enemy's main communications in the [Alban Hills]" were what the Allies might have done to enhance the chances of a successful bluff. Clark's watering down of that order—in positing the initial securing of the beachhead, before "advanc[ing] on [the Alban Hills]"—told Lucas not to take the risks required to maximize the likelihood of bouncing the enemy with a bluff. Lucas never thought a German retreat likely—whether induced by a bluff or not.

Alexander's conception of the Anzio bluff was predicated on "scar[ing] the Germans" and required that they be "fooled." He hoped that his enemy would think the VI Corps attack so substantial as to endanger the German Tenth Army on the Gustav Line, while not itself becoming vulnerable to counterattacks on its extended front. Unfortunately for the prospects of Shingle as a bluff, Wehrmacht commanders were rarely so fooled and, even more rarely, if ever, so scared.

The initial surprise of the Anzio landings did momentarily shake Kesselring to realize that he lacked the forces to prevent an immediate Allied seizure of Rome and did lead Tenth Army Commander Heinrich von Vietinghoff on January 22 to propose withdrawing from the Gustav Line.[185] Such a withdrawal was, however, immediately vetoed by Kesselring and was never more than minimally likely. The Germans reflexively responded to attacks—including assaults that surprised them—with counterattacks. By December 1943, they had prepared the contingent plan, Marder 1, to deal with an amphibious operation, like Shingle, on the Tyrrhenian Coast near Rome. Kesselring also had determined the steps he would take to counter landings near Genoa, Livorno, and Venice. The first actions he took to contain the beachhead at Anzio were those of Marder 1.[186]

Shingle, to succeed as a bluff, had to mislead Kesselring into thinking that it was in sufficient strength to hold a beachhead stretched to include the Alban Hills and/or Valmontone. Lucas evidently believed the likelihood that a bluffing advance would succeed to be so small and the probability of such a bluff being called with disastrous consequences so great as to justify his conservative actions.

In attempting to bounce Kesselring via bluff to the north of Rome woeful other-side perception has been seen: "Alexander's understanding of his enemy was at times shockingly deficient. Despite daily examples of German defensive intransigence, Alexander never seems to have grasped that his German counterpart was not the sort of commander to be intimidated."[187]

Game-Theoretic Perspectives on Anzio

While Operation Shingle was based on the belief that it would lead Albert Kesselring to retreat from the Gustav Line, the German field marshal also sought to anticipate likely Allied reactions to his own strategic moves. Where should he station his forces: if overwhelmingly on the Gustav Line, would the Allies undertake an amphibious bypass; if he weakened his Gustav-Line defenses by dispersing troops to repulse possible landings, would his enemy push through in the South?

When the battle at Anzio in the late winter of 1944 settled down into a sodden stalemate, each side speculated on what actions the other might take and on how its own initiatives would be responded to. Kesselring feared more landings and disposed north of Rome many divisions that might otherwise have strengthened his Tenth and Fourteenth Armies confronting the Allies on the Gustav Line and at Anzio.[188] Indeed, one plus of Operation Shingle, unmentioned in most histories, was that, in spurring German worries about another end run, it seems to have pulled troops away from their lines that would be attacked in May.[189]

Each side in 1943 and 1944 sought to draw to Italy from other fronts the divisions of its opponent, while limiting its own allotments to the peninsula. Would contemplated Allied drives northward toward the Po gain more in pulling Wehrmacht troops from Russia and France than they would cost of their own resources? Hitler and Kesselring faced the reverse of the question in pondering how resolutely to defend. As to which side in Italy, in seeking to draw in enemy forces, without having the same happen to itself, had more success historians have disagreed.[190] Such interconnected adversarial strivings are the lifeblood of game theory.

The belief of Churchill and Alexander that landing at Anzio would induce German retreat beyond Rome was based on poor other-side perception—in terms both of the military capabilities of the Germans and of their combative inclinations. Neither man seems to have expected that the response of their enemy at Anzio would be the same as in Sicily and at Salerno: a counterattack. The British Official History judged harshly the Allied OSP underpinning Shingle: "It was assumed ... that the threat to the communications of [their Tenth Army] would compel the Germans to withdraw from the Garigliano and Rapido Fronts. Never was an assumption more mistaken."[191]

Governmental Politics

The Allied premising of Shingle on an assumption that proved mistaken could be explained in part by the third of Graham Allison's models: that of governmental politics. His Model III viewed governmental decisions—and, by extension and even more, alliance decisions—as the results of bargaining games among persons with various powers. Foci for the model are the ways in which differences of personal position are resolved: ways that include both formally delegated authorities and the idiosyncratic interactions of decision participants.

Through the lens of the Governmental Politics Model, Shingle came about because: Churchill found in Brooke a decision ally of like mind; the CIGS persuaded the British Chiefs to back the operation; the Prime Minister ran his proposal by Eisenhower and other commanders in the

Mediterranean without meeting significant opposition; and the PM, with the preceding steps as substantiation of his position, then persuaded the POTUS to sign on. As is often the case for governmental and alliance decisions, there was no pre-specified procedure for deciding go-or-no-go to Anzio but, instead, sets of relevant expertises and authorities that were deftly wielded to closure by an experienced and expert practitioner of what Allison termed "bargaining games among players."[192] Allison found that "what determines each player's impact on results" includes "personal persuasiveness"—an important aspect of personality—and "control over information."[193] The decision on Anzio illustrated these points.

The structure of Allied command in late 1943 indicated that the decision on Anzio might have been most appropriately made by any one of four generals: Eisenhower, as Mediterranean commander until the end of the year; Henry Wilson, his successor; Alexander; or Clark. Instead, more than by any or all of them, it was made by a politician with a military background. The forceful personality of the Prime Minister loomed as mountainously over the decision on Anzio as did the Alban Hills over the beachhead. Anzio was seen for Churchill as "a unique opportunity ... to fulfill a lifelong fantasy by taking charge of a military operation and—at least temporarily—playing the role of a commanding general."[194] The PM combined indomitable will, rhetorical brilliance, and military experience with an officious compulsion to have a determinative hand in matters mammoth and minute. Hitler had an even stronger version of the same trait and freedom as well from the procedural constraints that reined in Churchill's urges. The Prime Minister mocked the Führer's interference in operational details but candidly confessed to the dictator's predilection in himself: "Yes. That's just what I do."[195] He prized this perk of position.

This attribute of Britain's first face in the war irked Western generals. Eisenhower was unhappy with Churchill's determination to have Shingle, which he thought constituted having "practically taken tactical command in the Mediterranean."[196] Brooke judged that "Winston never had the slightest doubt that he had inherited all the military genius of his great ancestor"[197]: John Churchill, the First Duke of Marlborough—the victor in 1704 over the French at Blenheim, about whom in the 1930s the Prime Minister had written a biography of six volumes. With, in addition to ancestry, a military education and participation in three earlier wars, Winston was judged "supremely confident of his ability to discuss grand strategy with the General Staff as much more than an interested and occasionally inspired amateur: he saw himself as their equal."[198]

This conclusion was, perhaps, understated—as the Prime Minister was also noted to have thought the British War Office, through war after war, to be unimaginative, sclerotic of mind, and inept.[199] Few have ever agreed more heartily than Churchill with Clemenceau's bon mot that war is a matter "too serious to entrust to the military." Nor was he alone in thinking little of British officers. Harold Macmillan, who dealt with many of them in the war, judged that the chiefs of staff of both the UK and U.S. chose as their subordinates mediocrities "too stupid to be employed in any operational capacity." Alan Brooke also voiced such disparagements, believing that many of his nation's most promising young officers had died in the Great War, with the result that "half our Corps and Divisional Commanders are totally unfit for their appointments."[200]

Britain's soldiers returned the scorn of their political superior. Alan Brooke's predecessor as Chief of the Imperial General Staff, Sir John Dill, urged him in January 1943: "You must come to some agreement with the [American generals] ... you cannot bring the unsolved problem up to the Prime Minister and the President. You know as well as I do what a mess they would make of it."[201] In the spring of 1944, Dill wrote Brooke—whom he knew to share his thoughts: "It is a thousand pities that Winston should be so confident that his knowledge of the military art is profound when it is so lacking in strategical and logistical understanding and judgment."[202]

Just as the soldiers belittled the military acumen of the national leaders, the latter had minimal regard for the political and diplomatic savvy of their generals. War Secretary Henry Stimson recorded in his diary on June 22, 1942, the reaction of Roosevelt to a memorandum of George Marshall's staff criticizing Operation Gymnast: "the President referred rather caustically to the paper ... saying that they had gone into politics to defend their position, basing their views upon the flimsiest kind of report from a Vice Consul."[203]

A self-assured personality can manipulate organizational structures. Brooke, in August 1943, wrote to his diary:

> Winston made matters almost impossible, temperamental like a film star, and peevish like a spoilt child. He has an unfortunate trick of picking up some isolated operation and without ever really having looked into it, setting his heart on it. When he once gets in one of those moods he feels everybody is trying to thwart him and to produce difficulties. He becomes more and more set on the operation brushing everything aside, and when planners prove the operation to be impossible he then appoints new planners in the hope that they will prove that the operation is possible.[204]

Brooke added, further on in that diary entry, that "[Winston] is quite the most difficult man to work with that I have ever struck, but I should not have missed the chance of working with him for anything on earth."[205]

The personal presence of the Prime Minister swayed decision-making groups: "the War Cabinet found it much easier to say 'no' to Churchill when he was out of the country." Instances included its vetoing in his absence his proposals: in August 1942, to appoint General Sir Claude Auchinleck to a new position; in May 1943, to occupy the Azores; and, that December, to name Harold Alexander as the overall ground commander for Overlord.[206]

Comparably consequential to personality in influencing governmental-politics decisions is control over information: by limiting who knows what. British generals sought to shield themselves from Churchill's meddling by denying him data. CIGS Brooke confessed to divulging as little as possible to his PM, feeling that "the more you tell that man about the war, the more you hinder the winning of it."[207] Auchinleck, in February 1942 the Commander-in-Chief of British Forces in the Middle East, purposely withheld in his official reports information on the strength of his armored forces facing the Afrika Korps: he did not want the Prime Minister, who as Minister of Defense was his superior, to have the numbers. He explained this in a side communication to Brooke that included the figures he had not sent Churchill.[208]

Mark Clark, although not present at Churchill's Tunis conference on Anzio, believed that information had there been withheld and torqued to influence the decision. He reported that Churchill, in his strong-arm advocacy of the landing, had insisted that the basic determination on it be made before intelligence reports—which "would under normal military conditions have been a deciding factor in ordering the Anzio attack"—were presented to the conference.[209] Even in their diminished, post-decision role, Clark sensed that these reports were not straightforwardly presented. While conceding the general excellence of British intelligence officers, he questioned their candor: "sometimes they were overly optimistic about a difficult job to be done, in order to hearten the troops.... I felt that their estimate of the Anzio situation was deliberately made optimistic because it was shaped to fit the decision already made at Tunis."[210]

To control information is to dictate decisions. Hitler's restrictions on the information he allowed his top subordinates has been thought "an essential feature of his exercise of power, for it meant that no one could argue with him on a basis of equal knowledge." The Führer ordered, for instance, that his foreign officers not be given military reports; nor his generals, diplomatic news.[211] Hitler met separately with his top functionaries and could silence diplomats and economic ministers with military considerations and generals with foreign-policy and economic imperatives.

Conclusions

That spins in memoirs are signs of bad decisions and bad outcomes was seen for Anzio, as also for Dieppe, Oran, and Messina. That the war histories of Churchill and Eisenhower downplayed their own roles and magnified those of others in deciding on Anzio suggests their unhappiness both with the launching of Shingle and with the results obtained.

Also suggestive of missteps is the positive spinning of results, which may be variously achieved. After Dieppe, one mode was to move the goalposts: while most of the operational objectives of Jubilee were slighted in the later accounts of decision participants, such subsidiary aims as luring the Luftwaffe out to fight and learning tactical lessons were raised to primary status. A related way to put lipstick on fiasco was taken in drawing attention away from the disastrous deaths in the harbor of Oran by overstating and highlighting the valor of Allied sailors and soldiers. Messina memoirs took yet another tack: the overdone touting of negligible plusses by Cunningham and Tedder in boasting of what their boats and planes had done.

Fair judgment of the decision to undertake Shingle must avoid outcome bias: must not be influenced by the consensus of historians that the Allies would most likely have been better off not mounting the operation. It must also avoid the hindsight bias of reasoning via selective consideration of the information available to the decision makers that factors responsible for the disappointing results should have been better foreseen.

Taking circumstances into account and striving to avoid outcome and hindsight biases, the Christmas-Day determination to launch Operation Shingle should be deemed acceptable—neither irrefutably good nor blatantly bad. The disparaging assessments cited above of the decision are overly harsh.

Winston Churchill and Dwight Eisenhower need not have exerted themselves as much as they did to downplay their roles in the decision on Anzio.

Less generally agreed on are the ratings of the meta-decisions: whether the deliberative process was sound, whether the authority to commit to the operation was suitably allocated and well exercised. The thinking and the discussions that led to Anzio could have been better. But, in an imperfect world, that is always so. Whether the overall process was as efficient and as wise as might have been expected—given the fatigues and strains of the participants, what they knew and did not, the pressures of time, the inevitable distortions of message between what was meant to be conveyed and what was understood—may be and has been debated.

Particular historical attention has been directed to the role played by Churchill. While the decision makers of Anzio did not put numbers on their probability estimates, values, and prospective gains, costs, and risks of their options, they did ponder non-quantitatively all such factors. Mark Clark and John Lucas thought, nevertheless, that Winston Churchill had perverted process. Had, as Lucas suggested, "the same amateur"—with his eloquence, his domination of meetings, his bullying of subordinates, his manipulation of bureaucratic channels, his charming of Roosevelt, and his insuppressible urge to meddle in military matters—forced his pet plan on the generals? Clark's account of the Christmas conference was in line with the misgivings of Lucas: Churchill "overrode all objections, including Eisenhower's.... The Prime had again demonstrated his ability to force decisions."[212]

Had the Prime acted inappropriately and had his impact on Anzio been for the better or for the worse?

Clark believed that "in the case of Anzio, political rather than military considerations dominated ... it became necessary to shape the military scheme to fit the political decision."[213] Psychological, political, and diplomatic considerations have long been considered appropriate influences on actions in war—including George Washington's 1776 attack on Trenton, Robert E. Lee's invasions of the North in 1862 and 1863, and, in 1942, the Allied landings in North Africa. Whether or not they should have been taken into account with respect to Anzio and, if so, to what extent would seem to have been best determined not by the generals, but instead by Churchill and Roosevelt acting on counsel from military and diplomatic advisors. This was done—with Churchill playing the lead and Roosevelt the assenting role. With the non-military aspects having been pushed by Churchill, the generals still had a veto: regardless of personality, psychology, politics, and foreign relations, Shingle would not have happened if a critical mass of military men had not thumbs-upped.

A case against Churchill on Anzio, based on unproven hypotheses, may be made. The Prime Minister has been ascribed motives not identical with those of the rest of the Western-Allies coalition: to increase the renown and credit bestowed on UK forces; to minimize UK casualties; to further the British Imperial agenda; and to have the egotistic, officious satisfaction of influencing military decisions. Had he had such incentives with respect to Shingle, he might have invoked diplomatic considerations as a way of getting the military to go along with his strategy. It would not have been easy for a general to counter Churchill's argument that likely effects on Spain and Turkey made Shingle essential.

We do not know the extent to which Clark may have been right in asserting that politics and diplomacy had impelled Shingle. Nor do we know if Churchill at Tunis was moved by any impulse other than to optimize the prospects of Allied victory. In the absence of compelling evidence to the contrary, it seems not inappropriate that he be given the benefit of the doubt.

The weight of both the military judgments by those involved and subsequent critiques indicate that Shingle was a not-unreasonable venture and that none of its decision makers did anything flagrantly bad.

Epilogue: The Science of Deciding, the Theory of Games and War

The Planning Fallacy

Anticipatory overoptimism, although largely ignored in writings on the war, underlay events in each of the chapters here: to British minds in the American advocacy of a cross-Channel assault in 1942; in the amateurish sanguineness that crashed at Dieppe; in the unrealistic hopes to take Tunis soon after landing in North Africa; in the sunny assurances of the air forces and navies that Axis escape at Messina could be interdicted; in the expectations of many for the results of landing at Anzio.

Winston Churchill, Franklin Roosevelt, and Dwight Eisenhower also showed awareness during the war of this behavioral trait that decision scientists later would label. The tactic of Churchill to "agree in principle and let the difficulties manifest themselves, as they will certainly do, in the discussion of ways and means" was based on decades of experience with planning-fallacy phenomena: such gung-ho-ness as that of George Marshall in April 1942 must erode as specifics were pondered. Franklin Roosevelt, wanting Torch before the November elections, sensed that his stipulation in July of landings by October 30 might not avail against the tendency of tasks to take too long. Dwight Eisenhower on July 9, 1943, in a cable to George Marshall noted one aspect of the planning fallacy that he had come to recognize: "it seems to be an invariable rule that every venture soon consumes more of our assets than initial calculations allotted to it."[1]

While the overconfidence central to the planning fallacy has preceded and caused many a disaster, decision scientist Daniel Kahneman also noted one benefit: "resilience in the face of setbacks." Such staunchness has value not only in war, but also, Kahneman believed, in scientific research, where both optimism and "a delusional sense of significance" he found to be vital to success. "In essence," Kahneman wrote, "the optimistic style involves taking credit for successes but little blame for failures"[2]—which inclination is not foreign to military and other memoirs.

Ways of Influencing and Resolving Decisions

To the various approaches taken to sway decisions and to reach agreements noted in Chapter 2, others were added.

One was having greater staff support. The Americans and British came to Casablanca in January 1943 with conflicting thoughts on grand strategy. After occasionally contentious debate, the British generally had their way—most notably in achieving Allied emphasis for the year in the Mediterranean, featuring as the next step the invasion of Sicily. Alan Brooke felt afterward that "our ideas prevailed almost throughout"[3]; U.S. General Albert Wedemeyer, that "we came, we listened and we were conquered." Wedemeyer ascribed the relatively weak decision influence of the U.S. at Casablanca to the supporting staff of the UK: "They swarmed down upon us like locusts, with a plentiful supply of planners and various other assistants, with prepared plans to insure that they not only accomplished their purpose but did so in stride and with fair promise of continuing in the role of directing strategy the whole course of this war."[4]

Not only did the British come to Morocco with an arsenal of prepared reports, but, when the conferees needed new papers, those too were UK-produced. While Roosevelt had told Marshall that he only wanted five or so American staffers in Morocco, the British came with a shipful: the 6,000-ton HMS *Bulolo,* replete with telecommunications, files, and office facilities. The American military "blamed their own inferior preparation and Staff work" for their "defeat at the hands of the British."[5] They vowed that it would not happen again.

Another tactic leading to American defeat at Casablanca was relentless repetition. Alan Brooke described the meeting of the Combined Chiefs on January 16, 1943:

> I had again to put forward all the advantages of our proposed Mediterranean [strategy] and counter arguments in favour of a French Front plan. It is a slow and tiring business which requires a lot of patience. [The U.S. chiefs] can't be pushed and hurried, and must be made gradually to assimilate our proposed policy … all matters have to be carefully explained and reexplained before they can be absorbed. And finally the counter-arguments put forward often show that even then the true conception has not been grasped and the process has to be started again.[6]

Four days later, after having begun "to despair of our arriving at any sort of agreement," in "one of the most difficult tasks I have had to do," Brooke recorded that "now we have got practically all we hoped to get when we came here!"[7]

How much logical persuasion swayed the decisions of the war is not easily judged: to what extent at Casablanca, for instance, did Brooke and the UK prevail because the U.S. eventually grasped the reasoning typed into memoranda and voiced in conference sessions—versus just being worn down by and yielding to relentless British reiterations?

While having more staff may favorably tilt decision outcomes, dismissing staff may make agreements more possible. The plenary meetings of the Combined Chiefs grew so that the UK and U.S. sides each came to have thirty or so attendant officers seated behind the principals. On May 19, 1943, in Washington, the bi-national chiefs were at loggerheads. Marshall then proposed that the supporting officers be dismissed and that the subsequent discussion be considered "off the record." With only the chiefs of staff and a secretary remaining in the room, Brooke related that "a heart to heart talk" resulted in "a bridge across which we could meet. Not altogether a satisfactory one, but far better than a break-up of the Conference." This procedure would be adopted several more times when discussions reached impasses and, per Brooke, "always helped to clear the air." Brooke "felt that frequently Marshall did not like shifting from some policy he had been briefed in by his staff lest they should think he was lacking in determination"[8]: flexibility was easier for him in a staffers-cleared room.

Extending the idea of reducing formality to ease agreement was sharing leisure. Successor to the Casablanca Conference was, in May 1943 in Washington, that of Trident. The British there were intent on further nailing down a joint commitment to the Mediterranean; the Americans were determined not to be again pushed around by their Allies and not to become so stuck in the Middle Sea as to postpone indefinitely a cross–Channel attack. Perhaps anticipating such disharmony, Marshall had arranged for conferees to make a luxurious weekend visit to restored

Colonial Williamsburg—dinner there featuring such items as Terrapin à la Maryland, simmered for two days in its own juices and washed down with 1929 Heidsieck Dry Monopole champagne. Marshall "urged all of them to forget about the future for the time being and let their thoughts dwell on that interesting period in the past when Williamsburg was the capital of England's most important colony."[9] The high officers wined, dined, birded, reminisced about hunting, and swam together. The getaway has been likened to the modern "common business practice" of "'getting to know you' weekends."[10] After two days of letting down their hair and of not talking about the 60-ton Tiger Panzer in the room, the military chiefs returned to Washington and reconvened. The interlude was judged, however, to have had no appreciable effect in softening the stances of Trident participants—with the conference considered, all in all, "one of the most ill-tempered and rancorous of all the wartime summits."[11]

Selecting decision participants unlikely to be rancorous or dissenting may ease the way to desired agreement. Similarly to doubters about Dieppe having been excluded from the decisions on Operation Jubilee, Mark Clark and John Lucas, known to have had reservations about Anzio, were thought "incredibly ... absent" from the decision conference of January 8, 1944, in Marrakesh. Neither of "the two men most vitally concerned with Shingle ... had even been invited."[12] John Lucas wrote that "why I was not allowed to attend in person I have never known as no reason was ever given me." He could only send two men of his staff.[13] The deck was stacked against disagreement.

When disagreers are present, they may be prevailed against by creating coalitions to outvote them. Churchill and Roosevelt, political beings that they were, knew legislative decision-making: lining up and holding together critical masses of support. Marshall and Stimson in June 1942 evidently believed that, by acting together, they could improve their chances of kiboshing Gymnast. Later that month, the American and British chiefs joined in rejecting the North African operation. Churchill and Roosevelt, however, met separately and proved the most telling decision coalition to be that of the two national leaders, as they kept alive the possibility of Gymnast. Brooke felt that Churchill "in later Conferences ... always feared that we should 'frame up' (he actually accused me in those terms one day) with the American Chiefs of Staff against him. He knew the Americans could carry the President with them and he feared being opposed by a combined Anglo-American block of Chiefs of Staff plus President."[14]

Legislative coalitions often are made by lobbying. Decision participants in the war sought at times to line up support for their positions before approaching other DMs—as Montgomery in August 1944 visited Bradley to confirm his assent to a northern single-thrust strategy, which was not given—before pitching it to Eisenhower. Roosevelt in July 1942 lobbied Hopkins to win his backing for Gymnast. The Presidential advisor had, the previous month, joined Marshall in opposing Churchill's push for North Africa. By July 16, however, when he and Marshall flew to London, Hopkins had been turned around by FDR in private meetings and was primed to act as his agent. The visit one month earlier of Mountbatten to Washington was a Prime-Ministerially-arranged mission to lobby Roosevelt against Sledgehammer and for both Gymnast and Jupiter.[15]

Lobbying and the winning of decision votes benefit from the persuasiveness of the words used. Few have been the historical moments when rhetorical eloquence set strategy in war. 205 BCE saw one such instance when Publius Scipio—later Africanus—bested Fabius Maximus in a debate before the Roman Senate and won its permission to invade Africa. The stirring broadcasts of Winston Churchill in the late spring of 1940 strengthened the resolve of Britain—from her poorest streets to her highest councils—to continue its war against Hitler.

The military decision makers of World War II seem, though, rarely to have been swayed by cogent or moving speeches. Churchill's unmatched way with words may in his meetings with Roosevelt in December 1941 and June 1942 have led the President to favor Operation Gymnast, but Roosevelt may well have wanted it before being pitched by his guest.

Churchill spoke well before the assembled military men on Christmas 1943 and his pitch may well have persuaded some of them to back Operation Shingle or to mute their opposition to it. During that meeting, Admiral John Cunningham (successor to his cousin Andrew as commander of Allied navies in the Mediterranean) said, "'You know, Prime Minister, this operation is fraught with great risks'—whereupon the Prime Minister turned on him and said, 'Admiral, of course, there is risk, but without risk there is no honour, no glory, no adventure,' whereupon John Cunningham crumpled up because no admiral of the fleet could admit he wasn't interested in honour, glory or adventure."[16]

At other times, however, the ideals and images movingly evoked by the Prime Minister did not avail. Late in 1943, he urged with passion to George Marshall, whose lapels he held, an invasion of Rhodes: "'His Majesty's Government can't have its troops standing idle. Muskets must flame' (and more fine English like that)." The U.S. Army chief in responding forwent eloquence: "Not one American soldier is going to die on [that] goddamned beach."[17] The Prime Minister's emotional words the next August to dissuade Eisenhower from invading southern France—that he might be impelled to go to the King and "lay down the mantle of my high office"[18]—also did not have their intended effect.

When rhetoric fails to avail, recourse may be had to ire. Churchill, in a British Chiefs of Staff meeting with cabinet officers present on December 4, 1941, proposed to send ten air squadrons to Russia. The Chief of Air Staff disagreed. Per Brooke's diary:

> This produced the most awful outburst of temper, we were told that we did nothing but obstruct his intentions, we had no ideas of our own, and whenever he produced ideas we produced nothing but objections, etc., etc! Attlee pacified him once, but he broke out again, then Anthony Eden soothed him temporarily, but to no avail. Finally he looked at his papers for some 5 minutes, then slammed them together, closed the meeting and walked out of the room.[19]

(Upon the publication of Brooke's diaries/memoirs, Churchill cut off all further contact with him.[20] Brooke, having become Viscount Alanbrooke, had resented what he saw in Churchill's memoirs as the unjust minimization of the roles of himself and of the British Chiefs.[21]) Anger can, at times, pay off. In August of 1942, Stalin said that Western reluctance to open a true second front indicated fear of the Germans. Churchill, per the British Official History, first "showed remarkable self-restraint under the Russian taunts, but after a time ... replied with passion. He was disappointed to find no 'ring of comradeship' in the discussions. His outburst appears to have been salutary, and the conversation soon turned to less inflammatory topics."[22]

At times in history, decisions may be unswayable by tactics, rhetoric, or wrath: they may derive instead from innate compulsion. Just as Alexander of Macedon perceived his life purpose to be to conquer Persia and Hannibal, his to fight Rome; Adolf Hitler may similarly have been internally driven to send his armies east—the pros and cons never having been weighed, no Plan Bs ever having been seriously considered, and the possible consequences being damned: "the plan to attack Russia was buried so deep within the Nazi DNA that it could not be stopped. The Führer invaded Russia because that was what he had been put on earth to do."[23] In this view, the explanations offered by the Führer to his generals—that intelligence indicated that the Soviets planned to attack Germany and were growing ever stronger, that Russia might stop the delivery of the 150,000 tons of oil that Germany received monthly from Romania, that victory in the East would lead Britain to give up the fight—however much truth they may have contained, were not so much considered reasons as plausible and/or invented pretexts.[24]

Public Opinion

Setting the context for the influencing and resolving of decisions throughout the war was the backdrop of public opinion: the landings in North Africa were impelled by Roosevelt's sense of what his people wanted; Dieppe, Sicily, Salerno, and Anzio were attacked in part to gratify American, British, and Canadian publics and to show that not all (just most) of the ground fighting was being left to the Russians.

High officers at times disregarded, at others invoked, public opinion. Alan Brooke knew that the citizens of the Allies early in 1942 thought that their armies should be battling toward Berlin.[25] He judged such thinking ignorant and best ignored. George Marshall in December 1941 advised against landing at Casablanca because a reverse "would have a very detrimental effect on the morale of the American people."[26] Seven months later, the U.S. Army chief advanced as one argument for shifting forces to the Pacific "that it would be highly popular throughout the U. S., particularly on the West Coast."[27] Douglas MacArthur, two months earlier, had also urged greater effort in the Pacific, because it would "satisfy American public opinion."[28] When, unhappily, Marshall acquiesced to Gymnast, he explained "that apparently our political system would require major operations this year in Africa."[29] Years later, he said, "We failed to see that the leader in a democracy has to keep the people entertained.... The people demand action. We couldn't wait to be completely ready."[30] Dwight Eisenhower summed up that "public opinion wins war"[31] and devoted much time to interacting with reporters.

Later military decisions were also based on what might upset or please the people: Montgomery's insistence on the frontal attack at Dieppe; the Royal Navy's refusal to have a capital ship bombard Dieppe; Alexander's conservative campaign in Sicily, because those back home might be too dismayed by defeats; Eisenhower's replacing Montgomery as overall ground commander in Normandy because of disgruntled Americans.

More though than their admirals and generals, the heads of state heeded public sentiment. They also felt that they should inspire, instruct, and occasionally manipulate the emotions and thoughts of their nations: in Churchill's Empire-rallying exhortations of 1940, Roosevelt's fireside-chat reviews of the global situation, FDR's misleading descriptions of pre-war events, and WSC's pressures for enhanced highlighting of British deeds in Italy.

Political scientist Richard Neustadt judged that an American President, to achieve success, "must be effective as a teacher to the public."[32] Making Neustadt's point by example, by excelling as Teacher in Chief, was Franklin Roosevelt: from the first days following his inauguration in 1933 in explaining why Americans could trust their banks; through his warnings in the mid–1930s of the dangers posed to his nation by international-law-flouting dictatorships; to his defiant voicing of American resolve, notwithstanding the setbacks that must come, in the aftermath of Pearl Harbor.

Roosevelt in 1937 had sensed more than his country the dangers posed by the violent actions of Germany, Italy, and Japan and had sought to bring it to his concerned view. In a major address he called for a quarantine of the aggressor nations and found himself, to his dismay, exposedly out in front of his people. There was shock at a perceived shift in national policy and calls by isolationist congressmen for impeachment. "It's a terrible thing," Roosevelt lamented, "to look over your shoulder when you are trying to lead—and to find no one there."[33] Having served in the wartime administration of Woodrow Wilson, he had seen the price paid by that President for being too far ahead of the citizenry and resolved not to repeat that mistake.[34] Wilson also had erred, Roosevelt thought, in excluding Republicans from leadership in the Great War.[35] To broaden his base of popular support, FDR made prominent members of the GOP his Secretaries of the Navy and of War.

To gauge the temper of his nation, Roosevelt read five daily newspapers and chatted with informed persons throughout the country. When in Washington, he most days with congressmen, hosted groups of visiting constituents, and held two informal press conferences each week.[36] He courted the scribes, "calling them by their first names, teasing them about their hangovers, exuding warmth and accessibility." Their coverage, despite the enmity toward FDR of their publisher bosses, was judged "generally full and fair"[37]—their columns instrumental in securing for him popular support. One of many missions of Eleanor was to chat with broad spectra of Americans and to report back to her husband on their conditions and thoughts. After speeches to the nation, Roosevelt would receive hundreds of telegrams. He would read them and would be heartened when the percentages that were approving were high.[38]

In the spring of 1940, with the crushing of Belgian, British, and French armies by the Wehrmacht, Roosevelt sensed a shift in the mood of Americans: they had become worried—if not so much as he—that the defeat of Britain would imperil themselves. He became willing to override the counsel of his military to extend aid to Churchill's nation, but still felt that he had to be cautious. His nation (by 88 to 12 percent) did not want to be in the war, but also wished (by 60 to 40 percent) to support England, even at the risk of becoming a combatant.[39] With political adroitness, Roosevelt spoke to his nation on the evening of December 29, 1940. He noted that the Nazis had announced their intentions to dominate the entire world and urged that the U.S. become "the great arsenal of democracy." By providing "the implements of war, the planes, the tanks, the guns, the freighters" to "Britain and the other free nations which are resisting aggression," America would stay at peace: "Our national policy is not directed toward war. Its sole purpose is to keep war away from our country."[40] By pitching these bellicose actions as the best way to stay out of the conflict, Roosevelt won the support of his public. That support enabled the passage three months later of the Lend-Lease Act—which authorized U.S. provision of war matériel, without immediate compensation, to Britain, China, and, later, Russia.

On September 11, 1941, Roosevelt announced in a radio address to the nation that the U.S. Navy would henceforth shoot on sight at any Axis submarines discovered in the North Atlantic in areas where they might prey on shipping to Britain: "when you see a rattlesnake poised to strike, you do not wait until he has struck before you crush him." To sell his public on the new policy, the President took liberties with the truth. He described a recent U-boat attack on an American destroyer, the USS *Greer*, which he said "was carrying American mail to Iceland. She was flying the American flag. Her identity as an American ship was unmistakable." She, "when attacked, was proceeding on a legitimate mission."[41] The President neglected to mention that a British plane had discovered the submarine and had dropped depth charges on it, whereupon the *Greer* had trailed the German vessel for three hours before having a few torpedoes harmlessly fired at it. The sub may not have known that the *Greer* was American. A majority of Americans, after the speech, supported the "shoot-on-sight" directive.[42]

Roosevelt's "deviousness" of presentation on the incident, some have felt, was copied 23 years later by Lyndon Johnson in misdescribing an encounter between U.S. and North Vietnamese vessels to secure passage of the Gulf of Tonkin Resolution.[43]

In the year after the entry of the U.S. into the war, the President spoke five times to his nation—limiting himself to that number out of "dread ... that my talks should be so frequent as to lose their effectiveness."[44] He asked his listeners in advance of his talks to obtain maps of the world so that they could follow his explanations of global strategy. They emptied the stores of global maps. He acknowledged substantial losses from Hitler's U-boats and Japanese attacks and warned his audience that more were to be expected "before the turn of the tide." He spoke of the evils perpetrated by the Nazis and Japan and said that they would be defeated by an "overwhelming superiority" of production. He exhorted that "every American ... not stop work for a single day," while relying on "mediation, or conciliation or arbitration" to resolve all disputes. He recounted the heroic feats of individual American fighting men.[45]

The result was a nation inspired and determined to win the war and also one solidly behind its leader: throughout 1941 and 1942, Roosevelt's public approval ratings would range between 70 and 84 percent. Churchill's then were even higher: 78 to 93 percent.[46] These levels of popularity affected national decision-making. Richard Neustadt has found Presidential power to be based on the personal prestige of the Chief Executive: reputation and standing that stems from the perceived wisdom, consistency, and dependability of conduct and from popularity and that promotes the cooperativeness of executive officers and the Congress.[47] That the wartime President and Prime Minister were so highly esteemed by their nations enhanced their decision sway: reduced the resistance that Marshall, Stimson, and others could put up against Roosevelt's directives in the summer of 1942 and made it easier for Churchill, in pushing for Anzio, to win the sign-offs of the Mediterranean commanders of two nations.

In the next two wars of America—those of Korea and Vietnam—the influence of public opinion on national decisions would be even greater: limiting the military steps that could be taken and forcing ends to the fighting.

Weariness

The Himalayan standing of Winston Churchill in the opinion of his public was significantly based on his heroic brilliance in his first weeks as Prime Minister in 1940 in what he called Britain's "finest hour." In the deliberations of December 1941 through July 1942 that culminated in the commitment to Torch, historians have generally rated both Prime Minister and President as national decision makers at least as highly as their top officers. Whether the pushing of Churchill to land at Anzio was for better or worse and whether his futile attempts to cancel the landings in southern France were wise or unwise continue to be debated. His ineffectual attempts specifically to delay Overlord and generally to influence war decisions in 1944 and 1945 have been seen—by Roosevelt and historians—as out-of-touch and petulant.[48]

Did Britain's greatest Parliamentary war leader since the two Pitts, if not of all time, become dysfunctionally weary?

Researchers of the past half-century have inquired into the effects of fatigue on decisions. While their study subjects have most commonly been military personnel or junior physicians, their findings have been judged applicable as well to jet-lagged persons of business, emergency responders, and parents of newborns.[49] These investigations indicate that sleep deprivation: impairs the functioning of the prefrontal and orbitofrontal regions of the cerebral cortex; worsens mood; erodes vigilance; lowers confidence; induces hesitancy; decreases verbal fluency; weakens creative thought; increases risk-seeking propensities; and generally degrades the ability to make decisions, especially those under uncertainty.[50] Both compensatory effort based on awareness of one's drowsiness and caffeine have been found of limited value in combatting fatigue.[51]

Speculations have been advanced as to the consequences of weariness in the war. Alan

Brooke attributed Churchill's eruption in Cabinet on December 4, 1941, to his "over-working himself and keeping too late hours."[52] Harold Macmillan met with Churchill on Christmas 1943, after the Prime Minister had dictated his telegram plugging Operation Shingle to Roosevelt. He described Churchill as "obviously *very* [emphasis in original] tired." Macmillan was also, though, impressed by the "amazing power of recovery" of "this astonishing man, who had been at the point of death a few days before."[53]

Best-placed to judge the vitality of the Prime Minister was his physician, Sir Charles Wilson, who in 1943 became Lord Moran. On December 27, 1941, in the White House, Churchill had a heart attack. Wilson knew the textbook treatment to be six weeks in bed but feared that letting the world know the coronary status of his patient "could only be disastrous." Believing that, should the PM know his own state of health, "his work would suffer," Moran would keep the diagnosis to himself. Two days later in Ottawa, Wilson asked Churchill not to lift a heavy object, which led the PM to worry again about his heart. Fearing that cardiac concern would distract his patient from preparing for his speech the next day to the Canadian Parliament, Wilson refused his next request that his pulse be taken: "You're all right. Forget your damned heart."[54] In December 1943, Churchill, described by Lord Moran, as "very tired," asked his physician, "Can't you give me something so that I won't feel so exhausted?"[55] Later, "he came to me more than once in the last year of the war complaining of exhaustion and it was plain that he was nearly burnt out."[56]

Churchill and Roosevelt saw the droop in each other. FDR, on March 18, 1942, wrote to WSC:

> I know you will not mind if I tell you that you ought to take a leaf out of my playbook. Once a month I go to Hyde Park for four days, crawl into a hole, and pull the hole after me. I am called on the telephone only if something of really great importance occurs. I wish you would try it, and I wish you would lay a few bricks or paint another picture.[57]

Fourteen months later, in Washington in May 1943, the two leaders were again together and the POTUS showed himself less inclined than previously to be convinced by the PM. Churchill asked Moran, "Have you noticed that the President is a very tired man? His mind seems closed; he seems to have lost his wonderful elasticity."[58] Treasury Secretary Henry Morgenthau believed he knew why Roosevelt "was tired. He has had ten days of arguing with Churchill, and the man is exhausted."[59]

Often feeling the same, Alan Brooke repeatedly described himself as "dog-tired."[60] In September 1943, after a few days off, he felt "that nothing less than a six months' leave could really restore the drive and vitality to pick up this burden again."[61] Non-restorative of his powers, Brooke felt, were his evenings spent as a guest of the Prime Minister in his country retreat of Chequers in Buckinghamshire. Eisenhower described the usual routine there: "Dinner would be followed by a short movie and then, at about 10:30 PM, business conferences would begin. These sometimes lasted until three the next morning."[62] (Eisenhower would rise the next mornings at his customary 6:45.[63]) Brooke recalled the "desperate longing for bed" that this Churchillian schedule produced.[64]

For George Marshall, who believed that "no important decision was ever taken after four o'clock in the afternoon,"[65] such hours were especially unwelcome. The American chief's "face," wrote Brooke of Marshall's first visit to Chequers, "was a study.... He was evidently not used to being kept out of his bed till the small hours of the morning and not enjoying it much.... I wonder how he would have liked to work permanently with Winston, and be kept out of bed three or four nights a week."[66]

Marshall worried that Eisenhower overworked. Harry Butcher described Ike in mid–July of 1942 as tired on the evenings of days that had featured "steady grind[s] of appointments."[67] It got worse. With Hopkins and Marshall in London later that month, Eisenhower was working eighteen-hour days and occasionally skipping lunch to get Marshall the papers he wanted.[68]

Marshall directed Butcher in January 1943

> to take care of Ike, keep him out of the office as much as possible, get him home early, get a masseur, have him rubbed down every evening before dinner, make him take a little nap before dinner, make him get a place where he can ride horseback or get some form of exercise, and, in general, do things that relax his mind and body, so he can have a fresh point of view while meeting ever-pressing decisions.[69]

Eisenhower complied somewhat with Marshall's wishes but still had moments of observed and admitted weariness—which led his doctors in August 1943 to order bed rest for a number of days.[70] His especial tiredness in Egypt in November 1943 and on the eve of Overlord was also noted.[71] General John Lucas, who had seen much of Eisenhower in 1943, recorded that December that "Ike looked well but much older."[72] On December 29, Marshall cabled Eisenhower that it was "important that you be fresh mentally and it certainly will not be if you go straight from one great problem [the Mediterranean Theater] to another [Overlord]. Now come on home and see your wife and trust somebody else for twenty minutes."[73] Eisenhower complied and took the first two weeks of 1944 off from the war to return to the U.S.

The barrage of V-1 rockets against England, begun in mid–June of 1944, not only inflicted 20,000 casualties but also deprived millions of sleep. Upon being alerted that the buzz-bombs were coming, Londoners—including Eisenhower and his staff—scurried to shelters. Not until early August, when the command post of the Supreme Commander was moved to Normandy, would he and his officers again have uninterrupted nights of sleep.[74]

Eisenhower was sensed to be in "the depths of despair," when, on July 25, Allied bombers mistakenly bombed their own troops. Around this time, he also "suffered several bad headaches, complained about his blood pressure and, in a rare mood of fatigue, spent one morning in bed" and was "depressed."[75]

Contributing to such physical and emotional decline of Eisenhower may have been not only too little sleep but also his cigarettes. He had begun smoking as a cadet at West Point and, during the war, puffed away each day up to four packs of unfiltered Camels. His cigarettes likely helped him at times to maintain a high level of performance through his long days—as nicotine, by triggering the release of dopamine, epinephrine, and glucose, is known to enhance attention, alertness, memory, and motor abilities.[76] These short-term positives of Eisenhower's habit came, however, with downsides: smoking in general increases not only the long-term risks of cancer and cardiovascular disease, but also heightens immediate sense of stress.[77] Stress in turn has been causally linked to anxiety, headaches, gastrointestinal upset, impaired sex drive, sleep difficulty, irritability, and depression. In 1949, a physician advised Eisenhower to reduce his smoking to one pack per day. After a few days, however, of such limited puffing, he decided that quitting would be better and never smoked again.

The extents to which the woes of Eisenhower in the war arose from his weariness and his smoking and the effects of them on his decisions are not known.

One decision that has been put down to mood was Omar Bradley's consent on August 14, 1944, to have George Patton send two-plus corps toward the Seine. The author of the American Official History judged that this "approval flowed from his self-esteem, which was growing markedly, a result not only of [recent] American success ... but also of the complimentary remarks from high-ranking American officers on his perspicacity and tactical skill."[78] Described that month as "fluctuating between flaming independence and depressing doubt," Bradley "attempted to play the role of the bold leader, then was troubled by doubt."[79] Insufficient sleep on the part of the army commander may have underlain such moods, as well as Patton's diagnosis on the fifteenth that Bradley was "suffering from nerves."[80] Patton generalized: "Tired officers are always pessimists."[81]

To avoid such effects of fatigue, Bernard Montgomery prioritized sleep. A subordinate recalled that, at 9:30 PM, he regularly headed off to bed and that, apart from once at El Alamein, he was not awoken.[82] In August of 1942, when visited by Churchill in Egypt, the newly-appointed Eighth Army Commander went to bed at his usual time—ducking out on the late-hour sessions of his nation's leader.[83] Even Montgomery, however, was later felt to have grown weary. A biographer noted that Patton's rude slur for the Briton in December 1945—"a tired little fart"—was partly on target: for "Monty was indeed tired."[84] He had been dragging at least since late 1943.[85] In July 1940, Churchill had dined with Montgomery and was surprised to find him a teetotaler. The general told the Prime Minister that he "neither drank nor smoked and was 100 percent fit." Churchill "replied in a flash, that he both drank and smoked and was 200 percent fit."[86] Churchill died at 90; Montgomery, at 88.

For the man whom Churchill made a field marshal, fitness—the mental being tied to the physical—was a priority. Montgomery insisted on rigorous training, whatever the weather and not just for soldiers in the field. All staff officers under forty were required once each week to run seven miles. Upon being informed of a physician's warning that such a run might well cause the death of one pudgy colonel, Montgomery's response was that such a death in training would be better than one in the midst of battle.[87]

Montgomery's opposing general in Africa could relate to his flagging and dragging: Albert Kesselring in early 1943 thought that Erwin Rommel "was physically worn out and psychologically fatigued ... a tired old man."[88]

George Patton in August 1943—on the grounds of fatigue—relieved Generals Terry Allen and Theodore Roosevelt, Jr., as first and second in charge of the U.S. First Division in Sicily.[89] Both, after rest, would be returned to command. Roosevelt came ashore on Utah Beach on June 6, 1944, with the first wave of U.S. troops—for which he would receive the Congressional Medal of Honor. He died of a heart attack, at 56, one month later. Allen would die at 81.

John Lucas noted his lack of sleep in Anzio and repeatedly recorded there in his diary his sense of stress: "The strain of a thing like this is a terrible burden. Who the hell wants to be a general."[90] Alexander was thought to have had Clark relieve Lucas primarily because of the physical toll Anzio was taking on him.[91]

Age

Years worsen fatigue.

Sleep researchers comparing persons aged 20 to 25 with others aged 40 to 60 have found that the older subjects claimed to have been less impaired by sleep deprivation, when they actually had had greater declines in attention and cognitive functioning.[92]

Early in 1942, Alan Brooke noted that First Sea Lord Sir Dudley Pound occasionally dozed off in meetings, looking "like an old parrot asleep on his perch."[93] Pound was then 64 and had an undiagnosed brain tumor. He not only administered the Royal Navy and represented it on the British Chiefs of Staff, but also slept on a camp bed at the Admiralty, the better to oversee the battle against the U-boats. With his torpor worsening and having suffered a stroke, Pound in September 1943 resigned as First Sea Lord. On October 21, 1943—the 138th anniversary of

Trafalgar—at 66, he died. Many thought that Briton's first sailor "had worked himself into an early grave."[94]

Franklin Roosevelt knew his own declining vigor and cut back in the 1940s his hours of work, but also allowed Churchill to keep him up late and thrice attended conferences across the Atlantic that sapped his strength. In Tehran in late 1943, the President was described as "inept. He was asked a lot of questions and gave the wrong answers."[95] At Yalta in February 1945, the President "intervened very little in the discussions, sitting with his mouth open ... [his] shrewdness has gone, and there is nothing left."[96] Nine weeks later, Roosevelt died—perhaps, like Pound, a victim of the war.

Napoleon judged in 1805, in which he turned 36: "A man has his day in war as in other things; I myself shall be good at it for another six years, after which even I shall have to stop." His last successful campaign was that of Wagram, in his fortieth year.[97]

For military leaders of acknowledged excellence over the centuries, their ages of peak achievements were: Alexander, 21 to 25; Hannibal, 29 to 31; Scipio, 27 to 34; Caesar, 42 to 55; Gustavus, 35 to 37; Marlborough, 52 to 58; Frederick, 33 to 50; Nelson, 38 to 47; Napoleon, 26 to 39; Wellington, 34 to 46; Lee, 55 to 57; and Grant, 39 to 42. While Alexander, Hannibal, Scipio, and Napoleon dazzled before thirtieth birthdays; Caesar, Marlborough, and Lee showed military brilliance still possible after 50. Other successful commanders in their later years were Timur (Tamerlane), who was 66 at Ankara; Moltke, 70 at Sedan and still Chief of Staff of the world's best army at 88; Hindenburg, 67 at Tannenberg; and MacArthur, 70 at Inchon.

Chronological age does not precisely measure youthfulness. Napoleon saw, and proved, that exertion quickens aging: few, if any, have ever worked as hard as he. He died at 51. His antagonist, William Pitt the Younger, began his 19 years as prime minister at 24, and died, exhausted, at 46. Wellington, in contrast, mixed work with recreation, showed 46th-year energy at Waterloo, and lived to 83. Marlborough assumed command at a youthful 51 and, ten tiring years later, laid it down at a worn-out 61. Lee, similarly, in the four years of America's Civil War, seemed to have aged multiples of that time. Both Marlborough and Lee commented, as their wars wore on, on their senses of decline in vitality and skill. Marlborough would outlive his war by nine years and would die at 72; Lee, by five years and at 63.

The ages on December 7, 1941, of leading decision makers were: Adolf Hitler, 52; Winston Churchill, 67; Franklin Roosevelt, 59; Alan Brooke, 58; George Marshall, 60; Dwight Eisenhower, 51; Bernard Montgomery, 54; Harold Alexander, 49; Omar Bradley, 48; Mark Clark, 45; Andrew Cunningham, 58; Maurice Gamelin (France's first general in early 1940), 69; Albert Kesselring, 56; Red Army Marshal Ivan Konev, 43; John Lucas, 51; Douglas MacArthur, 61; Erich von Manstein (thought by many the best general of the Third Reich), 54; Louis Mountbatten, 41; Benito Mussolini, 58; George Patton, 56; John Roberts, 49; Red Army Marshal Konstantin Rokossovsky, 44; Erwin Rommel, 50; Joseph Stalin, 62; Arthur Tedder, 51; Red Army Marshal Aleksandr Vasilevsky, 46; Maxime Weygand (who succeeded Gamelin as supreme French commander in May 1940), 74; and Georgy Zhukov (thought Russia's best general in the war), 45. Of those who died natural deaths, Churchill lived over 23 more years; Roosevelt, over three more; Brooke, 21; Marshall, seventeen; Eisenhower, 27; Montgomery, 24; Alexander, 27; Bradley, 39; Clark, 42; Cunningham, 21; Gamelin, sixteen; Kesselring, eighteen; Konev, 32; Lucas, eight; MacArthur, 22; Manstein, 31; Roberts, 21; Rokossovsky, 26; Stalin, eleven; Tedder, 25; Vasilevsky, 25; Weygand, 23; and Zhukov, 32. Hitler lived another three years, before taking his own life; Mountbatten, another 37 years, before being assassinated by the Irish Republican Army; Mussolini, another three, before being killed by Italian partisans; Patton, another four, before dying of a road accident; and Rommel, another two, before being made to kill himself.

None of the five main nations in the European war—France, Germany, Russia, the UK, and the U.S.—showed adeptness in identifying and promoting young military ability. (Of the five, Russia—in the rise to preeminence of Konev, Rokossovsky, Vasilevsky, and Zhukov—might seem to have done best. This, however, may well have owed less to superior Soviet talent-scouting in junior officers than to Stalin's having had shot in the late 1930s 78 of his 88 top commanders.[98]) Strategic excellence in war has been considered related to skill in chess. The last ten generally-recognized world chess champions became such at an average age of less than 30.[99] Their ages, plus the early feats of Alexander, Hannibal, Scipio, and Napoleon, suggest that all five nations might have done well to have given more decision authority to their best younger officers.

Both the UK and the U.S. had in the nineteenth century put young men into high positions. Wellington had at 39 commanded the forces of Britain in Portugal: her main army. Jeb Stuart had at 29 led the cavalry of Lee's Army of Northern Virginia. Philip Sheridan, lauded by Grant as the best general of the war, had at 33 commanded the cavalry of the Army of the Potomac.

Georges Clemenceau, upon becoming Premier Minister in 1917, found that many of France's generals "were too old and exhausted to lead properly." Pitilessly, he cashiered them.[100] Clemenceau was then, perhaps, especially aware of the deficits due to age, being 76 himself.

George Marshall in October 1939 similarly judged that "the present general officers of the line are for the most part too old to command troops in battle under the terrific pressures of modern war." He said that he would give them opportunities to show what they could do, but would sack those who did not perform well. Only one of the senior generals of the U.S. Army in September 1939, when Marshall became its chief, Walter Krueger, would command men in battle in the war.[101] (Heading the U.S. Navy at that time was the Chief of Naval Operations, Harold Stark (born in 1880), whom Eisenhower considered "a nice old lady."[102])

One way for Marshall to test ability was the war exercise. His own professional ascent had benefited from the proficiency he had shown in war games held in 1910 in Texas, in 1912 in Connecticut, and in 1914 in the Philippines.

In September 1941, 400,000 U.S. soldiers participated in Louisiana and Texas in a simulated military encounter. Eisenhower thought that "the beneficial results of that great maneuver were incalculable … it speeded up the process of eliminating the unfit; it brought to the specific attention of seniors certain of the younger men who were prepared to carry out the most difficult assignments."[103] Of the 42 in that game who commanded divisions or larger units, only eleven would command in the war. The abilities shown in that exercise by Eisenhower and Patton were judged vital to their promotions.[104] (Shortly after his impressive performance in Soviet war games in January 1941, Georgy Zhukov was made Chief of the USSR General Staff.[105])

Tiredness compounded by age impaired decisions. The United Kingdom, in the late fall of 1941, dispatched the new, strong, and swift battleship HMS *Prince of Wales,* escorted by the battlecruiser HMS *Repulse,* to the South China Sea. Per Churchill: "They had been sent to these waters to exercise that kind of vague menace which capital ships of the highest quality whose whereabouts is unknown can impose upon all hostile naval calculations."[106] The decision process was described: "The First Sea Lord [Pound], who was growing old and tired, and the Chiefs of Staff Committee, of which he was chairman, felt unable to withstand" the arguments for sending the two ships to the Far East.[107] Lacking air protection, the two were on December 10 sunk by land-based Japanese bombers. Churchill wrote that, on learning of this, "In all the war I never received a more direct shock."[108]

*   *   *

What should the fighting nations best have done with respect to the ages of their officers?

It is likely that all militaries in the war would have done better to have mandated retirement at a set age, perhaps at 50. For the U.S., this would have meant that such tired and bumbling old-sters as Lloyd Fredendall, Ernest Dawley, and Courtney Hodges would not have commanded the nation's armies. Historian Rick Atkinson described the three men. Fredendall, born in 1883 and in command at the American debacle at Kasserine, was "short, stocky and opinionated.... Unen-cumbered with charisma, [he] substituted bristling obstinacy.... On the telephone, [he] employed a baffling code, which he often abandoned in mid-conversation whenever he and his auditor had become sufficiently confused." Dawley, born in 1886, was "a stocky, cautious artilleryman" and "a decorated protégé of George Marshall in the Great War," who, in charge at Salerno on September 10, 1943, was soon "exhausted and off balance" and relieved of command. Hodges, born in 1887, "was the wrong general" at the head of the U.S. First Army in 1944–5. While "capable enough during the pursuit across France," by October 1944 he "was worn by illness, fatigue, and his own shortcomings—'an old man playing the game by the rules of the book, and a little confused as to what it was all about,' a War Department observer wrote."[109]

Had the places of such past-their-primes leaders been taken instead by such talented younger men as Joseph Collins, James Gavin, Matthew Ridgway, and Lucian Truscott—born in 1896, 1907, 1895, and 1895, respectively—unknown numbers of young American lives would likely have been saved. George Marshall would have done better to have gone much further than he did in culling the long-in-tooth from the ranks.

But mandating retirement at fifty would also have cost the nation the services in the war of such men as Marshall himself, Dwight Eisenhower, Douglas MacArthur, and George Patton—whose performances have been judged superb. A still better approach would have been—and would be for future militaries—to base promotions, demotions, retentions, and retirements much more than was the case on extensive, repeated testing of all officers, while also taking into account maturity, experience, and other qualities not well shown in test settings. Tests should simulate command conditions. If officers in war would have to perform when short of sleep, then tests should include rest deprivation. Tests need not be on the 400,000-man scale of the Louisiana-Texas exercise of 1941. With far fewer persons, officers could be tested on their abili-ties to optimize the performances of their top lieutenants and of their rank and file; to promote subordinates and to form efficient teams; to direct information gathering; to make judgments of overall situations based on limited reports; and to make prospectively best decisions when what is happening is unclear.

Not only the personnel, but also the tactical and strategic thinking of the military should be repeatedly challenged and tested. The growing bureaucratization of armed forces has brought with it the shortcomings of entrenched officialdom: red tape, adherence to fixed rules, inhibiting of initiative, and resistance to change. George Patton and Dwight Eisenhower, in the years after the First World War, butted their heads against the obstinate myopia of traditional thinking. Both men, seeing the potential of tanks, published articles in the *Infantry Journal* describing the strategic possibilities opened up by these new weapons. Eisenhower was ordered—with the threat of court-martial—not to publish any more such heretical thoughts: the foot soldier, not any new-fangled tracked vehicle, was to play the key role in future wars. Patton was told the same.[110] Brig-adier General Billy Mitchell was in 1925 court-martialed and demoted for what senior officers deemed excessive touting of the potential of planes in war.

The American war games of 1941 helped to show which hallowed military doctrines had been rendered obsolescent by advancing technology and which new methods—notably motor-ized infantry and tactical air support for armor—held promise.

To too great an extent men achieved high authority in the militaries of the 1940s based on how well they had done in the Great War, on their abilities to endure decades of slow advancement while not ruffling feathers or irking superiors by challenging prevailing orthodoxy with new ideas, on ingratiating themselves with peers and with those who made promotions (Patton was deemed masterful at "bootlicking"[111]), and on getting others to pen glowing reports about them.

The warring nations could and should have done better. Much was learned about the abilities of officers from war exercises conducted by Britain, Germany, the Soviet Union, and the United States. All would have gained to have taken such testing further and to have allocated command authority far more on test-displayed performance.

Decision Fatigue, Food and Sex

Modern research indicates that George Marshall may have been onto something in making his tough calls no later than by four in the afternoon.

Deciding tires.

Studies have found that periods of making choices reduce our self-discipline, our ability to persevere with mental tasks, and our sales resistance—all manifestations of *decision fatigue*.[112] In one study, Israeli judges were found to be more than seven times more likely to grant parole in cases heard early in the morning, than in similar cases late in the afternoon. They were also more than three times as likely to grant parole just after than just before lunch. Given that the chance of recidivism makes it riskier to grant than to deny parole, the actions of the judges were explained by their greater risk-aversion after extended stretches of deciding and when they had less sugar in their blood.[113]

It is possible that, just as physical exertion tires privates and limits how many miles they can march in a day, generals may have limited willingness to take decision risks: chancing hazardous steps may deplete their reserves of daring and make later audacity less likely—as may also have happened with the Israeli parole judges. Dwight Eisenhower noted that Bernard Montgomery had been criticized for overcaution at the end of 1942 and in early 1943 in pursuing Rommel's Afrika Korps.[114] The future field marshal had, for 13 days at El Alamein, persevered through the ups and downs of what would be the banner battle of his career. Having hazarded so much for so long may have drawn down his store of boldness.[115]

Researchers have learned that, after having exerted ourselves to make decisions we tend: to persevere less when encountering frustration; to procrastinate; to rely more on the advice of others; to avoid compromising, which requires more psychic effort; and to simplify our choices by restricting ourselves to a single criterion—such as "just give me the cheapest"—instead of making tradeoff judgments.[116]

Barack Obama in 2012 revealed awareness of such decision-scientific findings:

"You'll see I wear only gray or blue suits," he said. "I'm trying to pare down decisions. I don't want to make decisions about what I'm eating or wearing. Because I have too many other decisions to make." He mentioned research that shows the simple act of making decisions degrades one's ability to make further decisions.... "You need to focus your decision-making energy."[117]

One example given of decision fatigue was the choice made by New York Governor Eliot Spitzer—an "executive whose willpower has already been depleted by making decisions all day long," who was presumed to have been viewing "pictures of young women, many in transparent lingerie"—to engage a prostitute. One study found that showing men pictures of attractive women sharply increased their preference for immediate over future rewards.[118]

Such research suggests that generals pondering actions with possible near-term gains but also longer-term downsides may be the more likely to undertake them, if they recently have viewed comely women.

The effects of women on male generals have long been speculated on. Napoleon and Wellington had mistresses on campaign. One of Napoleon's leading marshals, André Masséna, brought a ladylove—the wife of a captain on his staff—in 1810 and 1811 on his campaign in Portugal. Uncharacteristic delay in his pursuit of Wellington's Anglo-Portuguese army was ascribed to the fatigue of his amour—although he reported it to his Emperor as a need to await supplies. After retreating from Wellington's Lines of Torres Vedras, the marshal's reflection was: "What a mistake I made in taking a woman to the war."[119]

Eisenhower's driver, Kay Summersby, in memoirs written after his death and as she was herself dying, recounted her unconsummated love affair in the later years of the war with the Supreme Commander.[120] She reported that "many, probably most, of Ike's top staff officers [in Algiers] had mistresses."[121] She was herself "one of the very few people who knew every general—and every general's girl friend."[122] In August of 1944, as their armies raced across France, Eisenhower and Bradley relaxed in the evenings by playing bridge with Summersby and another young woman.[123] The next March, a worn-down Eisenhower was sensed to be near collapse and was persuaded to spend a few days with Summersby, Bradley, two other women, and a few others in a villa on the French Riviera.[124] (Per Roosevelt's daughter Anna, her brother, "FDR, Jr., had developed a terrific crush on Kay Summersby, General Eisenhower's beautiful young driver." FDR himself, after spending time with the general and his driver, had concluded that the two were lovers.[125])

Allegations linked George Patton and Jean Gordon, daughter of the half-sister of the general's wife, Beatrice. Jean was 29 years younger than George, who, in Hawaii in the mid–1930s, one biographer wrote, "fell hard [for Jean], made a damned fool of himself, and nearly wrecked his marriage."[126] The affair was said by some intimates—and denied by others—to have resumed in the summer of 1944 when Gordon came to England and to have continued when, that September as a Red Cross nurse assigned to the Third Army, she went to France. After the war and the death of George, Beatrice said to Jean, "May the Great Worm gnaw your vitals and may your bones rot joint by little joint." Days later, on January 8, 1946, Jean Gordon killed herself.[127]

Marlene Dietrich, occasionally hardy and heroic in her visits to front-line Allied soldiers, said that she had shared the bed of Patton.[128]

The effects of female companionship on the military decisions of Eisenhower, Bradley, Patton, and others is not known.

Groupthink

In addition to two-person, private relationships, multi-individual interactions in meetings may also sway decisions. Inclinations toward overconfidence and the planning fallacy, decision science has found, may be strengthened when choices are made not by single decision makers, but by plural persons conferring.

Groupthink has been defined as

a quick and easy way to refer to a mode of thinking that people engage in when they are deeply involved in a cohesive group, when the members' strivings for unanimity override their motivation to realistically appraise alternative courses of action.... Groupthink refers to a deterioration of mental efficiency, reality testing, and moral judgment that results from in-group pressures.[129]

In his book of that title, Irving Janis found groupthink in the collective decision-making that had preceded the American surprise at Pearl Harbor, the drive of United Nations forces into North Korea, the attempted invasion of Cuba at the Bay of Pigs, and the escalation of the Vietnam War. One historian also diagnosed groupthink in both the UK and the U.S. after the visit of Hopkins and Marshall to London in April 1942 and among the Torch planners of Washington four months later.[130]

The scenario reviewed by Janis with greatest similarity to the deliberations that culminated in Operations Jubilee, Torch, and Shingle was that of the Bay of Pigs: the CIA-plotted and -pushed invasion of Cuba. Its goal was to overthrow the increasingly Marxist government of Fidel Castro, who had come into power in Havana in January of 1959. Two days after the inauguration of John Kennedy on January 20, 1961, his administration commenced formally debating the proposed operation, the planning for which had begun under Dwight Eisenhower. On the seventeenth of April, 1,400 Cuban exiles went ashore on the south coast of the island. None of their four supporting supply ships could land—all having been sunk or chased off by the Cuban air force. The invaders were soon attacked and surrounded by 20,000 of Castro's troops and 1,200 of them—most of those who had not been killed—were on April 19 taken prisoner.

The operation had had about as slim a chance of success as had the foredoomed landings at Red, White, and Blue Beaches at Dieppe. The Kennedy Administration had deludedly thought that the extensive American support for the exiles provided by the Central Intelligence Agency, air force, and navy of the U.S. could be denied behind the assertion that the invaders were just Castro-despising refugees, acting on their own. The lie was at once seen through—which made the military debacle a foreign relations disaster as well. John Kennedy soon asked, "How could I have been so stupid to let them go ahead?"[131] The U.S. would later pay a ransom of food and medical supplies valued at $53 million to Cuba to free the 1,113 surviving invaders. This bungle of the new administration contributed to the scorn that Nikita Khrushchev had for the young President and may have led him to send nuclear missiles to Cuba. The episode was rated "among the worst fiascos ever perpetrated by a responsible government."[132]

The decision-making for the Bahia de Cochinos had much along groupthink lines in common with that behind the landings at Dieppe. In each case, the decision-making circle included, in the words of Janis in writing of Kennedy's group, "some of the most intelligent men ever to participate in the councils of government."[133] Awareness of being among other intelligent men in overall concurrence was taken to mean that risks could be disregarded. (Decision scientists have found that groups, via discussion, become more risk-seeking and more excessively confident than their individual members.[134]) The result, in both 1942 and 1961, was that decision participants signed on for the projected operations not after having thought critically and independently but, instead, by relying on the consensual judgments of respected others.[135] Those judgments, however, sounded more consensual than they were, inasmuch as decision participants refrained from voicing worries out of concern for their personal positions and from fear of incurring disapproval,[136] while dissenters were in both instances told to keep to themselves their negative thoughts and questions.[137] The blinkered thinking symptomatic of groupthink was rendered less open to challenge by the imposition of secrecy. In 1961, this meant that many who might have seen flaws in the planned operation—including CIA and State Department experts on Cuba—never were consulted.[138]

There also were differences between the two groupthink scenarios. While admirals Harold Baillie-Grohman and Bertram Ramsay and generals Bernard Montgomery and John Roberts expressed reservations about Rutter/Jubilee, all highest-ranking advisors of John Kennedy approved the Bay of Pigs plan.[139] The approvals were given in several sessions of an ad hoc decision-making committee convened by Kennedy. That committee consisted usually of three cabinet officers, two White House staffers, three military chiefs, the director and deputy director of the CIA, as well as occasional others. The President, while voicing skeptical concerns, allowed the CIA officials to control the discussion. Whenever objections were raised, he turned to them for refutation.[140] After Arkansas Senator J. William Fulbright spoke to the group and predicted the diplomatic damage that would in fact ensue, Kennedy asked committee members, in turn around the table, to state their positions. Defense Secretary Robert McNamara voiced his approval of the invasion and was followed by other assents. Later decision research has shown that such open, ordered straw votes foster *cascades:* sequences in which group members, revealing their positions one by one, are influenced by those who have gone before them, giving early speakers outsized influence on the outcomes.[141] The problem is exacerbated when persons of high status—such as McNamara—speak early. Kennedy stopped the process before it reached Arthur Schlesinger, Jr., whom he knew to side with Fulbright.[142]

Cass Sunstein and Reid Hastie in 2015 addressed multi-person decision-making pitfalls in *Wiser: Getting Beyond Groupthink to Make Groups Smarter* and made points of pertinence to the decisions on Dieppe, Anzio, and the Bay of Pigs. Many leaders, in Sunstein's experience, "tend to command agreement"[143] and often have a *halo effect:* the attribution of excessively positive qualities including special astuteness in deciding.[144] Many in the councils of decision throughout the war sensed a glowing circle above the head of Winston Churchill. Haloed leaders seeking not information or analysis but acquiescence—Churchill in Tunis on Christmas 1943 may have been in quest of all three—in persons of lower standing may induce their self-silence. It was felt that the recent string of successes of John Kennedy had lent the members of his Bay of Pigs advisory group a euphoric sense of invulnerability, which stifled dissent.[145]

Dissent also is difficult, Sunstein found, when it entails differing with colleagues who are congenial, articulate, or of high status. In groups with such persons, others hold back from incurring personal risks or disapproval by expressing disagreement.[146] To maximize pertinent data for decision-making groups and to optimize their critical thinking, their leaders should "not allow irrelevant social factors such as status, talkativeness, and likability" to affect deliberations.[147] "Confident or dominant personalities ... regardless of the quality of their contributions" have disproportionate impact on decisions.[148] The deliberations on Rutter/Jubilee did not lack men of such temperaments: for Rutter, Bernard Montgomery was not to be withstood; for Jubilee, John Hughes-Hallett. Richard Bissell, Deputy Director of the CIA, played such a role and had such influence on the Bay of Pigs. When such persons are recognized as authorities, others defer to them and silence themselves.[149] In addition to their demeanors of mastery, Montgomery and Bissell had expertise sensed as paramount.

In the presence of such daunting experts, those of low status in decision-making groups are, Sunstein found, especially likely to self-silence.[150] The Canadian participants in the Dieppe decision—generals Andrew McNaughton, Henry Crerar, and John Roberts—were, by virtue of their Maple-Leafness, of lower standing. Despite their demonstrated prowess and achievements in the earlier war, Canadians were not treated well by some Britons. Like other dominions, Canada was thought to have been considered by Churchill but a subservient colony and source of manpower[151]; its Prime Minister, Mackenzie King, was disdained by Churchill and taken for granted[152]; bogus claims of limited space were momentarily asserted to bar Canadian generals from presence in a room in which decisions were being made on an operation in which their men predominated in number; Andrew McNaughton was in July 1943 by Harold Alexander denied permission to visit a Canadian division in Sicily—which led one American to wonder "how the British had ever succeeded in holding together an empire when they treated the respected military representative of its most important Commonwealth [sic] so rudely."[153] Neither McNaughton, Crerar, nor Roberts sought significantly to sway the decisions on Dieppe. It is likely that, had they done so, they would have had—per later research on groupthink[154]—little effect.

Sunstein described ways in which the downsides of groupthink may be limited. One entailed being alert to the dangers of *happy talk:* the inclination of group members mutually to reinforce and to mouth comforting, sunny views of their prospects.[155] Happy talk was imposed on high officers in Operation Jubilee and by Dwight Eisenhower on December 19, 1944—when he ordered in a meeting to respond to initial German successes in the Ardennes, "There will be only cheerful faces at this conference table." Happy talk can have the advantages of preventing disabling disheartenment and of inspiring improved performance. It may also, however, worsen decisions by downplaying risks and exaggerating possible benefits.

One way to counter such optimistic spinning is to promote anxiety in decision-making. Sunstein divided leaders into the two categories of the complacent and the anxious: the former being positive, confident, perhaps effervescent; the latter, "may be optimistic, nice, even enthusiastic ... but they are also troubled by concern, skepticism and doubt."[156] George Patton in Sicily and Normandy exemplified the complacent general—ideal for situations in which flanks need not be fretted; John Lucas at Anzio, the anxious officer most needed when risks lurk.

Giddy talk may also be reined in by focusing on numbers: instead of allowing Panglossian assurances to set the tone, asking for data and for estimates of possible positive and negative effects and their likelihoods. One form of quantification endorsed by Sunstein and mandated by the U.S. federal government for evaluating proposed regulations is *cost-benefit analysis:* expressing the pluses and minuses of actions in monetary terms and comparing them.[157] CBA is—along with such other disciplines as game theory, cost-effectiveness analysis, risk-benefit analysis, and systems analysis—one of several that contribute to decision science. CBA has been considered "an indispensable safeguard against" not only the types of individual biases that decision scientists have identified, but also against group malfunction—inasmuch as its numerical-data grounding "imposes real discipline" and "a reality check."[158] The rigorously-empirical approach of cost-benefit analysis and its sibling disciplines might have improved the non-decision at Messina. Numerical analysis might instructively have compared the likely effects of having Allied planes interdict German flight from Sicily versus bomb the rail yards of mainland Italy. Such comparisons might have brought better decisions and outcomes.

An alternative tactic noted by Sunstein to achieve reality checking is to arrange for uncowed expressions of opinion. Instead of cascade-fostering, sequential, open votes, groups might provide for anonymous statements of opinion or secret ballots.[159] Decision researchers have noted the benefits in corporate settings of promoting a "*culture of candor* in which employees are comfortable expressing their varied perspectives"—at times to the point of "vehemently argu[ing] their positions," even "yelling at each other."[160] They also have recommended that group leaders initially refrain from revealing their thinking and might well follow the custom of Japanese corporations in having members speak in reverse order of status[161]—sharply differing from the Bay of Pigs deliberations, in which McNamara made an early statement of position and Kennedy's chairmanship signaled his leaning. In the American Civil War (for instance, on the evening of July 2, 1863, at General George Meade's headquarters at Gettysburg), voting in councils of war had proceeded from junior to senior officers—perhaps to limit groupthink risk.

Anxiety may be promoted and groupthink complacency sobered by commissioning dissent. John Kennedy, in the Cuban Missile Crisis of 1962, had his brother, Attorney General Robert, be devil's advocate against an early, bellicose consensus. RFK's criticism was so effective as to unsettle the incipient meeting of minds—possibly averting war.[162] Assignment of a devil's-advocacy role may, however, seem patently artificial and therefore prove ineffective. To avoid this pitfall, suggested improvements include formally recognizing devil's advocacy as a vital decision-group process, with rotated assignment to it,[163] and *red-teaming:* a military term for having a sub-group oppose in a simulated situation a favored option or make a best case against it.[164]

Another related antidote to over-optimism in decisions is the *premortem:* asking that, when a decision has nearly been made, it be assumed to have ended in disaster and that a short account of the disaster be written.[165] Premortems might have foreseen enough of what went wrong at Dieppe and in Cuba to have lessened or prevented those misadventures. Both dissents and questions were judged to have been discouraged in deciding on Shingle—as searches in the records of those deliberations found no inquiries about what might go wrong and that "hardly anyone [with the few exceptions of 'junior staff officers whose misgivings were quickly dismissed or ignored'] dared challenge Churchill" or his presumptions.[166]

Franklin Roosevelt believed that groups can act more wisely than individuals: that involving others in deciding can help avoid error. The powers, statures, and occasional haloes of U.S. Presidents induces, however, in their advisors both happy talk and self-silencing. To maximize the net benefits of multi-person counsel for Presidential decisions requires that ways be found to skirt such pitfalls of groupthink. In this vein, one lauded practice of FDR was to indicate agreement with persons of conflicting positions, thereby encouraging them to make best cases for their favored options—after hearing which he decided.[167] He did not insist on Gymnast until after having heard the worst that George Marshall and Henry Stimson could say about it.

Expertise

What John Kennedy was said to have learned, above all, from the Bay of Pigs "was never to rely on experts."[168]

Cass Sunstein also addressed an issue common both to decision-making groups and to individual DMs: how best to use expertise—which he defined as the ability "to make winning bets on the future."[169]

Such predictive skill was a focus too of Daniel Kahneman, who cited one study in which the chief financial officers of large companies predicted future stock prices. The 11,600 forecasts collected showed that when the forecasts predicted price rises, more drops than rises occurred, and vice versa. More worrisome, though, to Kahneman than the finding of negative predictive accuracy was that the CFOs had no sense of the worthlessness of their forecasts, thinking them vastly more accurate than they were: not only did they have "no clue," they were also clueless about their cluelessness.[170]

One study of expert judgments cited by both Kahneman and Sunstein was that of Philip Tetlock: *Expert Political Judgment: How Good Is It? How Can We Know?* Tetlock reported the results of interviewing 284 persons whose professions constituted "commenting or offering advice on political and economic trends"[171]—from whom he obtained tens of thousands of predictions. The glimpses of these mavens into the future in their areas of purported expertise were largely worthless: but negligibly better than those of a hypothetical, dart-throwing chimpanzee.[172] These experts, though, when shown how weak their performance was, mustered an impressive array of excuses.[173] However poor many experts may be at predicting events, they may yet prove to be, after they have occurred, eloquent in discoursing on their inevitability.

The research results of decision science help to explain these findings. Experts, like everyone else, are subject to what Kahneman has termed *hindsight bias:* misremembering our earlier thoughts in such a way that, for events that have occurred, we think we had thought them more likely than was the case and, for possibilities that did not happen, the reverse.[174] Hindsight bias contributes to the *illusion of validity:* persistence, despite evidence of past errors in forecasts, in acting as if each particular prediction will be borne out.[175] This illusion derives significantly from overestimated understanding of the past: people are endlessly inventive and often skillful in constructing coherent, plausible, perhaps-persuasive narratives of what caused what: we "see the world as more tidy, simple, predictable, and coherent than it really is."[176] In consequence, "the illusion that we understand the past fosters overconfidence in our ability to predict the future."[177]

The tendency of experts, like others, to ignore or to scant uncertainty is strengthened by the desires of their audiences that they radiate self-assurance. As Kahneman put it: "an expert worthy of the name is expected to display high confidence." He cited a medical study which showed that "clinicians who were 'completely certain'" of their diagnoses were wrong 40 percent of the time.[178] We want our physicians to seem certain: we turn away from those who candidly confess their reservations to seek others of greater exuded sureness. Experts who most project unwarranted overconfidence are the most likely to advise decision makers and to be interviewed by the media.[179] Widespread judicial error has been diagnosed in mistaking witness confidence for reliability—in part because the U.S. Supreme Court has advised judges and juries, in assessing the weight to be accorded to testimony, to take into account the level of confidence projected. Knowing that self-proclaimed certainty enhances credibility, lawyers prompt their witnesses to state and restate how sure they are.[180] Sunstein summarized: "confidence trumps accuracy."[181]

To derive best guidance from experts, Sunstein advised: taking into account the track records of individual experts as forecasters and weighting more heavily the thoughts of these with greater demonstrated accuracy (such "evidence" being "a much better guide than an impressive self-presentation")[182]; having experts make best cases for conflicting propositions[183]; and heeding the collective input of many knowledgeable persons, rather than identifying and then relying on a single best one.[184] (Other decision scientists have found that, in gauging uncertainty, it is well to consult at least three experts but that, after a half dozen have weighed in, there is little expected additional gain from the judgments of any more.[185])

John Kennedy was thought to have sensed well how much he might rely on, or disregard, experts in the Cuban Missile Crisis, but not so well before the Bay of Pigs—at which time (a year-plus earlier) he said that he had been under the illusion "that the military and intelligence people have some secret skill not available to ordinary mortals."[186]

Winston Churchill and Franklin Roosevelt struck astute balances in dealing with their experts. Churchill, given his background, had significant basis for valuing his own military judgments at least as highly as those of his officers and had "unwillingness to put full reliance on military expertise."[187] Nevertheless, he still, after taking his best shots in debates and memoranda at changing their minds, ultimately acquiesced to their unswayable positions—with the years-long pondering of possible operations in Norway a prime example. Roosevelt, even after his years as Assistant Secretary of the Navy in the earlier war, knew that he could not match the specialized proficiencies of his admirals and generals. He did, however, pit them against one another—which was useful both in understanding the extent of uncertainty among them and in enabling him to exert authority by deciding for those whom he judged to have made the better cases. On matters of foreign relations and U.S. public opinion, he deemed his own judgments superior to those of his military.

Also excellent in exercising considered reliance on expertise was Dwight Eisenhower. That he okayed the disastrous attempt to take the harbor of Oran against the advice of U.S. Admiral Andrew Bennett likely owed more to his concern for his relations with the British than to ill-judged dependence on the expertise of UK Admiral Sir Bertram Ramsay. In tracking the accuracy of weather forecasts before June 6, 1944, Eisenhower anticipated the recommendations of later decision scientists to track and to measure the predictive accuracy of experts.

On May 29, 1944, Air Chief Marshal Sir Trafford Leigh-Mallory—arguably the leading authority on the airborne component of Operation Overlord—became concerned that Erwin Rommel had moved a division into the planned drop-zone for the 82nd Airborne Division. Even though the landing zone was then moved, Leigh-Mallory wrote and met with Eisenhower to urge that the drop and glider landings be canceled. He predicted that as many as 80 percent of the planes and gliders might be lost and foresaw the "futile slaughter" of both the 82nd and 101st Airborne Divisions. At most 30 percent of the forces landed by glider would, he thought, be able to act effectively.[188]

Eisenhower wrote in his memoirs: "It would be difficult to conceive of a more soul-racking problem" than that posed by "my technical expert." Had Leigh-Mallory been correct, the landings on Utah Beach would have been doomed, perhaps entailing "a gigantic failure, possible Allied defeat in Europe." He withdrew to his tent to mull alone: "Professional advice and counsel could do no more."[189] He then did what decision science would have recommended: reflected on the experiences of past airborne actions in Sicily and mainland Italy and considered the counsel not only of Leigh-Mallory but also of other airborne officers and of Omar Bradley who had been more optimistic. He decided to go ahead with the drops and glider landings.[190] Leigh-Mallory would report to Eisenhower on June 6 to admit with relief that his dire predictions had been monumentally wrong and to commend his commander for his decision: only 21 of 816 C-47 transport planes and 100 gliders—2.3 percent—had been shot down.[191]

Numbers

That Cass Sunstein urged tracking predictive accuracy and, to limit groupthink, quantifying decision components accords with decision science and game theory—a main tool and organizing principle of which has been numerical specification. World War II was more quantified than any conflict ever had been. Allied decision makers knew well the numbers of their own soldiers, support personnel, casualties, weapons, ammunition, artillery rounds (173,941 were fired by the U.S. Fifth Army in the first 24 hours of its attack in May 1944 on the Gustav Line[192]; 476,413 for the British 13th Corps on that and the next five days[193]), bombs, vehicles, and supplies. They generally refrained, however, from putting numbers on their uncertainties and never did on their values.

The strategic debate that had led to Torch had occasionally invoked probability estimates. On July 22, 1942, Marshall presented to the British Chiefs his plan to establish a foothold later that year on the Cotentin Peninsula—to be held until the spring, then expanded. Brooke responded that there was "no hope" of maintaining the lodgement through the winter.[194] While the Americans at times spoke as if the probability—p—that the foothold could be kept was 1.0 (100 percent),[195] Brooke's "no hope" meant a p of zero. These assertions—ps of 1.0 and 0.0—were not so much judgments of likelihood as declarations of certainty, obviating probabilities. They may also have been made to project senses of masterful expertise: to have given qualified judgments and non-extreme numbers, would have impressed less and would have lessened the satisfied comfort that self-certain proficiency can induce. Given these extreme positions, it might have been helpful for the two sides to explain their respective lines of reasoning, to discuss the key factors and, perhaps, to arrive at modified probability estimates between the two poles of p = 0.0 and p = 1.0.

Rough intermediate numbers appeared the next month. Marshall, on August 14, cabled Eisenhower that the elimination of landings in French Morocco would reduce the chances of success to "less than a fifty-fifty chance"—although just how success was defined was unclear. Eisenhower responded the next day that, if neither the French nor the Spanish resisted, there would be a "better than fair chance of success."[196] His aide, Harry Butcher, that day put "the chances of making successful initial landings" at "better than even."[197] UK strategists, in arguing against the French Moroccan component of Torch, held that the Atlantic surf in November would be—with probability of four in five—too treacherous for the landings near Casablanca. By the next April, Eisenhower was again using imprecise words instead of numbers, estimating that, should the Germans put over two divisions into Sicily, Operation Husky would have "scant promise of success."[198]

Whether attaching numbers to the chances and the values of outcomes would have improved the decisions reviewed here may be debated.

The Case Against Numbers

The quantifications of decision science and game theory might indeed in the war have worsened the decision processes. Numbers, when asked for, are not always freely or candidly given. Alan Brooke was said to have felt that, as Chief of the Imperial General Staff, his responsibilities included keeping his "doubts or fears ... from his colleagues." Needing to appear confident of victory, Brooke "confid[ed] his fears to his journal," which enabled him "the more easily to hide them from his colleagues, whose morale was sustained by the sight of a consistently sanguine commander."[199] He wrote on May 27, 1944: "The hardest part of bearing such responsibility is pretending that you are absolutely confident of success when you are really torn to shreds with doubts and misgivings."[200]

Brooke and others sharing his ideal of leader comportment would not willingly have revealed their quantified doubts. High officers might also have had personal, service-based, or national reasons for preferring certain options over others, about which they would not want to be numerically specific. Had such decision participants have had to state the personal estimates sought by decision scientists and game theorists, they might have given positively-tilted figures for operations they wanted and negatively-shaded numbers for those they disfavored—or uncandid probabilities of 1.0 and 0.0 intended to put over or to quash alternative actions (and/or to signal their own, certainty-radiating proficiency). Such behavior would be *gaming* the process,[201] would corrupt decision science and game theory, and would defeat their purpose.

Other downsides of basing decisions on quantified analyses are: that discussions centering on hard numbers might lower the level of cordiality and the spirit of cooperation; that such numbers might give misleading impressions of greater certainty and confidence than are warranted[202]; and that, when some decision aspects can be more easily quantified than others, the former might acquire more influence.[203]

Differences across decision participants complicate applying numerical decision science and game theory. That people have variant modes of reasoning and divergent bases for their judgments means that, however much effort is devoted to achieving consensus, material disagreement on the probabilities and values of various outcomes is unlikely to be eliminated.

Many military officers, moreover, would prefer to make their strategic decisions as had admirals and generals over the centuries, rather than to concede sway to analytic methods and thereby to persons more experienced with them.

The Case for Numbers

Napoleon, decision scientists and game theorists would note with approval, had quantified battle chances. He estimated, on the morning of Waterloo, the likelihood of French victory at 90 percent. When, in the early afternoon, the Emperor learned that 30,000 Prussians were arriving to menace his right, he saw his prospects for prevailing fall to 60 percent.[204]

As ways to communicate, to bound, and to understand uncertainties and, ultimately, to reach best decisions in their presence, decision scientists and game theorists would have quantified probabilities and values. They would have asked what probability Churchill had in mind in his judgment that Anzio "should be decisive"; just how great was the "great chance" of success of which Alexander and Clark were confident; just how small, the "little chance" of the same success foreseen by Lucas and Truscott[205]; how estimates of such likelihoods had been arrived at; what the components of the uncertainties were and how they might have been combined to yield ultimate, adjusted figures, with noted ranges of ineradicable disagreements about them. Did the Prime Minister's "should be" mean sixty percent likely? Eighty percent? No one asked and Churchill never said. Perhaps the thinking was that, throughout the range of possible probabilities implied by the Prime Minister's words—maybe 55 to 90 percent—the decision to invade was indicated and that more precision was therefore unneeded.

On the other hand, differences within the interpretative range of Churchill's words could have changed the decision on Anzio: the amphibious operation might have been judged worth undertaking if its chances of proving decisive were eighty percent, but not if only sixty percent. Invoking decision science and game theory to guide the deliberations on Shingle might, in quantifying probabilities and values and in encouraging discussion of the disagreements revealed, have led the decision participants to better understandings—and, possibly, to improving or to calling off the landing.

Or not.

Alan Brooke tended not to name numbers, while Eisenhower used elastic wording like "better than fair chance" and "scant promise" suggestive of intermediate probabilities. Brooke, in contrast, to come across the more convincingly and in line with projecting the self-assurance that people want in their experts, took hard, extreme positions: "no hope" and "absolutely confident of success"—implying probabilities of 0.0 and 1.0. The CIGS believed that it was generally better to speak so that $p = 0.0$ or 1.0 was understood, when he believed the true probabilities to be, say, 0.14 or 0.91. Decision scientists concede that it is occasionally advantageous to act as though $p = 0.0$ or 1.0, even if such is not the case,[206] but would also argue that optimal decision-making often requires best quantified estimates of intermediate probabilities.

Possibly more than canceling the minuses of quantified decision science and game theory may be their pluses. One is that, by providing a framework for proponents and opponents of possible actions to make their best pitches to each other, the explicitness of numbers may lead to better mutual understandings and to better discussions of modifications and alternatives. Systematic thinking through the consequences of the uncertainties voiced by decision participants—such as weather contingencies, enemy reactions, possible battle events, and other aspects of good and bad luck—may lead to best senses of how likely various outcomes might be. Similar discussion and analysis might assist in making aggregate judgments on such difficult value tradeoffs as own-side versus enemy casualties versus logistical consequences versus political considerations. Individual decision makers might disagree with such aggregate judgments, but might nevertheless benefit from such processes to come to their own personal conclusions on likelihoods, values, and best actions.

It is often not possible, after any amount of analytic effort, decision-participant reflection, and group discussion, to reach even a near consensus on event likelihoods, outcome values, and best choices. It should, though, be noted that, in the absence of quantified decision-scientific or game-theoretic analysis—as in the actual strategic determinations made in the war—all the same factors would have had to be considered. Better decisions are the more likely to result when attempts are made to couch event probabilities in numbers, to express in quantified terms just how much better or worse certain possible results are than others, and to choose among options with the aid of rigorously calculated comparisons than—as historically has been the case—when contingencies and values are discussed and pondered in imprecise and impressionistic words.

It would seem that, had they been encouraged to do so, the decision makers of the war could easily have thought and spoken in terms of numerical probabilities. Many of them, in challenging each other with gambles, showed familiarity with chances and odds. Before the Allied bombardment and capture of the Mediterranean island of Pantelleria between Tunisia and Sicily, Churchill and Eisenhower bet on how many Italians were there. Churchill thought a maximum of 5,000; Eisenhower more. They agreed that the Prime Minister would pay the general one franc for every one hundred Italians over 5,000. When more than 11,000 were captured, Eisenhower won 65 francs.[207] Churchill and Brooke, in September 1942, "had a standing bet"—as to whether the German drive through the Caucasus would reach Baku. The PM reported that he—doubting that Baku would fall—"used to chaff [the CIGS] weekly at Cabinet: 'How is our bet going this week?'"[208] Churchill won the wager. On September 8, 1944, in response to the report of the Joint Intelligence Committee predicting German surrender by December 1, the Prime Minister noted multiple sources of uncertainty and asserted: "It is at least as likely that Hitler will be fighting on January 1 as that he will collapse by then."[209]

Montgomery, in predicating success in Sicily on "60 or 70 percent luck," showed familiarity with the types of probability and quantification with which decision scientists and game theorists deal. Eisenhower on October 11, 1943, bet Montgomery five pounds that the war would be over by Christmas of 1944.[210] Admiral John Cunningham, three days before the VI Corps landed at Anzio, told General John Lucas, "The chances are seventy to thirty that by the time you reach Anzio, the Germans will be north of Rome."[211] In August 1944, British general Miles Dempsey offered to bet Omar Bradley that his 21st Army Group would beat Bradley's 12th Army Group to the French village of Argentan.[212] At about the same time, high officers haggled over wagers at numerical odds that the war would be over by Armistice Day.[213]

Principals, Agents, Asymmetric Information, Command Unity and Coalitions

Militaries have long pondered the optimization of command—which became the more challenging when battlefields grew so large that no general could see more than fractions of them. Granting too much independence to subordinates had the downside that they might not do what their superiors wanted—as Jean-Baptiste Bernadotte in the Jena Campaign and Richard Ewell at Gettysburg disappointed Napoleon and Lee.

But overly centralized command has downsides of its own, many arising from the asymmetries of information between superiors as principals and subordinates as their agents. For the general to decide well what the small-unit leader should do requires that the former learn the details of the situation confronting the latter. To ensure that the small unit does as directed and has its missteps corrected requires that it be monitored. The requisite communications take time and effort and may break down.

The solution arrived at and applied in German armies from the 1860s through 1945 was to decentralize, to combine in a delicate balance independence of action at lower levels with broad-brush control from above—based on the principle that one man cannot effectively exercise direct command over any unit larger than a company.[214] The training maneuvers in the 1920s and 1930s of the Weimar military sought "to give the lower commanders ... experience in decisionmaking under conditions of mobile warfare."[215] The German approach contrasted sharply with the French "system of elaborate plans and highly centralized control in the hands of higher leaders"—of which the Germans spoke "laughingly." (A reaction similar to that that the men of the Wehrmacht would have on reviewing the detailed attack plan for Dieppe.) The Reichswehr instead "went about it in a completely different manner—by developing tactical proficiency in all officers and men, 'encouraging individual enterprise and initiative,' keeping orders from superiors to an absolute minimum."[216] The higher commander set the overall missions, but "left the choice of means up to his subordinates, trusting to their best judgment."[217] The result was "a system of command that stood behind many of the German successes in both world wars."[218]

Credit for these successes should be given both to the tactical training of the lower officers and to their ethos of doing what their superiors wanted—thereby minimizing agency losses. Decentralized decision-making in the mode of the Wehrmacht becomes less effective when such an ethos is absent, when subordinates act with impunitous autonomy.

Of the four strategic situations reviewed here, Dieppe has been judged a bad Allied decision and Messina, a bad non-decision. Significantly implicated in both cases were violations of command unity. The dispersion and confusion of authority contributed to tragic agency losses: 4,000 casualties to no purpose at Dieppe and scores of thousands of German escapees at Messina.

Why had this happened?

Notwithstanding his urging of command unity in Washington in December 1941, George Marshall did not instill in American officers unstinting obedience to all superiors of whatever nations—with the result that such U.S. generals as Omar Bradley and Mark Clark felt free to disobey and to act independently of their British bosses. In August 1944, Marshall took a step that might have seemed to further unitary command: placing Bradley directly under Eisenhower, whom he would heed, instead of under Montgomery, whom he at times ignored. Marshall acted, though, not so much for a trimmer and more effective line of authority as, instead, from a main threat to command unity—national sensitivity: he did not want the Briton to continue reaping the credit for the triumphs of American troops.

For those clearly subordinate to him, Eisenhower promoted the unity of command that he preached. After Kasserine, he fired his British intelligence chief, replacing him with the also-British general Kenneth Strong. He gave Strong "complete authority over all American and British officers on my [Strong's] staff; if I thought anyone was not making the grade or was creating difficulties I was fully empowered to sack him on the spot whatever his nationality."[219] Omar Bradley credited Eisenhower in Africa with determination "to spare no severity in punishing those who tried to shield their insubordinate activities under the flags of their respective nations."[220]

But Eisenhower did not—indeed could not—exert fully his authority over his own British subordinates. He understood that Montgomery, as an imperial hero, was not to be ordered about by a green gringo and that the subordinates inserted under him at Casablanca were meant to weaken his control of the boots, boats, and bombers of Husky. He did not in Sicily rile his ally by being overly directive of his high British officers. Alexander, similarly, did not irk the U.S. by insisting from Clark in Italy unquestioning compliance with orders. The results were, on the one side, that no serious threats ever arose to the retention by Eisenhower and Alexander of their commands but, on the other, that the Allied victories achieved at Messina and in mainland Italy were less than they might have been.

(Albert Kesselring did not sense that the disunity of Allied command had enabled his successful extraction of Axis troops at Messina. He resented that Hermann Göring in July 1943—from East Prussia, a thousand-plus miles from Sicily—had exercised control of the Axis air forces in Italy. Kesselring "always envied the clear-cut command system on the enemy's side—where there was one Commander-in-Chief for a theatre, and he had everything under command."[221] This was the reverse of the way that Eisenhower saw it.)

In contrast to the delicacy with which Eisenhower and Alexander treated the officers of their allies was the insubordination and gracelessness of Montgomery. In late December 1944, he let Brooke know that he was keeping the British War Office fully informed of his operations, while withholding these reports from Eisenhower, his direct superior. On the twenty-ninth, he sent to Eisenhower an order for him to sign restoring Montgomery to control over all ground operations in the West, since "you cannot possibly do it yourself"—otherwise, "without one man directing and controlling ... we will fail again [as in the Ardennes]."[222] This self-serving appeal for command unity fell on deaf ears. Atop this was Montgomery's recently not having attacked when Eisenhower had thought that he had agreed to. The American Supreme Commander, having had enough, determined to cable the Joint Chiefs that either he or Montgomery had to go. Forewarned of this, the field marshal ate crow and kept his command.

When there is more than one principal and when two or more co-principals have different priorities, tensions arise in designating common agents and in assigning objectives to them. Such tensions are particularly evident in military coalitions. All co-principals want agents sharing their goals and answerable to them to be designated; after agents have been designated, the co-principals seek to assign their own objectives to them and to give more authority to those agents who most share their goals. These phenomena in military alliances have resulted in fragmented commands.

Winston Churchill, in writing of the First Duke of Marlborough, remarked that "the history of all coalitions is a tale of the reciprocal complaints of allies."[223] Churchill's ancestor, the agent early in the eighteenth century of Britain, Holland, and the Habsburg Empire, commanded under constraints placed on him by his principals and in the context of their often acting for their own interests. In the spring of 1945 when dismayed that Eisenhower was not doing what he wished, Brooke recalled what Churchill had said: "There is only one thing worse than fighting with allies, and that is fighting without them!"[224]

The member nations of war coalitions typically have had their own commanding generals as their top agents. The priorities of these generals were to cooperate with their other national counterparts to achieve the common goals of the alliances, but also to serve their narrower national interests. Without unified command, ill-coordination and catastrophes have resulted. French generals in the First World War said that, based on their own frustrated experiences, their admiration for Napoleon dropped upon realizing that he had so many times fought against coalitions.[225] From Bonaparte's first advance toward Montenotte in 1796 to his last toward Waterloo in 1815, he targeted the points where opposing national armies were joined—knowing that their reactions, lacking common command, would be disjointed.

The shortcomings of coalitions without unified commands may, however, be reduced if not eliminated, by an ethos in individual commanders of doing what is best for the overall coalitions. Historical examples include the actions for the common causes of Prince Eugene at Blenheim and of Field Marshal Gebhard von Blücher at Waterloo.

It has been observed that, in the Second World War, the importance of command unity "might seem obvious in retrospect, but at the time it involved each nation giving up long-established and much prized autonomy of action."[226] Unity of command, insofar as it entails having the officers of another nation defer to those of ours, is an eminently good idea; if the reverse, the principle has negative luster. Our generals are, after all, better than theirs; theirs can learn so much from serving under ours; the overall goals of the coalition will be so much more efficiently achieved, if our officers are in control. When interests are not identical—as was the case for Churchill's Britain and Roosevelt's America—ours are especially to be preferred to theirs. For individual admirals and generals, unity of command is the way things obviously should be for subordinates, but not so good an idea when applied to obeying superiors.[227]

On the Western Front in the Great War, the French predominated in number, which gave them the preeminent right to exercise any overall command; in the next war, the Americans outnumbered the British, and were first in line for concentrated clout. Command unity in the former case would transfer authority from the British and Americans to the French; in the latter, from the British to the Americans. In both cases, those nations standing to gain in authority by unifying command deemed it a compelling tenet; those whose power it would reduce thumbed it down.

In 1918, the French wanted to train the newly-arriving U.S. doughboys and to distribute them among their armies. The Americans insisted on their own training and on constituting an independent force. The combination of American incompetence and refusal to take French advice was thought by the men of Clemenceau to have led to 25,000 unnecessary American deaths.[228]

British opposition to command unity in the earlier world war was expressed by the Chief of the Imperial General Staff, William Robertson. He argued that soldiers fight better under their own generals and that command unity might favor one ally over others.[229] Churchill, one war later, opposed the American push for a supreme commander of Overlord: "The general may well be below the level of his task, and has often been found so."[230] Eisenhower summed up:

> Alliances ... have often done no more than to name the common foe, and "unity of command" has been a pious aspiration thinly disguising the national jealousies, ambitions and recriminations of high-ranking officers, unwilling to subordinate themselves or their forces to a commander of different nationality or different service.[231]

In any coalition, allies must weigh how large a price they are willing to pay in terms of overall military efficiency so that their high officers will not have to obey wholeheartedly their superiors of another nation. In Europe between 1942 and 1945, a not-insignificant price was paid.

The Potential Value of Decision Science and Game Theory Between Dieppe and Anzio

If, for each of the decisions reviewed here, decision makers had consulted with advisors who somehow knew all that decision science and game theory have learned through 2019, different actions might have been taken.

The methods of the two disciplines would have stimulated numerical specification. Estimates of how many men, ships, landing craft, planes, tanks, guns, shells, jeeps, trucks, casualties, rations, and days it would take to achieve military objectives had guided strategic discussions. Had probabilities and values also been specified, the critical factors of decisions would have come into sharper focus, along with better senses of their relative importance and of the uncertainties entailed. Such explicitness might well have accelerated the decision process of Gymnast/Torch and have led to better choices for Dieppe, Messina, and Anzio.

Hard, explicit numbers might well have assisted decision participants in prioritizing their objectives. Management researchers have documented tendencies to reduce multiple goals to single objectives and have often found that such narrowing of purpose enhances organizational performance. War requires more-rapid changes of sub-goal priorities than does business. Corporations with the overall goal of maximizing profit transition among their subgoals of pushing different product lines. Generals with the paramount objective of victory in war alter their strategic and tactical foci. Chief executive officers of companies typically have orders of magnitude more time than do generals to make such decisions.

When the landings on Sicily became secure beachheads, Allied decision makers should at once have switched their attention on the island to maximizing the removal of Germans from the war. That they never adequately made this shift owed in part to the distraction of two other important subgoals: getting Italy out of the war and invading the mainland. Best generalship required real-time balancing of these subgoals and judicious distribution of attention among them—which the Germans achieved, but the Allies did not. Decision-scientific quantification of relative subgoal importance, updated at least daily in ongoing battles, might usefully have guided the Allied leaders.

One vital subgoal of generals is that of securing information. They need to determine what resources should be put into reconnaissance and other data-gathering activities. Decision science and game theory have developed methods: to gauge how much it is worth prospectively to obtain specific data to guide decisions[232]; by applying other-side perception, to understand how beneficial it is to deny information to one's enemy and to induce enemy belief in disinformation; and to determine the optimal amounts of effort that should be devoted to reconnaissance patrolling, interpretation of radio intercepts, aerial surveillance, and the like. Attention to information values might have led the Allies to upgrade their security measures to prevent the losses of their battle plans to their enemies at Dieppe and Anzio.

When information is insufficient or misleading, surprises occur. The Western Allies, in many ways, excelled in surprising their enemies—both positively and negatively: their enemy had not anticipated where the attacks of November 1942, July 1943, and January and June 1944 would be made; it had also feared amphibious invasions of Norway after Britain's retreat from it in 1940 and in Italy after Anzio that never were launched. Game-table analysis—a method of game theory—helps to estimate the value of surprise in adversarial settings; behavioral decision research, to anticipate the likely reactions to it.

Allied decision makers significantly misanticipated the reactions of their enemy to Torch and Shingle: Adolf Hitler's commitment of forces to Tunisia and Albert Kesselring's quick containment of the landings at Anzio. Game-scenario simulations and decision-scientific findings of risk-seeking behavior when confronting possible losses would have enabled better predictions of enemy countermoves.

The actual predictions of enemy responses and the estimations of enemy force strengths and positioning were made less accurate by biases and common errors that have, since the war, become better understood. Faulty situation assessments were, for instance, submitted to Allied commanders before the battles of Dieppe, Kasserine, and the Ardennes. They could have been made more accurate had intelligence officers known about and borne in mind two common behavioral traits: *confirmation bias:* giving more credence to information in line with preconceptions[233]; and *conservatism bias*—the inclination to revise best estimates insufficiently to incorporate new information.[234] Both biases may be exacerbated by the tendency noted by decision scientist Max Bazerman that "even well-trained, honest professionals view and interpret data in self-serving ways."[235]

Optimal weighing of information may also be hindered by groupthink phenomena. To optimize the gathering and consideration of data, important potential sources must be tapped and must not be inappropriately silenced or ignored. Attention to the pitfalls of multi-person deliberations might have led to better decisions on Dieppe and Anzio.

Those decisions would likely have been improved if command had been unified. The principle of a single, controlling cerebrum—flouted in most alliances—might have been promoted through quantification of its consequences. A multi-national review of Operation Husky, possibly urged by George Marshall and acquiesced to by Alan Brooke, might have concluded that fractionated authority had enabled the escape of tens of thousands of Germans at Messina and might then have strengthened an ethos of obedience to superiors—with likely significant benefits in later battles.

Better Decisions in Conflicts to Come

Experience over recent decades with decision science and game theory in many settings has indicated how they might be of value to the armed forces of the future. An initial step would be to teach the basics of DS and GT in war colleges. Military decision makers will benefit from having learned: how to focus on and to improve meta-decisions—to make it more likely that strategic choices are being made by the best persons, in the best settings, without debilitating fatigue, with appropriate incentives and responsibilities, taking reasonable amounts of time, and in the best ways; how to conceptualize their highest-level objectives and how intermediate-level objectives contribute to higher and sometimes compete with and sometimes complement each other; how to recognize what types of confrontational scenarios they may be in, whether zero-sum or non-zero-sum or of studied game types; how to generate lists of action alternatives; how to pare such lists to manageable size with minimal loss of value; how to use schematic and analytic aides to structure their thinking[236]; how to optimize the allocation of time and resources in securing different types of information and in misleading opponents; how to quantify and to compare components of value; how to estimate outcome likelihoods; how to become comfortable and effective in acting amid uncertainty; how to determine the expected values likely to be realized by different options; and how to make prospectively-best choices based on such analysis.

One specialty area of decision science on which the UK and the U.S. in the war generally did well, but with unfortunate exceptions, was that of generating action alternatives. Imaginatively-generated Allied ideas in the war included deceptive measures and artificial harbors. The Allied leaders in 1941 and 1942 considered a broad range of options before settling on Gymnast/Torch. Later historians have not suggested that other important possibilities were overlooked. The Allied commanders in Sicily in 1943, however, largely failed to identify and to focus on steps that might have prevented German flight.

Many have observed that the conventional-warfare mindset of the U.S. military in the Second World War—because of its limited sets of strategic and tactical ideas—proved unsuitable for the asymmetric fighting that would ensue in Vietnam, Iraq, and Afghanistan. When success is measured more in terms of winning allegiance than of destroying divisions, fundamental contemplation of objectives and of best ways of securing them in the presence of societal and diplomatic constraints can be beneficial. The enhanced formulation of alternatives based on values and objectives has been studied and urged by decision scientists Ralph Keeney and Paul Kleindorfer.[237] It has been found that better sets of action alternatives are obtained when several persons enumerate decision objectives, whereupon composite lists of them stimulate identifying options.[238]

Such applications of decision science and game theory seem best carried out not by specialized teams, but instead by having widespread understanding of the principles and perspectives of the disciplines. Large organizations have encountered frustrations in mobilizing teams—both internal and external—of decision-scientific and game-theoretic experts to address their challenges. Such efforts have entailed substantial commitments of resources and attention and have often been poorly understood by decision makers unaccustomed to such approaches.[239] The resultant gains may at times have been exceeded by the costs. Rather than recruiting squads of specialized experts, it has been found better to have the basic concepts of decision science and game theory—through education, training, and example—be diffused and "embedded" throughout institutions: to become "a common language" and "a part of their organization's DNA."[240] Such corporations as Chevron and General Motors have taken this approach.[241]

Practical applications of analyses work best when the level of complexity is carefully chosen. Modern computers enable decision-analytic and game-theoretic modeling at levels of mathematical refinement orders of magnitude beyond what was possible in the 1940s. Decision scientists have, however, found that quantitative intricacy can become so great as to worsen decisions[242] and that decision makers may prefer less analytic refinement, if that will ease the cognitive demands on themselves.[243] Additional complexity, if it promises gains exceeding costs—among which confusion, the time required of decision makers to reach sufficient understanding, and decision delay ought not to be overlooked—should be accepted; if not, it should not be.[244]

Seeking the optimal level of analytic complexity should be part of a general effort to tailor analysis to context. Decision analysis was originally developed "to assist major organizations in making large, one-of-a-kind decisions."[245] In this mode, it might usefully have guided the deliberations on Gymnast/Torch, Rutter/Jubilee, Husky, and Shingle. Such decisions could be addressed by forming specialist teams to model the situations, to identify the risks, to quantify the uncertainties, and to estimate and to value the expected results of alternatives. While such ad hoc teams have had successes in business contexts, they have typically not maintained relevance and worth after the unique circumstances for which they were pulled together had been dealt with. They have often been succeeded by nimbler, faster methods less demanding of organizational resources.[246]

The type of formal decision-scientific/game-theoretic group that might usefully have guided the men of Christmas 1943 in determining whether or not to undertake Operation Shingle would have been too slow and cumbersome to have assisted John Lucas in choosing best defenses to German counterattacks on the Anzio beachhead. Generals in rapidly-changing, ongoing battles might, though, benefit from having one or two decision scientists or game theorists, in perhaps as little as five minutes, share their thoughts. Decision scientists recognize that the scrutiny they direct at other managerial processes should also examine their own activities: "the effort involved in analysis must be justified by prospective gains"[247]—on which decision makers should be the judges.

An essential further burden to "the effort involved in analysis" is the time required of decision makers to reach sufficient understanding. DMs have competing priorities for their attention—to focus conscientiously on all of which would require more hours than days have. The amounts of time decision makers should devote to soliciting, digesting, and heeding the advice of specialists in decision science and game theory should depend on how much value they derive from that time, as compared to what they might get from other activities. The decision makers should be the judges of this.

While decision makers should themselves determine their best allocations of time, decision consultants can usefully advise them in this. The latter, having observed what decision makers do and having estimated the returns at the margin of minutes put into alternative activities, including rest, may recommend which should be expanded and which cut back.

An often-overlooked aspect of allocating time is that devoted to securing information. The concept of the expected value of information can assist in deciding when it is best to hold off on acting until better situational understanding can be achieved and when it is best to bite the bullet (most typically for U.S. soldiers in 1942 through 1945, the full-metal-jacket, .30-caliber round) without any further delay. Significant hurdles to the efficient gathering and processing of information are groupthink phenomena. Procedures in conferences should be developed to ensure that information is considered in rough proportion to its likely importance, without the inappropriate squelching of any via groupthink. Intelligence officers should heed the finding that, in most organizations including the military, "selective attention, noise, and overload" is "the common state"[248]: they should continually ask themselves how their situation estimates might be best updated upon receiving new reports, while avoiding such pitfalls as confirmation or conservatism biases.

In focusing on—as has been done here—the optimization of decision making, it must be recognized that it is but one responsibility of soldiers, sailors, and flyers. Others include administering, reporting, executing orders, motivating subordinates, coordinating with peers and allies, and serving superiors. Dissimilar settings place variant emphases on the components of performance: the best commander for exploiting battlefield breakthroughs might not be the first choice for directing the defense of a precarious beachhead or for imposing order on an occupied region.

The diversity of requisite decision skills should be recognized. One type of acumen was needed in July 1942 to settle on the best grand-strategic option for the Western Allies. Not the same is the ability to take quick, perhaps-instinctive actions in fluid battle moments affording little time for reflection. Yet another dimension of decision competence is the ability to select best persons for the challenges at hand. The militaries of many nations have for centuries pondered and wrestled with these issues. Decision science and game theory can learn much from—and also improve on—judgments made by armed forces over the centuries of how best: to identify and to select persons of high promise; to test and to identify those whose promotions will maximally serve organizational goals; to train, to motivate, and to provide systems of support to upgrade performance; to determine when—taking into account age, fatigue, and indicators of proficiency—to promote, to demote, to relieve, or to retire.

A particular challenge of both analysis and training is to determine and to instill in officers optimal levels of risk aversion. Many have judged that American generals, from North Africa to Iraq, have been over-cautious, that, if more daring, they would have done better. That conclusion, however, provides but incomplete guidance: best would be to specify not just the direction but also the extent of desirable change. The prevalent sense in military histories that bolder is better should be tempered with the awareness that audacity can be excessive.

Whenever decision science and/or game theory are undertaken, "periodic 'look-backs' to earlier decision efforts to see what can be improved" are recommended.[249] Intelligence officers and other experts should be primarily rated on the revealed accuracy of their assessments and predictions—with minimal weight given to the elegance of their excuses for why their reports and recommendations were wrong. Actions against enemies might be based on best presumptions of opponent actions or on worst-case fears or on game-theoretic randomization or in other ways. Analysis of track records will shed light on which approaches work best and on which individual officers had most-consistently-accurate other-side perception.

In invoking decision-scientific and game-theoretic perspectives, decision makers should critically scrutinize the track records of those two disciplines just as those do those of other approaches: asking themselves whether the roles that decision science and game theory play are justified by the results they achieve and if they should be expanded, redirected, or cut back.

Chapter Notes

Epigraphs

1. Moran, *Struggle,* 20.
2. Larrabee, *Commander,* 644.
3. Chandler, *Papers III,* 1564n. Eisenhower responded on 11/13/1943: "I am unable to say whether or not the records of my office are sufficiently explicit to establish, in every case, reasons for decisions taken." Chandler, *Papers III,* 1563.
4. Sorensen, *Decision-Making,* xi, xiii.

Prologue

1. *Command,* 67.
2. Allied radar had detected the German convoy. This information, however, never reached these Allied boats.
3. Bryant, *Turn,* 508.
4. Daniel Kahneman and Amos Tversky. "Intuitive Prediction: Biases and Corrective Procedures." *Management Science* 12(1979): 313–27.
5. A synopsis based on Kahneman (*Thinking,* 250) and Sunstein (*Wiser,* 1).
6. Mellers, "Learned," 357.
7. Brown, *Rational,* 134.
8. Roberts, *Storm,* 603. Atkinson (*Guns,* 637) gave stronger numbers to the same point: "Soviet forces... killed roughly nine times more Germans than the United States and Britain combined."

Chapter 1

1. The French had rejected a British ultimatum that they make their ships unusable by the Germans.
2. Gilbert, *Second,*
3. Neillands, *Dieppe,* 33.

4. Keegan, *Normandy,* 121.
5. *Hinge,* 106.
6. Hamilton, *Making,* 548.
7. Villa, *Unauthorized,* 120.
8. Neillands, *Dieppe,* 12. Zuehlke (*Dieppe,* 36) noted that others considered it successful, but did not advance his own judgment on whether the gains had been worth the losses.
9. Stacey, *Six Years,* 325. Stacey (326, 340) called Dieppe generally "well documented," but found the record of its planning "far from complete"—forcing him to rely on non-contemporary papers and participant memories. Other authors, led by Villa (*Unauthorized,* 35), have expressed dismay and suspicion that the surviving files on the raid, from April through August of 1942, were so scanty.
10. Hamilton, *Making,* 548.
11. Stacey, *Six Years,* 330, 347.
12. Zuehlke, *Dieppe,* 53. Montgomery told Goronwy Rees (*Bundle,* 139), his personal representative to COHQ for Rutter, that Roberts was "not much good." Hamilton (*Making,* 556) also reported that Montgomery "had no high opinion" of the general.
13. Villa, *Unauthorized,* 227.
14. UK Chiefs of Staff Committee. *Minutes.* No. 42: 5/13/1942, 5. Rutter seems never to have been considered by the Combined Chiefs of Staff. Stacey, *Six Years,* 325.
15. Ziegler, *Mountbatten,* 187.
16. Gwyer, *Strategy,* 676. Four paragraphs—about one seventh of the document—addressed such raids: their advantages, details, and resource requirements.
17. Stacey, *Six Years,* 335.
18. These approvals may have been pro forma: Zuehlke (*Dieppe,*

64) considered that McNaughton and Crerar had, early in May, irrevocably given the go-ahead.
19. *Memoirs,* 70.
20. Neillands, *Dieppe,* 113–4.
21. *Hinge,* 458.
22. Neillands, *Dieppe,* 114.
23. *Hinge,* 457.
24. Churchill, *Hinge,* 458. Gwyer (*Strategy,* 639) stated that the Chiefs "approved a new directive to" Mountbatten on 7/27/1942. The minutes of the Chiefs of that (No. 76) and other dates recorded no such approval—perhaps out of concerns for security. Villa (*Unauthorized,* 46), finding such lack of documentation unprecedented, concluded that the Chiefs had never consented to Jubilee, that the decision to mount the raid had been made "by Mountbatten, without authority," and that Churchill, who had not recalled these events, had based his account of them on false memories coaxed into him by Mountbatten and Hughes-Hallett. Allison (*Essence,* 270) agreed with Villa that Jubilee had not been authorized. Neillands (*Dieppe,* 119–20) and Zuehlke (*Dieppe,* 368) considered and rejected as not credible the possibility that Mountbatten and Hughes-Hallett had pulled off Jubilee without higher consent—largely because Churchill, Brooke, and their staffs had kept close tabs on all such undertakings. Brooke, vigilant that the British Chiefs not be circumvented, had not indicated that that had happened.
25. Stacey, *Six Years,* 344.
26. Neillands, *Dieppe,* 115.
27. Stacey, *Six Years,* 345.
28. Stacey (*Six Years,* 328), based on an "unsigned account" of September 1942, made this one of two

COHQ plans. Others (Robertson, *Shame,* 51; Ziegler, *Mountbatten,* 188; Zuehlke, *Dieppe,* 43) have stated that the lone COHQ plan called only for peripheral attacks.

29. With few written records—none from before April 14, 1942 (Stacey, *Six Years,* 327–8)—many accounts of Dieppe's planning derive from the recollections of Mountbatten and Hughes-Hallett. Hamilton (*Making,* 549) wrote that "Mountbatten later claimed to have disliked the idea of a frontal assault on Dieppe." Hamilton did not mention that Montgomery had played any role in this decision, nor did he deny it. Robertson (*Shame,* 51), Ziegler (*Mountbatten,* 188), Villa (*Unauthorized,* 11, 185), Neillands (*Dieppe,* 99, 102), and Zuehlke (*Dieppe,* 44–6) made Montgomery the main decision maker for the frontal attack. Lovat (*March,* 274–5) ascribed responsibility for it not to Montgomery, but to Paget.

30. Neillands, *Dieppe,* 124. All times are given in terms of British Summer Time, one hour ahead of Greenwich Time.

31. Earlier plans had called for a longer raid, with re-embarkation not to occur until dark. Neillands, *Dieppe,* 93.

32. Neillands, *Dieppe,* 97.

33. Stacey, *Six Years,* 336–7.

34. Robertson, *Shame,* 184–5.

35. Villa, *Unauthorized,* 125.

36. Stacey, *Six Years,* 374.

37. Robertson, *Shame,* 247, 249, 253.

38. Stacey, *Six Years,* 363; Robertson, *Shame,* 242.

39. Stacey, *Six Years,* 389.

40. Stacey, *Six Years,* 368. The 227 fatalities include eighteen as POWs.

41. Robertson, *Shame,* 265.

42. Robertson, *Shame,* 218, 265.

43. Zuehlke, *Dieppe,* 366–7.

44. Even from Green Beach, where the invaders were relatively successful and where there was less enemy targeting of the radiomen, Roberts had no reports to guide his decisions on committing his reserves. Robertson, *Shame,* 329.

45. Stacey, *Six Years,* 381.

46. Robertson, *Shame,* 329.

47. E.g., Neillands, *Dieppe,* 233.

48. Stacey, *Six Years,* 382.

49. Stacey, *Six Years,* 381.

50. Montgomery, *Memoirs,* 70.

51. Stacey, *Six Years,* 388.

52. Robertson, *Shame,* 399.

53. Weinberg, *World,* 360.

54. Neillands, *Dieppe,* ix.

55. Those, for instance, of J. F. C. Fuller, B. H. Liddell Hart, and John Keegan (who had earlier written several pages of scathing commentary on it in his *Six Armies in Normandy*).

56. *Hinge,* 459.

57. Butcher, *Three Years,* 67.

58. *Crusade,* 199.

59. *March,* 271, 278.

60. Blumenson, *Battle,* 69; Weinberg, *World,* 360; Murray, *Won,* 413; Atkinson, *Dawn,* 70; Neillands, *Dieppe,* 265; Overy, *Why,* 166; D'Este, *Warlord,* 577; Roberts, *Masters,* 272; Hastings, *Winston's,* 269; Corrigan, *Second,* 502; Beevor, *Second,* 340; Zuehlke, *Dieppe,* 3.

61. This definition represents general current understanding, in line with the 2007 usage ("Personal," 68) of Howard Raiffa. The terms "decision science" and "decision analysis" have often been considered synonymous. To the extent that they differ, "decision analysis" has been understood to be more quantitatively focused and "decision science," to have a broader and more qualitative scope. A 2007 statement of the purpose of decision analysis—"to assist decision makers to make better decisions" (Edwards, "Introduction," 5)—applies as well to decision science. The term "decision analysis" is thought (Miles, "Preface," xii) to have been first used by Ronald Howard in 1966. The term "decision theory" has been applied (Miles, "Emergence," 21) to the writings of Blaise Pascal in 1670 and Jeremy Bentham in 1789 and has appeared in such titles as Abraham Wald's *Statistical Decision Theory* (NY: McGraw-Hill, 1950) and Ward Edwards' "Behavioral Decision Theory" (*Annual Review of Psychology, 12* (1961), 473–98)—taking, respectively, statistical and psychological perspectives.

62. One cannot, in war as in other fields, undertake all actions that promise net-positive results (good-outcomes-on-net). When one is undertaken, the net benefits of others that are not are lost—which are *opportunity costs*

and are implicitly taken into account in determining whether a good-outcome-versus-alternatives has been achieved.

63. As noted by decision scientist Rex Brown. *Rational,* 141.

64. Churchill and Mountbatten, in 1950 as the former prepared his war memoirs, had divergent thoughts on what should be said about the raid. Mountbatten objected to Churchill's early-draft relating of the losses suffered, his ascription of reviving Rutter as Jubilee to Mountbatten, and his mention that there was no written record of highest-level approval of Jubilee. Mountbatten recounted to Churchill events that the Prime Minister might have remembered but did not and squelched mention of Churchill's questions of December 1942 about what had happened. Lord Louis had his way: his substantially rewritten version of Churchill's account of Dieppe would be what Churchill would publish in *The Hinge of Fate.* Villa, *Unauthorized,* 36–9.

65. Robertson, *Shame,* 407.

66. Neillands, *Dieppe,* 267.

67. Zuehlke, *Dieppe,* 369.

68. Roskill, *Offensive,* 119; *Peace,* 164.

69. Stacey, *Six Years,* 401–2.

70. Wilmot, *Europe,* 110, 186, 181. To provide this fire, the British developed different types of specialized tanks, which on June 6, 1944 they used effectively. Omar Bradley declined to use most of these—showing, per Wilmot (265), "short-sightedness," which had "terrible consequences" on Omaha Beach.

71. Villa, *Unauthorized,* 201.

72. Roberts, *Masters,* 273.

73. Villa, *Unauthorized,* 3.

74. *Memoirs,* 71.

75. *Command,* 72. Truscott (*Command,* 533–4) considered that "Dieppe... proved the practicability and feasibility of the amphibious invasions we were then planning." He "was convinced" that Dieppe could have been taken and held—had that been the operational goal, instead of a one-tide, land-loot-and-leave.

76. Ziegler, *Mountbatten,* 190; Zuehlke, *Dieppe,* 115. A slightly different version of this conversa-

tion was given by Stacey (*Six Years,* 337). Both Hughes-Hallett and Mountbatten attested to this back and forth—with the difference that Mountbatten had the Prime Minister putting the question to himself.

77. Truscott, *Command,* 55; Stacey, *Six Years,* 325. Admiral Sir Bertram Ramsay sent this to Mountbatten.

78. Stacey, *Six Years,* 391.

79. Corrigan, *Second,* 417, 293.

80. D'Este, *Warlord,* 578.

81. Beevor, *Second,* 340.

82. Gilbert, *Road,* 211.

83. Wilmot, *Europe,* 110.

84. Mosley, *Backs,* 314. Villa (*Unauthorized,* 157) thought that Churchill, Mountbatten, and Portal saw continental raids "as a way to defuse pressure for an early Second Front."

85. Churchill, *Hinge,* 298.

86. Churchill, *Hinge,* 305.

87. Villa, *Unauthorized,* 72.

88. Corrigan, *Second,* 284.

89. Stacey, *Six Years,* 406–7.

90. *Hinge,* 459.

91. Liddell Hart, *Other,* 313, 383.

92. Stacey, *Six Years,* 408.

93. Gwyer, *Strategy,* 643; Ziegler, *Mountbatten,* 192.

94. Beevor, *Second,* 340.

95. Senger, *Neither,* 127, 139.

96. Kahneman, *Thinking,* 203. Kahneman was more pessimistic than other decision scientists about avoiding the consequences of outcome bias—which he judged "makes it almost impossible to evaluate a decision properly—in terms of the beliefs that were reasonable when the decision was made." The related term of *resulting* is commonly used in tournament bridge. Resulting occurs when a player makes a good bid on expectation that turns out badly and is criticized for it or a rash or a timid bid that turns out well, winning praise. The leading periodical of the game, the *Bridge World,* runs in each issue its "Master Solvers' Club," in which bidding problems are posed and discussed. While many of these problems are taken from past tournaments, the *Bridge World,* to avoid resulting, generally does not mention what happened: its goal is to identify actions that are best on expectation, not those that happened to be best in specific, actual situations.

97. The situation would be muddied—and made the more difficult for result-based rating of decisions—if the attempted fourth-down conversion failed, but the team still won or if it succeeded, but the team lost.

98. Howard, "Foundations," 33.

99. Roberts, *Masters,* 273.

100. Gwyer, *Strategy,* 641.

101. Hamilton, *Making,* 546.

102. Keegan, *Normandy,* 120–1.

103. D'Este, *Warlord,* 578.

104. Roberts, *Storm,* 290, 319.

105. Zuehlke, *Dieppe,* 362.

106. Stacey, *Six Years,* 399; Lovat, *March,* 278; Hamilton, *Making,* 552; Neillands, *Dieppe,* ix, 5, 271; Hastings, *Winston's,* 269; Zuehlke, *Dieppe,* 366.

107. Ziegler, *Mountbatten,* 195.

108. Stacey, *Six Years,* 335. Crerar had written to McNaughton that, were he in Roberts' place, "I should have no hesitation in tackling [the raid]."

109. 70.

110. Hamilton, *Making,* 552.

111. Zuehlke, *Dieppe,* 148–9.

112. Zuehlke, *Dieppe,* 144.

113. Neillands, *Dieppe,* 272.

114. Robertson, *Shame,* 51; Zuehlke, *Dieppe,* 369.

115. Stacey, *Six Years,* 404.

116. Villa, *Unauthorized,* 12.

117. Hamilton, *Making,* 554.

118. Neillands, *Dieppe,* 13.

119. Zuehlke, *Dieppe,* 99.

120. Stacey, *Six Years,* 391.

121. Neillands, *Dieppe,* 97.

122. Stacey, *Six Years,* 398.

123. Stacey, *Six Years,* 391.

124. Zuehlke, *Dieppe,* 44.

125. Whether Montgomery initially proposed the landing at Puys is unclear. Per Zuehlke (*Dieppe,* 43–4), he did. Per Robertson (*Shame,* 51), COHQ had recommended this assault to him.

126. Neillands, *Dieppe,* x.

127. Robertson, *Shame,* 401.

128. Stacey, *Six Years,* 400; Neillands, *Dieppe,* 124.

129. *March,* 273.

130. Roberts, *Masters,* 273.

131. Ziegler, *Mountbatten,* 186.

132. Stacey, *Six Years,* 398.

133. Zuehlke, *Dieppe,* 362.

134. Stacey, *Six Years,* 395; Zuehlke, *Dieppe,* 366.

135. Stacey, *Six Years,* 355.

136. Stacey, *Six Years,* 358, 359.

137. Stacey, *Six Years,* 350.

138. Stacey, *Six Years,* 350–1.

139. Zuehlke, *Dieppe,* 166–7.

140. Neillands, *Dieppe,* 3.

141. Gwyer, *Strategy,* 641.

142. Stacey, *Six Years,* 369.

143. Stacey, *Six Years,* 375.

144. Robertson, *Shame,* 239.

145. Stacey, *Six Years,* 401.

146. Stacey, *Six Years,* 386.

147. Stacey, *Six Years,* 392.

148. *Hinge,* 458–9.

149. Stacey, *Six Years,* 392–3.

150. Stacey, *Six Years,* 357.

151. E.g., Zuehlke, *Dieppe,* 157.

152. E.g., Ziegler, *Mountbatten,* 193; Roberts, *Masters,* 273.

153. Robertson, *Shame,* 400.

154. Zuehlke, *Dieppe,* 155–7. Per Brown (*Bodyguard,* 85), the Allies were duped by a German deceptive operation to believe that Dieppe was defended by but 1,400 mediocre troops of the 110th Infantry Division, when in fact over 5,000 men of the strong 302nd Infantry Division were there.

155. Stacey, *Six Years,* 358.

156. Neillands, *Dieppe,* 166–7.

157. *March,* 270, 274. Robertson, *Shame,* 307. Hastings Ismay agreed. Gilbert, *Road,* 212.

158. Stacey, *Six Years,* 380.

159. Zuehlke, *Dieppe,* 291.

160. Churchill, *Hinge,* 457; Neillands, *Dieppe,* 99, 210.

161. Zuehlke, *Dieppe,* 254.

162. Robertson, *Shame,* 178, 344.

163. *March,* 275.

164. In a poll of 4/1/1942, 50 percent of Britons expressed dissatisfaction with their government's conduct of the war; 67 percent wanted British offensive operations in 1942. Gallup, *Poll,* 328.

165. Villa (*Unauthorized,* 69) has suggested that Stalin saw the infeasibility of an early Second Front: his continuing calls for it deriving from a desire for more matériel.

166. Per Mountbatten, the British Chiefs of Staff, the Combined Chiefs, and the War Cabinet were then urging large-scale raids. Stacey, *Six Years,* 325.

167. Stacey, *Six Years,* 341.

168. Villa, *Unauthorized,* 11.

169. Villa, *Unauthorized,* 11; Zuehlke, *Dieppe,* 48. Message delivered by representatives of Montgomery, in his absence, at the planning meeting of April 25.

170. Villa, *Unauthorized,* 95.

Villa (96) thought the RN's position illogical: denying battleship support out of concern for impacts on public morale, while being oblivious that such denial would heighten the chances of incurring "a morale-crushing defeat."

171. *Hinge*, 393.

172. Stacey, *Six Years*, 412.

173. Hamilton, *Mantle*, 395.

174. Villa, *Unauthorized*, 121.

175. Ziegler, *Mountbatten*, 175; Villa, *Unauthorized*, 121.

176. Villa, *Unauthorized*, 121.

177. Villa, *Unauthorized*, 122.

178. Villa, *Unauthorized*, 149.

179. Villa, *Unauthorized*, 157.

180. Villa, *Unauthorized*, 92–3.

181. Stacey, *Six Years*, 335.

182. Robertson, *Shame*, ix, 110.

183. Hamilton, *Making*, 555.

184. Hastings, *Winston's*, 269.

185. Zuehlke, *Dieppe*, 147.

186. Neillands, *Dieppe*, 112.

187. Zuehlke, *Dieppe*, 131.

188. Villa, *Unauthorized*, 198.

189. Villa, *Unauthorized*, 199; Zuehlke, *Dieppe*, 129, 131.

190. Neillands, *Dieppe*, 103.

191. Gwyer, *Strategy*, 639.

192. Villa, *Unauthorized*, 22. To Villa (21), the Prime Minister was "notorious for denying anything but formal responsibility for disasters," while "always ready to accept praise" for triumphs. Villa (50) urged that Churchill's role in Dieppe be critically evaluated.

193. *Unauthorized*, 21–2. Perhaps, however, Villa suggested, the Prime Minister reflected that any scapegoating might call into question his own actions, which led him to recount the raid as a success.

194. While Robertson (*Shame*, viii) primarily faulted Montgomery and Mountbatten for the raid, Lovat (*March*, 274) blamed Paget for the frontal assault at Dieppe. Hamilton (*Making*, 553) considered Montgomery and Brooke to be the only two soldiers in Britain with the clout to kibosh a tragically bad idea. Villa (*Unauthorized*, 245) wrote that "if anyone could have stopped the Dieppe raid it was the Canadian commander, General McNaughton." Neillands (*Dieppe*, ix, 278) lamented the absence of the "moral courage" needed to call off the raid and thought (97) that, when the heavy preliminary bomb-

ing was dropped, both Mountbatten and Roberts could and should have pulled the plug.

195. Russo, *Traps*, 5.

196. Kleindorfer, *Decision*, 126.

197. Stacey, *Six Years*, 324.

198. Robertson, *Shame*, 266; Neillands, *Dieppe*, 35.

199. Arguable exceptions were men like Keyes and others who had been involved in the raid of April 23, 1918 on the Belgian port of Zeebrugge—since which time, however, the technologies of warfare had been transformed.

200. *Making*, 546–7. Neillands (*Dieppe*, 32, 34–5) also wrote of Mountbatten in but marginally softer terms.

201. Robertson, *Shame*, 144, 189.

202. Villa, *Unauthorized*, 198.

203. E.g., Robertson, *Shame*, 184–5.

204. Robertson, *Shame*, 140.

205. How much of a role in the decision on Dieppe Paget had and whether he was on net for or against it have been disputed by historians. Hamilton (*Making*, 549) thought that the raid on Dieppe "was born" in an agreement on roles and responsibilities struck on March 21, 1942 between Mountbatten and Paget. While Hamilton (*Making*, 549) considered Paget at first "keen" for the raid, Robertson (*Shame*, 103) wrote that in June he thought little of it and Villa (*Unauthorized*, 193) reported his having in early July advocated cancellation.

206. Stacey, *Six Years*, 338.

207. Zuehlke, *Dieppe*, 117.

208. Villa, *Unauthorized*, 231.

209. Reynolds, *Command*, 344–5.

210. If, instead of basing his attempt to cancel Jubilee on the supposition of blown security, he had instead notified other decision makers that reanalysis in the light of latest intelligence indicated likely calamity—as Hamilton (*Making*, 555) speculated may have been his reconsidered mindset—he might have succeeded.

211. Villa, *Unauthorized*, 170.

212. Hamilton, *Making*, 555.

213. Hamilton, *Making*, 551. Even if factually correct—just what Hamilton meant by "formally attended" is not clear—this state-

ment gives the misleading impression that Montgomery had been less involved than was the case. In a meeting with COHQ members in April 1942, he had called their work amateurish. Zuehlke, *Dieppe*, 44. The COH (Stacey, *Six Years*, 336) reported his attendance at "some of the planning meetings." It also (329) related that one result of the meeting between Montgomery and McNaughton on April 30, 1942 was agreement that the former "should proceed with the preparation of plans." Subsequently, per the COH (336), Montgomery had not delegated, but had "kept [the responsibility for planning Rutter] in his own hands." Montgomery himself (*Memoirs*, 69) stated that he had been "made responsible for the Army side of the planning."

214. Hamilton, *Making*, 524–5.

215. Zuehlke, *Dieppe*, 129–30.

216. Villa, *Unauthorized*, 197–8; Zuehlke, *Dieppe*, 109, 130.

217. Villa, *Unauthorized*, 198.

218. Reynolds, *Dress*, 106.

219. He was, per Robertson (*Shame*, ix), a "fine officer," "conveniently at hand" as "a scapegoat;" per Neillands (*Dieppe*, 233, 271) "most unjustly" scapegoated, having been "no more or less to blame than any other of the senior participants." Churchill's account of Dieppe (*Hinge*, 457–9) did not mention Roberts.

220. *Unauthorized*, 3.

221. Corrigan, *Second*, 502; Brown, *Bodyguard*, 80. Brown judged that Churchill's resurrection of Rutter as Jubilee on July 15 was to "convince the Americans that Sledgehammer would be a disaster."

222. Brown, *Bodyguard*, 75. Brown considered and rejected the possibility that this had occurred because the London Controlling Section (in charge of strategic deceptions) and operation planners were ill-coordinated, perhaps owing to the conditions of "super-secrecy." He was left with the explanation "that Rutter was intended as a sacrificial operation from the very beginning"—as part of a campaign to trick the Germans into fearing an invasion of France. Brown (81) also related that measures to deceive the enemy "about the purpose and destination" of Rutter/Jubilee were pro-

posed and vetoed. On August 15, six British commandos made "a typical small irritation raid" at Barfleur, 100 miles west of Dieppe. Brown (86) wondered if this incident, "on the very eve of Jubilee," had been a mistake, which he thought unlikely, or whether "the British *wanted* [emphasis in original] the Germans to be alert and nervous along the Channel coast."

223. Villa, *Unauthorized,* 234.

224. Bryant (396) did—on what basis is not clear—credit the "restraining hand" of the CIGS with having helped limit the scope of the raid.

225. Moran, *Churchill,* 73.

226. Villa, *Unauthorized,* 94; Bryant, *Turn,* 387; Danchev, *Diaries,* 310.

227. Brooke's diary (Danchev, *Diaries,* 317) on September 1 recorded that he had dined that day with Henry Crerar, who "gave me a very good account of the Dieppe raid and of its difficulties. The casualties were undoubtedly far too heavy—to lose 2,700 men out of 5,000 on such an enterprise is too heavy a cost."

228. Gwyer, *Strategy,* 642–3.

229. Matloff, *Strategic: 1941–1942,* 366. A BOH (Howard, *August 1942,* 219) similarly characterized the reactions to Dieppe of US Army planners.

230. Howard, *August 1942,* 219.

231. Mountbatten told the Combined Chiefs of Staff on 1/22/1943 that "the overriding lesson of Dieppe" was the need in amphibious operations for "discipline, training, and tactical flexibility." The report of the British Joint Planning Staff considered by the Chiefs the same day held that the organization of small-scale raids could "be adequately dealt with... on the same lines as was the Dieppe raid." U.S. Department of State, *Foreign,* 690, 790.

232. Danchev, *Diaries,* 442.

233. Villa, *Unauthorized,* 234.

234. Raiffa (*Decision,* 27–9, 107) gave a historically-classic exposition.

235. The decision makers might, for example, have thought it 20-percent likely that German artillery would have been positioned in the cliffs in ways that the reconnaissance planes would have detected—

in which case, the divisions planned to land at Red and White Beaches would have been shifted to Green Beach, thereby reducing the number of Canadian casualties by 400. The roughly-estimated EVI of 80 (= (0.2)(400)) casualties saved would have been compared with the costs and risks of the reconnaissance flights to judge whether they should have been undertaken. To avoid tipping off the defenders, the Allies would have sent reconnaissance planes not just to Dieppe, but also to many other points between Brest and Rotterdam. The costs and risks of such other flights should also have been considered.

236. Brooke may, it could be speculated, have thought that Rutter/Jubilee would have a 30-percent chance of persuading the US to postpone Roundup/Overlord until 1944, with a saving of 200,000 casualties. The EVI of 60,000 casualties avoided would have justified Jubilee.

237. Robertson, *Shame,* 400–1.

238. Allison, *Essence,* 17.

239. Allison, *Essence,* 143.

240. Allison, *Essence,* 255.

241. Allison, *Essence,* 5.

242. Allison, *Essence,* 6.

243. Allison, *Essence,* 263.

244. Allison, *Essence,* 6.

245. Wilmot, *Europe,* 181–3; Stacey, *Six Years,* 403–4.

246. *Memoirs,* 70–1.

247. Stacey, *Six Years,* 399.

248. Stacey, *Six Years,* 399.

Chapter 2

1. A converted American cutter, with a history of patrolling to catch bootleggers on the Great Lakes. It had been transferred to Britain under Lend-Lease and renamed.

2. Roberts, *Storm,* 301.

3. Atkinson, *Dawn,* 106.

4. Gwyer, *Strategy,* 16–7.

5. Matloff, *Strategic: 1941–1942,* 55.

6. The Franklin D. Roosevelt Presidential Library and Museum, Franklin D. Roosevelt, Papers as President: The President's Secretary's File, 1933–1945, Series 1: Safe File, Box 1: American-British Joint Chiefs of Staff: "Joint Board Estimate of United States Over-All Production Requirements-9/11/1941, 1, 10, 14, 17.

7. Hamilton, *Mantle,* 109.

8. Hamilton, *Mantle,* 110.

9. Churchill, *Grand,* 482–3.

10. Churchill, *Grand,* 561.

11. Churchill, *Grand,* 562.

12. Churchill, *Grand,* 574–6.

13. Churchill, *Grand,* 574.

14. Churchill, *Grand,* 589.

15. U.S. Department of State, *Foreign,* 72.

16. Matloff, *Strategic: 1941–1942,* 105–6.

17. U.S. Department of State, *Foreign,* 172.

18. Churchill, *Grand,* 624.

19. U.S. Department of State, *Foreign,* 163. For months to come, the two names, "Gymnast" and "Super-Gymnast," would be used interchangeably.

20. U.S. Department of State, *Foreign,* 185–91, 196.

21. U.S. Department of State, *Foreign,* 208. A report of the Planning Committee of the US and UK Chiefs of Staff dated January 14 made May 25 the earliest possible date to begin loading for "SUPER-GYMNAST, as originally planned." The committee also, though, reported that 12,000 UK and 12,000 US troops could be landed at Casablanca and Algiers by March 28. U.S. Department of State, *Foreign,* 263–4.

22. *Grand,* 608–9.

23. *Second,* 315–6. Comparably laudatory of the committee was Pogue (*Ordeal,* 283–4).

24. Churchill, *Grand,* 608–9.

25. Bryant, *Turn,* 254.

26. "The most complete unification of military effort ever achieved by two allied nations." Wilmot, *Europe,* 99.

27. Churchill, *Hinge,* 168; Matloff, *Strategic: 1941–1942,* 176.

28. Churchill, *Hinge,* 175.

29. Chandler, *Papers I,* 118.

30. The operational names were occasionally confused. On May 27, 1942, for example, Roosevelt asked Churchill what had been discussed with Molotov about Bolero. Churchill noted that: "By 'Bolero' the President meant 'Sledgehammer', in 1942. This was fully comprehended by us." In his account of a May 1942 meeting with Brooke, Eisenhower had referred to "Bolero," when it seemed that he meant Roundup. Roberts, *Masters,* 174. The min-

utes of the British Chiefs of Staff of June 30, 1942 (p. 3) noted continuing confusion with the Americans over just what "BOLERO" and "ROUND-UP" referred to. Churchill did not like the name "Roundup"—originally chosen by the British (Pogue, *Ordeal,* 315)—for being boastful, but dared not change it, lest the Americans think it portended a shift in attitude. He resigned himself to "hop[ing] it does not bring bad luck." Churchill, *Hinge,* 394.

31. Roberts, *Masters,* 133.

32. Churchill, *Hinge,* 283.

33. Churchill, *Hinge,* 289–90.

34. Sherwood, *Roosevelt,* 556.

35. Gwyer, *Strategy,* 619.

36. The Franklin D. Roosevelt Presidential Library and Museum, Franklin D. Roosevelt, Papers as President: The President's Secretary's File, 1933–1945, Series 4: Departmental Correspondence, Box 83: War—Marshall, George C., 1941–1942, 4.

37. U.S. Department of State, *Foreign,* 428, 467.

38. Danchev, *Diaries,* 267.

39. Hamilton, *Mantle,* 297–8.

40. Sherwood, *Roosevelt,* 590.

41. Churchill, *Hinge,* 342–3.

42. Roberts, *Masters,* 202.

43. Churchill, *Hinge,* 343–4; Ismay, *Memoirs,* 254–5. Brooke (Bryant, *Turn,* 329) had a variant recollection: Marshall himself had brought Roosevelt the telegram.

44. *Hinge,* 343–4.

45. Churchill, *Hinge,* 344.

46. Marshall later said that he had acted to cement UK support for Roundup. Pogue, *Ordeal,* 333.

47. Churchill, *Hinge,* 526.

48. U.S. Department of State, *Foreign,* 478–9.

49. *Hinge,* 398.

50. Moran, *Churchill,* 48. Americans, led by Marshall, had, per Hopkins (Moran, *Churchill,* 102), a conflicting view of the effects of Tobruk: they had gone to see PM and POTUS at the White House intent on securing agreement to undertake Sledgehammer but somehow—they were unsure just how—the disaster in Libya had led them to agree to send men and ships meant for the cross-Channel operation instead to the British Eighth Army in Egypt.

51. Sherwood, *Roosevelt,* 592.

52. Roberts, *Masters,* 364.

53. *Hinge,* 390–1.

54. Field Marshal Sir John Dill's cable to Churchill of 7/15/1942. Churchill, *Hinge,* 396.

55. Pogue, *Ordeal,* 342.

56. Sherwood, *Roosevelt,* 604. The paper was dated July 16.

57. Sherwood, *Roosevelt,* 603.

58. *Hinge,* 237.

59. Keegan, *Second,* 316.

60. Danchev, *Diaries,* 283.

61. Roberts, *Masters,* 247–8, 251, 576. Brooke wrote in his diary on July 15 that "Hopkins is for operating in Africa, Marshall wants to operate in Europe and King in the Pacific." Bryant, *Turn,* 341. The British sensed that Hopkins reflected the position of Roosevelt.

62. Pogue, *Ordeal,* 346.

63. Pogue, *Ordeal,* 346–7.

64. Pogue, *Ordeal,* 347.

65. Bryant, *Turn,* 346. Marshall, when interviewed 14 years later had a variant recollection: when the possibility of proceeding without Cabinet approval was raised, "I blew the hell out of that and said unless the cabinet agreed I wouldn't go along. A compromise wording was worked out." Pogue, *Ordeal,* 347.

66. One American Official History (Howe, *Northwest,* 13–14) made 25 July more than 24 July the day of decision—for it was on the later date that the Combined Chiefs formally accepted Marshall's proposal. Churchill (*Hinge,* 404), Brooke (Danchev, *Diaries,* 284–5), Eisenhower (Chandler, *Papers IV,* 2064), and another AOH (Matloff, *Strategic: 1941–1942,* 280–1) judged that the key date of UK-US concurrence was the twenty-fourth.

67. Churchill, *Hinge,* 404.

68. Gwyer, *Strategy,* 684–5. Per the memorandum of the Combined Chiefs: "if the situation on the Russian front by 15th September indicates such a collapse or weakening of Russian resistance as to make 'ROUND-UP' appear impracticable of successful execution, the decision should be taken to launch [Torch]."

69. Matloff, *Strategic: 1941–1942,* 282.

70. Churchill, *Hinge,* 405.

71. Howe, *Northwest,* 13–4.

72. Matloff, *Strategic: 1941–1942,* 282.

73. That with highest expected value.

74. If the costs of deciding on the details of the various options—in terms of both resources and time—were negligible, this sequencing would be suboptimal: best versions of all strategic alternatives should first be determined, then compared in choosing among them. In practice, it may be most convenient and cost-effective to decide first among the main options, before refining that selected.

75. Matloff, *Strategic: 1941–1942,* 206.

76. Matloff, *Strategic: 1941–1942,* 147.

77. Matloff, *Strategic: 1941–1942,* 100.

78. Matloff, *Strategic: 1941–1942,* 178.

79. Matloff, *Strategic: 1941–1942,* 158.

80. Matloff, *Strategic: 1941–1942,* 308–9.

81. Matloff, *Strategic: 1941–1942,* 163. In April, American and British planners disagreed: the former judging troop transports "the limiting factor;" the latter, cargo shipping. Matloff, *Strategic: 1941–1942,* 180.

82. Matloff, *Strategic: 1941–1942,* 186.

83. Matloff, *Strategic: 1941–1942,* 312.

84. Matloff, *Strategic: 1941–1942,* 163.

85. Matloff, *Strategic: 1941–1942,* 227.

86. Matloff, *Strategic: 1941–1942,* 117.

87. Matloff, *Strategic: 1941–1942,* 189.

88. Matloff, *Strategic: 1941–1942,* 217.

89. Matloff, *Strategic: 1941–1942,* 304–5.

90. Matloff, *Strategic: 1941–1942,* 310.

91. Matloff, *Strategic: 1941–1942,* 312.

92. Roberts, *Masters,* 574.

93. U.S. Department of State, *Foreign,* 78; Churchill, *Hinge,* 393–4.

94. Churchill, *Grand,* 483, 486, 561.

95. *Crusade,* 43. Lieutenant General Leslie McNair, on 1/15/1942, urged landings in Freetown, Sierra Leone and Dakar, Senegal. Chandler, *Papers I,* 56n.

96. Reported by Alan Brooke in Washington on June 19, 1942. U.S. Department of State, *Foreign,* 424–5.

97. Stacey, *Six Years,* 324.

98. U.S. Department of State, *Foreign,* 435.

99. Sherwood, *Roosevelt,* 610.

100. Chandler, *Papers I,* 409.

101. Giraud had, months earlier, proposed this to De Gaulle, who had thought it infeasible. De Gaulle, *L'Unité,* 19. Giraud also demanded that Torch be placed under his supreme command.

102. Pogue, *Ordeal,* 402. Roosevelt, when told that the landings would have to be delayed until after the elections, did not object. His press secretary, Steve Early, when informed by a Marshall aide on the eve of the invasion—after the electoral victories of the Republicans—of its imminence, responded: "You tell me that now, you son of a bitch? Why, oh, why couldn't you have done it a week ago." Mosley, *Marshall,* 212.

103. *Masters,* 199.

104. Churchill, *Hinge,* 478.

105. Howe, *Northwest,* 27.

106. Matloff, *Strategic: 1941–1942,* 287.

107. Bryant, *Turn,* 400.

108. Matloff, *Strategic: 1941–1942,* 288.

109. WSC to FDR of 8/27/1942. Churchill, *Hinge,* 475. Brooke, off with Churchill to Egypt and Russia, had not been a party to this proposal. In his first meeting with the British Chiefs upon his return, he sided more with Washington than with London: prioritizing Casablanca, questioning the wisdom of landing at Philippeville and Bône, but also in favor of attacking Algiers. Howard, *August 1942,* 125–6. The proposal of Eisenhower of 8/22/1942 was to land at Oran, Algiers, and Bône, but not at Casablanca. Howard, *August 1942,* 121.

110. The proposal of the US Joint Chiefs of 8/25/1942. Matloff, *Strategic: 1941–1942,* 291. Howard, *August 1942,* 124.

111. Morison, *Contributions,* 5.

112. Hamilton, *Mantle,* 320.

113. *Blast,* 160. A poll of mid-1939 reported that, for 26 percent of the French, the US was the country they liked best; for 23 percent of the French, England. Gallup, *Poll,* 167.

114. *Hinge,* 478.

115. Churchill, *Hinge,* 477.

116. *Kriege,* Book I, Chapters I, III.

117. *Thinking,* 256. Russo (*Traps,* 79) reached the same conclusion.

118. Chandler, *Papers I,* 606; Patton, *War,* 354.

119. Lewis, "Obama's." The last two quoted sentences paraphrased the President.

120. Liddell Hart, *Second,* 332.

121. Matloff, *Strategic: 1941–1942,* 175.

122. Lucas, *Algiers,* 32.

123. Churchill, *Grand,* 578.

124. U.S. Department of State, *Foreign,* 259.

125. Wilmot, *Europe,* 59.

126. Burdick, *Germany's,* 52.

127. Burdick, *Germany's,* 63, 104.

128. Burdick, *Germany's,* 150, 152, 160, 162, 173, 177, 183–6.

129. Eisenhower, in mid-October 1942 invoking other-side perception, judged that "a wise move for the Germans, particularly in the event of a successful TORCH, would be a deliberate move in Spain." On 11/2/1942, he reported to Marshall that "the purpose of the reserve corps, now under training in the United Kingdom, is to provide us a quick means of intervening in case of hostile Spanish reaction." Such need, he thought, would persist until 75 days after the Torch landings. Chandler, *Papers I,* 620, 652.

130. Ismay, *Memoirs,* 261.

131. Sherwood, *Roosevelt,* 595.

132. Bryant, *Turn,* 236–7.

133. Churchill, *Hinge,* 59.

134. Butcher, *Three Years,* 72.

135. U.K. War Cabinet, *Chiefs of Staff Committee: Minutes of Meetings:* CAB 79/56/23 (4/9/1942): 2.

136. Churchill, *Hinge,* 432.

137. Chandler, *Papers I,* 393.

138. U.K. War Cabinet, *Chiefs of Staff Committee: Minutes of Meetings:* CAB 79/56/25 (4/14/1942): 2.

139. U.S. Department of State, *Foreign,* 466.

140. Matloff, *Strategic: 1941–1942,* 280.

141. Butcher, *Three Years,* 32; Matloff, *Strategic: 1941–1942,* 276, 280, 282; Hamilton, *Mantle,* 354. Churchill in September 1942 said that he was "very much astonished to find out that TORCH practically eliminates any opportunity for a 1943 ROUNDUP." Chandler, *Papers I,* 570.

142. "North Africa," 152.

143. Butcher, *Three Years,* 58.

144. Morison, *Contributions,* 24; Bryant, *Turn,* 432.

145. Chandler, *Papers II,* 872.

146. Pogue, *Ordeal,* 273.

147. *Grand,* 596–7.

148. *Blast,* 144.

149. Morison, *Contributions,* 17.

150. Stimson, *Active,* 436.

151. Sherwood, *Roosevelt,* 590.

152. The words of Bryant (*Turn,* 233), expressing his own and Brooke's view. Brooke's diary entry (Danchev, *Diaries,* 248) of 4/14/1942: "[Hopkins and Marshall] have not begun to realize all the implications of this [Bolero-Sledgehammer-Roundup] plan and all the difficulties that lie ahead of us!"

153. E.g., Hamilton, *Making,* 520.

154. Stoler, *Allies,* 40–1.

155. Roberts, *Masters,* 139.

156. Hamilton, *Mantle,* 297.

157. Marshall's strategic plan, as presented to the British in April 1942, held that, if "[t]he situation on the Russian front becomes desperate... [Sledgehammer] should be considered as a sacrifice in the common good." Gwyer, *Strategy,* 680. Roosevelt in June 1942 proposed to Mountbatten such a step. Stimson, *Active,* 423.

158. Roberts, *Masters,* 215.

159. Roberts, *Masters,* 215, quoting Max Hastings.

160. Hastings, *Winston's,* 241–3.

161. Churchill, *Grand,* 440–1.

162. Bryant, *Turn,* 398.

163. *Dawn,* 28. With respect to Sledgehammer, what Marshall had been saying in London in April was: "This is what should be done and you are the ones who should do it." He admitted to Roosevelt that he had in England been "greatly embarrassed by the fact that we

could propose only 2½ divisions to participate in a cross–Channel operation by September 15." Chandler, *Papers I*, 280.

164. Stimson, *Active*, 437.

165. Stimson, *Active*, 419; U.S. Department of State, *Foreign*, 475.

166. Stimson, *Active*, 417.

167. Roberts, *Masters*, 128–9.

168. UK Chiefs of Staff Committee. *Minutes*. No. 9: 3/17/1942.

169. Keegan, *Second*, 313.

170. Churchill, *Closing*, 257.

171. *Hinge*, 310.

172. Bryant, *Turn*, 287.

173. Roberts, *Masters*, 156.

174. Pogue, *Ordeal*, 318.

175. *Hinge*, 289–90.

176. *Memoirs*, 250.

177. Pogue, *Ordeal*, 320.

178. Roberts, *Masters*, 158–9.

179. *Winston's*, 232. Other British writers in the same vein were Leonard Mosley (*Marshall*, 204–5), Sir John Keegan (*Second*, 313), Andrew Roberts (*Masters*, 157–9, 576), and Nigel Hamilton (*Mantle*, 331).

180. *Contributions*, 24.

181. Roberts, *Masters*, 90.

182. Roberts, *Masters*, 90.

183. Danchev, *Diaries*, 284.

184. Roberts, *Masters*, 392.

185. Bryant, *Turn*, 314.

186. Sherwood, *Roosevelt*, 568–70.

187. *Hinge*, 304–5. Churchill would, on November 11, 1942, state to the Commons that "one object" of the releases "was to deceive the enemy." Robertson, *Shame*, 397. It is not clear that the Soviet Union knew of this intent.

188. Churchill, *Hinge*, 442.

189. Roberts, *Masters*, 176.

190. Roberts, *Masters*, 175.

191. Sherwood, *Roosevelt*, 569.

192. Gwyer, *Strategy*, 660.

193. Gwyer, *Strategy*, 622; Sherwood, *Roosevelt*, 582.

194. Roberts, *Masters*, 198.

195. Churchill, *Hinge*, 392.

196. Hamilton, *Mantle*, 105. Roberts (*Masters*, 561) also saw FDR more than WSC as the initiator of Gymnast/Torch.

197. Blumenson, *Patton*, 510.

198. Stoler, *Allies*, 68.

199. Colville, *Fringes*, 624.

200. Matloff, *Strategic: 1941–1942*, 269.

201. Matloff, *Strategic: 1941–1942*, 268–9.

202. *Active*, 425.

203. Pogue, *Ordeal*, 340–1. Robert Sherwood (*Roosevelt*, 594) in 1946 had thought that it had been "far more than a bluff in General Marshall's mind."

204. *Mantle*, 337, 339.

205. *Mantle*, 336.

206. *Mantle*, 340.

207. Pogue, *Ordeal*, 340–1.

208. Roberts, *Masters*, 233.

209. *Mantle*, 339, 341, 345.

210. Hamilton, *Mantle*, 343; The Franklin D. Roosevelt Presidential Library and Museum, Franklin D. Roosevelt, Papers as President: The President's Secretary's File, 1933–1945, Series 4: Departmental Correspondence, Box 84: War—Stimson, Henry L., 1942.

211. Roberts, *Masters*, 235–9.

212. Pogue, *Ordeal*, 359; Hamilton, *Mantle*, 359.

213. Hamilton, *Mantle*, 366, quoting Stimson's diary entry of 8/7/1942. Pogue (*Ordeal*, 348) dated the meeting and diary entry one day earlier.

214. Hamilton, *Mantle*, 366.

215. This could have been done by assigning numerical values to possible outcomes, summing the products of such values multiplied by their estimated chances of being realized to calculate expected values, and opting for the alternative of highest expected value.

216. *Generals*, 458.

217. *Generals*, 447.

218. Goodwin, *Ordinary*, 65.

219. Goodwin, *Ordinary*, 65.

220. Moran, *Struggle*, 71.

221. Davis, *Soldier*, 396.

222. Warlimont, *Inside*, 267.

223. Warlimont, *Inside*, 271.

224. Keegan, *Second*, 340.

225. Churchill, *Hinge*, 558.

226. Kesselring, *Memoirs*, 139. Credit for the confusion of the Axis goes in part to the success of the Allies in spreading disinformation pointing in wrong directions. Playfair, *Destruction*, 136.

227. Atkinson, *Dawn*, 76–7.

228. Atkinson, *Dawn*, 71.

229. Atkinson, *Dawn*, 77.

230. Eisenhower, *Crusade*, 107.

231. *Hinge*, 578.

232. Howe, *Northwest*, 679.

233. Figures rounded off further from those of Atkinson (*Dawn*, 159), who noted their imprecision.

234. Playfair, *Destruction*, 172. Per Howe (*Northwest*, 683), 20,975 German troops came into North Africa in November 1942.

235. Howe, *Northwest*, 291.

236. Atkinson, *Dawn*, 173.

237. Atkinson, *Dawn*, 173.

238. Atkinson, *Dawn*, 178.

239. Liddell Hart, *Second*, 336.

240. Liddell Hart, *Second*, 336.

241. Atkinson, *Dawn*, 240.

242. Ellis, *Brute*, 296.

243. D'Este, 392–4. Eisenhower had ordered deployment of a concentrated, mobile reserve behind a thin line of screening and reconnaissance units. Eisenhower, *Crusade*, 126. Fredendall, however, had not so positioned his men and Eisenhower had not imposed his will. Reserves instead were strewn in inadequate clumps behind the front and defeated one by one.

244. *Hinge*, 659.

245. Atkinson, *Dawn*, 536–7. The total was that given by Alexander (*Memoirs*, 39) and Eisenhower (*Crusade*, 157). The American Official History (Howe, *Northwest*, 666) put the number at 275,000; Warlimont (*Inside*, 313) of Hitler's HQ, at 300,000. Liddell Hart (*Second*, 431) thought all three numbers too high, inasmuch as Axis ration strength in April had been less than 180,000. Eisenhower (*Crusade*, 156) estimated 125,000 captured Germans.

246. *Hinge*, 564.

247. E.g., Morison, *Contributions*, 25; Gilbert, *Road*, 260; Boog, *Global*, 794; Roberts, *Masters*, 291.

248. Howe, *Northwest*, 677.

249. *Hinge*, 564.

250. Hobbs, *Dear*, 88.

251. Hobbs, *Dear*, 92, 93.

252. Playfair, *Destruction*, 525–6.

253. Butcher, *Three Years*, 244.

254. *Crusade*, 116.

255. Playfair, *Destruction*, 188.

256. A self-tout: "bold," in military-speak, connotes "laudable."

257. *Crusade*, 116, 118.

258. Atkinson, *Dawn*, 180, 182–3, 191. Liddell Hart (*Second*, 337, 338) also criticized Anderson's cautious slowness and Beevor (*Second*, 393), his non-concentration.

259. Hamilton, *Master*, 232.

260. Beevor, *Second*, 393.

261. Bryant, *Turn*, 430.

262. Hamilton, *Master,* 139.

263. Atkinson, *Dawn,* 246.

264. Bryant, *Turn,* 455. More specifics on the shortcomings of Eisenhower's performance in North Africa were not to be found in Brooke's diary, in the expansion of the diary by Bryant, or in the minutes of the Casablanca session (U.S. Department of State, *Foreign,* 655–62) in which Eisenhower's authority was trimmed.

265. Howe, *Northwest,* 29–30.

266. Howe, *Northwest,* 371.

267. *There,* 159.

268. *Memoirs,* 157.

269. Morison, *Sicily,* 218.

270. See other types of this bias in Chapter 4 and the Epilogue.

271. Meyer, "TORCH," 152.

272. Keegan, *Second,* 316; Murray, *Won,* 299; Overy, *Why,* 53; Roberts, *Masters,* 250, 579; Hastings, *Winston's,* 232; Corrigan, *Second,* 296; Beevor, *Second,* 385; Hamilton, *Mantle,* 342.

273. Roberts, Masters, 579.

274. Keegan, *Second,* 316.

275. Truscott, *Command,* 49.

276. Sherwood, *Roosevelt,* 607.

277. The UK and US seem to have differed significantly not only on the probabilities estimated for the success of an early cross-Channel attack but also on the values of possible outcomes: the Americans being the more willing to increase Western-Ally casualties by tens of thousands, if that would aid the Soviets and bring earlier victory; the British the less dissatisfied to have the Germans and Russians continue to kill each other and the less willing to incur additional Western-Ally casualties to reduce those of the Russians.

278. U.S. Department of State, *Foreign,* 431.

279. Butcher, *Three Years,* 29.

280. Roberts, *Masters,* 287; Atkinson, *Dawn,* 61.

281. *Crusade,* 71.

282. E.g., Morison, *Contributions,* 28–9; Beevor, *Second,* 385; Hamilton, *Mantle,* 103.

283. *Active,* 427.

284. Hamilton, *Mantle,* 357–8.

285. Hobbs, *Dear,* 55.

286. *Hinge,* 548.

287. *Blast,* 161.

288. Butcher, *Three Years,* 145.

289. Pogue, *Ordeal,* 415.

290. *Diaries,* 177.

291. Murray, *Won,* 273.

292. *Second,* 341–2.

293. Danchev, *Diaries,* 344–5.

294. *Grand,* 586.

295. Roberts, *Masters,* 221.

296. Murray, *Won,* 299; Atkinson, *Dawn,* 296–7; Roberts, *Masters,* 579.

297. Moran, *Churchill,* 130–1.

298. Moran, *Churchill,* 157.

299. Roberts, *Masters,* 479.

300. *Active,* 436.

301. Howe, *Northwest,* 683.

302. Liddell Hart, *Rommel,* 365; Warlimont, *Inside,* 272, 308; Boog, *Global,* 793.

303. Schumann, *Umschwung,* 128.

304. Liddell Hart, *Rommel,* 419.

305. Warlimont, *Inside,* 308.

306. Warlimont, *Inside,* 308, 310.

307. Warlimont, *Inside,* 310.

308. Howe, *Northwest,* 601–2, 645; Schumann, *Umschwung,* 129.

309. *Memoirs,* 156–7.

310. *Hinge,* 591.

311. Roberts, *Storm,* 310.

312. E.g., Macmillan, *Blast,* 259; Murray, *Won,* 298.

313. Schumann, *Umschwung,* 111.

314. Howe, *Northwest,* 673.

315. Boog, *Global,* 794; Schumann, *Umschwung,* 111.

316. Warlimont, *Inside,* 307.

317. Liddell Hart, *Rommel,* 426.

318. Warlimont, *Inside,* 314.

319. Atkinson (*Dawn,* 539)—with Bryant (*Turn,* 501) in basic agreement—sided with Hitler against the AOH: holding that the fighting in Tunisia had kept "the Mediterranean closed an extra half-year."

320. *Grand,* 586.

321. Weinberg, *World,* 434–5.

322. Von Neumann, John, "Zur Theorie der Gesellschaftsspiele," *Mathemathische Annalen 100:* 295–320. 1928. Oversimplifying, the theorem states that in any zero-sum game of two opponents, there is an expected game value—call it V—such that each opponent has a strategy, perhaps using probabilistic moves, that will ensure that its expected outcome is no worse for it than V.

323. *Kriege,* Book I, Chapter I.

324. The War of the American Revolution, which essentially ended with the surrender of Lord Cornwallis at Yorktown and led to British recognition of American independence, was more zero-sum than that of 1812, which ended in a negotiated settlement yielding neither side its full war aims. The American Civil War, which in 1865 ended slavery and secession, was more zero-sum than the Austro-Prussian War of the next year, terminated after seven weeks of conflict by a peace settlement that granted Prussia hegemony in Germany but no Austrian territory and that would eventually lead to the alliance of the two main combatants. The First World War had begun with each participant seeking zero-sum victory and had ended when all parties realized how non-zero-sum the devastation was and agreed to an armistice.

325. Axelrod, *Evolution,* 73–87.

326. Reinhard Selten, an occasional game-theoretic collaborator with Harsanyi, also shared the 1994 prize.

327. *Memoirs,* 127.

328. Davis, *Game Theory,* 27–30; Neumann, *Games,* 111es.

329. Davis, *Game Theory,* 28.

330. Rapoport, *Two-Person,* 92.

331. Davis, *Game Theory,* 52. Rapoport, Anatol, and Carol Orwant. "Experimental Games: A Review." *Behavioral Science 7:* 1–37. 1962.

332. *Grand,* 516.

333. Atkinson, *Guns,* 98.

334. Wilmot, *Europe,* 336.

335. Westphal, *West,* 162.

336. Blumenson, *Patton,* 320.

337. Grant, *Memoirs,* 157.

338. Mawdsley, *Thunder,* 264.

339. See, for instance, Anatol Rapoport and Albert M. Chammah, "The Game of Chicken," *American Behavioral Scientist 10:* 10–28, 1966; Dixit, *Games,* 9es.

340. The situation may be depicted as a game table:

	Driver B	
	Swerve	**Continue Straight**
Swerve	0, 0	−1, 1
Driver A		
Continue Straight	1, −1	−1000, −1000

Non-Zero-Sum Game-Table Depiction of Chicken

For each combination of plays by the two drivers, the outcome values are shown as ordered pairs: the first number is that of Driver A; the second, that of Driver B.

341. *Strategy,* 124.

342. *Common Sense and Nuclear Warfare.* NY: Simon and Schuster, 1959, 30.

343. Churchill (*Hinge,* 698) disagreed: "No one could doubt the magnitude of the victory of Tunis. It held its own with Stalingrad."

344. U.S. Department of State, *Foreign,* 539, 560.

345. Roberts, *Masters,* 322.

346. Churchill, *Hinge,* 666. It is possible that the Prime Minister was positively glossing to Stalin. In the same message, he said that the UK and US were working toward "a cross-Channel operation in August." If delayed, "it will be prepared with stronger forces in September." To his War Cabinet on January 20, Churchill (*Hinge,* 612) had mentioned such a possible action in less positive terms: the build-up of forces in the UK would "go ahead as far as our commitments allow, with a view to a 'Sledgehammer' of some sort this year or a return to the Continent with all available forces if Germany shows definite signs of collapse."

347. Churchill, *Hinge,* 654.

348. Churchill, *Hinge,* 668.

349. Bryant, *Turn,* 482.

350. Howe, *Dear,* 106.

351. Churchill, *Hinge,* 677.

352. Kesselring, *Soldat,* 210.

353. Liddell Hart, *Rommel,* 422.

354. Kahneman, *Thinking,* 334. One example illustrating these behavioral patterns given by Kahneman (334–5) entailed choices between A = $240 for sure and B = a lottery ticket offering a one-quarter chance of gaining $1,000 and a three-quarters chance of gaining nothing, with expected monetary value (EMV) of $250; and between C = losing $750 and D a three-quarters chance of losing $1,000 and a one-quarter chance of losing nothing, an EMV of losing $750. 73 percent of the research subjects chose A and D. To choose A, preferring a sure amount less than the EMV of the lottery, shows risk aversion: to choose D, preferring a

lottery with EMV of minus $750 to that amount of certain loss is risk-seeking.

355. *Thinking,* 317, 318–9.

356. Per historian Gordon Corrigan (*Second,* 302): "He had got his victory and he was not going to risk throwing it away" via risky attempts to destroy Rommel's retreating Afrika Korps.

Chapter 3

1. Churchill, *Closing,* 38.

2. Morison, *Sicily,* 215.

3. Morison, *Sicily,* 215n; D'Este, *Bitter,* 514.

4. *Closing,* 4–8.

5. Garland, *Sicily,* 417n; Churchill, *Closing,* 38.

6. Bradley, *General's,* 191.

7. *Soldat,* 222.

8. *Memoirs,* 162.

9. D'Este, *Bitter,* 597, 607.

10. Churchill, *Closing,* 39.

11. This figure is intermediate among those in various sources. The AOH (Garland, *Sicily,* 416n) gave the low number of 39,569, which may have excluded those who left before the main evacuation; the BOH (Molony, *Sicily,* 182), 60,000; Morison (*Sicily,* 214n), 52,346, of whom 13,500 were wounded; and L. Clark (*Anzio,* 13), 53,000.

12. Garland, *Sicily,* 416n; L. Clark, *Anzio,* 13.

13. Morison, *Sicily,* 215n.

14. Churchill, *Closing,* 38–9.

15. Per the AOH (Garland, *Sicily,* 410), between 70,000 and 75,000; the BOH (Molony, *Sicily,* 182), 75,000; D'Este (*Bitter,* 523), 62,000.

16. Among those questioning the wisdom of launching Husky have been Baldwin (*Battles,* 228) and Mitcham (*Sicily,* 309–10). Eisenhower at Casablanca had recommended attacking Sardinia before Sicily. Chandler, *Papers II,* 1230.

17. Butcher, *Three Years,* 352–3.

18. Butcher, *Three Years,* 387.

19. *Crusade,* 183.

20. *Crusade,* 177.

21. *Crusade,* 178.

22. *Memoirs,* 167, 169.

23. Warlimont, *Inside,* 345.

24. Mitcham, *Sicily,* 285.

25. Liddell Hart, *Rommel,* 427–8.

26. Molony, *Sicily,* 91.

27. Mitcham, *Sicily,* 308.

28. *Bitter,* 548. The British had brought back 3.6 percent (25 of 704) of their tanks at Dunkirk (Wilmot, *Europe,* 33)—versus 38 percent (47 of 125) for the Germans at Messina.

29. D'Este, *Bitter,* 526.

30. Mitcham, *Sicily,* 308.

31. Garland, *Sicily,* 413, 421.

32. Ambrose, *Supreme,* 226. Among those whose conclusions could be so characterized were: Fuller, *Second,* 265; Morison, *Sicily,* 218–9; Pond, *Sicily,* 211; Liddell Hart, *Second,* 446; Bradley, *General's,* 198; Hamilton, *Master,* 349; Keegan, *Second,* 349; Ellis, *Brute,* 307; Blumenson, *Battle,* 61; Murray, *Won,* 303; Atkinson, *Day,* 55; and Hastings, *Inferno,* 434.

33. Hastings, *Inferno,* 435.

34. Senger, *Neither,* 146.

35. D'Este, *Bitter,* 283, 287.

36. Blumenson, *Patton,* 287.

37. Blumenson, *Patton,* 304.

38. Kesselring, *Soldat,* 221.

39. Pond, *Sicily,* 209, 215.

40. *Crusade,* 178–9.

41. D'Este, *Bitter,* 190.

42. The Germans were more taken in by the ruse than the Italians, who continued to believe that Sicily would be the next Allied target. D'Este, *Bitter,* 190. On July 7, the Joint Intelligence Committee of the UK had reported that the Axis expected landings in Sicily. Goodman, *Joint,* 129.

43. Hamilton, *Master,* 296.

44. Roskill, *Offensive,* 130; D'Este, *Bitter,* 231.

45. Churchill, Cunningham (Churchill, *Closing,* 32), Roskill (*Offensive,* 129), and Alexander (*Memoirs,* 107) thought that the lack of opposition owed in part to Allied achievement of surprise—to which the foul weather contributed. Bradley (*General's,* 182) thought his enemy not in the least surprised—with which Kesselring (*Memoirs,* 162) agreed.

46. Strong, *Intelligence,* 131; Bradley, *General's,* 164; D'Este, *Bitter,* 113. It was not good for the Allies that, as Morison (*Sicily,* 202) noted, "the terrain was perfect for an orderly withdrawal... There were any number of Thermopylae where

Axis units could, and did, fight tough rear-guard actions." Both sides foreknew the topography: the Allies nevertheless launched Husky; had the ground less favored a staged retreat, the Wehrmacht would not have defended as it did.

47. Kesselring, *Memoirs,* 165.

48. Liddell Hart, *Other,* 356. Heinrich von Vietinghoff also thought that such attacks could easily have succeeded. D'Este, *Bitter,* 526. This account of Kesselring runs counter to what he wrote in his memoirs—(163) in which he claimed, puzzlingly and without explanation, to have deemed Calabrian landings after July 12 no longer a worry. One reason they were not initially attempted was the limited range of land-based air cover: Allied air bases in Malta, Pantelleria, and Tunisia were too distant. Once, however, the Allies were operating out of Sicilian airfields, Axis worries about their Calabrian rear should have increased—as indeed General Emilio Faldella, chief of staff to Guzzoni, wrote that they did. Pond, *Sicily,* 213.

49. Garland, *Sicily,* 69.

50. Garland, *Sicily,* 258–9, 262.

51. Roberts, *Masters,* 389. A case for the reverse of this judgment may be made: such landings might not only have been challenging, but also risky for the Allies. The Germans would, at Salerno in September and at Anzio in January, rapidly bring in troops from far parts to attack and to imperil the beachheads. They might have reacted similarly, had the Allies in July landed on either side of the Strait of Messina.

52. Pond, *Sicily,* 212.

53. Liddell Hart, *Second,* 440.

54. *Memoirs,* 105.

55. Alexander, *Memoirs,* 105; Montgomery, *Memoirs,* 162.

56. Lamb, *Montgomery,* 26; D'Este, *Bitter,* 556.

57. Garland, *Sicily,* 422–3.

58. Hamilton, *Master,* 304.

59. Hamilton, *Master,* 324.

60. *General's,* 188; *Soldier's,* 135.

61. Garland, *Sicily,* 422. Atkinson (*Day,* 124) thought that Alexander's order, in preventing Patton from taking Enna by July 16, "baleful," but for a different reason: it enabled the escape of the Germans in western Sicily.

62. Molony, *Sicily,* 111.

63. *General's,* 188.

64. D'Este, *Bitter,* 557.

65. Blumenson, *Patton,* 325.

66. *Memoirs,* 169. D'Este (*Bitter,* 416) favored a variant, directing Patton even more to his right, to drive "northeast towards Mount Etna, trapping the main German forces between the Americans and Eighth Army... followed by a drive to the northeastern coast and Messina."

67. *Soldat,* 226.

68. Montgomery had planned for an amphibious right hook on the night of July 16/17, but first postponed, then canceled it. D'Este (*Bitter,* 396) deemed the cancellation "inexplicable... Had Montgomery carried out his original intention he would, at a single stroke, have regained the initiative and been in control of the coastal route to Messina."

69. Liddell Hart, *Second,* 446.

70. Pond, *Sicily,* 211.

71. Garland, *Sicily,* 366–7.

72. Truscott, *Command,* 235–40.

73. Garland, *Sicily,* 404–5.

74. D'Este, *Bitter,* 482.

75. *General's,* 197.

76. Hamilton, *Master,* 362.

77. Roskill, *Offensive,* 121.

78. Molony, *Sicily,* 181.

79. Roskill, *Offensive,* 152.

80. Roskill, *Offensive,* 143.

81. Montgomery, *Memoirs,* 164.

82. *El Alamein,* 90. In his later memoirs, Montgomery (169) regretted that there had not been "close co-ordination of the land, air and sea effort."

83. Roskill, *Offensive,* 146; Garland, *Sicily,* 379.

84. Garland, *Sicily,* 381.

85. *Sailor's,* 556.

86. *Memoirs,* 162.

87. Morison, *Sicily,* 216.

88. *War,* 71.

89. *Command,* 543.

90. D'Este, *Bitter,* 398.

91. Cunningham, *Sailor's,* 553, 556; Tedder, *Prejudice,* 452.

92. *Bitter,* 549. D'Este (549n) called Alexander's "among the least candid and useful of the many memoirs to appear after the war." He also disputed Tedder's numbers: while the air chief had, for instance, claimed the destruction on August 5 of 24 enemy vessels, the Germans actually had lost that day but one ferry, while suffering seven injuries. D'Este exempted from his indictments of memoirs those of Eisenhower and Montgomery. Eisenhower's candor, however, came not in his memoirs, but in an unguarded remark to a friend. He would subsequently refrain from saying such things and his memoirs would be positively spun. Both his and Montgomery's memoirs sped briskly past Allied fumblings in Sicily.

93. Garland, *Sicily,* 422–3. The BOH (Molony, *Sicily,* 89) phrased it that "rightly or wrongly the orders were interpreted to mean that Alexander had less than complete confidence in the capabilities of his American troops."

94. D'Este, *Patton,* 513.

95. Bradley, *General's,* 190.

96. Atkinson, *Dawn,* 183, 258.

97. D'Este, *Patton,* 514—citing the unpublished memoirs of Leese.

98. Churchill, *Closing,* 37.

99. Garland, *Sicily,* 417.

100. Molony, *Sicily,* 174; Hamilton, *Master,* 348; Garland, *Sicily,* 379, 421.

101. Mitcham, *Sicily,* 294.

102. Bradley, *Soldier's,* 134; Montgomery, *Memoirs,* 168–9.

103. Molony, *Sicily,* 174.

104. D'Este, *Bitter,* 529.

105. D'Este, *Bitter,* 547n. Strong's memoirs (*Intelligence,* 139) were terse—and, per D'Este, untruthful—on this point: "Early in August we deduced that the enemy was contemplating evacuation and by the second week of the month they had indeed started to pull out."

106. E.g., Morison, *Sicily,* 219; Pond, *Sicily,* 211–2; Mitcham, *Sicily,* 294; D'Este, *Bitter,* 539–40, 544.

107. Roberts, *Masters,* 577; Beevor, *Second,* 499.

108. One historian who did make this point was Atkinson (*Day,* 55), who saw in the preoccupation of the Allied commanders with the Tunisian campaign the cause of the bad outcome at Messina.

109. Chandler, *Papers II,* 1266.

110. Chandler, *Papers II,* 1306.

111. Roberts, *Masters,* 577. Beevor (*Second,* 499) agreed, calling the evacuation of 110,000 enemy an "oversight" that owed to Marshall.

112. Hamilton, *Master,* 348–9. Hamilton also faulted Eisenhower for not calling a meeting on forestalling Axis escape until August 9, by which time little could be done.

113. Bradley, *General's,* 168.

114. Roskill, *Offensive,* 150.

115. Hamilton, *Master,* 313. Brooke in late 1943 thought Alexander "a very, very, small man and cannot see big... I shudder at the thought of him as a Supreme Commander!" Danchev, *Diaries,* 473.

116. Hamilton, *Master,* 301, 304, 312, 319, 322.

117. E.g., Jackson, *Alexander,* 218, 226; D'Este, *Fatal,* 28, 55; Mitcham, *Sicily,* 180; Hastings, *Inferno,* 433.

118. Among them: Tedder as quoted in Atkinson, *Day,* 161; Pond, *Sicily,* 212; Garland, *Sicily,* 411; Bradley, *General's,* 188, 193, 194; and D'Este, *Bitter,* 396.

119. Hamilton, *Master,* 315, 317, 328.

120. Hamilton, *Master,* 321–3.

121. *General's,* 192–3.

122. Hamilton, *Master,* 323. Hamilton also blamed Patton's chief of staff, General Hobart Gay, for withholding from his army commander Alexander's order to drive north instead of northwest toward Palermo. It is possible that Patton was complicit in his not acknowledging getting the order until entering Palermo.

123. Quoted in Pond, *Sicily,* 220; Garland, *Sicily,* 423. Hastings (*Inferno,* 433) agreed.

124. Morison, *Sicily,* 202.

125. Roskill, *Offensive,* 149.

126. Pond, *Sicily,* 211.

127. D'Este, *Bitter,* 538.

128. *Command,* 204; *General's,* 178; Garland, *Sicily,* 421.

129. *General's,* 178.

130. Down on the air forces were Garland, *Sicily,* 411; Baldwin, *Battles,* 231; and Jackson, *Alexander,* 225; on the navies, Baldwin, *Battles,* 232; Warner, *Cunningham,* 210; and D'Este, *Fatal,* 28.

131. *Sicily,* 218–9.

132. Bryant, *Turn,* 454.

133. Bryant, *Turn,* 458.

134. Garland, *Sicily,* 420.

135. *Three Years,* 346.

136. Atkinson, *Guns,* 406.

137. Howe, *Northwest,* 260, 364; Playfair, *Destruction,* 179.

138. Liddell Hart, *Rommel,* 376, 384, 397, 421.

139. *Crusade,* 126. Eisenhower pitched the drive toward Sfax in his cables of 12/29/1942 and 1/12/1943 to the Combined Chiefs of Staff and the British Chiefs of Staff. Chandler, *Papers II,* 871–2, 901–2.

140. Atkinson, *Dawn,* 286.

141. Butcher, *Three Years,* 243.

142. Bradley, *General's,* 164. Tedder, *Prejudice,* 428–30. Churchill also noted that Eisenhower, previously so confident in urging a cross-Channel attack, which would have been met by many more than two divisions, had evidently changed his tune and lamented "these pusillanimous and defeatist doctrines." Tedder, *Prejudice,* 429.

143. Blumenson, *Patton,* 240, 242, 244, 248.

144. Blumenson, *Patton,* 245.

145. D'Este, *Bitter,* 75. Perhaps indicative of Gairdner's insignificance was that, in a top-secret message from Eisenhower to Alexander of 3/23/1943, his name was twice misspelled as "Gardner." Chandler, *Papers II,* 1055.

146. Tedder, *Prejudice,* 431.

147. D'Este, *Bitter,* 545; Hamilton, *Master,* 348; Roskill, *Offensive,* 150; Garland, *Sicily,* 421.

148. "Overview," 2.

149. Pratt, "Overview," 3.

150. Pratt, "Overview," 3, 5.

151. "Economics," 44–5.

152. For instance by Corrigan (*Second,* 302).

153. D'Este, *Eisenhower,* 604. Churchill, on the last day of 1943 in the vein of these criticisms of Meade and Montgomery, "chided" Eisenhower on his reservations about Operation Shingle: "he hoped that the guarding of such reputation for success as I had established had not made me a cautious soldier." D'Este, *Eisenhower,* 473.

154. *Wise,* 94.

155. "Economics," 42–3.

156. Macmillan, *Blast,* 308–9. Eisenhower cabled Marshall on 8/4/1943 his exasperation with Churchill: "When things are going rather badly," the theater commander could concentrate on the demands of battle; "when things get going rather well... some of the individuals who are responsible for

running the war begin to take an enormous interest in its detailed direction. I have in mind just now the recent activity of the Prime Minister in firing telegrams here and to the President about every little detail." Chandler, *Papers II,* 1316–7.

157. "Economics," 48–50.

158. United States Joint Chiefs of Staff, *Joint,* A-2.

159. Hope, *Unity,* 1.

160. Summers, *Strategy,* 192–204; Cohen, *Supreme,* 183; Hope, *Unity,* 14.

161. The US fought alongside British and French forces, but chose to call itself an "Associate," rather than an "Ally," of them.

162. U.S. Department of State, *Foreign,* 92–3.

163. Roberts, *Masters,* 79.

164. Roberts, *Masters,* 81.

165. Churchill, *Grand,* 597.

166. Ferrell, *Diaries,* 59.

167. Boog, *Global,* 795.

168. Bryant, *Turn,* 454–5.

169. Bryant, *Turn,* 335, 505–6; *Triumph,* 195. For Brooke, however, MacArthur—whom he thought "the greatest general of the last war"—was an exception. Bryant, *Turn,* 560.

170. Butcher, *Three Years,* 258.

171. Hobbs, *Dear,* 99–100.

172. Reynolds, *Command,* 332.

173. *Prejudice,* 443.

174. *Prejudice,* 444.

175. Bryant, *Turn,* 454.

176. Hope (*Unity,* 15 note 2) found that "French, Russian, and British lists of the principles of war [in the inter-war period] never mention 'unity of command.' The closest foreign principles are the principle of 'unity of effort' in French doctrinal circles, and the principle of 'cooperation' in British doctrine."

177. Kimball, *Churchill, I,* 254.

178. D'Este, *Bitter,* 71.

179. D'Este, *Bitter,* 124.

180. Kesselring, *Memoirs,* 165. General Siegfried Westphal (*West,* 144) confirmed the "wrath" of Wehrmacht headquarters at Kesselring's order.

181. D'Este, *Fatal,* 481n.

182. The simplified game-theoretic perspective might have been depicted in the form of a zero-sum game table like the following:

		Germans	
		Run: Briskly Withdraw their Troops from Sicily	Reinforce: Send More Troops to Sicily to Slow the Allied Conquest
Allies	Deliberately Proceed Messina	29	26
	Aggressively Act to Prevent German Escape	60	87

Hypothetical, Zero-Sum-Game-Table Depiction of the Strategic Choices in July and August 1943, with the Numbers Representing Roughly-Conjectured Expected Outcome Values, which the Allies Sought to Maximize and the Germans to Minimize.

The outcome values have not been precisely calculated but are roughly conjectured in line with the general understanding of the situation. The outcome values may be thought of as those of the Allies on a 0-to-100 scale on which

0 = the value of a hypothetical scenario in which the Allies take two full months to clear Sicily of all enemy and suffer 60,000 casualties while inflicting 16,000 German; and

100 = the value of a hypothetical scenario in which the Allies inflict 55,000 German casualties, while suffering 24,000, and have all of Sicily in one month.

The actual outcome of 22,400 Allied casualties, 11,000 German, and 38 days to take the island is taken to be the expected result of the Allied deliberateness and the German reinforcement that actually occurred and to have a value of 26, as seen in the upper right of the game table. The game table presumes that the Germans had the same expected outcome values for the four possible combinations of decisions, but wished to minimize them.

183. Jackson, *Alexander*, 222–3.
184. Liddell Hart, *Other*, 364.
185. Ricks, *Generals*, 71.
186. Blumenson, *Patton*, 566.
187. Weigley, *Eisenhower's*, 729. Blumenson ("America's," 3) similarly judged US leaders in the war

"generally workmanlike rather than bold, prudent rather than daring." They "stay[ed] within the odds, the safe way of operating, and refrained from opting for the imaginative and the unexpected. Very few of their operations were brilliant."

188. Ricks, *Generals*, 118.
189. *Generals*, 351.
190. *Generals*, 118, 449.
191. Allison, *Essence*, 145.
192. Allison, *Essence*, 177.
193. Fisher, *Cassino*, 222–3. Fisher's exact numbers were 43,560 Allied casualties to 38,024 German (for slightly different dates across the various armies). He misadded his own numbers—neglecting in his totting up 3,355 casualties of British soldiers serving in Mark Clark's Fifth Army—and stated an Allied total of 40,205 casualties.
194. Atkinson, *Day*, 55. Atkinson noted that this would prevent both reinforcement and retreat. He judged that, still engaged in Tunisia during the early planning for Husky, the commanders were so focused on getting seven divisions ashore and capturing airfields and ports that their attention did not extend to Messina.
195. E.g., by Kleindorfer, *Decision*, 305.
196. See, for instance, Edwards, "Experiments;" Keeney, *Decisions*; and Edwards, "Multiattribute."
197. Kleindorfer, *Decision*, 343.

Chapter 4

1. Chandler, *Papers III*, 1485. This optimism was based largely on intercepted Wehrmacht messages, before Kesselring changed Hitler's mind, decoded by Ultra, indicating German intention to retreat beyond Rome. D'Este, *Eisenhower*, 457–8.
2. Atkinson, *Day*, 248.
3. Chandler, *Papers III*, 1497. By October 21, Alexander, as his forces came up against the enemy positions, was reporting similarly that the campaign for Rome would be "long and costly... a 'slugging match.'" Atkinson, *Day*, 255.
4. Atkinson, *Day*, 254.
5. M. Clark, *Risk*, 290.
6. Atkinson, *Day*, 323.
7. Blumenson, *Salerno*, 293.
8. Blumenson, *Salerno*, 294.
9. Churchill, *Closing*, 379.

Brooke, on January 20, 1944, felt "a special responsibility for [Shingle] as I resuscitated it after my visit to Italy." Bryant, *Triumph*, 99.
10. *Blast*, 368.
11. Matloff, *Supreme: 1943–1944*, 415; Blumenson, *Salerno*, 298. Per Reynolds (*Command*, 394), "Anzio would not have happened without [Churchill]." Per Hastings (*Winston's*, 356), it was "the last important operation which sprang from the personal inspiration of the prime minister." George Marshall in 1949 "recalled that he had had nothing to do with the Anzio decision." After the decision, he had agreed to let certain units "remain in the Mediterranean for Anzio." Matloff, *Supreme: 1943–1944*, 415n, 416.
12. Molony, *1st April*, 2. Lord Moran, in Marrakesh with Churchill in January 1944, wrote in his diary (*Churchill*, 169–70): "the P.M. has a bright idea. He is organizing an operation all on his own... a landing behind the lines at Anzio."
13. *Thinking*, 345. See also Russo, *Traps*, 24 and Arkes, "Sunk Cost," 97–8, 105, 107–8.
14. Kahneman, *Thinking*, 363–74. Barbara J. McNeil et al. ("On the Elicitation of Preferences for Alternative Therapies." *N Engl J Med* 306: 1259–62. 1982) found the same tendencies among ambulatory patients, graduate students, and physicians.
15. Churchill, *Closing*, 386–7. Lord Beaverbrook, an intimate of Churchill, asserted that a main motive of the Prime Minister, unmentioned in this missive to Roosevelt, was that success at Anzio might convince the US to delay Overlord "until it would be little more than a mopping-up operation." Roberts, *Masters*, 460.
16. Churchill, *Closing*, 384.
17. Reynolds, *Command*, 389.
18. *Closing*, 378.
19. *Closing*, 378–9.
20. Butcher, *Three Years*, 494.
21. *Crusade*, 212.
22. *Crusade*, 212–3.
23. *Crusade*, 213.
24. "Lucas," 203–4.
25. On 10/25/1943, 10/29/1943, 10/31/1943, and 11/4/1943. Chandler, *Papers III*, 1529, 1539, 1545, 1549.
26. Atkinson, *Day*, 318.

27. Thompson, "Lucas," 203–4.

28. For instance, by Blumenson, *Salerno*, 297 ("all agreed on the desirability") and Lloyd Clark, *Anzio*, 65 ("to a man giving Shingle their unqualified support"). Strong (*Intelligence*, 170), in contrast, reported that Eisenhower had thought Shingle "somewhat risky," but was persuaded by Churchill "somewhat against his better judgement to make two divisions available."

29. Hamilton, *Master*, 515.

30. Lucas, *Algiers*, 295n. Per the AOH (Blumenson, *Salerno*, 312), the Germans in mid-January had 150,000 men in their Tenth Army; a reserve force of 24,000 in and near Rome; 70,000 in northern Italy; and 25,000 "in hospitals or on other assignments."

31. L. Clark, *Anzio*, 73—who put the German total at 23.

32. Between January 17 and 19, while these preliminary attacks were occurring, practice landings—as had been the case for Operation Rutter in June 1942—were being bungled. These rehearsals for Shingle incurred the loss of 40 landing craft and ten artillery pieces. Molony, *Sicily*, 650.

33. M. Clark, *Risk*, 223. Graham (*Tug*, 151) considered a possible decision point unmentioned by other authors: the option that Alexander and Clark had, after the repulse on the Rapido, of canceling Shingle. They deemed such a move, however, "after all the fuss and the concessions made by the Combined Chiefs of Staff... impossible: it would have cost both their heads." Instead, they "blindly" left in place the orders previously given to Lucas.

34. Molony, *Sicily*, 686.

35. Atkinson, *Day*, 355.

36. *Closing*, 436.

37. *Risk*, 244.

38. Atkinson, *Day*, 353. Julian Thompson ("Lucas," 189) presumed that George Marshall "must have intervened" on behalf of Lucas.

39. Lucas, *Algiers*, 3.

40. Cable to Marshall of 12/17/1943. Chandler, *Papers III*, 1604–5. Eisenhower reiterated this plan for command succession on 12/29/1943 and 1/18/1944. Chandler, *Papers III*, 1631, 1664.

41. Atkinson, *Day*, 429.

42. *Risk*, 244.

43. Atkinson, *Day*, 353–4.

44. Atkinson, *Day*, 428.

45. Lucas, *Algiers*, 310.

46. Per his son, Colonel John P. Lucas, Jr., the death was unrelated to the trying time in Italy: General Lucas had in China after the war contracted amoebic dysentery, the treatment for which had resulted in a blood clot that had caused his collapse on a dance floor, followed soon by his death. D'Este, *Fatal*, 421.

47. Atkinson, *Day*, 355.

48. Blumenson, *Salerno*, 356.

49. Lucas, *Algiers*, 333; Atkinson, *Day*, 355. Clark also had General Donald Brann personally convey this message to Lucas. Blumenson, *Anzio*, 63; Blumenson, *Salerno*, 356.

50. Lewin (*Ultra*, 285) argued that this should not have been a surprise, given that Allied intelligence had predicted, "with what proved to be remarkable accuracy," both minimal German resistance on 1/22/1944 and Kesselring's subsequent reinforcements. Both Alexander (*Memoirs*, 126) and Truscott (*Command*, 309), however, attested to surprise in the Allied command, summarized by the American Official History, (Blumenson, *Salerno*, 358) that "everyone had expected the landing to be bitterly opposed." The British Official History (Molony, *Sicily*, 658) concurred.

51. Kesselring, *Memoirs*, 192. Kesselring's actions and explanations of them may exemplify what Kahneman (*Thinking*, 202–3) has described as "hindsight bias"—discussed in the Epilogue.

52. Kesselring, *Memoirs*, 193.

53. Per the AOH (Blumenson, *Salerno*, 319), Canaris had said this "several days earlier"; per Brown (*Bodyguard*, 421) and Schumann (*Zerschlagung*, 130), on January 21, the eve of the landing.

54. Graham, *Tug*, 149–50.

55. D'Este, *Fatal*, 133.

56. Churchill, *Closing*, 426.

57. Atkinson, *Day*, 363. Mark Clark's (*Risk*, 231) figures were 50,000 men and 5,200 vehicles.

58. Atkinson, *Day*, 363.

59. Molony, *Sicily*, 686.

60. Lucas, *Algiers*, Chart No. 1, based on Fifth Army and VI Corps intelligence reports, after page 329. These figures excluded support personnel. Per Molony (*Sicily*, 669), VI

Corps had, by 1/29/1944, landed 69,000 men, 508 guns, 237 tanks, and 27,250 tons of supplies. D'Este (*Fatal*, 146) had 71,500 Germans on that date facing 41,000 Allies and, three days later (*Fatal*, 185), 95,000 Germans versus 76,000 Allies.

61. Per the AOH (Blumenson, *Salerno*, 390), the British on January 31 took Campoleone. Map XXXVI: D+9 of Lucas (*Algiers*, after page 353) placed the Allied lines beyond the village. The BOH (Molony, *Sicily*, 676–7), however, stated that the attack had only "gained the railway which ran [through Campoleone] on an embankment. Losses were heavy and several attempts to cross the embankment, which greatly impeded the tanks, failed... Campoleone remained in German hands." Map 37 of the BOH showed the repulse of an attack beyond the embankment east of Campoleone and put British lines at the close of their advances of January 29 through 31 south of the village and the railway. The accounts of Atkinson (*Day*, 396) and Lloyd Clark (*Anzio*, 152) accorded with that of the BOH: the enemy kept the village.

62. Atkinson, *Day*, 412, 415. Per the AOH (Blumenson, *Salerno*, 392), 100,000 Allies versus fewer than 90,000 Germans; per Lloyd Clark (*Anzio*, 158), just under 100,000 Germans against 76,400 Allies.

63. Molony, *Sicily*, 724, 752.

64. Atkinson, *Day*, 421.

65. Blumenson, *Salerno*, 420.

66. Blumenson, *Salerno*, 424.

67. Gavin, *Berlin*, 77.

68. Lucas, *Algiers*, 295.

69. Blumenson, *Salerno*, 356.

70. Atkinson, *Day*, 418.

71. *Algiers*, 353.

72. Pogue, *Victory*, 332–3. Marshall had, on February 18, radioed his dissatisfaction with Lucas to General Jacob Devers, the highest-ranking US officer in the Mediterranean, urging him to "[l]et nothing stand in the way of procuring the leadership of the quality necessary." The US Army Chief of Staff, customarily ruthless in dismissing the underperforming, apparently had conflicting thoughts about Lucas, of whom he had previously held a high opinion. On March 1, 1944, he would suggest to Eisenhower the possibility of having Lucas assist in Overlord.

D'Este, *Fatal,* 420–1, 538 n23. Rawson, *Eyes,* 44–5. Eisenhower did not do so.

73. Alexander, *Memoirs,* 126. Martin Blumenson (*Anzio,* 116) speculated that, had the February attacks at Cassino succeeded, the generalship of Lucas might not have been criticized.

74. Marshall on 3/1/1944 cabled Eisenhower his understanding derived from Jacob Devers that Lucas had been relieved because "he looked old and completely tired out. All were agreed that he had done everything that could have been done with the means available." Rawson, *Eyes,* 44.

75. Moloney, *Sicily,* 762.

76. *Closing,* 426.

77. Blumenson, *Salerno,* 355.

78. *Closing,* 426; Westphal, *West,* 158.

79. *Memoirs,* 194.

80. Atkinson, *Day,* 370.

81. Bryant, *Triumph,* 107n. Alexander in his memoirs made points both ways: first (125) wondering "what our position would have been if fresh German divisions had found us stretched from Anzio to the Alban Hills," inasmuch as Lucas had held on only "with difficulty" in the significantly more defensible actual positions; then, on the next page, asserting that the "clear" explanation of "what went wrong" was that Lucas had "missed his opportunity by being too slow and cautious. He failed to realize the great advantage that surprise had given him."

82. Truscott, *Command,* 50.

83. Atkinson, *Day,* 371.

84. *Risk,* 232.

85. *Command,* 311.

86. *Command,* 549.

87. Molony, *Sicily,* 686; D'Este, *Fatal,* 7, 404–5; Nicolson, *Alex,* 232–3; Atkinson, *Day,* 371–2.

88. Blumenson, *Salerno,* 427.

89. *Second,* 271.

90. Roberts, *Storm,* 396. The others in essential agreement: Morison ("But for General Lucas's much criticized caution," VI Corps would likely have suffered "destruction in detail." *Sicily,* 381); D'Este ("The notion that Lucas could have [cut Highway 6] with the forces at his disposal and maintained a link to Anzio is ludicrous in the extreme." *Fatal,* 403); and Hastings ("The

likeliest outcome of a dash for Rome from Anzio would have been the destruction of Lucas's corps." *Winston's,* 357). One year earlier (*Masters,* 459), Roberts had called the decision of Lucas "a costly mistake." Another three historians (Liddell Hart, *Second,* 529; Murray, *Won,* 382; Corrigan *Second,* 411) took an intermediate, straddling, position: that Lucas might have missed a decisive opportunity but also might have saved his army from ruin.

91. See, for instance, Raiffa, *Decision,* 21–7, for a monetary situation; Weinstein, *Clinical,* 53–61, in a medical setting.

92. M. Clark, *Risk,* 237; Molony, *Sicily,* 687; D'Este, *Fatal,* 135, 403; L. Clark, *Anzio,* 324; Roberts, *Storm,* 396. D'Este went further than the others in holding that Lucas, in not having sought to take Cisterna and Albano—six miles north of Campoleone—within 48 hours after landing had made "a serious mistake."

93. Blumenson (*Anzio,* 134), citing Mark Clark, was on the optimistic side of this issue, thinking that securely holding the two villages might have dissuaded German attack: "In this case—purely speculation, of course—the Germans would have had to fall back from Cassino and probably beyond Rome."

94. Lucas, *Algiers,* 335.

95. Atkinson, *Day,* 368.

96. M. Clark, *Risk,* 231.

97. M. Clark, *Risk,* 233.

98. Bryant, *Triumph,* 102.

99. Bryant, *Triumph,* 102.

100. *Storm,* 394.

101. *Storm,* 395.

102. *Memoirs,* 126.

103. Bryant, *Triumph,* 107.

104. Colville, *Fringes,* 674.

105. *Algiers,* 307, 310.

106. *Algiers,* 344.

107. *Algiers,* 319.

108. *Algiers,* 325, 346.

109. Bidwell, in Barnett, *Generals,* 282; Atkinson, *Day,* 371.

110. D'Este, *Fatal,* 421.

111. *Command,* 549.

112. *Closing,* 426.

113. *Closing,* 437.

114. *Closing,* 432. Churchill had said a slightly different version of this to Brooke and Eisenhower on February 29, 1944. Bryant, *Triumph,* 116.

115. D'Este, *Warlord,* 665.

116. Fuller, *Second,* 271: "this dismal failure;" Blumenson, *Anzio: the Gamble that Failed,* title; Greenfield, *Strategy,* 41: "failed dismally;" L. Clark, *Anzio,* 322: "a special place in the pantheon of audacious military schemes that failed;" Roberts, *Storm,* 394: "a drawn-out, costly failure;" Hastings, *Winston's,* 356: "one of the biggest Allied failures of the war."

117. *Closing,* 437.

118. *Closing,* 534.

119. *Closing,* 539–40.

120. *Command,* 550–1.

121. D'Este, *Fatal,* 266.

122. *Crusade,* 213.

123. Blumenson, *Salerno,* 392.

124. *Crusade,* 264.

125. M. Clark, *Risk,* 239. Atkinson, *Day,* 421; Roberts, *Storm,* 394.

126. 124.

127. D'Este, *Fatal,* 266.

128. Lucas, *Algiers,* 305.

129. *Command,* 550–1.

130. Blumenson, *Salerno,* 349.

131. Blumenson, *Salerno,* 347.

132. Blumenson, *Salerno,* 327. Clark subsequently ascribed responsibility for the Rapido attack to Alexander, but this seems not to have been the case. Blumenson, *Salerno,* 349. Blumenson (*Salerno,* 350) suggested alternatively sending the American forces that attacked over the Rapido instead to extend the British bridgehead over the Garigliano. This change would, however, he judged, have been "difficult if not altogether impossible," because of the challenges in mingling units of the two nations. D'Este (*Fatal,* 82) ascribed Clark's non-exploitation of the British bridgehead to his not wanting the British to "gain the credit for breaking the Gustav Line."

133. Fisher, *Cassino,* 545.

134. Blumenson, *Breakout,* 700.

135. Blumenson, *Salerno,* 427.

136. Churchill, *Closing,* 435.

137. Moran, *Churchill,* 145.

138. *Risk,* 208.

139. *Risk,* 237.

140. *Memoirs,* 125.

141. *Command,* 306–7.

142. *Memoirs,* 125.

143. M. Clark, *Risk,* 229. To Lucas's worries about rapid German response, Alexander had replied that Allied air would prevent it. (David Eisenhower, *Eisenhower,* 124.)

144. Truscott, *Command,* 306. Clark (*Risk,* 229) reported his Fifth Army G-2's view differently: reporting that it had predicted enemy resistance to the Anzio landing and that the Germans "would pull back only if they were defeated on one of the two fronts."

145. *Command,* 298.

146. Lucas, *Algiers,* 305.

147. *Risk,* 228.

148. Truscott, *Command,* 298.

149. Atkinson, *Day,* 324.

150. Atkinson, *Day,* 325.

151. Lucas, *Algiers,* 322.

152. L. Clark, *Anzio,* 173.

153. Atkinson, *Day,* 417.

154. D'Este, *Fatal,* 245.

155. Blumenson, *Salerno,* 419.

156. Graham, *Tug,* 156.

157. As paraphrased by Blumenson, *Anzio,* 134.

158. Butcher, *Three Years,* 506.

159. Lucas, *Algiers,* 334.

160. Lucas, *Algiers,* 359.

161. Lucas, *Algiers,* 366.

162. *Three Years,* 465.

163. Molony, *Sicily,* 661.

164. Molony, *Sicily,* 664–5.

165. Molony, *Sicily,* 672.

166. Reynolds, *Command,* 393.

167. Churchill (*Closing,* 385) called Clark's absence "an oversight which I regret." The BOH (Molony, *Sicily,* 772) judged the absence of Brooke and Clark from the decision conferences in Tunis and Marrakesh "perhaps unfortunate," in that they might have brought to the table the requisite tactical analysis. Questions have arisen—see the Epilogue—as to whether the absences of Clark and Lucas from these two conferences were indeed accidental.

168. Blumenson, *Salerno,* 425.

169. *Command,* 329.

170. *Risk,* 209.

171. *Crusade,* 202–3.

172. D'Este, *Warlord,* 658; Moran, *Struggle,* 188.

173. 191. The German edition of Kesselring's memoirs (*Soldat,* 265) made the point more strongly, asserting that the Allies had neglected many opportunities to put his forces in serious difficulties with such landings.

174. L. Clark, *Anzio,* 325.

175. Morison, *Sicily,* 336, 381; D'Este, *Fatal,* 400–1. Morison (381) concluded that "'a correct strategic move' Anzio certainly was not;"

D'Este, that "Anzio was doomed before the first LST sailed from Naples," for which Churchill had "culpability."

176. Molony, *Sicily,* 771, 772.

177. Per Clark's Deputy Chief of Staff, General Sir Charles Richardson (Atkinson, *Day,* 356), "complete nonsense from its inception;" per Shelford Bidwell (Barnett, *Generals,* 282) (who also, though, thought the operation "muddled in execution"— presumably by others than Lucas, whom he defended.), "the plan was basically unsound;" per Lloyd Clark (*Anzio,* 65), "a fundamentally flawed concept."

178. D'Este, *Fatal,* 401; Thompson, "Lucas," 203.

179. Blumenson, *Anzio,* 137. For this shunning of the gamble that he thought the central premise of Shingle, Blumenson also (*Anzio,* 189) assigned blame to Clark. D'Este (*Fatal,* 406) quoted assentingly Blumenson's take on the bluff, but also wrote that "the evidence suggests that it would have ended very badly."

180. *Games,* 189.

181. That bluffing in fact occurs in such games—sometimes successfully—may derive from imperfect understanding or psychological advantage. You might initiate an attack on my king that you know cannot succeed—in hopes that I do not understand the situation as well as you or that I so respect your skill as to be unsettled by your moves and therefore do not take my best line of play.

182. Schelling, *Strategy,* 34.

183. Schelling, *Strategy,* 23–36; McMillan, *Games,* 46–67.

184. Latimer gave as illustrations: Julius Caesar in 52 BCE crossing the Allier River against Vercingetorix by concealing two legions, sending off four others arrayed to look like his whole force of six legions, then having the first two legions emerge from hiding to build a bridge over the stream; the men of William the Conqueror at Hastings in 1066 feigning disordered flight in order to lure pursuers, who were then turned on and defeated in detail; John Churchill, the first Duke of Marlborough, in 1704 feinting toward Strasbourg before marching to the Danube, where he would with Prince Eugene of Savoy win the

Battle of Blenheim; Frederick II of Prussia in 1757 at Leuthen feinting toward the Austrian right, while moving most of his army, concealed by terrain, to attack the enemy left; Napoleon at Austerlitz in 1805 feigning weakness on his right to entice his Austro-Russian foes to attack it, whereupon French troops emerged from hiding to assault the thinned enemy center; and, in the spring of 1962, Confederate general John Magruder, with a fraction of the strength of Union general George McClellan, slowing the advance of the latter toward Richmond via various ruses to make his army seem more numerous.

185. Graham, *Tug,* 149.

186. Molony, *Sicily,* 587–8, 661; Thompson, "Lucas," 198.

187. D'Este, *Fatal,* 401.

188. Fisher, *Cassino,* 40.

189. Conversely, it could be argued that the Germans, invoking OSP, might have sensed the actual Allied disappointment with Shingle and should have inferred that it made further amphibious moves less likely.

190. Blumenson (*Anzio,* 19) and Baldwin (*Battles,* 229) deemed the question of who, in Italy, had been tying down whom to be unanswered. Liddell Hart (*Second,* 536) argued that the numbers—the Allies having 30 divisions to 22 German and twice as many men in their push toward and past Rome—indicated that the Allied strategy "had not proved a good strategic investment." Keegan (*Second,* 319) agreed. Roberts (*Masters,* 459) held the opposite: that the reinforcements Hitler sent to Anzio and the Gustav Line meant "denuding himself" of the forces needed to oppose Overlord—which "disproves Basil Liddell Hart's theory."

191. Molony, *Sicily,* 774.

192. Allison, *Essence,* 6.

193. Allison, *Essence,* 300.

194. D'Este, *Fatal,* 93.

195. Moran, *Churchill,* 170.

196. Butcher, *Three Years,* 465.

197. Bryant, *Turn,* 335.

198. Roberts, *Masters,* 16.

199. Roberts, *Masters,* 16–7.

200. Hastings, *Winston's,* 222.

201. Bryant, *Turn,* 450.

202. Roberts, *Masters,* 471.

203. U.S. Department of State, *Foreign,* 437.

204. Danchev, *Diaries,* 450.

205. Danchev, *Diaries,* 451; Bryant, *Turn,* 592.

206. Reynolds, *Command,* 331, 388.

207. Roberts, *Masters,* 101.

208. Roberts, *Masters,* 100–1.

209. *Risk,* 228.

210. *Risk,* 228–9.

211. Wilmot, *Europe,* 162.

212. *Risk,* 205–6.

213. *Risk,* 228.

Epilogue

1. Chandler, *Papers II,* 1247.

2. *Thinking,* 263–4.

3. Bryant, *Turn,* 459.

4. *Reports!,* 192.

5. Roberts, *Masters,* 337.

6. Danchev, *Diaries,* 360.

7. Danchev, *Diaries,* 364.

8. Bryant, *Turn,* 509.

9. Roberts, *Masters,* 364.

10. Roberts, *Masters,* 362.

11. Roberts, *Masters,* 366.

12. D'Este, *Fatal,* 97–8.

13. *Algiers,* 292.

14. Bryant, *Turn,* 514.

15. Matloff, *Strategic: 1941–1942,* 234–5.

16. Oral history interview of Field Marshal Lord Harding of Petherton, in December 1943 chief of staff to Alexander. D'Este, *Fatal,* 98–9. Carver (*Harding,* 123) related that this exchange occurred a week later in Marrakesh.

17. Pogue, *Victory,* 307.

18. Butcher, *Three Years,* 639.

19. Bryant, *Turn,* 239.

20. Brown, *Bodyguard,* 803.

21. Reynolds, *Command,* 408, 518.

22. Gwyer, *Strategy,* 661.

23. Roberts, *Storm,* 144. Ian Kershaw (*Fateful,* 56, 63) agreed.

24. Liddell Hart, *Talk,* 171; Roberts, *Storm,* 142; Hastings, *Inferno,* 138.

25. A poll in Great Britain in the early spring of 1942 found 50 percent "dissatisfied with the Government's conduct of the war" and 67 percent to "favor an offensive operation this year." Gallup, *Poll,* 328.

26. U.S. Department of State, *Foreign,* 130.

27. Matloff, *Strategic: 1941–1942,* 268.

28. Matloff, *Strategic: 1941–1942,* 215.

29. Matloff, *Strategic: 1941–1942,* 272.

30. Pogue, *Ordeal,* 330.

31. D'Este, *Eisenhower,* 322.

32. *Presidential,* 84.

33. Rosenman, *Working,* 167.

34. Goodwin, *Ordinary,* 23.

35. Rosenman, *Working,* 190.

36. Neustadt, *Presidential,* 313

37. Goodwin, *Ordinary,* 26.

38. Sherwood, *Roosevelt,* 298.

39. Polls conducted on 12/1–6/1940 and 12/18–23/1940. Gallup, *Poll,* 256.

40. Franklin D. Roosevelt, "On National Security. December 29, 1940. Radio Address of the President, Delivered from the White House." Web-accessible at http://docs.fdrlibrary.marist.edu/122940.html .

41. Franklin D. Roosevelt, "On Maintaining Freedom of the Seas. September 11, 1941. Radio Address of the President, Broadcast from the White House." Web-accessible at http://docs.fdrlibrary.marist.edu/091141.html .

42. A poll conducted on 9/19–24/1941 reported 56 percent approval, 34 percent disapproval, and ten percent without opinion. Gallup, *Poll,* 299.

43. Goodwin, *Ordinary,* 278.

44. Goodwin, *Ordinary,* 320.

45. Franklin D. Roosevelt, "On Progress of the War. February 23, 1942. Address of the President, Broadcast over a Nationwide and Worldwide Radio Hookup." Web-accessible at http://docs.fdrlibrary.marist.edu/022342.html. Franklin D. Roosevelt, "On Our National Economic Policy. April 28, 1942. Radio Address of the President on the Subject of Total War and Total Effort." Web-accessible at http://docs.fdrlibrary.marist.edu/042842.html.

46. Cantril, *Public,* 106, 756.

47. *Presidential,* 71–2.

48. Roberts (*Masters,* 431) described Roosevelt in late 1943 as "gradually becoming less enamoured of Churchill." The Prime Minister, per Brooke, was then evincing "new feelings of spitefulness" toward the US for the preponderance of its power over that of the UK. Winston "became inclined at times to put up strategic proposals which he knew were unsound purely to spite the Americans." Danchev, *Diaries,* 473. Per Hastings (*Winston's,* 312, 398, 400): "Churchill's standing in American eyes would decline steadily between the summer of 1943 and the end of the war;" the Prime Minister after Normandy's D-Day engaged in "further pointless wrangles with the Americans" and was sent by Roosevelt "a headmasterly rebuke... for appearing to concede to the Russians a lead role in Romanian affairs;" while WSC's badgering of FDR to nix Anvil was "woeful" and "extremely tactless."

49. McKenna, "One night," 251; Whitney, "Feedback," 753.

50. Harrison, "Impact," 236–40, 246–7; Venkatraman, "Sleep," 603, 608; Whitney, "Feedback," 745, 753. McKenna ("One night," 250) found that sleep-deprived persons are more risk-seeking when contemplating possible gains, but more risk-averse for potential losses.

51. Harrison, "Impact," 240, 246; Whitney, "Feedback," 753.

52. Bryant, *Turn,* 239.

53. *Blast,* 368–9.

54. Moran, *Churchill,* 17–20.

55. Moran, *Churchill,* 157.

56. Moran, *Churchill,* ix.

57. Churchill, *Hinge,* 178.

58. Moran, *Churchill,* 103.

59. Roberts, *Masters,* 373.

60. For instance, on July 25, 1942 (after reaching the decision on Torch); on August 20, 1942 (after a day of troop inspections and conferences in Egypt); and on January 16, 1943 (at Casablanca). Bryant, *Turn,* 347, 389, 448.

61. Bryant, *Triumph,* 20.

62. *Crusade,* 241.

63. Chandler, *Papers I,* 587.

64. Bryant, *Turn,* 242.

65. Mosley, *Marshall,* 202.

66. Bryant, *Turn,* 242.

67. *Three Years,* 17.

68. Butcher, *Three Years,* 29–30.

69. Butcher, *Three Years,* 247.

70. To be promoted to colonel in the regular army, the Supreme Commander, who had been made an acting four-star general in February, on August 10 had a physical. It resulted in his being ordered to bed—which he left temporarily the next day to host to dinner six visiting US senators. Added to his other responsibilities was that of hosting "civilian notables." In October 1942—with

the visits of Eleanor Roosevelt (he would meet her at Paddington Station) and Treasury Secretary Henry Morgenthau impending—he complained about this to Marshall. Chandler, *Papers I,* 607. The problem would persist: Butcher (*Three Years,* 431) would report that Ike's 10/17/1943 "was spent largely with visiting firemen [two cabinet secretaries and one special envoy]."

71. Morgan, *Past,* 179; Summersby, *Eisenhower,* 146-7.

72. *Algiers,* 273.

73. D'Este, *Eisenhower,* 473.

74. *Eisenhower,* 171.

75. Summersby, *Eisenhower,* 169-170.

76. Heishman, Stephen J., et al. Meta-analysis of the acute effects of nicotine and smoking on human performance. *Psychopharmacology (Berl).* 210(4): 453-69, 2010.

77. Moylan, Steven, et al. How cigarette smoking may increase the risk of anxiety symptoms and anxiety disorders: a critical review of biological pathways. *Brain Behav.* 3(3): 302-26. Mishra, Aseem, et al. Harmful effects of nicotine. *Indian J Med Paediatr Oncol.* 36(1): 24-31, 2015.

78. Blumenson, *Battle,* 220.

79. Blumenson, *Battle,* 267-8.

80. Blumenson, *Patton,* 511.

81. *War,* 354.

82. Hamilton, *Master,* 97.

83. D'Este, *Warlord,* 592.

84. Horne, *Monty,* 284.

85. Brooke observed on 12/14/1943: "Monty is tired out." Lamb, *Montgomery,* 56.

86. Montgomery, *Memoirs,* 64.

87. Chalfont, *Montgomery,* 119; Horne, *Monty,* 37.

88. Roberts, *Storm,* 311.

89. Butcher, *Three Years,* 376.

90. *Algiers,* 328.

91. Blumenson, *Anzio,* 134-5.

92. "Impact," 247.

93. Danchev, *Diaries,* 226.

94. Roberts, *Masters,* 419.

95. Moran, *Struggle,* 140.

96. Moran, *Struggle,* 223.

97. It follows that decision makers, in deciding, should take into account their own vitality. Similarly to Churchill's judging (Reynolds, *Command,* 393) that his own "advancing years" had contributed to his inability to monitor and to spur Shingle to success, Robert E.

Lee, late in 1863, had lamented (Freeman, *Lee,* 357) that a maneuver had failed: "I am too old to command this army... we should never have permitted those people to get away." Lee and Churchill ought to have considered the likely effects of their years on the execution of their decisions.

98. Montefiore, *Stalin,* 226.

99. Mikhail Botvinnik, Mikhail Tal, Tigran Petrosian, Boris Spassky, Robert Fischer, Anatoly Karpov, Garry Kasparov, Vladimir Kramnik, Viswanathan Anand, and Magnus Carlsen had an average age of 29.4—based on subtracting their birth years from the years in which they became champions.

100. Cohen, *Supreme,* 64.

101. Larrabee, *Commander,* 101.

102. D'Este, *Eisenhower,* 297.

103. *Crusade,* 11.

104. Pogue, *Ordeal,* 162-3.

105. Mawdsley, *Thunder,* 38.

106. *Grand,* 547.

107. Bryant, *Turn,* 220. Per British Official Naval History author C. S. Roskill, Churchill had proposed the action. The resistance of Pound and others, articulated in multiple meetings, was overridden. Moran, *Struggle,* 101n.

108. *Grand,* 551.

109. *Dawn,* 273-4; *Day,* 212-3; *Guns,* 310-1. In Eisenhower's 2/1/1945 ranking of 38 high officers, Hodges was eleventh: behind corps commanders Leonard Gerow (eighth) and Joseph Collins (ninth), but ahead of army group commander Jacob Devers (24th). Chandler, *Papers IV,* 2467-8. Gerow, a graduate of the Virginia Military Institute, had known Eisenhower since 1915 and was thought "Eisenhower's closest friend." Collins, graduating two years behind Eisenhower from West Point, had been a friend of his there. Devers had graduated from West Point in Patton's class of 1909 and had in 1943 displeased Eisenhower—who was subsequently said to have had "ill feelings" toward him. D'Este, *Eisenhower,* 483, 486.

110. D'Este, *Eisenhower,* 151-2.

111. D'Este, *Eisenhower,* 252.

112. Baumeister, *Willpower,* 91-2, 94, 103-4.

113. Baumeister, *Willpower,* 96-9. Shai Danziger, et al., "Extraneous factors in judicial decisions," *Pro-*

ceedings of the National Academy of Sciences of the USA 108(17): 6889-6892, 2011.

114. *Crusade,* 178. Marshall thought "the pursuit of Rommel across the Desert... slow." Roberts, *Masters,* 541. Authors who have criticized the post-El-Alamein deliberateness of Montgomery include Liddell Hart, *Second,* 305, 413, 421; Horne, *Monty,* 55; Roberts, *Storm,* 301; Hastings, *Inferno,* 363; and Beever, *Second,* 379.

115. Some rock climbers feel that they have limited willingness to make risky moves, which can be exhausted after leading a few dangerous pitches—even though their physical strength might remain high.

116. Vohs, "Making Choices;" *Willpower,* 102-4.

117. Lewis, "Obama's."

118. Baumeister, *Willpower,* 88-90, 107.

119. Longford, *Wellington,* 224, 247.

120. In Algiers in 1943, the two would "listen to some records, have a couple of drinks, smoke a few cigarettes and steal a few kisses—always conscious that someone might walk in at any moment." Flying to the Cairo Conference in November 1943 in a C-54 cargo aircraft among others who had fallen asleep, they were "two adults necking in a darkened plane... dreamily content." Months after the war, they were "kissing, holding hands and being quite indiscreet." Morgan, *Past,* 157, 176, 268.

121. *Past,* 153.

122. *Past,* 274.

123. Summersby, *Eisenhower,* 172.

124. Morgan, *Past,* 244-5.

125. Goodwin, *Ordinary,* 480.

126. D'Este, *Patton,* 359.

127. D'Este, *Patton,* 743-5, 806.

128. Atkinson, *Guns,* 415-6.

129. Janis, *Groupthink,* 9. William Whyte, Jr., in 1952 had coined the term.

130. Roberts, *Masters,* 167, 260.

131. Janis, *Groupthink,* 16.

132. Janis, *Groupthink,* 13.

133. *Groupthink,* 14.

134. Sunstein, *Wiser,* 52, 78.

135. Janis, *Groupthink,* 37.

136. Janis, *Groupthink,* 32, 39.

137. Janis, *Groupthink,* 40-1.

138. Janis, *Groupthink,* 32.

139. Janis, *Groupthink,* 15.

140. Janis, *Groupthink,* 42.

141. Sunstein, *Wiser,* 57–75. The pros and cons for managers of information cascades—relying on the prior judgments of others—are discussed by Oberholzer-Gee in "Learners."

142. Janis, *Groupthink,* 42–3.

143. Sunstein, *Wiser,* 36.

144. Sunstein, *Wiser,* 22. Kahneman (*Thinking,* 82) defined the term as, "the tendency to like (or dislike) everything about a person—including things you have not observed."

145. Janis, *Groupthink,* 35.

146. Sunstein, *Wiser,* 23.

147. Sunstein, *Wiser,* 134.

148. *Wiser,* 68.

149. *Wiser,* 35.

150. *Wiser,* 41.

151. Hastings, *Winston's,* 199. Roberts (*Masters,* 273) expressed surprise at the lack of influence, despite their immense contributions, the Canadians had on war decisions.

152. Moran, *Churchill,* 20–1; Hastings, *Winston's,* 313. Churchill may in part have been reacting to King's disapproval of his own behavior: his intake of alcohol before noon and his flouting of rationing regulations in insisting on having both fish and meat in wartime dinners. Moran, *Churchill,* 20; Hastings, *Winston's,* 173.

153. Butcher, *Three Years,* 368. Brooke wrote that Alex had been "apparently" acting on "Monty's wishes." Brooke himself "felt inclined to tell [McNaughton] that he and his government had already made more fuss than the whole of the rest of the Commonwealth concerning the employment of Dominion forces!" He also judged it "typical of Alex not to have the strength of character to sit on Monty and stop him being foolish." Danchev, *Diaries,* 431–2.

154. Sunstein, *Wiser,* 41.

155. *Wiser,* 9–10, 109.

156. *Wiser,* 10.

157. Thompson, *Benefit-Cost,* 1–2. The term is synonymous with *benefit-cost analysis.*

158. Sunstein, *Wiser,* 140–2.

159. Sunstein, *Wiser,* 120.

160. Zeckhauser, *Wise,* 44–5.

161. Russo, *Traps,* 152. In deliberations of the US Supreme Court, in contrast, the Chief Justice first presents his views on each case, followed by the other justices in order of seniority—with no one speaking a second time until all have spoken once. Zeckhauser, *Wise,* 66.

162. Janis, *Groupthink,* 268; Sunstein, *Wiser,* 116.

163. Kleindorfer, *Decision,* 218. Russo (*Traps,* 159) gave similar advice.

164. Sunstein, *Wiser,* 117–9.

165. Kahneman, *Thinking,* 264. Kahneman credited origination of the concept to Gary Klein. Russo (*Traps,* 112) similarly urged pretending that contemplated projects become fiascos and listing reasons why—which he termed "prospective hindsight."

166. D'Este, *Warlord,* 653.

167. Sunstein, *Wiser,* 5, 115–6.

168. Schlesinger, *Thousand,* 296.

169. *Wiser,* 157.

170. *Thinking,* 261.

171. *Expert,* 239.

172. Tetlock, *Expert,* 51.

173. Tetlock, *Expert,* 129–37.

174. Kahneman, *Thinking,* 202–3.

175. Kahneman, *Thinking,* 211.

176. Kahneman, *Thinking,* 204.

177. Kahneman, *Thinking,* 218.

178. *Thinking,* 263.

179. Tetlock, *Expert,* 62–3.

180. Russo, *Traps,* 78.

181. *Wiser,* 158.

182. *Wiser,* 163–4.

183. This point being implicitly made in Sunstein's approval of Roosevelt's methods, devil's advocacy, and red-teaming. Kleindorfer (*Decision,* 218) recommended engaging extramural experts known to espouse conflicting positions.

184. *Wiser,* 161–3.

185. Hora, "Eliciting," 148.

186. Janis, *Groupthink,* 31.

187. Cohen, *Supreme,* 110.

188. Wilmot, *Europe,* 243; Ambrose, *Supreme,* 406–7.

189. *Crusade,* 246. Eisenhower also had Leigh-Mallory put his reservations in writing so that, should they be disregarded and the disaster he foresaw ensue, he would not be blamed.

190. *Crusade,* 247.

191. Butcher, *Three Years,* 566–7, 570; Atkinson, *Guns,* 50.

192. M. Clark, *Risk,* 277.

193. D'Este, *Fatal,* 347.

194. Danchev, *Diaries,* 283.

195. Eisenhower, in a memorandum of 7/17/1942, gave personal estimates "of a fairly successful landing of the leading division" at "about 1 in 2; of finally establishing a force of 6 divisions in the area... about 1 in 5." In the memorandum dated five days later laying out the American case for Sledgehammer of which Eisenhower was the main author, certain, assertive language ("Successful offensive action this fall will provide valuable training and experience...") was mixed with hedged admission of possible disaster ("Cherbourg is proposed as the first objective because the prospect of initial tactical success appears greatest in that area, and the prospect of sustaining ourselves... appears favorable."). Chandler, *Papers I,* 390, 403.

196. Matloff, *Strategic: 1941–1942,* 288–9.

197. *Three Years,* 58.

198. Bradley, *General's,* 164.

199. Roberts, *Masters,* 22.

200. Bryant, *Triumph,* 144.

201. Matheson ("From Decision Analysis," 446) reported in applications of DS cases of "manipulating the weights to get your favorite projects funded, rather than providing real insight into which course of action should be taken"—a pitfall also noted by Kleindorfer (*Decision,* 227).

202. As noted by decision scientist Rex Brown (*Rational,* 11).

203. Brown (*Rational,* 140) gave the examples in environmental-protection analyses of frequent undervaluations of intangible aspects, while focusing on "more readily measured cost outcomes, thus tipping the scales against regulation."

204. Chandler, *Napoleon,* 1076. The Emperor said this, at the height of the battle, to one of his marshals, Nicolas Soult. His words may be more significant as an indication of the terms in which he thought than as his candid judgment of the situation. To serve his ends, he had had untruths communicated to his soldiers and published in his journals. The numbers he told Soult may have been distorted to hearten the marshal, or other listeners, or himself.

205. Truscott, *Command,* 306.

206. E.g., Kahneman, *Thinking,* 256.

207. Chandler, *Papers II,* 1232.

208. Churchill, *Hinge,* 514.

209. Churchill, *Triumph,* 171.

210. Butcher, *Three Years,* 722.

211. Lucas, *Algiers,* 321–2. D'Este, *Fatal,* 109.

212. Bradley, *Soldier's,* 374.

213. Hansen, diary entry of 8/10/1944. A bet had been made "for armistice day at 10 to 1 rate and I offered to purchase his bet for at 5 lbs on a 2 lb bet but he declined."

214. Van Creveld, *Command,* 144–5.

215. Citino, *Path,* 184.

216. Citino, *Path,* 99–100.

217. Citino, *Path,* 61.

218. Van Creveld, *Command,* 144.

219. Strong, *Intelligence,* 114.

220. *Soldier's,* 18.

221. Liddell Hart, *Other,* 369–70.

222. Atkinson, *Guns,* 471.

223. *Marlborough: His Life and Times: Volume V: 1705–1708,* NY: Charles Scribner's Sons, 1936, 1937, 246.

224. Danchev, *Diaries,* 680.

225. Cohen, *Supreme,* 68.

226. Roberts, *Masters,* 67.

227. These viewpoints have been shared by diplomats. Otto von Bismarck, as an ambassador, freelanced at will; as Reichskanzler, he forbade such independent actions.

228. Cohen, *Supreme,* 75–6.

229. Cohen, *Supreme,* 72.

230. Cohen, *Supreme,* 111–2.

231. Ambrose, *Supreme,* 83.

232. See, for instance, Raiffa, *Decision,* 27–32, 157–81—numerical demonstrations of how information values should be calculated; Weinstein, *Clinical,* 131–67—determinations of information values in medical settings; Thompson, Mark S. Decision Analytic Determination of Study Size: The Case of Electronic Fetal Monitoring. *Medical Decision Making 1(2):* 165–179, 1981—an application showing how DS may determine the optimal numbers of subjects in medical studies; and Thompson, *Decision,* 41–70—a discussion of information values in the context of social program evaluation.

233. Kleindorfer *(Decision,* 113) defined it as "the inclination to search for evidence that confirms rather than refutes our favorite hypotheses." Decision scientists who have documented its widespread prevalence include Russo, *Traps,* 75–6; Kahneman, *Thinking,* 81, 324, 333; and Sunstein, *Wiser,* 139.

234. Meyer, "Bumbling," 48. An influential early documentation of this bias was given by Ward Edwards ("Theory").

235. Bazerman, *Surprises,* 80.

236. Among the best-known and most-widely-used of such aides are decision trees and game tables.

237. Keeney, *Value-Focused,* throughout; Kleindorfer, *Decision,* 52–62.

238. Siebert, "Creating." The study subjects, university students in business, when faced with common career decisions, did not consider many significant alternatives. When provided with master lists of objectives, the subjects came up with significantly more alternatives that they judged to be of high quality.

239. Matheson, "From Decision Analysis," 419–20.

240. Matheson, "From Decision Analysis," 421; Spetzler, "Building," 451, 457.

241. Spetzler, "Building," 461–7.

242. E.g., Spetzler, "Building," 460.

243. Luce, "Emotional," 20.

244. This accords with the position of Brown (*Rational,* 147), who (132) advocated making decision analyses "as useful as possible while costing the least analytic effort."

245. Matheson, "From Decision Analysis," 419.

246. Matheson, "From Decision Analysis," 419–21.

247. Brown, *Rational,* 134.

248. Bazerman, *Surprises,* 102.

249. Spetzler, "Building," 457.

Bibliography

Adams, John A. *General Jacob Devers: World War II's Forgotten Four Star*. Bloomington, IN: Indiana University Press, 2015.

Alexander, Harold. *The Alexander Memoirs 1940–1945*. London: Cassell, 1962; Barnsley, S. Yorkshire: Frontline, 2010.

Allison, Graham, and Philip Zelikow. *Essence of Decision: Explaining the Cuban Missile Crisis*. NY: Addison-Wesley, 1999.

Ambrose, Stephen E. *Eisenhower: Soldier and President*. NY: Simon & Schuster, 1990.

Ambrose, Stephen E. *Eisenhower. Volume One: Soldier General of the Army President*. NY: Simon & Schuster, 1983.

Ambrose, Stephen E. *The Supreme Commander: The War Years of General Dwight D. Eisenhower*. NY: Anchor Books, 1969, 1970.

Arkes, Hal R., and Catherine Blumer. "The Psychology of Sunk Cost," pp. 97–113 in Connolly, et al., *Judgment*.

Arrow, Kenneth J. "The Economics of Agency," pp. 37–51 in Pratt and Zeckhauser, *Structure*.

Atkinson, Rick. *An Army at Dawn: The War in North Africa, 1942–1942*. NY: Henry Holt, 2002.

Atkinson, Rick. *The Day of Battle: The War in Sicily and Italy, 1943–1944*. NY: Henry Holt, 2007.

Atkinson, Rick. *The Guns at Last Light: The War in Western Europe, 1944–1945*. NY: Henry Holt, 2013.

Axelrod, Robert. *The Evolution of Cooperation*. USA: Basic Books, 1984.

Baldwin, Hanson. *Battles Lost and Won: Great Campaigns of World War II*. NY: Harper & Row, 1966.

Barnett, Corelli, ed. *Hitler's Generals*. NY: Grove Weidenfeld, 1989.

Baumeister, Roy F., and John Tierney. *Willpower: Discovering the Greatest Human Strength*. NY: Penguin, 2011.

Bazerman, Max H., and Michael D. Watkins. *Predictable Surprises: The Disasters You Should Have Seen Coming, and How to Prevent Them*. Boston: Harvard Business School Press, 2004.

Beevor, Antony, *The Second World War*. NY: Little, Brown, 2012.

Binder, L. James. *Lemnitzer: A Soldier for His Time*. Washington: Brassey's, 1997.

Blumenson, Martin. "America's World War II Leaders in Europe: Some Thoughts." *Parameters 19(4)*: 2–13, 1989.

Blumenson, Martin. *Anzio: The Gamble that Failed*. London: Weidenfeld and Nicolson, 1963.

Blumenson, Martin. *The Battle of the Generals: The Untold Story of the Falaise Pocket—The Campaign that Should Have Won World War II*. NY: Morrow, 1993. Paginations differ across editions.

Blumenson, Martin. *Breakout and Pursuit: The United States Army in World War II: The European Theater of Operations*. Washington, D.C.: Center of Military History, United States Army: 1961; Atlanta, GA: Whitman Publishing, 2012.

Blumenson, Martin. *The Patton Papers: 1940–1945*. Boston: Houghton Mifflin, 1974.

Blumenson, Martin. *Salerno to Cassino: The United States Army in World War II: The Mediterranean Theater of Operations*. Washington, D.C.: Center of Military History, United States Army: 1969, 1993.

Boog, Horst, Werner Rahn, Reinhard Stumpf, and Bernd Wegner. *Germany and the Second World War: Volume VI: The Global War: Widening of the Conflict into a World War and the Shift of the Initiative 1941–1943*. Translated by Ewald Osers et al. Stuttgart: Deutsche Verlags-Anstalt, 2001; Oxford, UK: Clarendon, 2001.

Bradley, Omar N. *A Soldier's Story*. NY: Henry Holt, 1951; Modern Library, 1999.

Bradley, Omar N., and Clay Blair. *A General's Life*. NY: Simon & Schuster, 1983.

Brown, Anthony Cave. *Bodyguard of Lies*. NY: Harper & Row, 1975.

Brown, Rex. *Rational Choice and Judgment: Decision Analysis for the Decider*. Hoboken, NJ: Wiley, 2005.

Bryant, Arthur. *Triumph in the West: A History of the War Years Based on the Diaries of Field-Marshal Lord Alanbrooke, Chief of the Imperial General Staff*. Westport, CT: Greenwood Press, 1959.

Bryant, Arthur. *The Turn of the Tide: A History of the War Years Based on the Diaries of Field-Marshal Lord Alanbrooke, Chief of the Imperial General Staff*. Garden City, NY: Doubleday, 1957.

Burdick, Charles B. *Germany's Military Strategy and Spain in World War II*. Syracuse, NY: Syracuse University Press, 1968.

Butcher, Harry C. *My Three Years with Eisenhower: The Personal Diary of Captain Harry C. Butcher, USNR, Naval Aide to General Eisenhower, 1942 to 1945*. NY: Simon & Schuster, 1946.

Cantril, Hadley, ed. *Public Opinion: 1935–1946*. Princeton, NJ: Princeton University Press, 1951.

Carver, Michael. *Harding of Petherton, Field Marshal*. London: Weidenfeld and Nicolson, 1978.

Chalfont, Alun. *Montgomery of Alamein*. NY: Atheneum, 1976.

Chandler, Alfred D., Jr., ed. *The Papers of Dwight David Eisenhower*. Vols. I-IV. Baltimore: Johns Hopkins Press, 1970.

Chandler, David G. *The Campaigns of Napoleon*. NY: Macmillan, 1966.

Churchill, Winston S. *The Second World War: Volume III: The Grand Alliance*. Boston: Houghton Mifflin, 1950.

Churchill, Winston S. *The Second World War: Volume IV: The Hinge of Fate*. Boston: Houghton Mifflin, 1950.

Churchill, Winston S. *The Second World War: Volume V: Closing the Ring*. Boston: Houghton Mifflin, 1951.

Churchill, Winston S. *The Second World War: Volume VI: Triumph and Tragedy*. Boston: Houghton Mifflin, 1953.

Citino, Robert M. *The Path to Blitzkrieg: Doctrine and Training in the German Army, 1920–39*. Boulder, CO: Lynne Rienner, 1999; Mechanicsville, PA: Stackpole Books, 2008.

Clark, Lloyd. *Anzio: Italy and the Battle for Rome—1944*. NY: Grove Press, 2006.

Clark, Mark W. *Calculated Risk*. NY: Harper, 1950; NY: Enigma, 2007.

Clausewitz, Carl von. *Vom Kriege*. Berlin: Dümmlers Verlag, 1832. Internet accessible at http://www.clausewitz.com/readings/VomKriege1832/TOC.htm. Translations by the present author.

Cohen, Eliot A. *Supreme Command: Soldiers, Statesmen, and Leadership in Wartime*. NY: Free Press, 2002.

Colville, John. *The Fringes of Power: 10 Downing Street Diaries 1939-1955*. NY: Norton, 1985, 1986.

Connolly, Terry, Hal R. Arkes, and Kenneth R. Hammond, eds. *Judgment and Decision Making: An Interdisciplinary Reader. Second Edition*. NY: Cambridge University Press, 2000.

Corrigan, Gordon. *The Second World War: A Military History*. NY: St. Martins's, 2010.

Cunningham, Andrew Browne. *A Sailor's Odyssey: The Autobiography of Admiral of the Fleet Viscount Cunningham of Hyndhope*. NY: E. P. Dutton, 1951.

Danchev, Alex, and Daniel Todman, eds. *War Diaries: 1939-1945, Field Marshal Lord Alanbrooke*. London: Weidenfeld & Nicolson, 1957, 1959, 2001.

Davis, Kenneth S. *Soldier of Democracy*. NY: Doubleday, Doran, 1945.

Davis, Morton D. *Game Theory: A Nontechnical Introduction*. NY: Basic Books, 1970, 1983.

De Gaulle, Charles. *Mémoires de Guerre: L'Unité: 1942–1944*. Paris: Librairie Plon, 1956.

D'Este, Carlo. *Bitter Victory: The Battle for Sicily, 1943*. NY: Harper, 1988, 1989, 1991, 2008.

D'Este, Carlo. *Eisenhower: A Soldier's Life*. NY: Henry Holt, 2002.

D'Este, Carlo. *Fatal Decision: Anzio and the Battle for Rome*. NY: Harper, 1991, 1992, 2008.

D'Este, Carlo. *Patton: A Genius for War*. NY: HarperCollins, 1995.

D'Este, Carlo. *Warlord: A Life of Winston Churchill at War, 1874-1945*. NY: HarperCollins, 2008.

Dixit, Avinash, and Susan Skeath. *Games of Strategy*. NY: Norton, 1999.

Edwards, Ward. "The Theory of Decision Making." *Psychological Bulletin 51*: 380–417, 1954.

Edwards, Ward, and J. Robert Newman. "Multiattribute Evaluation," pp. 17–34 in Connolly, et al., *Judgment*.

Edwards, Ward, and Marcia Guttentag. "Experiments and Evaluation: A Reexamination." Pp. 409–63 in *Evaluation and Experiment: Some Critical Issues in Assessing Social Programs*, edited by C. A. Bennett and A. A. Lumsdaine. NY: Academic Press, 1975.

Edwards, Ward, Ralph F. Miles, Jr., and Detlof von Winterfeldt, eds. *Advances in Decision Analysis: From Foundations to Applications*. NY: Cambridge University Press, 2007.

Edwards, Ward, Ralph F. Miles, Jr., and Detlof von Winterfeldt. "Introduction," pp. 1–12 in Edwards, et al., *Advances*.

Eisenhower, David. *Eisenhower: At War 1943-1945*. NY: Random House, 1986.

Eisenhower, Dwight D. *Crusade in Europe*. Baltimore: Johns Hopkins University Press, 1948.

Ellis, John. *Brute Force*. NY: Viking Penguin, 1990.

Fisher, Ernest F, Jr. *Cassino to the Alps. USAWWII*. Washington, D.C.: U. S. Army, 1977.

Freeman, Douglas Southall. *Lee*. A one-volume abridgment by Richard Harwell of the four-volume *R. E. Lee*. NY: Charles Scribner's Sons, 1934, 1935, 1961.

Fuller, J. F. C. *The Second World War: 1939–45: A Strategical and Tactical History*. London: Eyre and Spottiswoode, 1948; third impression: NY: Duell, Sloan, and Pierce, 1954; USA: Da Capo Press, 1993.

Gallup, George H. *The Gallup Poll: Public Opinion 1935-1971: Volume One: 1935-1948*. NY: Random House, 1972.

Garland, Albert N., and Howard McGaw Smyth, assisted by Martin Blumenson. *Sicily and the Surrender of Italy: The United States Army in World War II: The Mediterranean Theater of Operations*. Washington, D.C.: Office of the Chief of Military History, United States Army: 1965.

Gavin, James M. *On to Berlin: Battles of an Airborne Commander 1943-1946*. NY: Viking, 1978.

Gilbert, Martin. *The Second World War: A Complete History*. London: Weidenfeld & Nicolson, 1989.

Gilbert, Martin. *Winston S. Churchill: Volume VII: Road to Victory 1941-1945*. Hillsdale, MI: Hillsdale College Press, 1986, 2013.

Goebbels, Josef. *The Goebbels Diaries*. Translated and edited by Louis P. Lochner. London: Hamish Hamilton, 1948.

Goodman, Michael S. *The Official History of the Joint Intelligence Committee. Volume I: From the Approach of he Second World War to the Suez Crisis*. Abington, Oxfordshire: Routledge, 2014.

Goodwin, Doris Kearns. *No Ordinary Time*. NY: Simon & Schuster, 1994.

Graham, Dominick, and Shelford Bidwell. *Tug of War: The Battle for Italy 1943–45*. London: Hodder & Stoughton, 1986; Barnsley, South Yorkshire: Pen & Sword Books Limited, 2004.

Grant, U. S. *Personal Memoirs of U.S. Grant*. NY: Charles L. Webster, 1885; Da Capo Press, 1982.

Greenfield, Kent Roberts. *American Strategy in World War II: A Reconsideration.* Baltimore: Johns Hopkins, 1963.

Greenfield, Kent Roberts, ed. *Command Decisions.* NY: Harcourt, Brace, 1959.

Gwyer, J. M. A., and J. R. M. Butler. *Grand Strategy. Volume III: June 1941—August 1942.* London: Her Majesty's Stationery Office, 1964.

Hamilton, Nigel. *The Mantle of Command: FDR at War: 1941–1942.* NY: Houghton Mifflin Harcourt, 2014.

Hamilton, Nigel. *Master of the Battlefield: Monty's War Years 1942–1944.* NY: McGraw-Hill: 1983.

Harriman, W. Averell and Elie Abel. *Special Envoy to Churchill and Stalin.* NY: Random House, 1975.

Harrison, Yvonne, and James A. Horne. "The Impact of Sleep Deprivation on Decision Making: A Review." *Journal of Experimental Psychology: Applied 6(3):* 236–49, 2000.

Hastings, Max. *Inferno: The World at War, 1939–1945.* NY: Vintage Books, 2011.

Hastings, Max. *Winston's War: Churchill 1940–1945.* NY: Vintage Books, 2009.

Hobbs, Joseph P. *Dear General: Eisenhower's Wartime Letters to Marshall.* Baltimore: Johns Hopkins, 1971.

Hoch, Stephen J., Howard C. Kunreuther, and Robert E. Gunther. *Wharton on Making Decisions.* NY: Wiley, 2001.

Hope, Ian. *Unity of Command in Afghanistan: A Forsaken Principle of War.* Carlisle, PA: Strategic Studies Institute, 2008.

Hora, Stephen C. "Eliciting Probabilities from Experts," pp. 129–153 in Edwards, et al., *Advances.*

Horne, Alistair, with David Montgomery. *Monty: The Lonely Leader, 1944–1945.* London: Macmillan, 1994.

Howard, Michael. *History of the Second World War. United Kingdom Military Series. Grand Strategy. Volume IV: August 1942-September 1943.* London: Her Majesty's Stationery Office, 1972.

Howard, Ronald A. "The Foundations of Decision Analysis Revisited," pp. 32–56 in Edwards, et al., *Advances.*

Howe, George F. *Northwest Africa: Seizing the Initiative in the West. USAWWII.* Washington, D.C.: U. S. Army, 1957.

Ismay, Lord. *The Memoirs of General the Lord Ismay.* NY: Viking, 1960.

Jackson, W. G. F. *Alexander of Tunis as Military Commander.* London: B. T. Batsford, 1971.

Janis, Irving L. *Groupthink: Psychological Studies of Policy Decisions and Fiascoes.* Boston: Houghton Mifflin, 1982.

Kahneman, Daniel. *Thinking, Fast and Slow.* NY: Farrar, Straus and Giroux, 2011.

Keegan, John. *The Second World War.* NY: Penguin, 1989.

Keegan, John. *Six Armies in Normandy: From D-Day to the Liberation of Paris.* NY: Viking, 1982; Penguin, 1983.

Keeney, Ralph L., and Howard Raiffa. *Decisions with Multiple Objectives: Preferences and Value Tradeoffs.* NY: Wiley, 1976.

Kershaw, Ian. *Fateful Choices: Ten Decisions that Changed the World, 1040–1941.* NY: Penguin, 2007.

Kesselring, Albert. *The Memoirs of Field-Marshal Kesselring.* Trans. William Kimber, Ltd. UK: William Kimber, Ltd., 1953; Novato, CA: Presidio Press, 1989.

Kesselring, Albert. *Soldat bis zum Letzten Tag.* Bonn: Athenäum, 1953; Germany: Verlag Siegfried Bublies, 2000. Translations by the present author.

Kimball, Warren F. ed. and commentator. *Churchill & Roosevelt: The Complete Correspondence: I. Alliance Emerging: October 1933—November 1942.* Princeton, NJ: Princeton University Press, 1984.

Kimball, Warren F. ed. and commentator. *Churchill & Roosevelt: The Complete Correspondence: II. Alliance Forged: November 1942—February 1944.* Princeton, NJ: Princeton University Press, 1984.

Kimball, Warren F. ed. and commentator. *Churchill & Roosevelt: The Complete Correspondence: III. Alliance Declining: February 1944—April 1945.* Princeton, NJ: Princeton University Press, 1984.

Kleindorfer, Paul R., Howard C. Kunreuther, and Paul J. H. Schoemaker. *Decision Sciences: An Integrative Perspective.* NY: Cambridge University Press, 1993.

Lamb, Richard. *Montgomery in Europe 1943–45: Success or Failure?* London: Buchan & Enright, 1983.

Larrabee, Eric. *Commander in Chief: Franklin Delano Roosevelt, His Lieutenants, and Their War.* NY: Simon & Schuster, 1987.

Latimer, Jon. *Deception in War.* Woodstock, NY: The Overlook Press, 2001.

Leahy, William D. *I Was There.* NY: Whittlesey House, 1950.

Lewin, Ronald. *Ultra Goes to War: The First Account of World War II's Greatest Secret based on Official Documents.* London: Hutchinson & Co., 1978.

Lewis, Michael. "Obama's Way." *Vanity Fair October 2012.* Internet-accessible at http://www.vanityfair.com/news/2012/10/michael-lewis-profile-barack-obama .

Liddell Hart, B. H. *The German Generals Talk.* NY: Quill, 1948, 1975, 1979.

Liddell Hart, B. H. *History of the Second World War.* NY: Paragon Books, 1970.

Liddell Hart, B. H. *The Other Side of the Hill.* London: Cassell, 1948, 1951, 1973.

Liddell Hart, B. H., ed. *The Rommel Papers.* Trans. Paul Findlay. NY: Harcourt, Brace, 1953.

Longford, Elizabeth. *Wellington: The Years of the Sword.* NY: Harper & Row, 1969.

Lovat, Lord. *March Past: A Memoir by Lord Lovat.* London: Weidenfeld and Nicolson, 1978.

Lucas, John P. *From Algiers to Anzio.* Unpublished manuscript. Archived in the US Army Heritage and Education Center in Carlisle, PA.

Luce, Mary Frances, John W. Payne, and James R. Bettman. "The Emotional Nature of Decision Trade-Offs," pp. 17–35 in Hoch, et al., *Wharton.*

Luce, R. Duncan, and Howard Raiffa. *Games and Decisions: Introduction and Critical Survey.* NY: Wiley, 1957.

Macmillan, Harold. *The Blast of War: 1939–1945.* NY: Harper & Row, 1967, 1968.

Marshall, George C., and H.R. Stark. "Joint Board Estimates of United States Over-All Production Requirements," web-accessible at docs.fdrlibrary.marist.edu/psf/box1/t04a02.html .

Matheson, David and James E. Matheson. "From Decision Analysis to the Decision Organization," pp. 419–50 in Edwards, et al., *Advances*.

Matloff, Maurice. *Strategic Planning for Coalition Warfare: 1943–1944: The United States Army in World War II*. Washington, D.C.: Office of the Chief of Military History, United States Army, 1959.

Matloff, Maurice, and Edwin M. Snell. *Strategic Planning for Coalition Warfare: 1941–1942: The United States Army in World War II*. Washington, D.C.: Office of the Chief of Military History, United States Army, 1953.

Mawdsley, Evan. *Thunder in the East: The Nazi-Soviet War 1941–1945*. London: Hodder Arnold, 2005.

McKenna, Benjamin S., et al. "The effects of one night of sleep deprivation on known-risk and ambiguous-risk situations." *Journal of Sleep Research 16*: 245–52, 2007.

McMillan, John. *Games, Strategies, & Managers*. NY: Oxford University Press, 1992.

Mellers, Barbara, and Connson Locke. "What Have We Learned from Our Mistakes," pp. 351–74 in Edwards, et al., *Advances*.

Meyer, Leo J. "The Decision to Invade North Africa (TORCH) (1942)." Pp. 129–53 in Greenfield, ed., *Decisions*.

Meyer, Robert J., and J. Wesley Hutchison. "Bumbling Geniuses: The Power of Everyday Reasoning in Multistage Decision Making," pp. 37–61 in Hoch, et al., *Wharton*.

Miles, Ralph F., Jr. "The Emergence of Decision Analysis," pp. 13–31 in Edwards, et al., *Advances*.

Miles, Ralph F., Jr., and Detlof von Winterfeldt. "*Preface*," pp. xi-xiii in Edwards, et al., *Advances*.

Mitcham, Samuel W., Jr., and Friedrich von Stauffenberg. *The Battle of Sicily: How the Allies Lost Their Chance for Total Victory*. Mechanicsburg, PA: Stackpole Books, 1991.

Molony, C. J. C., et al. *History of the Second World War. United Kingdom Military Series. Mediterranean and Middle East. Volume V: The Campaign in Sicily 1943 and The Campaign in Italy 3rd September 1943 to 31st March 1944*. London: Her Majesty's Stationery Office, 1973.

Molony, C. J. C., et al. *History of the Second World War. United Kingdom Military Series. Mediterranean and Middle East. Volume VI: Victory in the Mediterranean: Part 1: 1st April to 4th June 1944*. London: Her Majesty's Stationery Office, 1984, 1986.

Montefiore, Simon S. *Stalin: The Court of the Red Tsar*. London: Weidenfeld and Nicholson, 2003.

Montgomery, Bernard Law. *El Alamein to the River Sangro; Normandy to the Baltic*. NY: St. Martin's Press, 1947, 1948, 1974.

Montgomery, Bernard Law. *The Memoirs of Field-Marshal the Viscount Montgomery of Alamein, K.G.* Cleveland: The World Publishing Co., 1958.

Moran, Lord. *Churchill: Taken from the Diaries of Lord Moran: The Struggle for Survival: 1940–1965*. Cambridge, MA: Houghton Mifflin, 1966.

Morgan, Frederick. *Peace and War: A Soldier's Life*. London: Hodder and Stoughton, 1961.

Morgan, Kay Summersby. *Past Forgetting: My Love Affair with Dwight D. Eisenhower*. NY: Simon & Schuster, 1976.

Morison, Samuel Eliot. *American Contributions to the Strategy of World War II*. London: Oxford, 1958.

Morison, Samuel Eliot. *History of United States Naval Operations in World War II. Volume IX: Sicily—Salerno—Anzio: January 1943—June 1944*. Boston: Little, Brown, 1954; Edison, NJ: Castle Books, 2001.

Mosley, Leonard. *Backs to the Wall*. NY: Random House, 1971.

Mosley, Leonard. *Marshall: Organizer of Victory*. London: Methuen, 1982.

Murray, Williamson, and Allan R. Millett. *A War to Be Won: Fighting the Second World War*. Cambridge, MA: Harvard, 2000.

Neillands, Robin. *The Dieppe Raid: The Story of the Disastrous 1942 Expedition*. London: Aurum Press, 2005.

Neustadt, Richard E. *Presidential Power and the Modern Presidents: The Politics of Leadership from Roosevelt to Reagan*. NY: The Free Press, 1990.

Nicolson, Nigel. *Alex: The Life of Field Marshal Earl Alexander of Tunis*. London: Weidenfeld and Nicolson, 1973.

Oberholzer-Gee, Felix. "Learners or Lemmings: The Nature of Information Cascades," pp. 273–86 in Hoch, et al., *Wharton*.

Overy, Richard. *Why the Allies Won*. London: Jonathan Cape, 1995; Pimlico, 2006.

Paget, Lord. *March Past*. London: Weidenfeld and Nicolson, 1978.

Patton, George S., Jr. *War as I Knew It*. Boston: Houghton Mifflin, 1947, 1975, 1995.

Playfair, I. S. O., Molony, C. J. C., et al. *Mediterranean and Middle East. Volume IV: The Destruction of the Axis Forces in Africa*. London: Her Majesty's Stationery Office, 1966.

Pogue, Forrest C. *George C. Marshall: Ordeal and Hope 1939–1942*. NY: Viking, 1966; Penguin, 1993.

Pogue, Forrest C. *George C. Marshall: Organizer of Victory 1943–1945*. NY: Viking, 1973; Penguin, 1993.

Pond, Hugh. *Sicily*. London: William Kimber, 1962.

Pratt, John W., and Richard J. Zeckhauser. "Principals and Agents: An Overview," pp. 1–35 in Pratt and Zeckhauser, *Structure*.

Pratt, John W., and Richard J. Zeckhauser, eds. *Principals and Agents: The Structure of Business*. Boston: Harvard Business School Press, 1985.

Raiffa, Howard, "Decision Analysis: A Personal Account of How It Got Started and Evolved," pp. 57–70 in Edwards, et al., *Advances*.

Raiffa, Howard. *Decision Analysis: Introductory Lectures on Choices under Uncertainty*. Reading, MA: Addison-Wesley, 1968.

Rapoport, Anatol. *Two-Person Game Theory*. Ann Arbor: University of Michigan Press, 1966.

Rawson, Andrew. *Eyes Only: The Top Secret Correspondence Between Marshall and Eisenhower*. Brimstone Port Stroud, Gloucestershire: Spellmount, 2012.

Rees, Goronwy. *A Bundle of Sensations: Sketches in Autobiography*. London: Chatto & Windus, 1960.

Reynolds, David. *In Command of History: Churchill*

Fighting and Writing the Second World War. NY: Random House, 2005.

Reynolds, Quentin. *Dress Rehearsal: The Story of Dieppe.* NY: Random House, 1943.

Ricks, Thomas E. *The Generals: American Military Command from World War II to Today.* NY: Penguin, 2012.

Robert H. Ferrell, ed. *The Eisenhower Diaries.* NY: Norton, 1981.

Roberts, Andrew. *Masters and Commanders: How Four Titans Won the War in the West, 1941–1945.* UK: Allen Lane, 2008.

Roberts, Andrew. *The Storm of War: A New History of the Second World War.* UK: Allen Lane, 2009.

Robertson, Terence. *The Shame and the Glory: Dieppe.* Toronto: McClelland and Stewart, 1962.

Rosenman, Samuel I. *Working with Roosevelt.* NY: Harper & Brothers, 1952.

Roskill, S. W. *The War at Sea 1939–1945. Volume III: The Offensive: Part I: 1st June 1943 to 31st May 1944.* London: Her Majesty's Stationery Office, 1960.

Russo, J. Edward, and Paul J. H. Schoemaker. *Decision Traps: Ten Barriers to Brilliant Decision-Making and How to Overcome Them.* NY: Doubleday, 1989.

Schelling, Thomas C. *The Strategy of Conflict.* Cambridge, MA: Harvard, 1960.

Schlesinger, Arthur M., Jr., *A Thousand Days: John F. Kennedy in the White House.* Boston: Houghton Mifflin, 1965.

Schumann, Wolfgang, et al. *Deutschland im Zweiten Weltkrieg 3: Der Grundlegende Umschwung im Kriegsverlauf (November 1942 bis September 1943).* Cologne: Pahl-Rugenstein Verlag, 1979.

Schumann, Wolfgang, et al. *Deutschland im Zweiten Weltkrieg 5: Der Zusammenbruch der Defensivstrategie des Hitlerfaschismus an allen Fronten (Januar bis August 1944).* Cologne: Pahl-Rugenstein Verlag, 1984.

Schumann, Wolfgang, et al. *Deutschland im Zweiten Weltkrieg 6: Die Zerschlagung des Hitlerfaschismus und die Befreiung des deutschen Volkes (Juni 1944 bis 8 Mai 1945).* Cologne: Pahl-Rugenstein Verlag, 1985.

Senger und Etterlin, Frido von. *Neither Fear nor Hope.* Trans. George Malcolm. London: Macdonald, 1960, 1963.

Sherwood, Robert E. *Roosevelt and Hopkins: An Intimate History.* NY: Harper, 1948.

Siebert, Johannes, and Ralph L. Keeney. "Creating More and Better Alternatives for Decisions Using Objectives." *Operations Research 63(5):* 1144–58, 2015.

Sorensen, Theodore C. *Decision-Making in the White House.* NY: Columbia University Press, 1963.

Spetzler, Carl S. "Building Decision Competency in Organizations," pp. 451–68 in Edwards, et al., *Advances.*

Stacey, C. P. *Official History of the Canadian Army in the Second World War. Volume I: Six Years of War: The Army in Canada, Britain and the Pacific.* Ottawa: Queen's Printer and Controller of Stationery, 1955.

Stimson, Henry L., and McGeorge Bundy. *On Active Service in Peace and War.* NY: Octagon, 1947, 1948, 1971.

Stoler, Mark A. *Allies in War: Britain and America against the Axis Powers: 1940–1945.* London: Hodder, 2005.

Strong, Kenneth. *Intelligence at the Top: The Recollections of an Intelligence Officer.* Garden City, NY: Doubleday, 1969.

Summers, Harry G., Jr. *On Strategy: A Critical Analysis of the Vietnam War.* Novato, CA: Presidio Press, 1982; NY: Dell, 1984.

Summersby, Kay. *Eisenhower Was My Boss.* NY: Prentice-Hall, 1948.

Sunstein, Cass R., and Reid Hastie. *Wiser: Getting beyond Groupthink to Make Groups Smarter.* Boston: Harvard Business Review Press, 2015.

Tedder, Lord. *With Prejudice: The War Memoirs of Marshal of the Royal Air Force.* Boston: Little, Brown, 1966.

Tetlock, Philip E. *Expert Political Judgment: How Good Is It? How Can We Know?* Princeton, NJ: Princeton University Press, 2005.

Thompson, Julian. "John Lucas and Anzio, 1944," pp. 188–214 in Brian Bond, ed., *Fallen Stars: Eleven Studies of Twentieth Century Military Disasters.* London: Brassey's, 1991.

Thompson, Mark S., *Benefit-Cost Analysis for Program Evaluation.* Beverly Hills: Sage, 1980.

Thompson, Mark S., *Decision Analysis for Program Evaluation.* Cambridge, MA: Ballinger, 1982.

Truscott, L. K., Jr. *Command Missions.* NY: E. P. Dutton, 1954.

United Kingdom Chiefs of Staff Committee. *Minutes of Meetings (O) nos. 1–89 1942 Jan. 9-Aug 13.* http://discovery.nationalarchives.gov.uk/browse/r/h/C387131.

United States Department of State. *Foreign Relations of the United States: The Conferences at Washington, 1941–1942, and Casablanca, 1943.* Washington: USGPO, 1968.

United States Joint Chiefs of Staff. *Joint Operations.* Joint Publication 3–0, 17 January 2017.

Van Creveld, Martin. *Command in War.* Cambridge, MA: Harvard University Press, 1983.

Venkatraman, Vinod, et al. "Sleep Deprivation Elevates Expectation of Gains and Attenuates Response to Losses Following Risky Decisions." *Sleep 30(5):* 603–9, 2007.

Villa, Brian Loring. *Unauthorized Action: Mountbatten and the Dieppe Raid.* Toronto: Oxford University Press, 1989.

Vohs, Kathleen D., et al. "Making Choices Impairs Subsequent Self-Control: A Limited-Resource Account of Decision Making, Self-Regulation, and Active Initiative." *Journal of Personality and Social Psychology 94(5):* 883–98, 2008.

Von Neumann, John, and Oskar Morgenstern. *Theory of Games and Economic Behavior.* Princeton, NJ: Princeton University Press, 1944.

Warlimont, Walter. *Inside Hitler's Headquarters 1939–45.* Trans. R. H. Barry. Novato, CA: Presidio, 1962, 1964.

Warner, Oliver. *Cunningham of Hyndhope: Admiral of the Fleet.* London: John Murray, 1967.

Wedemeyer, Albert C. *Wedemeyer Reports!* NY: Henry Holt, 1958.

Weigley, Russell F. *Eisenhower's Lieutenants: The Campaign of France and Germany 1944–1945. Bloomington: Indiana University Press, 1981.

Weinberg, Gerhard L. *A World at Arms: A Global History of World War II. Second Edition*. NY: Cambridge University Press, 1994, 2005.

Weinstein, Milton C., and Harvey V. Fineberg. *Clinical Decision Analysis*. Philadelphia: W. B. Saunders, 1980.

Westphal, Siegfried. *The German Army in the West*. London: Cassell and Co., 1951.

Whitney, Paul, et al. "Feedback Blunting: Total Sleep Deprivation Impairs Decision Making that Requires Updating Based on Feedback." *Sleep 38(5):* 745–54, 2015.

Wilmot, Chester. *The Struggle for Europe*. Old Saybrook, CT: Konecky & Konecky, 1952.

Winterbotham, F. W. *The Ultra Secret*. NY: Harper & Row, 1974.

Zeckhauser, Bryn, and Aaron Sandoski. *How the Wise Decide: The Lessons of 21 Extraordinary Leaders*. NY: Crown Business, 2008.

Ziegler, *Mountbatten*. NY: Knopf, 1985.

Zuehlke, Mark. *Tragedy at Dieppe*. Vancouver: Douglas & McIntyre, 2012.

Index